W9-ADR-662

Against Criminology

Against Criminology

Stanley Cohen

ST. JOSEPH'S UNIVERSITY

3 9353 00235 9741

HV
6028
.C55
1988

Transaction Books
New Brunswick (U.S.A.) and Oxford (U.K.)

Copyright © 1988 by Transaction, Inc.
New Brunswick, New Jersey 08903

All rights reserved under International and Pan-American Copyright Conventions. No part
of this book may be reproduced or transmitted in any form or by any means, electronic or
mechanical, including photocopy, recording, or any information storage and retrieval system,
without prior permission in writing from the publisher. All inquiries should be addressed
to Transaction Books, Rutgers — The State University, New Brunswick, New Jersey 08903.

Library of Congress Catalog Number: 87-16237

ISBN 088738-153-7 (cloth)

ISBN 0-88738-689-X (paper)

Printed in the United States of America

Library of Congress Cataloging in Publication Data

Cohen, Stanley.
  Against criminology.

  Bibliography: p.
  1. Crime and criminals.   I. Title.
HV6028.C55 1987   364   87-16237
ISBN 0-88738-153-7
ISBN 0-88738-689-X (pbk.)

One must belong to a tradition to hate it properly.

—Adorno

Contents

Preface

This is a selection of essays that I have written over the past fifteen years about certain aspects of criminology. If there are three orders of reality in the subject — first, the "thing" itself (crime and the apparatus for its control); second, research and speculation about this thing (description, classification, causal theory, normative and technical solutions to crime as a "problem"); and third, reflection about the nature of the whole enterprise itself — then these essays belong mostly to the third order. Their tone, that is, is introverted and reflective. They deal with the justifications and apologies for criminology: how it explains itself to itself and others; why it chooses some subjects, theories, and policies and not others; its endless proclamations about what its subject, scope, and purpose "should" be. In particular, I am concerned with the various internal schisms and the intellectual opportunities and problems opened up by the "new" criminologies of the past two decades.

I have not included here, then, work that reflects my substantive areas of interest over this period: in vandalism, delinquency and youth culture, deviance and the mass media, or most consistently, in prisons and changing systems and ideologies of social control. Most of my work in this last area has appeared in my recent book *Visions of Social Control*, and I saw no justification for reprinting the various papers leading up to this.

This volume would literally not have been possible without the initiative of Irving Horowitz. It was his idea to collect these essays, on the pragmatic grounds that most of them were not readily available to a North American readership and on the intellectual grounds that it would be worthwhile to try to find the common theme in my work.

The first response I gave to his intellectual query was that I was not aware of any such continuous theme, but were I to look for it, it would be my preoccupation with how liberalism — as a political doctrine and a way of making sense of the social world — has dealt with the problem of crime. My original title for this collection was "Crime, Punishment and the Liberal Imagination"—and this does indeed cover the implicit subject matter of most of these essays.

Criminology was born of post-Enlightenment liberalism, and every significant attempt to define its scope and purpose, every major twist in its convoluted inner dialogue, have been made within or in reaction to that original discourse. This is true in terms of its theoretical preoccupations (the limits of freedom and tolerance, the nature of responsibility and determinism, the possibility of devising rational solutions to social problems); its political allegiance (mainstream academic criminology has always been liberal; radicals and conservatives have to define themselves against this consensus); and also in terms of the everyday meaning of what it is to be "liberal" (we want to be nice, but people who do bad things must be punished). The great unwritten book in criminology is a serious examination of the basic principles of liberalism, their historical changes and mutations, their critics (internal, radical, and conservative), and how this relates to crime and punishment.

This is not such a book. Though I keep coming back to these problems (more often than I was aware of at the time), they demand more systematic attention than can be given by these disparate essays written for such different purposes. To have used the subject of liberalism as my organizing theme would be to pretend to a consistency that just is not there.

"Against Criminology," the title of this collection and of the essay (chapter 2) that sketches its context, is far more accurate. At a personal level it conveys my dissatisfaction with the existence of criminology as a separate subject and my marginal relationship to its major preoccupations. More important, it conveys the nature of the collective intellectual enterprise, begun some twenty years ago, to create what is conceived as either an alternative criminology or an alternative to criminology. Although these essays are personal—I certainly wrote them and, structuralist literary criticism notwithstanding, my intentions matter in understanding them—they should be seen as reflections of this collective endeavor. They are reports (particularly the early essays), that is, from an active participant rather than a detached observer.

As the sequence moves on the tone becomes somewhat more detached. I find myself subjecting the anti-criminology enterprise to the same "sociology-of-knowledge" stance that I sometimes recommend to be taken toward criminology itself. This stance would treat the structure and productions of criminology in the same way as the structures and productions of religion or art are treated by "their" sociologists. Most of what passes for criminology is like theology or literature: it is indistinguishable from what should be the object of its attention. We know well enough why the alternative position, "pure" detached knowledge, is both impossible and irresponsible. Nonetheless, something of this detached spirit is needed to sense the collective element in these essays. For this reason, I have not changed their content, tempting as this was, especially for those early essays (such as chapters 3 and 4), which now seem so brash, simplistic, and tendentious. But this is how we spoke and wrote.

Behind this collective facade, I am aware of my personal preoccupations. For one thing, even when dealing with the most arcane of theoretical issues, I was always conscious of a moral responsiblity to understand what *difference* our claims would make if taken literally. I remain a moral pragmatist, concerned not so much with formulating policy as with trying to show what choices our theories imply. Invariably, values and politics, not science, determine these choices. A second personal tone, especially after the early bravado of anti-criminology, is a certain tentativeness. I argue not just with the "enemy," nor even just with those who think like me, but with myself. In particular, I worry whether certain ideas are taken more or less seriously than they should be.

The essays in each part of the volume are arranged in chronological order. In the introductory Part One I start with a brief entry on criminology that was prepared for the *Social Science Encyclopaedia*. This introduces outsiders to such key terms as *classicism* and *positivism* that make up the discourse of theoretical criminology. It also restates my belief in the profound continuities that have informed the history of criminology, the belief I repeat each academic year to draw students away from the tyranny of the present. Chapter 2, which I wrote for this volume, takes a distant overview of its main themes. At the risk of repetition, it retells the story of the early attempt to break with mainstream criminology, the problems and opportunities that this break opened up, and then the current positions being negotiated in the struggle to define the proper character of the "discipline."

Part Two sets out some early programmatic statements of anti-criminology. Like chapters 3 and 4, these were aimed outward, trying to convince a general readership of the novelty and appeal of the emerging new paradigm or—like chapter 5—emphasizing a particularly novel element, in this case the hidden political meanings of crime and deviance. Chapter 6 repeats these exercises but sets out in more detail the nature of the difference between the old and emerging new criminologies, especially as this appeared in Britain at the time. Much of the critique and rhetoric in these essays is embarrassingly dated. The point of including them is to see which of these ideas turned out viable and productive, and which of them were to fade away.

Part Three starts with three essays (chapters 7, 8, and 9) that reflected my own immediate doubts about just where the whole enterprise was leading. Dealing respectively with social work, criminal justice, and delinquent youth culture, these essays consider the problems of translating theories into the language of recognizable social policy and reality. Chapters 10 and 11 continue this project but are more generally concerned with crime control and justice in the Third World. By the time I was writing chapters 12 and 13, anti-criminology not only was firmly established but was showing some surprising tendencies to reverse some of its earlier rhetoric and return to the terrain of mainstream criminology. I use the issues of decentralization and criminalization to examine a few of these twists. Chapter 14 returns to the Third World and to one of the earliest interests of the new criminology: trying to find the political significance of crime.

Most of the essays in Part Three reflect a tone of self-doubt, caution, even a certain retrenchment. If the early phase of anti-criminology was evangelical in its attempt to tell the Good Tidings to outsiders (general sociologists, social workers, political activists, even the general public), then these essays are more of an internal dialogue with my fellow travelers. This was also the point at which splits and disputes appeared within the revisionist ranks. We realized the obvious: that a negative stance toward the old criminology did not provide enough of a guide for knowing what should be put in its place. These essays were harder to write. As Sartre reminds us (but with a greater certainty than I would ever pretend): "When other people don't think as you do, it is difficult to prove them wrong, difficult and tiring. But when they share your point of view and you've got to explain that they're mistaken, it's hopeless."

Part Four consists of a single chapter (15), which was written as a short story (the first work of fiction, I believe, to appear *as such* in a serious sociological journal). This is less a "conclusion" to the whole volume than an expression of one of the nightmares induced by writing about other people's problems.

These essays were written originally for very different audiences: a television debate (chapter 4), an Open University course (chapter 6), and academic specialists on Africa (chapter 14), as well as a conventional sociological and criminological readership. This accounts for their inconsistency in style that I have made no effort to change. It also accounts, I'm afraid, for a certain degree of repetition and self-plagiarism: the same favorite ideas and references keep getting wheeled in. I have eliminated only the few more intrusive repetitions. Nor have I tried to rewrite the essays to look wise in the light of later knowledge and consciousness (I apologize particularly for writing of a world in which all criminals and all criminologists are always male). The only changes I've made are minor stylistic ones, such as restoring bits altered by zealous editors, standardizing the format of the references and footnotes, and cutting out some parochially British references.

I am indebted to Irving Horowitz for his persistent encouragement in putting this volume together and to all the good friends I have worked with over these years.

S.C.
January 1987

Part One

Introduction

1

Criminology*

There are two scriptural beginnings to the history of criminology, each marking out a somewhat different fate for the study of crime and its control. The first dates from the mid-eighteenth century and tells of the revolutionary contribution of Enlightenment thinkers like Beccaria (1738-1794) and Bentham (1748-1832) in breaking with a previously "archaic," "barbaric," "repressive," or "arbitrary" system of criminal law. This was the classical school. For these reformers, legal philosophers, and political theorists, the crime question was dominantly the punishment question. Their program was to prevent punishment from being, in Beccaria's words, "an act of violence of one or many against a private citizen"; instead, it should be "essentially public, prompt, necessary, the least possible in given circumstances, proportionate to the crime, dictated by laws." Classicism presented a model of rationality: on the one side, the free "sovereign" individual acting according to the dictates of reason and self-interest; on the other, the limited liberal state, contracted to grant rights and liberties, to prescribe duties, and to impose the fair and just punishment that must result from the knowing infliction of social harm.

This immaculate-conception account of the birth of classicism has been challenged by revisionist histories of law and the state. Dates, concepts, and subjects have been reordered. Classicism is now to be understood in terms of the broader rationalization of crime control associated with the emergence of the free market and the new capitalist order. But the preoccupations of classicism — whether they appear in utilitarianism, Kantianism, liberalism, anarchism, or indeed any political philosophy at all — have remained a constant thread in criminology. This is where the subject overlaps with politics, jurisprudence, and the history and sociology of the law.

A century after classicism, though, criminology was to claim for itself an-

* "Criminology" from *The Social Science Encyclopedia* (London: Routledge, 1985), pp. 173-175.

other beginning and another set of influences. This was the positivist revolution, dated in comic book intellectual history with the publication in 1876 of Lombroso's (1836–1909) *Delinquent Man*. This was a "positivism" that shared the more general social scientific connotations of the term (the notion, that is, of the unity of the scientific method) but that acquired in criminology a more specific meaning. As David Matza suggests in his standard sociologies of criminological knowledge,[1] criminological positivism managed the astonishing feat of separating the study of crime from the contemplation of the state. Classicism was dismissed as mere metaphysical speculation. The new program was to focus not on the crime (the act) but the criminal (the actor); it was to assume not rationality, free will, and choice but determinism (biological, psychic, or social). At the center of the criminological enterprise now was the notion of causality. No longer a sovereign being, subject to more or less the same pulls and pushes as his fellow citizens, the criminal was now a special person or member of a special class.

The whole of the past century of criminology can be understood as a series of creative, even brilliant, yet eventually repetitive variations on these late-nineteenth-century themes. The particular image conjured by Lombroso's criminal type — the atavistic genetic throwback — faded away, but the subsequent structure and logic of criminological explanation remained largely within the positivist paradigm. Whether the level of explanation was biological, psychological, sociological, or a combination of these ("multifactorial," as some versions were dignified), the Holy Grail was a general causal theory: Why do people commit crime? This quest gave the subject its collective self-definition: "the scientific study of the causes of crime."

At each stage of this search criminology strengthened its claim to exist as an autonomous, multidisciplinary subject. Somewhat like a parasite, criminology attached itself to its host subjects (notably, law, psychology, psychiatry, and sociology) and drew from them methods, theories, and academic credibility. At the same time, somewhat like a colonial power landing on new territory, each of these disciplines descended on the eternally fascinating subjects of crime and punishment and claimed them as its own. In this fashion criminological theories and methods draw on Freudianism, behaviorism, the Chicago school of sociology, functionalism, anomie theory, interactionism, Marxism, and much else. Each of these traces can be found in any current criminology textbook; it would be difficult to think of a major system of thought in the social sciences that would not be so represented.

All the time this positivist trajectory was being established, criminologists retained their interest in the question of punishment. If, in a sense, all criminology became positivist, then also all criminology remained concerned with "classical" matters. But instead of speculation about the limits and nature of the criminal sanction, this side of criminology (sometimes called "penology") took this sanction as politically given. True, there was (and still is) an important debate about whether the subject matter of criminology should be confined to conventional legal definitions of crime or shifted to include all forms of socially injurious conduct. The punishment question, however, was largely resolved in empirical terms: describing, analyzing, and evaluating the workings of the criminal justice system. Research findings were built up about the police, courts, prisons, and various other agencies devoted to the prevention, control, deterrence, or treatment of crime. This remains today the major part of the criminological enterprise.

Little of this, however, was "pure" empiricism. The classical tradition was alive in another sense: modern criminologists became the heirs of the Enlightenment beliefs in rationality and progress. Their scientific task was carried along by a sense of faith: the business of crime and delinquency control could be made not only more efficient but also more humane. As reformers, advisers, and consultants, criminologists claim for themselves not merely an autonomous body of knowledge but also the status of an applied science or even a profession.

It is this simultaneous claim to knowledge and power that links the two sides of criminology: causation and control. In positivism this is an organic link: to know the cause is to know the right policy. Recently, however, this link and its justification in the immaculate-conception history of positivism have been questioned. Histories of the emergence of the prison during the late eighteenth century and early nineteenth century have shown the dependence of control systems on theories of rehabilitation, behavior modification, and anomie well before their supposed "discovery" by scientific criminology. To critics like Foucault,[2] criminological knowledge has always been wholly utilitarian: an elaborate alibi to justify the exercise of power.

In the general climate of radical self-scrutiny that descended on the social sciences in the 1960s, criminology, too, began to fragment a little. There were three major attacks against the positivist hegemony, each in its peculiar and distinct way representing a return to classical questions.

First, labeling theory—a loose body of ideas derived from symbolic interactionism—restated some simple sociological truths about the relative nature of social rules and the normative boundaries that they mark. Crime was one form of that wider category of social action, deviance; criminology should be absorbed into the sociology of deviance. Beyond such conceptual and disciplinary boundary disputes, the very nature of the conventional quest for causality was regarded with skepticism. In addition to the standard behavioral question (Why do some people do these bad things?) there was a series of definitional questions: Why are certain actions defined as rule breaking? How are these rules applied? What are the consequences of this application? At times these definitional questions seemed to attain causal primacy; it was not that control led to deviance, but deviance to control. Social control agencies — with their organized systems of labeling, stigmatizing, and isolation — were meddlesome busybodies, making matters worse for society and its underdogs and outsiders. And behind the pretensions of scientific criminology was a simpleminded identification with middle-class values.

This liberal criticism of liberalism was to become harder and tighter in the second onslaught on mainstream criminology. This came from what has been labeled variously as "conflict," "new," "critical," "radical," or "Marxist" criminology. Drawing initially on some strands of labeling theory and conflict sociology and then on classical Marxist writing about law, class, and the state, these theories moved even further from the agenda of positivism. Traditional causal questions were either dismissed or made subservient to the assumed criminogenic features of capitalism. Legalistic definitions were either expanded to include crimes of the powerful (those social harms that the state licenses itself to commit) or else subjected to historicist and materialist inquiry. Labeling theory's wider notion of deviance was abandoned. Law was the only important mode of control, and the focus of criminology had to be shifted to the power of the state to criminalize certain actions rather than others. The analytical task was to construct a political economy of crime and its control. The normative task (that is, the solution to the crime problem) was to eliminate those economic and political systems of exploitation that gave rise to crime. The goal was a crime-free society, possible only under a different social order and impossible with the conceptual tools of bourgeois criminology.

The third critique of the positivist enterprise came from a quite different theoretical and political direction. Impressed by the apparent failure of the causal quest and of progressive policies such as treatment, rehabilitation, and social reform, a loose coalition of intellectuals appeared under such rallying calls as "realism," "back to justice," and "neo-classicism." Some of them are neo-liberals — and theirs is a note of sad disenchantment with the ideas and policies of progressive criminology. Some of them are conservatives (or neo-conservatives) — and theirs is a note of satisfaction about the supposed failures of liberalism. Both these wings harken back to classical questions; the notion of justice (or "just deserts") allows liberals to talk of rights, equity, and fairness, while it allows conservatives to talk about law and order, social defense, deterrence, and the protection of society. In neither case — but particularly for conservatives — is there much interest in traditional questions of causation.

Criminology is a subject with a complicated past and polemical present. Most criminologists are employed at the core of the enterprise, busy either describing, classifying, and explaining crime or else analyzing, evaluating, and advocating policy. At the periphery are various fascinating intellectual disputes about the subject's true content and justification. As Jock Young has recently shown,[3] the major schools of criminological thought are divided on quite basic issues:

the image of human nature, the basis of social order, the nature and extent of crime, the relationship between theory and policy. And if we move out of the Anglo-American cultures in which contemporary criminology has mainly flourished, even more fundamental differences appear. (A major and belated recent development has been the serious comparative analysis of crime and its control.)

But whether positivist or neo-classical, radical or conservative, detached intellectuals or disguised policemen, criminologists confront the same questions. All this diversity is a manifestation of a single tension: crime is behavior, but it is behavior that the state is organized to punish.

Notes

1. David Matza, *Delinquency and Drift* (New York: Wiley, 1964); and *Becoming Deviant* (Englewood Cliffs, N.J.: Prentice-Hall, 1969).
2. Michel Foucault, *Discipline and Punish* (London: Allen Lane, 1977).
3. Jock Young, "Thinking Seriously about Crime," in *Crime and Society*, ed. M. Fitzgerald et al. (London: Routledge & Kegan Paul, 1981).

2

Against Criminology

My relationship with criminology is, I suppose, some variety of what used to be called "repressive tolerance." Every attempt I have ever made to distance myself from the subject, to criticize it, even to question its very right to exist, has only got me more involved in its inner life. This is, of course, not just a personal experience but the shared fate of most of us who some twenty years ago embarked on a collective project of — no less — constructing an alternative to criminology. The more successful our attack on the old regime, the more we received Ph.D.'s, tenure, publishers' contracts, and research funds, appeared on booklists and examination questions, and even became directors of institutes of criminology and received awards from professional associations.

Again, all this was not peculiar to the anti-criminology enterprise. The Marcusean notion of repressive tolerance tells us of the extraordinary powers of modern capitalism to absorb, co-opt, and neutralize even the most radical attacks against it. This is the same point made (more forcibly and persuasively) in the theory of "recuperation," produced by the International Situationists in that most far-reaching of all critiques ever made of modern culture.

In retrospect, especially the retrospect allowed us by Foucault's rewriting of the history of the social sciences, all this was inevitable enough. Unlike in certain areas of natural sciences, it is impossible to construct a model that so fundamentally undermines all previous assumptions as to create a completely new discipline. With the exception perhaps of abolitionism, nothing produced by anti-criminology, neither the discovery of any new facts nor the creation of a new mode of understanding the old facts, came remotely near this type of paradigmatic or disciplinary revolution. The special history of the criminological discourse — the deep interpenetration between knowledge and power — makes this prospect even more unlikely than in any other branch of the social sciences. To be against criminology, it seems, one has to be part of it. Indeed, as we shall see, some influential members of the original anti-criminology cohort have

8

now decided to make a virtue of this apparent necessity, abandoning as wholly misconceived the attempt to construct an alternative discourse and returning instead to the citadels of the old criminology.

Whatever the justifications for this particular move, it must surely be true that the intellectual distance that is needed to comprehend the subject can be achieved only by a real immersion in its inner life. Thus, Adorno: "One must belong to a tradition to hate it properly." *Hate*, no doubt, is too strong a word, but *distance, detachment, marginality*, and *ambivalence* all convey closely enough the stance that some of us tried (or pretended) to cultivate toward the criminological tradition. At best, this stance was no more than the type of sociological perspective required to study any institution seriously, whether law, religion, medicine, or art. Sociologists "of" these areas are not lawyers, priests, doctors, or artists. At worst, though, this distancing led to a self-indulgent irresponsibility in which the internal problems, the "stuff" of criminology, were denied an existence at all — as if to say that people are not moved by religion or are not really sick.

The stuff of criminology consists of only three questions: Why are laws made? Why are they broken? What do we do or what should we do about this? To demonstrate that these questions are so often posed in the wrong way called for (and still calls for) an intellectual perspective that lies outside the ideology and interests of those who run the crime-control system and the academics they hire to help them. To explain away the significance of these questions, however, is not only to deny their perpetual intrinsic interest but also to forget what the crime problem means in modern societies such as Britain and the United States: the massive resources invested in crime control; the depths of insecurity, denial, and irrationality in "thinking about crime"; the awful costs and waste of human life that crime means to its perpetrators and victims.

The new criminologies of the past twenty years promised to combine both these interests: to be reflexive and critical, but also to answer questions of substance. The subsequent tensions between the new and the old (and then within the new) criminologies is as much a tension between these outsider and insider interests as it is a more obviously political battle between varieties of conservative, liberal, and radical positions.

The initial intellectual shape taken by the break (later to be called "inversion" or "left idealism") was a systematic attempt to overturn the taken-for-granted assumptions of the positivist criminological tradition. At the personal level what happened was a collective form of role distancing: a refusal to be identified as a criminologist "like the rest of them." Organizations were founded and postures were struck (chapters 3 and 6 chronicle some of this) that proclaimed alternative identities: "sociologists of deviance," "critical criminologists," and so on. And all the while a curiously ambivalent relationship — inside and outside — was maintained with the old criminology. When the Norwegian sociologist Nils Christie, a leading anti-criminologist and abolitionist, was invited to receive an honorary degree from the University of Sheffield and open its new Centre for Criminology, he began his speech by saying that our proper role should be to close, not to open, such centers.

More cruelly than "role distance," all this might be seen as merely a form of collective bad faith. We were attributing responsibility to something out there, the discipline of criminology, that in fact we were very much part of. A safe radicalism: making a good living by denouncing the very institution by which you live. "Anti-psychiatry," a product of the same era and culture was a parallel enterprise.

But there is more to the story than this. Repressive tolerance, recuperation, role distance, bad faith — these are all elegant enough concepts to help understand the project of alternative criminology in retrospect. These concepts, however, are reductionist in trying to explain what happened without taking the content of the debates seriously enough in its own terms. The internal twists of the emerging discourse — the actual disputes that took place as the new criminology tried to establish its identity — deserve attention as much as these detached views of its history. The study of crime, law, deviance, and social control remains one of the most fertile areas for the sociological imagination, and the ideas generated by anti-criminology are as interesting now as they always were: the reality of crime as a social problem, the possibility of creating a crime-free society, the relationships between crime and politics, the nature of social control.

The essays in this volume give something of both sides of the enterprise, that is, meta-reflections about what criminology should be doing as well as some idea of the substance of the theoretical conflicts themselves. But, as I note in the preface, the bias is more toward the reflective side. On the content of criminological theory, the best guide remains David Matza's *Becoming Deviant*. Without being polemical or evangelical (the tone of my Part One essays), this book gives a clear hermeneutic reading of the major theoretical possibilities open at the time (1969) to criminology and sociology of deviance.

If *Becoming Deviant* was the book for the end of the sixties, in its depiction of the permanent tensions in theorizing about crime and deviance, then Foucault's *Discipline and Punish* was surely the book for the end of the seventies. With these two books on a desert island, the intelligent student could easily arrive at the whole agenda of theoretical criminology. By simply ignoring the internal debates within the subject, Foucault bypasses them altogether. Instead, he locates the whole discourse of criminology in the particular combination of knowledge and power that marked the simultaneous evolution of the disciplinary power of the modern state and the emergence of human sciences. Despite the mass of theoretical and empirical objections mounting up against Foucault's "history of the present," it is now simply not possible to think of criminology in the same way. The theoretical agenda ahead is to combine this external view of the discourse with a serious account of its internal content.[1]

But this is to run ahead of our story. What this essay does is retell the history of revisionist thinking about crime and its control over the past twenty years, a history in which the subsequent chapters are some raw material. I emphasize here two particular theoretical connections: the first is the relationship between criminology and the evolving contradictions of liberalism; the second is the parallel between anti-criminology and various deconstructionist movements in literature, philosophy, and other areas of the human sciences over this time period.

Deconstruction

We have yet to understand what the sixties meant to the cohort of left-liberals who began their intellectual careers during that period. The "return of ideology," New Left, counterculture, cultural revolution, personal politics — none of these concepts quite make sense of the ways in which intellectual life was conceived and led. Those of us who belong to this generation are too close as participants to be very good observers. Some more detached cultural historians of years to come are needed to excavate these ideas.

In one tiny corner of the cultural map of the sixties, a group of academics in Britain, North America, and parts of Western Europe gathered themselves around the old subjects of crime and punishment, deviance and its control. What we started saying was mostly interesting and creative, sometimes extravagant and silly, always typical of the wider intellectual and political culture in which we lived. In retrospect the claims we made were much further than we thought from being scientific revolutions, paradigmatic changes, the discovery of anomalies, or whatever. They were much closer to the products of radical art movements such as Dada and surrealism, anti–art created by artists.

These essays describe some of the forms that this impulse took: the development within criminology, law, sociology, social work, and psychiatry of various radical, critical, or countercultures dedicated to reconstituting the discipline or profession; the establishment of social movements aimed at weakening, bypassing, or abolishing conventional structures of legality, punishment, control, and treatment; struggles by various deviant groups themselves against the institutions and ways of thinking that oppressed them. To understand the oppositional, confrontational nature of these movements and ideas, we need to reconstruct the way the old regime was viewed. At the risk of caricature, let me distinguish three levels of attack: *structures of control*; *knowledge and theory*; *politics*.

Structures of Control

The base of modern crime control systems was laid down in those great structural transformations that took place from the end of the eighteenth century to the beginning of the nineteenth century: the consolidation and centralization of crime control in the hands of the state; the categorization of deviant, criminal, and dependent groups into separate types, each eventually with its own system of knowledge and its own professional group that monopolized this knowledge and power; the segregation and incarceration of these criminal and deviant populations into closed-purpose, built institutions of care, treatment, or punishment.

These structures were of course criticized and modified long before the 1960s, but—for various reasons that are still being debated in the literature—it was only in these years that the criticism intensified, dispersed itself through a wide range of public opinion (including the very professionals running the system), and proclaimed that a set of genuine alternatives was possible. As I describe in *Visions of Social Control*, this criticism was also sustained by resonant ideologies in the wider culture: the return to community, a distrust of bureaucracies and professionals, a libertarian attack on the state. Parallel movements took place in areas of mental illness, old age, and other areas of the welfare system: all became subject to what I called a great "destructuring" impulse or vision. The resultant movements can be easily listed. In place of *centralized state control*: decentralization, delegalization, decriminalization, diversion, divestment, informal justice; in place of *classification and professionalization*: delabeling, deprofessionalization, decategorization, demedicalization, anti-psychiatry, self-help; in place of *segregation and incarceration*: decarceration, prison abolition, deinstitutionalization, community care (or correction or treatment).

The prefix *de* indicates what these movements had in common: the negative, destructive sense that the old structures were now discredited and had to be destroyed, "tear down the walls," in the imagery of the decarceration movement. There was also a powerful element of *re*: a looking back to an imaginary golden age of social control before those original great structures had been consolidated. The vision was of inclusion rather than exclusion: care and concern in the decentralized community, away from bureaucrats and professionals. Sometimes this was a project of liberal reform within the interstices of the social democratic state, for example, diversion as a way of bypassing the harsher reaches of the formal system or community control as a way of keeping some offenders out of prison. Sometimes the project was more radical: a breaking up of the power structures associated with the modern state and returning them to the people. Thus, a society "without law" or "without crime."

Knowledge and Theory

To the three taken-for-granted structures of crime control (centralization, classification, and segregation) can be added a fourth construction at the level of knowledge. This is the assumption that the proper object of criminology is the criminal. This is what we understand as the emergence of positivist criminology: the actor rather than the act becomes the object of "penality," the creature whose existence the whole of criminological theory has to explain. In Foucault's Left Bank rhetoric, this is the move from body to mind or, even more grandly, the arrival of the *soul* as the proper object of knowledge.

Even more explicitly than by visualizing alternative structures of control, it was at this level of knowledge that the new criminologies began their attack. The enemy was *positivism*, the word that became (as it did in the wider sociological culture) the all-purpose object of contempt. As my early chapters in Part Two show, *positivism* came to symbolize everything we did not like: scientism, technology, dehumanization, reification, and (a peculiarly strong theme) the personalization of social problems by seeing them through the lens of pathology and psychiatry.

As later self-criticism was to show, much of this attack took the form of a simple inversion of the assumptions of criminological positivism. At times, though, the three postsixties decontructionist paradigms — labeling theory, critical criminology, and abolitionism — appeared to be doing little more than rescuing crime from criminology and restoring it to the mainstream of sociology. There was nothing very startling, for example, in restating Durkheimian theory about the relativity of rules or in reworking interactionist ideas about social categorization. At other times it was the wider ideological connotation of positivism that was dominant: the attacks on determinism and reductionism; then, particularly, the attempt to cast a quite different role for the criminologist (not a technocratic "agent of social control" but a partisan armed with a liberal underdog sympathy and, later, a commitment to revolutionary social change). The chapters in Part Two record variations on these twin themes: the modest sociological and ambitious ideological.

Politics

There is a sense in which the whole of the anti-criminology movement was political. It was devoted to finding (or, rather, restoring) the political dimension in each of those three questions that constitute criminology: Why are laws made (not, self-evidently, to protect all but to serve particular political interests); Why do some people break laws (not, self-evidently, because these people are simply bad or because they cannot help themselves but for latent ideological reasons); How is the crime problem to be solved (not, self-evidently, by goodwill and rationality but according to political choices and preferences). In each case the point was to challenge the original achievement of positivism in separating crime from the state.

Now, although many other political traditions — conservative, anarchist (but not, noticeably, socialist or Marxist) — had something to say about the crime question, this enterprise was above all an examination of liberalism. All serious thinking about crime touches on the nature of liberalism. Conversely, every single principle of liberalism carries implications for how we think about crime. The birth of the classical school of criminology was identified with the same thinkers (Bentham, Beccaria, Mills) and the same principles that are associated with the formal birth of liberalism: limiting the power of the state, reducing punishment to its minimum, utilitarianism, civil rights and liberties. And, in a more complex way, the positivist revolution was also liberal: in its original rhetoric of humanization, progressivism, reform, and benevolence as well as its later guises of treatment, rehabilitation, Fabianism, and welfare statism.

The distinctively political decoding of criminology that emerged in the sixties must not, however, be understood as a simple "attack" on liberalism. Rather, it was a series of maneuvers on the territory historically shared between liberalism and criminology. The attack was also confusing because sometimes it *was* clearly antiliberal (in the name of a vague libertarianism and, later, a more explicit Marxism) but sometimes (often from the same source) really an internal dialogue between varieties of liberalism. These are some obvious areas where such debates converged:[2]

- *The individual and society.* Anti-criminology began its life with a complex (and confusing) set of maneuvers around the classic liberal image of the atomistic individual whose desires are pitted against the common interests of society. At times this image of the individual was reaffirmed in the person of the deviant with free will — as against the positivist image of determinism. At other times atomistic individualism was attacked by invoking the "fully social" deviant who could not be understood apart from society. And the liberal image of a consensual society based on the social contract was replaced by an extreme pluralism (the multiple social realities of deviancy theory) or by a social order that existed only because of coercion and repression.
- *The power of the state.* When classic liberalism pointed to the sources of restraint on individualism, the obstacles to the individual's freedom to choose, it was referring to constraints imposed by the state. Hobbes on "the silence of the law," Mills on the proper limits of the state — these original ideas all reappeared in the rhetoric of the sixties. Thus, in the debates about decriminalization and crimes without victims, liberals were accused of hypocrisy, of not taking their own principles seriously enough. Or else a

more extreme libertarian note was struck by affirming values of tolerance and diversity (doing your own thing) against the Leviathan of the state.

* *Humanism and benevolence.* A recurring note in anti-criminology was its attack on the pretensions of benevolence, especially in the form of the ideology of treatment and rehabilitation. At times this appeared to be a defense of classic liberal values of freedom and civil liberties against the intrusive (but cunningly disguised) powers of the therapeutic state. At times it was liberalism itself that was under attack, and bewildered liberals were told that their humane victories against conservatism (of which they were so proud) were no more than new forms of coercion.

* *Constitutionalism and the rule of law.* Here again, anti-criminology was to address a traditional set of liberal values with a characteristic ambivalence. On the one hand, the rule of law, due process, and civil liberties were reaffirmed against any arbitrary power. On the other, the whole notion of "rights" was denounced as mere ideology, a facade of formal equality to disguise and legitimate real social inequality.

* *Reformism and progress.* Liberalism was a credo of progress through gradual, incremental reforms. As against any conservative pessimism, there was a strong belief that through goodwill and enlightened knowledge things had got better, and would continue to do so. As against radical utopianism, the faith was that the means toward this progress lay in gradual, patient reforms — piecemeal social engineering rather than revolution or the promises of historicism. The new criminology denounced both these beliefs: the Whig, progressivist view of history was questioned, and all sorts of Dionysian and utopian visions entertained.

* *Science and rationality.* Classic liberalism shared with criminological positivism (and positivism in its wider meaning in the social sciences) a series of related beliefs about the nature of empirical knowledge: the distinction between fact and value, the possibility of separating the observer from the observed; the intrinsic value of reason and rationality. Each of these beliefs was challenged by anti-criminology: in the weak form by exposing the ideological nature of criminology, its hidden value agenda; in the strong form by denouncing all conventional methodology as ideological and insisting on the inevitability and desirability of a committed, "taking-sides" role for the observer.

And so on. The list could be expanded to include virtually all other major liberal principles: tolerance, community, privacy, the tentativeness of knowledge. In each case the anti-criminology attack was both a reflection and an exposure of the disarray and contradictions in the liberal tradition. Even if these connections were not made clear at the time, it was surely the "decline of Western liberalism" that gave the political content to anti-criminology: the deradicalization of the tradition, the rewriting of the theory of democracy in the cold war period, the evasiveness about questions of class and equality. When radical criminologists explicitly attacked liberalism—for example, its principle of "equality before the law" for being bogus; its theories such as Mertonian anomie theory for "not going far enough"—it was to highlight the contradictions between the professed principles of liberalism and its actual commitments. This is exactly the same indictment made by the more general critics of the liberal heritage: "The practise of liberalism has turned out to be a great deal less radical and subversive of established forms of inequality and oppression than one might expect if one looked only at liberal theory and accepted it at its own valuations."[3]

Putting Together the Pieces

Anti-criminology was, by definition, a highly self-conscious enterprise. It was not surprising, then, that very soon after its initial appearance it was marked by self-doubt, and eventually a series of major internal revisions. All sorts of metaphors have been used to understand such changes in intellectual history. When the scientific element is dominant, we look for progress, breakthroughs, new horizons, paradigmatic shifts; the cultural lends itself to talk about cycles, swings, and fashions; when the political is dominant, we talk of polarization, of moves to the extremes or to the center. None of this language quite conveys what was to happen to anti-criminology. The image that I prefer (and that applies to the social sciences in general) is that of a friendly parasite that grows by turning in on itself, constantly reproducing internally but also having to adapt to changes in its host organism ("society").

Thus, the initial changes in anti-criminology (largely esoteric and invisible to the outside world) appeared as it began to absorb the implications of its own creations. This was followed by a further set of mutations forced by having to reconsider its relationship to an external (mainly political) world. To use the alternative metaphor of deconstruction, this was the period of picking up the pieces that at first had been so casually thrown around. The chapters in Part Three—especially 7, 8, and 9 and then, at a later period, 12 and 13— record and comment on the products of this second phase.

Structures of Control

By the middle and more clearly by the end of the seventies, liberals and radicals—most of whom had participated in these destructuring movements themselves—began to publish evaluations of what had happened to the original vision. The conclusion, as I detail in *Visions of Social Control* and summarize in chapter 12, was dismal. Things simply did not turn out the way they should have. The visualized reforms had not been put into practice at all, or they had been put into practice for the wrong reasons, or they had been co-opted and absorbed in such a way as to completely blunt their radical edge. Not only had the old structures turned out more resilient than we had thought (rates of incarceration increased, professionals retained their power) but the "alternatives" now overlaid on the existing system had actually made matters worse: coercive social control is disguised, the net of state control widened, intentions made more opaque than ever.

There were many different ways, again as chapter 12 shows, of making sense of this sad tale. The putative failures of the sixties' vision could be attributed to faulty implementation; to a historical tension between "conscience" and "convenience"; to the voracious appetite of professionals for exploiting all reforms to serve their own interest; or finally, to underlying historical processes that always render mere reform irrelevant. As this "taking-stock" literature made itself heard and these various theories were debated, four relevant political responses began to emerge. First, "radical impossibilism," a restatement of the traditional belief that no progressive reforms are possible without a major restructuring of the whole political economic order; second, "liberal realism," a sense of caution, skepticism, and even despair, a further lowering of the (already diminished) liberal horizon; third, "reaffirmation," an attempt to show (as the European abolitionists are doing) just what a literal translation of the original vision would have to look like; fourth, "left realism," a retention of socialist principles, but this time with a willingness to engage in social reform, a determination to be "relevant," and a denunciation of the original vision as romantic and utopian.

I describe my own position as "cautious reaffirmation," somewhere between the third and fourth models. It is the growth of left realism, though, that demands our most serious attention in telling the story of anti-criminology. What is significant here is an almost complete reversal of the original enterprise. Criminal justice policy must be constructed on, rather than against, the familiar structures of social control. The police, the courts, the rule of law become structures to be defended and exploited (for working-class interests) rather than demystified. Above all, the victim is reintroduced on the scene as the major determinant of criminal justice policy. These policy preferences eventually become embodied into a whole new theoretical paradigm.

Knowledge and Theory

The original exercise of denouncing and inverting positivism (street crime is not the real problem, crime is rational social action, disorganization and pathology are not important, the criminologist must be a political activist, and so on) had already reached its apotheosis by the time Taylor, Walton and Young published *The New Criminology* in 1973. The ideas of the first phase were already being qualified, revised, or abandoned. This reassessment came from a more orthodox socialist tradition (including *The New Criminology* itself and its immediate successors) or from fellow-traveling liberals worried about their earlier excesses. More generally, all those involved in the original enterprise began to examine the implications of their earlier work. Chapters 7 and 8, dealing respectively with social work and criminal justice, are examples of the debates that emerged in this period. Although internal recriminations and differences were also beginning to emerge, most clearly between Marxists and others, this phase of reassessment was really the expression of a common paradox. We began to sense that although the original onslaught on the old criminology was made in the name of "relevance," the shape that the attack took was drifting so far away from common sense as to sound more and more irrelevant. Much of initial critique of "absolutism" remained theoretically justified, but it began to disintegrate the further it was translated into a political and moral agenda. There, all sorts of inconsistencies appeared (was the deviant a mismanaged, stigmatized underdog or a rational, cryptopolitical hero, or neither?). Sound methodological prescriptions (such as the need to achieve appreciation by suspending conventional value judgments) looked absurd when extrapolated into an overall moral position.

Critical criminology began to be trapped in its own pretensions. It had originally emerged because the spurious scientific claims of traditional criminology had served to remove crime from politics. We could hardly now let ourselves drift away from these very same political considerations. It would have been consistent to continue supporting the old positions: in political terms, revolutionary transformation rather than reform; in theoretical terms, a "pure" deconstructionism that denied all the ground rules of the accepted discourse. The problem, however, was that we wanted things both ways: on the one hand, to be critical, to continue demystifying the claims of common sense and of the accepted disciplinary paradigm; on the other, to be and to look relevant, to intervene in a world in which real political choices were made.

At first, this problem was not easily resolved. Some of us were comfortable just to articulate these ironies and paradoxes without offering an immediate way out. This, I suppose, is the tone of chapters 7, 8, and 9. Others quickly denounced the idealistic elements in their original work, and moved to a "harder," more conventional Marxism that reaffirmed traditional revolutionary politics and rephrased the crime question in political economy or historicist terms. Yet others retreated into a modified liberalism, confining themselves to the cautious, middle-range criticisms suggested by labeling theory. In Western Europe the full-blown abolitionist paradigm emerged; this took the original theoretical breakthrough literally, refused to be embarrassed by charges of idealism, romanticism, or utopianism, and got down to the theory and practice of alternative realities (such as decriminalization, conflict resolution, mediation and so on).

All these positions are still alive today. Very soon, however, the influential majority of "theoretical Marxists" realized that far from resolving the tension between criticism and relevance, this was merely to move further along the critical path. Thus began the series of developments that culminated in the appearance at the beginning of the eighties of the current and now dominant "left-realist" position. Chapters 12 and 13 allude to left realism, but let me set out again very schematically its main features: (1) Instead of demystifying the crime problem as a product of media myths, moral panics, or false consciousness, crime is now acknowledged to be a real problem. There is a rational core to the fear of crime. One cannot gloss over its antisocial impact, nor deny the existence of victims, nor ignore the demoralization and disorganization that are both the causes and products of predatory and violent crime. (2) Although the particular psychological form it took was misconceived, the original positivist enterprise of finding the causes of crime was fully justified. Just when mainstream criminology has abandoned these etiological questions in favor of a know nothing managerialism, so must radicals return to the obvious contexts in which crime emerges in modern capitalist society: poverty, racism, deprivation, social disorganization, unemployment, the loss of community. The empirical and theoretical agenda is to demonstrate against these causal links. (3) Older idealist notions, such as the elevation of the criminal into a "primitive rebel" or cryptopolitical actor, must now be finally repudiated. And historical (and especially historicist) analysis, although important for building a sociology of law, is no real substitute for solving the traditional problems of criminology.[4] (4) Radical criminology, then, must make itself politically relevant by operating on the very same terrain that conservatives and technocrats have appropriated as their own. It cannot afford to risk the errors of the sixties by allowing itself to be marginalized.

In short, left realism *is* realistic. It resolves the tensions between outside/inside, criticism/relevance by moving closer to the commonsense, public knowledge of what constitutes the crime problem. This, it is argued, is where any credible alternative to mainstream criminology must be constructed.

Politics

The heady mixture of well-meaning liberalism, romantic anarchism, and New Left-style Marxism that characterized the initial phase of anti-criminology could hardly hold together for very long. As I have just recorded, these ingredients were soon separated out. A theoretically purer Marxism, a visionary anarchism, reconstituted liberalism, and finally, left realism — all emerged as distinctive political stances against mainstream criminology. At the same time, and far more important than any of these changes within anti-criminology, the "mainstream" itself had undergone a remarkable political transformation. In response to increasing crime rates, the emergence of the New Right, the consolidation of discrete law and order campaigns into a permanent political stance, and the supposed discrediting of the optimistic, liberal solutions of the sixties, mainstream criminology nudged itself in various neoliberal, neoconservative, and old conservative directions, and emerged in its current managerial guise. The heritage of liberal criminology is denounced, the search for causes is proclaimed a waste of time (because this does not lead to immediately feasible forms of intervention), and solutions are sought in the restoration of traditional authority and in varieties of punishment, deterrence, and incapacitation. By no means all mainstream criminologists share this managerial perspective, but this—in the United States at least—is where much of the political noise is coming from.

Left realism and other similar revisions of the original critical paradigm are responses to the same political changes that gave rise to the conservative and managerial positions. Whether it goes by the name of "left realism" or not, this response is part of the more general realignment of radical thinking over the eighties. As commentators such as Lasch suggest,[5] instead of reasserting a pure left gospel, the "thoughtful" radical mood is to acknowledge the legitimacy of some of the concerns that underlie the growth of contemporary conservatism. Conservative issues are then appropriated and given a left liberal twist. In criminology this means jettisoning the embarrassing political baggage inherited from left idealist days, affirming a social democratic, egalitarian set of values, and calling for state intervention to combat the social conditions that cause predatory and violent crime. These maneuvers are, once again, taking place on the familiar terrain of liberal principles. The following are examples:

1. A final repudiation of the individualistic set of values that appeared in the traditional liberal conception of negative freedom (the absence of constraints) as well as the initial phase of anti-criminology. Doing your own thing is now exposed not just as bogus value (a set of rights that liberals conferred only to the private lives of the privileged classes) but as something not worthwhile achieving anyway. And the model of the individual-society relationship from which such values derive is seen as primitive. I record in chapter 13 some variants of this revisionist denunciation of the "bourgeois liberal" ideal of personal liberty, the notion that constraints on human freedom are wholly external. Feminist ideology has supplied a quite different mode of thinking (for example, about the difference between private and public realms, about what constitutes harm, damage, or victimization) and an alternative principle of "positive," emancipatory liberty. At the same time the older forms of non-interventionism and anti-statism are attacked not only for romanticizing and trivializing social problems but for lending themselves to the New Right campaign to free the market from state regulation, thus only exacerbating the causes of these problems.

2. A "defensive formalism" about rights, due process, constitutionalism, and the rule of law. Faced with the seeming onslaught against civil liberties from the New Right, radicals are increasingly adopting those traditional liberal causes abandoned by the more embittered, impoverished version of liber-

alism. As with questions about the individual and society and the power of the state, the issue of rights must be set in the context of deeply rooted tensions in the history of socialism. Lukes, for example, has recently analyzed the central paradox in Marxism about questions of morality.[6] On the one hand, there is the contemptuous dismissal of the language of rights, justice, and morality as mere ideology, anachronistic, historically determined, and illusory: the "ideological nonsense about rights [Rechts] and other trash," in Marx's words. Not only are ethical judgments subordinate to historical determinism, but Rechts arise to deal with a reality that Marxism demands to be abolished. In these terms — and in very similar terms to which The New Criminology looked forward to a society "without crime" — the objective of Marxism is to create a society in which the edifice of morality and rights is not necessary. On the other hand, though, as Lukes describes, Marxism abounds in (and depends on) moral judgments: in its vision of a better world, its moral condemnation of capitalist evils, its advocacy of moral values against pragmatic self interest, its morality of emancipation.

This general paradox about morality — but more specifically the distinctive issue of legality — is the context of current debates in radical criminology. Although liberal ideas of freedom are rejected as being too narrow and individualistic, they are not denied the status of being genuine freedoms. Formal equality is seen as a value to be protected, and not just an ideological mask to cover substantive inequality.

3. The antiscientific rhetoric so characteristic of the sixties attack on positivism has now been quietly dropped. Rationality is no longer denounced nor is positivist research methodology as such. Realists urge an eclectic use of any means that will justify their theoretical or political objectives. These include quantitative methods, such as victim surveys and correlational studies of crime patterns, as well as a reliance on official criminal statistics. The social constructionist paradigm, which emphasized the socially contingent and ideological character of such measurements of crime and directed attention instead to the constructing activities of social control agents, is now kept alive only by liberal sociologists working in the tradition of labeling theory.

4. The political tone is becoming more reformist and piecemeal, less utopian and visionary. It is not so much that the standard liberal critiques of utopianism and historicism (Popper, Berlin) have been accepted by the Left but, rather, that reformist politics has been split off from any such grand theoretical design. Faced by issues — ecology, personal life-style, feminism, nuclear disarmament — that are harder to categorize in conventional left/right terms, radicals have remained with the issues themselves. Left realists working, for example, in such areas as victims' rights or community control over the police hardly refer to any master blueprint. This mirrors a conflict not only between liberal and Marxist traditions but within Marxism. Realists represent the anti-utopian tendency in Marxism that denounced such thinking as futile speculation, evasions of the more urgent historical task of trying to transform the present.

These, again, are just four examples. We could continue through the catalogue of liberal values to see how closely the revisions in anti-criminology, at the levels of policy and theory, correspond to the wider dialogue within and against liberalism.

The Present Tension

Any attempt to explain the fate of anti-criminology must avoid a narcissistic exaggeration of its importance. True, these ideas were diffused with commitment and enthusiasm, and true, they reached the center of the criminological enterprise. But at no point has the theoretical or political momentum been strong enough to pose a real threat to the dominant tradition. Today's conservative criminologists are debating with the legacy of liberalism and need never even mention any more "radical" perspective. The pristine form of anti-criminology must look like pure science fiction to the hard realists of crime control.

Still, this episode demands attention, both in external terms as an exercise in the sociology of knowledge and in internal terms because the ideas themselves are valuable. There are some good and bad ways of explaining the initial appearance of anti-criminology and its later mutations. One line would see the original ideas as simple reflections of artifacts of the wider cultural idealism of the sixties, ideas that then became modified in light of the harsher political realities of the next decade. Or this trajectory could be seen in empiricist terms: new findings, variables, and results being added to complicate the original theory. Alternatively, both the early New Leftism and the later left realism (and other variations en route) can be seen as points in the century-long revision of Western socialism and Marxism. This political context is particularly important in Britain: left realism is a Labour Party criminology, produced by socialists moving from sectarian left groupings into the central political arena. Yet another explanation would be biographical: the increasing "responsibility" that is supposed to result from becoming middle-aged and getting tenure. We could also look for parallels in other intellectual movements. My favorite example (pretentious as it is) comes from Isaiah Berlin's wonderfully sympathetic studies of the nineteenth-century Russian intelligentsia.[7] He describes thinkers torn between a suspicion of absolutism and a yearning to discover another absolute, monolithic idea. Many drifted toward what he describes as a Russian habit of taking ideas to their extreme, even absurd conclusion, as if not to do so was a sign of moral cowardice. Similarly, the reaction against the absolutism of the old criminology itself tended toward absolutism, only to recover its balance in the face of its moral absurdity and political irrelevance.

Illuminating as some of these theories and comparisons might be, they are no substitute for taking the ideas themselves seriously. The smug note of these histories also carries the risk of an altogether premature burial of ideas that still demand attention. This applies particularly to the differences between the idealist, realist, and abolitionist projects—arcane and remote as they might sound to those impatient to get on with the business of "taking crime seriously." Before considering these differences, I shall set out the wider spectrum of styles available in academic criminology today. The single criterion of this typology is ideology. It does not take account of all sorts of other differences (theoretical, methodological), and there will be any number of criminologists who will not recognize themselves anywhere in this typology. This is an abstract rendition of some dominant modes of thinking and relating to the political world.

1. *Conservative.* The traditional conservative model stresses the primacy of law and order, a strengthening of the legal and penal system, classical doctrines of punishment such as deterrence, a moral crusade against permissiveness, and lack of authority as the sources of crime. The reconstituted, neoconservative version retains the values of the original but is more pragmatic, more selective about the use of state power, less ambitious or fundamentalist in its commitment to restoring a lost social hierarchy. It is more attracted to "scientific" alternatives, such as selective incapacitation and environmental manipulation, than to indiscriminate increases in punishment. Though drawing on traditional conservative theories about the causes of crime—decline of moral values, creeping permissiveness, lack of discipline in home and school—it is vague or skeptical about the possibility of any large-scale manipulation of such factors. Instead, we find appeals to "human nature," a revived Social Darwinism, and the new "science" of sociobiology.

2. *Managerial.* This style overlaps closely with neoconservatism but (in the same way as old-style liberal positivism pretended to be "scientific") it professes to be wholly nonideological, pragmatic, and technocratic. For this reason, it also attracts many neoliberals or those who see themselves as "liberal" in the commonsense sense. And unlike conservatism, which contains an explicit model of how society does and should work, managerialism professes no interest in traditional causal questions or understanding the social context of crime. All this, together with theories about the origins of the criminal sanction, is dismissed as time-wasting speculation. Energy is devoted to only one of the three criminological questions, that is, how to design an effective crime control policy. The criminologist becomes a systems engineer, a manager of crime. In the words of a recent correspondent to *The Criminologist* (the newsletter of the American Society of Criminology), "The role of the criminologist and the role of the justice system is to manage crime, to deal with the inevitable eternal crime problem in the most humane and equitable fashion possible." This expression of equity and justice, however, is invariably secondary to the utilitarian goal of crime prevention.

3. *Liberal.* There are three variants of liberalism now on the market. The most traditional version retains the program of presixties positivism — treatment, rehabilitation, reform, individualization — as if nothing had happened since then. This version is intact and strong in nonacademic settings (social work, therapy, probation, parts of the correctional system itself). It also dominates the "progressive" criminology exported to the Third World (see chapter 10) and countries such as Israel, which accept these ideas unquestioningly and where there is no critical tradition. The second variant is the neoliberalism that gained strength in the seventies, especially in the United States. This is skeptical about the treatment model and other general claims to be "doing good." It still advocates middle-level destructuring reforms in the spirit of labeling theory (diversion, community alternatives, selective decriminalization). It supports the due process rather than crime control model and is drawn to the original (liberal) version of the "back-to-justice" program. To the extent that it is more interested in social reaction rather than causality, it sometimes lends itself to managerialism.

A third variety of liberalism is now also emerging. Its theory of crime causation is virtually identical to that of left realism, but its overall political program and genealogy are closer to "genuinely" liberal or social democratic goals than the more explicit socialism, which is found in the self-conscious versions of left realism. We find a vigorous reaffirmation of rehabilitation against neoliberal, conservative, and ultraleftist dismissals. In opposition to the "nothing-works" doctrine, the potential is restated for properly organized programs, decentralized and integrated into the local community but dependent on state financial support. In addition, the standard sociological theories of crime causation — economic deprivation, alienation and powerlessness, the lack of meaningful employment, social dislocation — are reworked and translated into policies for strong state intervention. An outstanding example of this reinvigorated left liberalism is Currie's *Confronting Crime.*[8]

4. *Socialist.* The traditional version locates crime in the total system of inequality and dominance in capitalist society, rejects mere reformism, and looks toward a revolutionary change in the social order that will result in socialist legality. The reconstituted version is left realism. It professes to retain traditional Marxist theory about the history and nature of capitalism but brackets this off in order to mount a credible political alternative to managerialism and conservatism. It stresses the same causal nexus as the left-liberal sociological tradition restated by Currie — inequality, racism, unemployment, the destruction of community, the demoralizing effect of the free market — and advocates much the same social policies — within the criminal justice system and in the wider society. The theory, though, is more likely to invoke conventional Marxist concepts, and the policies (in Britain particularly) are more likely to be linked to ongoing party political and labor movement struggles.

5. *Abolitionist*. This is a position distinctive to criminology and has no obvious general political referent unless this be some version of anarchism.
It remains faithful to most of the components in the initial anti-criminology
vision. In particular, it takes as a literal truth—something to be translated
into social policy—the original set of insights about the relativity of the
criminal and penal law model as a form of categorization and social control. In contrast, therefore, to every other position, it refuses to accept the
centrality of the criminal law as a form of social control or "crime" as a
concept to define undesirable behavior. Punishment is seen at best as useless and at worst as dangerous. Abolitionists search for forms of control
and conflict handling outside the criminal justice system (negotiation, reconciliation, mediation, modes derived from tort or civil law). In contrast again
to all the other models, the power of professionals and the centralized state
is questioned and the vision of decentralized community control retained.
If punishment (the infliction of pain) is to be imposed at all, this is for absolute rather than utilitarian reasons.[9]

6. *Theoretical*. A final style must be distinguished, which, unlike all the others,
is not much interested in being "relevant" or, rather, does not use relevance
as a criterion for the construction of knowledge and theory. Drawing either
on conservative or liberal values about "knowledge for its own sake" or "pure
scholarship" or academic freedom, this is criminology that is content to
leave to others any political implications of its work. The commitment is
to sociology (however that might be interpreted) and to the integrity of knowledge as a value in itself, not subordinate to any other interests. The results
of this sort of work in criminology—descriptive, historical, theoretical—
might indeed be open to multiple and opposing interpretations. Alternatively, they might appear obviously (though implicitly) to either support
or else profoundly undermine existing social arrangements and ways of
thinking.

I must repeat that this classification is highly stylized and, except for the
most self-conscious ideologues who might indeed see the world in one or other
of these modes, does not allow for the intricate and contradictory ways in which
today's criminologists might arrange their worldviews. Most of us will abstract
and acknowledge truths from each position. On a whole range of issues—
doing good versus doing justice, detachment versus commitment, short-term
reforms versus long-term transformation—otherwise oppositional styles will
share a common front. And most important, choices will arrange themselves
quite differently in cultures and political systems outside the Anglo-Saxon and
Western European settings in which these styles emerged. As I note at the end
of chapter 10, preferences for any of these models or judgments as to which
is "progressive" are wholly contingent on historical and political reality. There
are some countries, Israel for one, that still support such preposterous schemes
as "clinical criminology" and where the news of twenty years ago has still to

reach; there are countries that still await the "classical," liberal attack on torture, brutality, and arbitrary power.

Even in our more familiar Western settings, however, the location of mainstream versus oppositional tendencies is somewhat more complicated than it was twenty years ago. In one sense the tendencies "against" which any opposition is constructed remain as clear as ever. Not, this time, traditional conservatism and unrepentant psychological positivism but the emerging conservative-managerial alliance. And out of date as the polemics of my early chapters sound, the "failure of criminology" is as apparent now as it was then. Conservative postures are as firmly entrenched as ever, and managerialism is more influential than liberal positivism ever was. To the outside world, criminology retains its academic reputation for combining scientific neutrality with humanitarianism, despite the fact that its status derives entirely from the exercise of power throughout the penal apparatus. And it retains its credibility as a policy-relevant science, despite the fact that in terms of *success* in dealing with the crime problem, it should long ago have been relegated to the status of alchemy, astrology, and phrenology. The same criticisms that could be mounted twenty years earlier against the methodology that guided the positivist search for causes can now be directed toward the obsession with effectiveness, evaluation, classification, "what works."[10] Who can still take seriously a scientific endeavor that has used millions of dollars of research funds to come up with this "state-of-the-art" finding: "While great caution must be exercised in making causal connections, it does appear on the basis of limited evidence that the rise and fall of crime rates may at least be tentatively correlated with a decrease or increase in the risk of imprisonment."[11]

There can be no doubt that managerial criminology is a weaker, theoretically more impoverished opponent than the positivist legacy as it appeared twenty years ago. By the same token, the combined force of the real alternatives — liberal, left realist, abolitionist, and good, old-fashioned sociological — is stronger than it ever was. Much as these positions differ from one another in theory, politics, and style, they share a commitment to keep alive the knowledge that managerial and conservative idealogues are trying to suppress. This knowledge is simple enough: it is *not* lack of knowledge or of the "right" technology that stops us confronting the crime problem:

> What seems on the surface to be technical arguments about what we can and cannot do about crime often turns out on close inspection, to be moral and political arguments about what we should or should not do; and these in turn are rooted in larger disagreements about what sort of society we want for ourselves and our children. . . . If we continue to tolerate the conditions that have made us the most violent of industrial societies, it is not because the problem is overwhelmingly mysterious or because we do not know what to do, but because we have decided that the benefits of changing those conditions aren't worth the costs.[12]

Vague as this statement might sound, it is quite clear when we go on to specify them, that these are precisely the "arguments," "disagreements," and "costs" that conservatives must oppose and managerialists must rule as irrelevant.

Behind this common front, there are obvious differences within the oppositional ranks. In the initial phase of anti-criminology, these differences were submerged, their appearance now is altogether healthy because it allows for a creative theoretical dialogue to emerge. Of particular interest is the dialogue between, on the one side, left realism and Currie's type of left-liberalism, and on the other, the tiny but theoretically vigorous European abolitionists.

In this context the strengths of the realist position are obvious. In political terms it is immediately responsive to the demands of victims, potential victims, and public opinion. And even if our starting point is good theory rather than responsive politics, it offers a vision that is sociologically faithful and that addresses a recognizable political reality. The crime question does not belong, somehow "naturally," to the Right. Crime and violence as we see them today in societies such as Britain and the United States are the products of a state of chronic disorder in social relationships, the results of well-studied structures of inequality, deprivation, and dislocation. These in turn are the products of the reconstructed capitalism of the postwar era and its current forms under Reagan, Thatcher, and their equivalents. Far from improving things, the current conservative solutions — more punishment, cutting back on welfare state provisions, maintaining unemployment, reaffirming old-fashioned individualism, the attempt to free the market from state regulation — can only make matters worse. If this is a deterministic theory, then let it be. As sociologists such as Currie show (yet again), no amount of explaining away of those "imperfect" correlations between crime and various indices of inequality and dislocation, nor any appeals to "human nature," nor another round of psychological explanation can remove the brute facts of the social order.

On all this, as well as much else, abolitionism is silent. Its preference for what is something close to labeling theory's project of dealing with reaction rather than behavior tends to obscure the importance of those standard sociological concerns, which are seen instead as forming an obvious, taken for granted background. The real social variable is not the conditions under which criminal behavior occurs but the conditions that allow for criminalization itself. Suggestive as this view continues to be, it unwittingly bypasses the wider political choices that have to be made.

The strengths of abolitionism are more theoretically subtle and less politically appealing, especially out of the boundaries of the smaller, more homogenous European societies in which the model has been nurtured. These are theoretical insights — in one sense the buried wisdom of the sixties sensibility — that should not be sacrificed for political expediency. No doubt to talk about the contingent nature of the label of crime or the historical specificity of punishment or the values of reconciliation all sounds a little remote to city dwellers protecting themselves from muggers and their children from dope dealers. This does not mean however that such talk should be abandoned. And besides these "thought experiments," abolitionists do indeed engage themselves with practical social policies. There is no good reason that all such policies should be guided by populism rather than a more fantastic sense of the possible.

As chapter 13 chronicles, this is part of the continuing dilemma about the proper object of criminology. The original idealist "moment," for all its excesses, was surely correct to question the easy congruence between the dictates of public opinion and the boundaries of the disciplinary paradigm. The realist colonization of this area of congruence (the constitution, that is, of working-class violence and theft as *the* crime problem), with the addition of domestic violence and the victimization of women, makes some good sense. But it comes close to denying any relevance to the whole historical and theoretical project of exposing and relativizing the terms of the dominant discourse. The litmus test is large-scale organizational crime committed by the powerful: organized crime, corporate crime, state crime. Realists tend to bracket this off as a "second front"; abolitionists, to ignore it altogether. In both cases books with titles such as "Confronting Crime" and "Taking Crime Seriously" remain misleading.

But this type of point-scoring for or against realism and abolitionism is not what I have in mind by a theoretical dialogue. We need a more sustained analysis of the tensions exposed by this contrast. Most such tensions belong not to criminology but to agelong sociological and political debates, which take on a distinctive shape only when confronting the subject of crime.

One example is the old debate between idealist and materialist tendencies in radical thought. Although it would be misleading to see abolitionism as simply idealist and realism as materialist, this is just the form that the dialogue often takes. This was prefigured more than half a century ago by Pashukanis:

> At the Hamburg Congress of Criminologists in 1905, von Hamel, a reputable representative of the sociological school, declared that the main obstacles to modern criminology were the three concepts of guilt, crime and punishment. If we freed ourselves of these concepts, he added, everything would be better. One might respond to this that the forms of bourgeois consciousness cannot be eliminated by critiques in terms of ideas alone, for they form a united whole with the material relations of which they are an expression. The only way to dissipate these appearances which have become reality is by overcoming the corresponding relations in practise, that is, by realizing socialism through the revolutionary struggle of the proletariat.[13]

Now, although abolitionists do somewhat more than trying to free themselves of concepts and realists do not talk much about the proletarian struggle, their differences are close enough to the classic idealist-materialist debate.

A second and allied issue, suggested also by Pashukanis's words, concerns the worth of utopian thinking. As I have noted, realism allies itself with the anti-utopian strand in classical Marxism that denounces such speculation as reactionary and futile. This strand accounts, as Lukes notes, for the relative poverty of imagination about what the future socialist society will actually look like. As I suggest in chapter 8, this makes it difficult to know exactly how crime and punishment will actually be dealt with in the future. My own answers at that time were altogether conventional and unimaginative. The realist answer now would be to repeat the anti-utopian reasons for not confronting such questions until the time is nearer. This results, as it did in classical Marxism, in a failure "to exploit the practical strengths of utopian thinking, bringing liberating non routine perspectives to bear upon intractable problems in the here and now."[14] One fundamental such "intractable problem" is punishment. Realism has much to say about causation, policing, legality, victimization, and prevention, but it remains silent about punishment, implicitly accepting the conventional view I present in chapter 8. For abolitionists, punishment is the heart of the matter. Their program of abolishing prisons and punishment, utopian as it sounds in the pejorative sense of the word, is certainly "liberating" and "non routine." It is the contrast between these modes of thinking that needs to be exploited.

A third issue concerns the power of the state. Realist policies, whether cast in the language of social democracy, welfare statism, or socialism, depend on a strong, interventionist state. If this is not supported as a good in itself, then it can be justified only in instrumental terms as the only possible way of dealing with crime now, or (the third rationale) in terms of the Trotskyist doctrine of the necessity of a strong state in order to guarantee the transition to socialism (whereupon the state apparatus will disappear).[15] These justifications are not explicitly discussed in the criminological literature, but it is clear that each one of them would be opposed by the more anarchistic element in abolitionism. The point, again, is not to argue on behalf of one ideology against another but rather to see how these esoteric debates within counter-criminology bear upon such standard political questions. As I note at the end of chapter 12, social control theory has hardly begun to absorb the serious work about the modern state being produced elsewhere in sociology.

A fourth, and allied, issue is the question of means and ends. Criminological theory in every form from classicism through to positivism and its critics has been dominated by utilitarian thinking. The justification for intervention — whether punishment, treatment, or whatever — is in terms of the supposed ends to be achieved. Marxism is also utilitarian in this ordinary sense of the relationship between means and ends, but in addition proposes a special type of "consequentialism" in which the ends justifies the means because the end *must* follow. In contrast, most abolitionists are drawn to absolutist rather than utilitarian theories. They would support policies for "their own sake," that is to say, because they embody or prefigure the desired end state. You do not support undesirable policies only because they may lead to desirable ends; similarly, you support policies congruent with your values even if they fail to lead to such ends as "reducing crime." In this respect the ideology is again closer to anarchism: in Emma Goldman's words, "No revolution can ever succeed as a factor of liberation unless the MEANS used to further it be identical in spirit and tendency with the PURPOSES to be achieved."[16] Both this ideological difference and the standard discussions of utilitarianism in moral philosophy and jurisprudence remain open for discussion.

Over and above such examples of the theoretical and political issues that the realist-abolitionist debate draw us toward, we might turn to that last style I distinguished: "detached," theoretical sociology. More than in any other field of sociology, the student of crime and its control suffers from the pressures and delusions of relevance, impact, the wish to be listened to by the powerful. But we cannot entrust all our work to these temptations. Our primary responsibility is to the values of rationality, skepticism, caution, and good sense without which the whole intellectual enterprise is doomed. The view that the more congruent a discipline becomes with the societal definition of its subject, the more it degenerates into a mere ideology need not necessarily be opposed to those values.

For a long time, though, these worldviews have been opposed to each other. Ordinary reason, so we have been persuaded to think, cannot grasp reality but is itself part of that reality and therefore yet another form of repression. Nor can science "get at" a reality to which it is itself subservient. The way we know (knowledge) is the way we control (power). The social sciences offer neither enlightenment nor emancipation and cannot be distinguished from ideology. We must finally free ourselves from the illusion that we can know the truth and use this knowledge to make things better.

This terrible news, as Steiner and others remind us, is part of the more general "dissent from reason" that has characterized a powerful line of Western intellectual thought over this century.[17] The attack is on the Cartesian, Comtean faith at the heart of the Western philosophical tradition, the faith that with enough time, goodwill, decency, and reason some right answers to human and social problems will emerge. Criminology was originally part of this same optimistic, confident tradition. It drew on the same great dream as did the other great nineteenth-century positivist systems. After World War I deeper forces were unleashed; the old confidence disappeared, the pessimistic and apocalyptic became commonplace. In Steiner's terms, intellectuals began to doubt the old "wager on rationality" of the Western philosophical tradition: "Yes, words are vague and imperfect; yes, there are problems of understanding each other; yes, language is full of traps, but finally when all is said and done, there is between the word and the world a real relationship."[18]

Beyond the great demystification projects of Marxism and Freudianism, Steiner argues, the "language revolution" was crucial: the breaking of the relationship between word and world. The anti-Enlightenment forces came not just from irrational instincts or historical inevitability. In speech criticism, in Wittgenstein, and then in the Frankfurt School, the basis was laid for the attack on objectivity and reason themselves. The idea now was that the attempt to establish the truth value of any claim was just ideology. From here, through a long and fascinating intellectual route, we arrive at structuralism, post-structuralism, Foucault, and the other deconstructionist movements in art, philosophy, literary criticism, and the social sciences.

The original anti-criminology movement was part of this same intellectual stream. Our values — touchingly — remained humanist, but our conceptual baggage was borrowed from the rhetoric of demystification and deconstruction. We said very similar things: progress is a myth, reason and objectivity are illusions, the word is not the world. The more the discipline appeared congruent with common sense, the more it was mere ideology. Thus, "crime" is not real, but the product of faulty categorization, moral enterprise, or class-based attribution in the interest of the powerful; "criminals" were not what they appeared to be, but were elevated into rebels or demoted into ordinary people just like everyone else, while the "real" criminals were invisible; the "crime problem" was the product of manipulation by the media and the powerful; "prostitution," "blackmail," and "theft" were just labels attached to transactions and social arrangements endemic to this society; "rape" was just an extension of normal male sexuality; the designation of some drugs rather than others as illicit was irrational, arbitrary, and prejudiced; "mental illness" was not really an illness but a myth, a metaphor, a label attached to certain people under certain circumstances; "benevolence" and "reform" were really hidden forms of coercion; psychiatry, social work, and treatment were all forms of social control; and so on. In each case the enterprise was the same, to show that the accepted word did not stand for the world as it really was.

We have seen something of what happened to this enterprise in criminology. This is not the place nor have I the competence to discuss the fate of deconstructionism elsewhere. There is no simple way out of this history, neither a primitivist retreat to common sense and an appeal to the "obvious" nor a total surrender to an epistemology that negates the whole of the social sciences. For criminologists, the only guarantee of avoiding either extreme is to remember the existence of their subjects — offenders and victims alike.

Notes

1. This is just the goal achieved by David Garland in the case of England at the end of the nineteenth century: *Punishment and Welfare: A History of Penal Strategies* (London: Gower, 1985).
2. Here, as throughout this chapter, I draw on Anthony Arblaster's recent valuable examination of classic liberal principles and their decline in the twentieth century: *The Rise and Decline of Western Liberalism* (New York: Basil Blackwell, 1984).
3. *Ibid.*, p. 91.
4. For an interesting review of recent historical work on crime, see Christopher Tomlins, "Whose Law? What Order? Historicist Interventions in the War against Crime," *Law in Context* 3 (1985): 130–47.
5. Christopher Lasch, "What's Wrong with the Right?" *Tikkun* Vol. 1 No. 1 (1986) pp. 23–29.
6. Steven Lukes, *Marxism and Morality* (Oxford: Clarendon Press, 1985).
7. See particularly, Isaiah Berlin, *Russian Thinkers* (London: Hogarth Press 1981).
8. Elliott Currie, *Confronting Crime: An American Challenge* (New York: Pantheon Books, 1985).
9. See Nils Christie, *Limits to Pain* (Oxford: Martin Robertson, 1981).
10. For a summary of these criticisms, see chapter 5 of my *Visions of Social Control* (New York: Basil Blackwell, 1985).
11. James K. Stewart, director, National Institute of Justice, calling for Solicited Research Programs (Washington, D.C.: U.S. Department of Justice, 1985).
12. Currie, *Confronting Crime*, p. 19.
13. E. Pashukanis, *Law and Marxism: A General Theory* (London: Ink Links, 1978), p. 184.
14. Lukes, *Marxism and Morality*, p. 46.
15. Lukes, (ibid., p. 159) quotes the early Trotsky:
    Under socialism there will not exist the apparatus of compulsion itself, namely the state: for it will have melted away entirely into a producing and consuming commune. Nonetheless the road to socialism lies through a period of the highest possible intensification of the principle of the state. . . . Just as a lamp before going out, shoots up in a brilliant flame, so the state, before disappearing, assumes the form of the dictatorship of the proletariat i.e. . . . the most ruthless form of state, which embraces the life of the citizens authoritatively in every direction.
16. Emma Goldman, *My Disillusionment with Russia*, quoted by Lukes, *Marxism and Morality*, p. 105.
17. George Steiner, *The Dissent from Reason* (Jerusalem: Bnei Brit, 1986).
18. *Ibid.*, p. 7.

Part Two

Redefining the Field

3

"Images of Deviance"*

There has always been some truth in the layman's charge that the sociologists' picture of the world is merely a more complicated representation of his own common-sense way of understanding things. One can also see why sociologists in their quest for academic respectability have bristled at such accusations and insisted on their subject's status as a "science." Such defensiveness, though, not only is misplaced in that sociologists need to break free from the chains of science but misses the point that the sociologists have to start off with the layman's picture of the world. This is not to say that they must take this picture as the truth, but, unlike natural scientists, they cannot afford to ignore it. They must look behind the picture and understand the processes of its creation before trying to paint over it and superimpose their own version of what is happening.

There is perhaps no subfield of sociology where this paradox is more clearly illustrated than in the study of crime, delinquency, and other forms of deviant behavior. A large amount of space in newspapers, magazines, and television and a large amount of time in daily conversation are devoted to reporting and discussing behavior that sociologists call deviant, behavior that somehow departs from what a group expects to be done or what it considers the desirable way of doing things. We read of murders and drug taking, vicars eloping with members of their congregations and film stars announcing the births of their illegitimate children, football trains being wrecked and children being stolen from their prams, drunken drivers being breathalyzed and accountants fiddling the books. Sometimes the stories are tragic and arouse anger, disgust, or horror; sometimes they are merely absurd. Whatever the emotions, the stories are always to be found, and, indeed, so much space in the mass media is given to deviance that some sociologists have argued that this interest functions to reassure society that the boundary lines between conformist and deviant, good and bad,

* Introduction to *Images of Deviance* (Harmondsworth: Penguin, 1971) pp. 9–24.

35

healthy and sick are still valid ones. The value of the boundary line must continually be reasserted; we can know what it is to be saintly only by being told just what the shape of the devil is. The rogues, feckless fools, and villains are presented to us as if they were playing parts in some gigantic morality play.

By using a very broad and abstract concept of deviance, this book (*Images of Deviance*) does not ignore what to the public are the most serious and obvious forms of deviant behavior; the chapters on drug taking, theft, and football hooliganism are evidence of this. But the concept of deviance itself does not include only such "headline social problems," nor does it by any means include only criminal or delinquent conduct. The term *deviance* itself is to blame for carrying this narrower connotation. If we look at some words that can mean roughly the same things as the verb *to deviate*, we find the more generic features of the concept: alter course; stray; depart from; wander; digress; twist; drift; go astray; change; revolutionize; diversify; dodge; step aside.

The possibilities to which words such as these alert us are usually ignored, and the layman's understanding of deviance is based on the more visible types that are classified and presented in the everyday realm. Pressed to explain the *fact* of deviation, the public will probably redirect the question by talking about the *type of person* the deviant is thought to be: brutal, immature, irresponsible, vicious, inconsiderate, degenerate. These labels are the traditional ones of sin and immorality onto which newer concepts have been uneasily grafted following the increase in prestige and credibility given to psychiatrically derived vocabularies. Thus, sexual offenders are not degenerate but sick; they have "kinks," "warped mentalities," or "twisted minds." These labels are comfortable ways of looking at things because they leave us with the satisfaction of knowing that the problem is somewhere out there. The fault lies in the individual's genetic composition, mind, family, and friends, or in society as a whole.

This leaves the public with broadly four types of response to deviance: it can be *indifferent*, the problem does not concern us, "let them do their thing"; it can *welcome* the deviance, heralding it, for example, as pointing the way for society to advance; it can be *punitive*, advocating deterrent and retributive measures, ranging from a fine to the death penalty; or finally, it can be *progressive*, advocating various treatment and therapeutic measures, ostensibly designed for the deviants' "own good." (This last type of response might, of course, only look more progressive and libertarian than the third, but some of the methods, such as electric shock, brain surgery, and compulsory hospitalization, could merely be authoritarian techniques of social control under the guise of benevolent technology.) In any event, all these responses are evaluated in terms of their success in eradicating the deviance or controlling it within manageable proportions.

Traditionally, criminologists have accepted a view of deviance not very far from all this. They have carried out research, spending millions in the process, to demonstrate the ways in which the deviant is supposed to be different from the nondeviant. They have tried to show, for example, and less successfully than most people assume, that the deviant's personality, family experience, or attitudes toward authority are significantly different from those of a normal counterpart and that these differences somehow cause the deviance. Measures of control or treatment that take such differences into account are then usually proposed. A vocal group of criminologists in the United States and Britain have gone a step further in proposing to extrapolate backward from such supposed differences in order to predict and hence pick out in advance those destined to occupy deviant roles. A certain amount of controversy was aroused at the beginning of 1970 when a New York psychiatrist, formerly President Nixon's physician, proposed that psychological tests should be given to all six-year-olds in the United States to uncover their potential for future criminal behavior. He went on to advocate massive psychological and psychiatric treatment measures for those children with criminal inclinations, suggesting further that those who persisted into their teens should be interned in special camps for conditioning. The controversy about these views, and the fact that they were apparently being received seriously by the U.S. government, occurred mainly because of the starkness with which they were expressed. They were not at all novel nor were they the idiosyncratic ramblings of a cranky scientist but, in fact, the logical conclusion of years of respectable theory and research shaped by the conception of the criminal as a particular type of person, understandable and treatable apart from society.

What sort of strategies could lead to such proposals? Let me give a crude example of how somebody working within this particular tradition makes such connections between research, theory, and policy. Last year an intelligent psychology student in a reputable university obtained his Ph.D. after a lengthy study of the degree to which long-term prisoners were capable of "abstract" as opposed to "concrete" thinking. He chose as his controls (i.e. a group drawn for comparative purposes from the normal population) men from a sheltered employment workshop in the area, and found that the prisoners were more likely to think in a "concrete" way. This meant that they scored — and his logic and statistics were impeccable — less well on a test of abstractness: when presented with objects such as miniature handcuffs, they were more likely to say things like "police" than to mention abstract notions such as "law and order." On the basis of this statistical demonstration our psychologist then went ahead to propose that group therapy of long-term offenders should be designed to help them think abstractly so that aims such as deterrence and rehabilitation should be meaningful to them. Presumably, the next step is to design a test for schoolchildren that will weed out all the concrete thinkers and help them to come to terms with the abstractness of reality.

Of course, not all research in the tradition to which contributors to this volume are reacting is as crude as this caricature. If so, our educational task would be much simpler. Nevertheless, the logic behind this research is alarmingly appealing to both the public and the policymakers, and is not altogether different from that which shapes more prestigious and sophisticated work, such as that by Gluecks in the United States and Eysenck in Britain. It is the logic whereby the "punishment-fits-the-crime" principle has been translated with a minimum of discomfort to the "treatment-fits-the-criminal" principle.

This psychological tradition cannot but have rubbed off on sociologists as they moved in to study deviance and social problems. Their accounts, though, turned out to be inherently more plausible, if only because they recognized the complexity of the social process involved in creating and shaping deviant patterns. One valuable line of theory, for example, has pointed to the ways in which delinquency may be generated by a society that holds out common goals for all to attain yet provides unequal access to the means for reaching such goals. Another body of research has provided a vivid and credible account of deviant styles of life and subcultures, and how individuals become involved in them. We know a fair amount, for example, about the world of the drug addict, the social organization of delinquent gangs, some of the patterns behind organized crime, how some women become involved in prostitution.

The mainstream of criminology, though, particularly in Britain, has identified with strategies, values, and aims remarkably close to what the public demands and expects and the implications of sociological theories have either not been made explicit or not permeated through. It would be surprising, given the close historical connection between criminology and control or welfare concerns, to find otherwise. More often than not these concerns have expressed themselves in "soft" ways, and students of crime and deviance are invariably accused of being do-gooders or sentimental busybodies. In these roles they have played an important part in removing the more barbaric irrationalities of our legal and penal system. But the welfare approach embodies a conception of deviance close to that of the general public's, and in their well-meaning attempts to educate prison officers, policemen, or magistrates, criminologists are playing out the role that society happily allocates to them.

In recent years, particularly in the United States, there has been a two-pronged attack on this way of looking at the subject. From the theoretical side, questions have been raised about the whole concept of deviance, and a sociological truism has been reasserted, namely, that deviance is not a quality inherent in any behavior or person but rests on society's reaction to certain types of rule breaking. The same act — shall we say a homosexual encounter — is not defined in the same way by all societies, nor are all persons breaking the rules (in this case the rules governing sexual encounters) officially defined and classified as deviants. One must understand deviance as the product of some sort of transaction that takes place between the rule breaker and the rest of society. Similarly, a "social problem" consists not only of a fixed and given condition but the perception and definition by certain people that this condition poses a threat that is against their interests and that something should be done about it. From the policy side, the issue about what sort of role criminologists or students of deviance should play has also been reanalyzed. Questions, always dormant, have been brought out into the open about what side they are on and what sort of value commitments their theories lead them to. When dealing with the phenomenon of violence, for example, these answers have had to be made in contexts such as those of the U.S. ghettos, in which the distinctions between ideological and criminal action have become increasingly blurred.

These are the sort of issues raised by what I will call the "skeptical approach" to crime, deviance, and social problems, the approach that was the common starting point for the contributors to this volume. We had all been students and subsequently teachers in these areas, and had completed or were busy doing research on topics such as drug taking, vandalism, organized crime, sexual deviance, debt collection, the Mods and Rockers, football hooliganism, police action, juvenile delinquency, physical handicaps, approved schools, prisons, suicide, and mental illness. We were all familiar with U.S. literature on deviance, and in some cases this had directly shaped our research. In any event we were all uneasy about the way our subject seemed to be going in Britain.

Our feelings about official criminology ranged from distrust of its orientation toward administrative needs and impatience with its highly empirical, antitheoretical bias, to simply a mild lack of interest in the sort of studies that were being conducted. Many such studies were useful, but useful for what? We were also unhappy with the apparent attempt to define criminology as a self-contained discipline that, in Britain, was being dominated by forensic psychiatrists, clinical psychologists, and criminal lawyers. In terms of having congenial people to discuss our work with, we found some of our sociological colleagues equally unhelpful. They were either mandarins who were hostile toward a committed sociology and found subjects such as delinquency nasty, distasteful, or simply boring, or else self-proclaimed radicals whose political interests went only as far as their own definition of "political" and who were happy to consign deviants to social welfare or psychiatry. For different reasons, both groups found our subject matter too messy and devoid of significance. They shared with official criminology a depersonalized, dehumanized picture of the deviant: he was simply part of the waste products of the system, the reject from the conveyor belt.

So — as our own theory might put it — we found ourselves with a common identity problem, and we needed a form of subcultural support. In July 1968 a few of us met and decided to form a group, with the initial intention of organizing some discussions around our areas of interest. Besides talking about such specific subjects (others have included middle-class violence, gambling, hippies, con men, and police relations with colored immigrants), some time has been spent working out a more general position in regard to the study of deviance. We have not been altogether successful in this, and we are probably more agreed on what we are *against* than what we are for. I think, though, that it is possible to distill from these discussions a number of themes that provide common ground. To a greater or lesser extent, these are the themes that run through the papers in this volume. Not all the contributors would agree with all these themes; neither, though, would they find them highly objectionable.

Connecting with the Public

If sociologists see their task as explaining the world in terms intelligible only to fellow sociologists, then they are welcome to do so. Let them not complain, though, that politicians, policymakers, social workers, and the mythical man in the street do not listen to them. Of course, the main reason they do not listen is not because of a communication problem but because sociologists have no position of power or say things contrary to dominant values; witness the willfully ignorant way in which the government has handled the drug addiction problem. But we can be credible only to the extent that we are intelligible. Without our talking down or being patronizing, the accounts and theories we give of deviance should be interesting and meaningful to the layman. Conversely, the accounts of deviance given by nonsociologists — schoolteachers, journalists, bartenders, police officers — should be of interest to us.

Looking at the Others

I have already pointed out that a cornerstone of the skeptical viewpoint was a concern with the reactions of society to those forms of behavior classified or classifiable as deviant. The research worker must question and not take for granted the labeling by society, or certain powerful groups in society, of certain forms of behavior as deviant or problematic. To say that society creates its deviance and its social problems is not to say that "it's all in the mind" and that some nasty people are going around creating deviance out of nothing, or willfully inflating harmless conditions into social problems. But it does mean that the making of rules and the sanctioning of people who break these rules are as much a part of deviance as the action itself. The concept of crime is meaningful only in terms of certain acts being prohibited by the state, and a problem can be a problem only to somebody. So, whenever we see terms such as *deviance* and *social problem*, we must ask, "Says who?"

A corollary of this is that we must observe the effect of certain types of social reactions and public policies. We know, for example, that forms of deviance such as drug taking, homosexuality, and abortion would be very different if they were not "criminalized." If marijuana smokers were reacted to merely with mild disapproval when they overindulged themselves, the "drug problem" would have a different shape, and the meaning of smoking to the individual would change radically. The effect of the prohibition is thus crucial. We must also be alerted to the effects of the reaction of others on the individual's concept of himself or herself. Indignation, punishment, and segregation from the community might mark the person out in a special way, and together with others in a similar position, the person might eventually act in ways that resemble society's stereotype of him or her. Of course, the labeling effect is by no means automatic; one can resist the label or only pretend to comply. Deviants can also act in such a way as to shape their own role and identity.

Not all the "others" are equally powerful to impose definitions of deviance or to enforce rules. By focusing on certain groups, such as the police, who play key roles in the processes of social control, we are able to see how abstract definitions are mediated through the everyday encounters between the deviant and society. We are interested in agents of social control in terms not of their efficiency or expertise but of their mediating, channeling or funneling functions, the ideologies that support them, and the unintended consequences of their actions. Even in the superficially nonproblematic area of suicide, the control agent's — in this case the coroner's — role can be usefully examined in this way. The whole organization of social control can be approached in terms of its two-way relationship to changes in the pattern of crime itself.

Deviance as a Process

Our young psychologist's discovery of criminals' concrete thought patterns was one move in the obsessive game of finding the Holy Grail that will tell us the secret of deviance. The deviant is seen as the product of certain forces, or as the possessor of certain characteristics, and one day, given time, skill, and of course research funds, we will know what these forces and characteristics are.

The only part left out of this picture is the deviants themselves and the fact that they arrive at their position and become the sort of persons they are through a series of processes observable elsewhere in life. It is these processes we are interested in, not just the initial pushes and pulls but the stages of involvement, disinvolvement, sidetracking, doubt, guilt, and commitment. If psychological characteristics such as concreteness, extraversion, neuroticism, and the rest are of any meaning at all, they must be related to the processes of becoming a deviant.

These processes, of course, take place only in a context. We have become very much aware that the skeptical position has exaggerated its differences from older sociological concerns by playing up the role of "others" in creating and perpetuating deviance and playing down the structural conditions in which various forms of deviance arise in the first place. Neither societal reactions to deviance nor the process of becoming deviant can be studied apart from the economic, educational, and class systems; institutions such as family, school, and leisure, and patterns of power, conflict, and diversity. In different ways the papers on sabotage, soccer hooliganism, and thieving highlight some of these contexts.

The Defense of Meaning

What to some of us is a very radical break from traditional perspectives is the concern to defend both a conception of deviance as meaningful action and the status of the meaning that the deviant gives to his own activities. The annihilation of meaning has occurred in two ways. The one is to use adjectives such as *meaningless, senseless, pointless, aimless,* or *irrational* to describe various sorts of deviance, for example, violence or vandalism. People cannot allow deviation to threaten their picture of what their society is about. Part of this picture involves recognizing and accrediting certain motives as legitimate; if these motives cannot be found, then the behavior cannot be tolerated but must be neutralized or annihilated. Thus, vandalism, unlike theft, cannot be explained in terms of the accredited motive of acquiring material gain, so it is described as motiveless. The only way of making sense of some actions is to assume that they do not make sense. Any other assumption would be threatening. We are very much concerned — the chapter on industrial sabotage raises this problem explicitly — with restoring meaning to behavior that has been stripped of it in this way.

The other sense in which we are concerned with meaning is to do justice to, or in David Matza's term to "appreciate," the deviant's own story. The social scientist, as well as the layman, is increasingly likely to dismiss such stories as, for example, "mere rationalizations." Deviants are told that whatever meaning they give to their actions, the outside observer, the expert, knows better. You get drunk because you "can't cope with reality"; you take part in a demonstration because you have "unresolved authority problems"; you smoke pot because of "peer-group pressures." The more you protest to the contrary, the more you do not understand yourself.

One of the most significant groups in our society responsible for annihilating deviance, in both senses, is the psychiatric profession. It has endowed commonsense statements, such as "The poor bastard must be out of his head to do something like that," with a spurious scientific validity. It has provided justifications for new social controls under the guise of therapy. It has legitimized the creeping tendency to write off or explain away political conflict or racial disturbances as being the work of "mere hooligans" or "the lunatic fringe."

It should be made clear that in talking about appreciating deviants' own accounts of their motives, we do not regard this as the only story. We are also wary of the trap of romanticizing deviance. To hail schizophrenics as saints is no less misleading than to dismiss them as the unfortunate products of a biochemical imbalance. Such romanticism is not a form of appreciation at all because it ignores the pathos, guilt, suffering, and unhappiness that might be part of the schizophrenic situation.

Deviance as Continuous and Permeating

Another way to emphasize the problematic nature of the concept of deviance is to note that many aspects of deviance are continuous with normal life. It is not only labeled vandals who break other people's property, not only professional con artists who con others into believing in or parting with something, not only blackmailers who use blackmail to exploit a position of strength. This is not to say that the very illegality of certain types of transactions or behavior is not crucial. On the contrary, the labeling of actions in certain terms puts them in a class of their own. What we mean by *continuity* is the need to be alerted to similarities between deviant and normal transactions.

Deviant values are also not altogether discontinuous with more accepted ones; deviants might only be taking conventional values to extremes or acting out, as David Matza has argued, private values that are subterranean to society. Deviants might justify their behavior by appealing to widely acceptable social motives: "I only did it for fun," or "Everyone else is doing it." One has to delineate the normal patterns, such as those of technology and leisure in the cases of thieving and soccer hooliganism, within which the deviance develops. Further, there are questions such as those posed in the chapter on blackmail: What sort of society is conducive to the persistence of blackmail as a worthwhile form of commercial enterprise, and under what conditions can this deviance begin to resemble certain forms of acceptable commercial activity?

The Political Implications of Studying Deviance

A conception of deviance is not simply a shorthand description. It carries within it a range of evaluative, moral, and practical implications. For too long criminologists have either ignored these implications or readily accepted the directions they pointed to. Both these strategies are theoretically and morally indefensible. Let us imagine a sociologist interested in race relations being asked by a city to study its race problem in order to discover the best way of getting rid of its colored residents. Most such sociologists in Britain would refuse the job and would probably see as the major theoretical issue the reason that the city should have posed the problem in this way. Their values would commit them to such a perspective.

In some cases of deviance and social problems the position is analogous. We would not accept a brief from a seaside resort to clear its beaches of beatniks, however much we are interested in the subject of beatniks. And if we were against laws prohibiting homosexual behavior, we would presumably not undertake research on how to make such laws more effective. But the decisions are usually more complicated than these or of a different order, and the position is only roughly analogous to the race relations illustration. The deviance might be of a nature or degree that we would find difficult to tolerate or accept, and indeed skeptical theorists can be accused of opting for studying forms of deviance (such as homosexuality) that are calculated anyway to elicit a progressive, liberal response. Research goals are also usually defined in more subtle ways than "making the law more effective," and as students of race relations have discovered, one can be "pure" enough in one's research or even explicitly come down on one side, only to have one's findings distorted or torn from their contexts by politicians and used for the other side. In the study of crime an additional political problem presents itself: vast amounts of the information required are controlled by such bodies as the prisons, police, and Home Office, and are subject to such sanctions as the Official Secrets Act. Research funds also usually come from bodies with clearly defined aims, and although the person who pays the piper does not always call the tune, his directions are not easy to ignore.

All these considerations imply, at the very least, that criminologist should be more honest and explicit about what their values are and what they are aiming to do. If they want to be technologists to help solve the state's administrative and political problems, let them say this. But, however interesting and commendable such research may be, there are surely some subjects where something else is required.

We are not all agreed among ourselves about this "something else." In some cases there is a clear imperative to reject the officially stated aims of social control and actively or by implication lend support to the deviant group. In other cases we might support official aims such as deterrence but be concerned to define the deviant as a different sort of person from that which he is supposed to be. In yet other cases we might unequivocally accept the aims and conceptions of the control system. Faced with acts including marijuana smoking, violent crime, and drunken driving, it is clearly meaningless to ask, "Are you for or against deviance?" The question in this form is both absurd and inhuman: absurd, because in the rendering deviance intelligible, this is not usually the most pertinent question; inhuman, because one's sympathies with the deviant — or if there is one, the victim — are very human and not reducible to such an abstract question.

There are yet other types of more conventionally defined forms of political action that our theories must at least force us to consider. In this respect the skeptical position — which often implies little more than a plea for a more tolerant attitude toward the deviant or reform at the level of specific institutions such as prisons or mental hospitals — might be less demanding than other complementary sociological positions. In the United States, for example, criminologists like Richard Cloward have followed through the implications of their theories which located delinquency in the disadvantaged positions of the working-class and black adolescent. In a recent article in the journal *Viet-Report*, Cloward considers various tactics to make the poor an effective force in shifting national priorities from the Vietnam war to domestic programs. He advocates techniques such as massive rent stoppages to bankrupt slum landlords, disruptive techniques to claim welfare rights, and other policies that come close to the advocacy of urban guerrilla warfare. I am not suggesting that such policies are necessarily applicable in Britain or that they are at all relevant to most forms of deviance; they do, however, confront social problems in a more direct and honest way than many sociologists here seem prepared to consider.

It should be made clear that in lumping together the police, the courts, correctional institutions, social work, and psychiatry as forms of social control one is not implying some sort of blanket moral condemnation of those associated with these institutions. The term *social control* is a neutral, analytical one that should not carry any such overtones. Not only do we recognize that, say, child care officers, approved-school housemasters, probation officers, and psychiatrists are involved in genuinely helping functions under usually frustrating and intractable conditions but we want to give such groups some support. We do not want to keep aloof from those who are doing our dirty work for us. Our support might take only the form of buttressing a latent ideology that some of these groups have already arrived at, but such support is very much needed if the dehumanizing tendency of the social sciences (statistical reductionism, people being seen as collections of symptoms, the worship of computers) is not to be replaced in the world of policy and practice.

Sociologists are increasingly becoming traders in definitions: they hawk their versions of reality around to whomever will buy them. There is a responsibility to make such definitions not only intelligible, consistent, and aesthetically satisfactory but also human.

4

The Failures of Criminology*

The public image of the criminologist is a very strange and shifting one: at times a Sherlock Holmes figure, sniffing around for clues; at times a white-coated scientist analyzing blood stains; at times a psychiatrist explaining a child's delinquency in terms of the child's unconscious desire to punish the mother; at times a softhearted do-gooder turning our prisons into holiday camps. And indeed, people calling themselves criminologists have appeared in Britain under all these and yet other disguises.

For now I'll ignore some of the more bizarre activities that go on under the name of criminology and include only those enterprises directed primarily toward understanding the causes of crime, either as an end itself or to use this knowledge as a means of prevention, control, or treatment. Sociologists, psychologists, and psychiatrists are the major contributors here. They are a small group — I could probably personally name most of them — but like leeches they live off a very large body on which they are wholly parasitic. In the same way that our courts, prisons, probation officers, and police "need" crime, so does the criminologist. The gap, though, between the real world of crime and the artificial world of criminology is enormous. One reason for this is that the mere existence of something called criminology perpetuates the illusion that one can have a general theory about crime causation. Our subject matter, however, is artificial in the sense that the sorts of conduct that are criminal are wholly determined by what a particular society happens to prohibit. To quote Antony Flew:

> If you choose to study earthworms, then you have every reason to expect that your
> subjects will have a great deal in common besides whatever it is which makes them

* "The Failures of Criminology" was originally a talk given on the B.B.C. Television Programme, "Controversy" in August 1973, and subsequently published in *The Listener*, 8 November, 1973, pp. 622–625.

46

count as earthworms. But if you set up as a criminologist you will be surprisingly fortunate if you discover any universal truths about crime and criminals save those which follow necessarily from the initial definitions.

Their "initial definitions" have given British criminologists two major preoccupations: trying to locate the cause of crime in the characteristics of the individual, and carrying out operational research on the control and penal systems (how to make the machine operate more effectively, for example, by devising better ways to classify prisoners and allocate them to different forms of treatment). As other perspectives — predominantly sociological — have been introduced, these two preoccupations have been wrapped up with ritualistic gestures toward the "role of society in creating crime," but the basic sociological truisms about this role have not really been recognized.

How *does* society create crime? First, societies may be structured in such a way that certain segments are more likely to contribute to the crime rate than others. There is no need to make any sweeping deterministic claims about "poverty causing crime" — an absurd simplification — but no amount of sophisticated research and theory can hide the fact that in Western industrial society, the bulk of official *recorded* crime is committed by those at the bottom of the socioeconomic ladder. This has something to do with the differences in opportunity, with pressures, with the experiences of frustration and hopelessness, and with relative (as opposed to absolute) deprivation, and it also, of course, is connected with the relative vulnerability of this group (and racial minorities) to the machinery of formal social control: arrest, sentencing, punishment. Our society will continue to generate problems for some segments within it, for example, working class adolescents, and then condemn whatever solution these groups find to their problems. We must also realize that some of our most cherished social values — individualism, masculinity, competitiveness — are the same ones that generate crime.

A second sense in which society creates crime, and this is, by definition, true of all societies, is that we make the rules whose infraction constitutes crime. Crime is simply behavior that violates the criminal law. It is a category that is not fixed and immutable. By definition a major cause of crime is the law itself; this is not to say that if we cease to treat behavior X — say, smoking dope — as a crime then it will disappear but that the effects of labeling certain disapproved behavior as crime is of crucial importance. Further, the *behavioral* questions, the ones criminologists are obsessed with — "Why did they do it?" — might be dead-end ones when compared with the *definitional* questions: Why is that rule there? How is it enforced? What are the consequences of this enforcement? Take again the dope-smoking example. If 80% of students on a campus smoke, the question is not "Why do they do it?" but "Why have those in power allowed such a law to remain?"

From the psychological bias in British criminology and the consequent inability to incorporate such sociological truisms most of its other failures follow. The Holy Grail of criminologists, the alchemist's stone for which they have been searching in the hundred years since Lombroso thought he found the secret of criminality in the shapes of Italian bandits' skulls, is the cause of crime. They have gone about this search in a remakably uniform, one might say ritualistic, way. Find the association between crime and characteristics of the individual, and then the problem is solved. The rallying call is "the criminal and not the crime," a call that was historically a liberal and humane advance but that has led (in Britain in particular) to a view of crime as a function of individual maladjustment.

And this view has fostered a research methodology disarmingly appealing but potentially distorting. You find a group of known offenders, usually in a prison or other institution, and call them the Experimental Group. You then find a group of supposed nonoffenders, match them in other characteristics, and call them the Control Group. And if the Experimental Group has more of quality X, say, being redheaded, then this quality is either a cause or an intervening variable onto which a causal theory is built. So red hair in itself may not cause criminality but may itself be caused, say, by eating carrots. Carrot eating then becomes the explanatory factor. Within this sort of logic and design — and over the years, with great ingenuity, statistical sophistication, sincerity, dedication, and good intentions — hundreds of thousands of unfortunate men, women, and children have been given lavish attention, to their amusement, indifference, or annoyance. They have had their brain rhythms recorded, their skulls measured, their naked bodies photographed and somatotyped, their attitudes to their mothers, fathers, and siblings closely questioned; they've had to fill in numerous forms, get their strength of grip measured, stare at inkblots, blink their eyes at the sound of buzzers, and so on.

The results of all this have been at best ambiguous, at worst dangerously misleading, and in the main quite useless except for a few laughs at how gullible public bodies can be in giving away research money. The methodological flaws in this type of research are well known. First, studies of crime in the so-called normal population (by simply asking people to report what crimes they have committed) reveals an incidence that must make all attempts at finding a reasonable control group of "nonoffenders" highly dubious. *Most* people have committed crimes that go unreported, and even official figures tell us that males in England now have a one-in-five chance of being arrested for an indictable offense before their fortieth birthday. Second, the composition of the so-called "Experimental Group" is also a problem. Its numbers are usually studied at a terminal point in their criminal career, that is, they have already been processed by the official control system. How does one know what criteria determine movement through the system (these might have nothing to do with the offense; we know, for example, that police are more likely to arrest boys who don't show them proper respect), and how does one know whether or not the characteristics being observed are the *results* rather than the cause of crime? To give an example: if you find that a group of institutionalized delinquents are more likely to come from broken homes than a matched control group, this does not necessarily mean that broken homes is a causal factor. The association *might* happen like this: suppose judges react differently to children from broken homes and that *this* counts for the likelihood of institutionalization, that is, only those from "bad" families are sent away. Another example: at one time the vogue in theorizing about the causes of drug addiction was to postulate that certain types of personalities — suspicious, insecure, and paranoid — were predisposed to this deviance. But where and when were these characteristics observed? In large U.S. state hospitals to which addicts were sent for compulsory treatment. Is it surprising that after years on the street trying to hustle supplies, avoid federal narcotics agents, and watch out for spies and agents provocateurs, addicts should present themselves as insecure, suspicious, and paranoid?

Such bizarre theories are still alive and well in Britain. Here is Dr. R. Cockett, the regional psychologist to the Home Office Prison Department, describing in 1971 drug takers in a Remand Centre:

> They were shown to be rather more suspicious and withdrawn than non drug-takers, more emotionally tense and excitable, and more radical or less conservative in temperament, but to have relatively poor self-sentiment formation — persistence, willpower, social effectiveness and leadership . . . less emotional maturity and tolerance of frustration . . . intrapunitiveness . . . a tendency towards paranoid feeling.

Working your way through decades of this sort of research, you cannot avoid the peculiar feeling that in fact you are reading the *same* research project over and over again. "We don't go in for the Lombrosian type of nonsense of measuring skulls anymore," protest our present-day criminologists. But they do: in 1971 an English criminologist began a study of the chromosome abnormalities in a random sample of 500 Borstal boys and a control group of 500 factory employees. The well-known psychologist Eysenck is currently being financed by the Home Office "to test theories about the susceptibility of certain personality types to the development of criminal tendencies," using (surprise!) a sample of prisoners and matched controls. This method has even been extended to try to *predict* delinquency: factors like "mothers' attitude negative" found in the delinquent group are taken as "warning signs" of early delinquency. The ludicrous writings of the Gluecks in the United States still claim that "predelinquency" can be spotted as early as the age of three.

Of course, not all searches for the philosopher's stone proceed along the same lines. A breakthrough hailed by criminologists here is the longitudinal study, whereby one follows a random group of children for several years. Let's look how this method turned out in Dr. Donald West's study of delinquent development, started in 1962 and one of the biggest single pieces of criminological research in the country. The study takes 400 South London boys at the age of eight to nine and follows them for eight years. It's concerned with the individual characteristics of boys likely to become delinquent. Fine, but what turns out to distinguish the poorly behaved boys from the rest? Well, the best predictor seems to be *family income inadequate*; this was "remarkably effective" in identifying the "problem prone minority." Hardly startling news.

But what measurements were these poor kids being subjected to? A Spiral Maze Test, a Body Sway Test (most boys hardly swayed; some found the test unpleasant and anxiety provoking), and — wait for it — the Pencil Tapping Test. In the last test the subject taps a pencil on a blank piece of paper for ten seconds, this reveals the extrapunitive personality type, and it was confidently expected that "boys with delinquent personalities would tend to scatter their dots more widely." Elsewhere psychiatric social workers rated the attitudes of the boys' unfortunate mothers. Forty-two boys were said to have "cruel, passive or neglecting mothers," and they were more than twice as likely to become early delinquents as the remainder of the boys. Looks impressive, but it was actually only 21 percent (nine boys) of this group who became delinquent. How was it that *most* of the boys with these awful mothers escaped trouble?

Obviously an improvement on the Control/Experimental Group methods, such studies are still trapped in their initial assumptions: delinquency is something "in" the person. But the opposite is true: delinquency is something "outside" the person. To paraphrase Laing: "No-one has delinquency like having a cold." Crime and delinquency are labels, not things in a person.

Let me make it clear that my objections are not to explanations at the psychological level as such; of course, personality and family factors are of critical importance. The problem is the peculiar direction these explanations have gone: toward a clinical model that either explicitly or implicitly regards crime as being like a disease. This model appears in strong or weak forms, and lies in the mainstream of British criminology. Here is a strong version (from D. J. Rees, president of the World Federation of Mental Health):

> It should be stressed that all failure to comply with the rules of the game, and indeed all anti-social behaviour, whether it is noticed merely in the nursery or comes eventually to the courts of the country is evidence of some psychological failure in the conduct of life. Crime . . . is the outward manifestation or sign of some disorder in the personality and character.

Weaker versions assert that crime is simply *like* mental disease or that *most* crime is a product of mental disease. The defects of this model are gross and manifest. To a philosopher, the argument is hopelessly muddled and based on an inappropriate epistemology. On a factual level there is no evidence that any significant part of crime is the product of disease and what evidence there is, is based on clinical experience with unrepresentative samples. To a sociologist, such a model cannot come to terms with the relativity of the law nor the extraordinary variations in crime from one society to another.

The consequences of accepting even the soft version are of major significance. Viewing criminals as sick leads to discrediting any meaning or motivations they offer for their actions. They are stripped of the dignity of *choosing* to act in the way they want to, and instead are seen as the victims of forces beyond their control. This stripping is not only undignified but empirically untenable. In only a very small minority of crimes can the action be said to meet such definitional criteria of illness as *incompetence* (a literal inability to inhibit the behavior in question) and *suffering*. But because the experts, the doctors, know best, they can prescribe (in the same way as they reach a "diagnosis" and "prognosis") the best treatment. So, under the guise of psychiatric benevolence and a humanitarian ideology, we are asked to approve new methods of social control: electric shock, brain surgery, indeterminate incarceration in special hospitals, behavior therapy, chemical castration. The illness model lends further credibility to prevention programs based on such misleading notions as "latent delinquency" and "predelinquency." We must do something about the "predelinquents," the "carriers of the virus." And use of a softer version of the medical model, the rhetoric of liberal reform, has led to such policy changes as the gradual replacement of a legalistic by a welfare model for dealing with juvenile offenders. What in fact the "child-saving movement" has succeeded in doing is extend the juvenile laws to activities that would not be offenses for adults and gradually deprive juveniles of legal protection. Instead of due process we have family courts nosing around to find "pathology." The clinical model of crime, then, is dehumanizing, inaccurate, and potentially dangerous.

Another way in which the causes of crime have been obscured lies in the refusal of British criminologists to recognize the political nature of their enterprise. I mean *political* in the very broadest sense of that term: we have a subject matter to study only because society makes rules, some people break them, and some are punished. Damage, victimization, exploitation, theft, and destruction carried out by the powerful are not only not punished but not called "crime."

These are matters intimately concerned with questions of values, political conflict, and power. Criminologists have retreated from this battlefield by pretending it doesn't exist. This is done under two guises: the Neutral Scientist pursuing a question for the pure truth or the State Technician, the social engineer who keeps the system running smoothly. Occasionally, the criminologist ventures forth as the Humanitarian Reformer, and in this guise has done much to eradicate some of the grosser irrationalities and barbarities of the legal and penal system. But there remains a poltical timidity that shuts out certain problems. There is, for example, a refusal to deal with the overreach of the criminal law. It is much easier only to carry out behavioral research (why does someone break the law?) than to ask why the law is there at all and how it is enforced. To take two specific areas: violence and white-collar crime. In analyzing the causes of violence, criminologists have not understood the problems raised by violence associated with various forms of ideological conflict (race, class, national, religious). For the public, the "violence problem" includes student militants, the Angry Brigade, the Northern Ireland conflict, and trade union picketing, as well as the couple of hundred murderers who have the criminologist's attention so lavishly bestowed on them as they wait in prisons or psychiatric hospitals. These are difficult areas and cannot be solved by the arbitrary grouping of some offenders as "criminal" and others as "political." In the face of these problems, criminologists either have tried to extrapolate straight from their traditional models (so militants suffer from "unresolved authority problems") or have abandoned the debate completely by saying that such questions are for political scientists to deal with.

The other area—which for a long time criminologists have recognized theoretically but never actually come to grips with—is the field of white-collar or "respectable" crime: tax evasion, fraudulent advertising, corruption of local authority officials, shady deals by big business, infringements of laws by drug companies. Every reliable assessment has shown that the financial loss and public damage from these sources is greater than from "ordinary" crime, but we are too timid to confront this fact. And certainly our old explanatory models won't work. Were those involved in the Watergate affair or local cases of political corruption just unconditional extroverts? Suffering from identity crises? Trapped in a criminal subculture? Why aren't criminologists busy giving *them* pencil-tapping tests and trying to find out whether they had "cruel, passive, or neglecting" mothers?

There is another, narrower, form of timidity: the lack of nerve in the face of centralized governmental control over research facilities in this country. Few criminologists in the United States or Scandinavia would tolerate the degree of power exercised by the Home Office over criminological research. Access to prisoners, police, or anyone else in the system is severely limited, and publication further restricted by the powers of the Offical Secrets Act. So we have a curious situation in which most criminological research is tame "house research" done by the Home Office's own research unit (which specializes in abstruse technical reports that haven't exactly shed much light on the crime problem). Most other research is directly financed, sponsored, or controlled by the Home Office.

For criminology, the fact that most research has been "agency determined" is a critical source of distortion. To get funds from the Medical Research Council to do research on the causes of polio is one matter: one takes for granted the aim of eradicating polio, and the virus in the test tubes has no feelings about the matter. But in studying crime causation one cannot take certain aims for granted; moreover, the correctional position, one that approaches the phenomenon with the sole aim of eradicating it, systematically interferes with any capacity to understand it. If one holds a view of the human being as an object, then agency-determined research into crime causation is defensible; otherwise, it must be an insidious if not always immediately visible source of distortion.

The three failures I have concentrated on arise from the psychological bias, the clinical model, and political timidity. But even in its own terms, criminology has failed to deliver the goods. To those of us in the social sciences looking for a sophisticated theoretical approach, British criminology has been hopelessly anachronistic and trapped in its own history. To the public, daily swamped by the media's hysterical and tendentious reporting about crime, the criminologist is just another softhearted do-gooder. And if the public *did* look at our literature, it would find this dry, full of jargon, technical, and without any sense of urgency. Finally, the point where I started, the criminologist's connection with the world of crime is getting increasingly remote: crime figures rise, the courts are overloaded, the prisons lurch from one crisis to another. We haven't delivered the goods because we have not comprehended, or more accurately we have *pretended* not to comprehend, the nature of the problem. We don't have to discover the physiology of the mosquito before we think of draining the swamp.

5

Protest, Unrest, and Delinquency: Convergences in Labels and Behavior*

In this paper I would like to speculate about some of the problems raised by the blurring of the boundary lines between, on the one side, action usually labeled as "protest," "unrest," and "dissent," and on the other, delinquency. I want to concentrate specifically on violent or disruptive behavior because this is where the blurring has become sharpest and the conceptual (and policy) problems, most acute. If such problems had not been forced upon us (as I believe they should have been) by taking the new "skeptical" perspective on deviance seriously, they have surely been forced upon us by the emergence of new forms of unrest and massive civil disorder, particularly in the United States and particularly on the campuses and in the black ghettos.

Traditionally, the categories within which criminologists have responded to violence have mirrored the way in which the public as a whole discriminates between kinds of violence. On the one hand, there are the conventional, traditionally defined delinquent and criminal forms of violence, and on the other, there is violence associated with clearly recognized types of ideological conflict: political, class, ethnic, racial ("unrest" or "protest"). This distinction has seemed a commonsense way of understanding the world, although no one, of course, can pretend that it has ever been watertight, either in the nature and contexts of the behavior itself or the societal responses to it. Just in terms of crowd violence, for example, the work of Rudé, Hobsbawm, and (in an opposite way) Le Bon, all point to obvious overlaps.[1] Recent years, though, have witnessed some significant convergences between these two traditionally insulated areas. These convergences have produced the realization that the distinction between the criminal and the ideological cannot be taken for granted. Indeed, it is highly problematic and is itself based on ideological and specifically political positions.

* "Protest, Unrest and Delinquency: Convergences in Labels and Behavior" from *Internations Journal of Criminology and Penology*, Vol. 1 (1973), pp. 117–128.

The Problem of Problems

Even though the differences between the ideological and the criminal or delinquent might seem obvious at first sight, it is less obvious that the divergence *within* the social sciences in talking about violence is entirely due to such differences. The divergence should be put in the context of the overwhelming definition of most forms of crime as social rather than political problems, and the general insulation of the study of crime and deviance from sociology as a whole. This insulation is all the more noteworthy because it was not apparent in the early years of sociology (for example, in Durkheim). It occurred partly because of the way sociological theory itself developed, with its stress on a consensus model of society in which divergences were explained away rather than explained. In the more mechanistic versions of such theories, aberrant forms of behavior were seen simply as rejects from the conveyor belt, not of any intrinsic interest. Most of the responsibility for this insulation, though, was on the side of "criminology," "social pathology," and "social problems," with their stress of reform, welfare, or control objectives.[2]

A series of discrete "conditions" — crime, delinquency, mental illness, suicide — was studied and written about, and policies were directed toward each. So, as Horowitz and Liebowitz point out in a critical recent article,[3] the premise that punishment and rehabilitation are the only two possible responses to deviance yields the conventional tendency to evaluate deviant behavior in therapeutic rather than political terms. Decisions regarding deviance are relegated to the area of "social policy and administration" rather than to overtly political arenas.

This tendency was picked up by Bramson in his comparison, and location in political terms, of European and U.S. theories of mass society.[4] He notes the U.S. tendency to study "social problems" (delinquency, crime, "minority problems") in terms of how to make intransigent individuals conform, and compares this to "the social problem" of European sociology, which encompassed, in Mannheim's words, "those problems which arouse our passions in everyday political and social struggles." Now, it is clear that the dilemmas in such subjects as criminology are not found to be particularly relevant (let alone passion arousing) for those social scientists concerned with today's political and social struggles. And policymakers, politicians, and members of the public can hardly be blamed for not seeing the point of all those dilemmas, theories, and mountains of research project.

The development in recent years, though, of the transactional or skeptical perspective on deviance marks the most promising potential direction in making theories of deviance what they always should have been: theories about society and therefore about politics, conflict, coercion, and other such "normal" concerns. This perspective cannot but allow us to see that the decision to treat deviance as a social problem is itself a political decision.

Despite the fact that these ideas were being expressed in sociology some time ago, the message is only now beginning to percolate through. One reason is the very real behavioral and definitional merging of these areas. Not for the first time, the real world has begun to intrude on all those neat classifications, typologies, and interdisciplinary distinctions. So, Horowitz and Liebowitz, using the obvious backdrop of the U.S. ghettos, go as far as conceding that the distinction between political marginality and social deviance is becoming obsolete. Behavior that in the past was conceived as deviant is now assuming well-defined ideological and organizational contours. The politicization of groups such as drug takers and homosexuals is only the most obvious manifestation: any attempt to resist stigmatization and manipulation in the name of therapy or punishment is a self-conscious move to change the social order, and in any conception of the political process in terms other than looking at such matters as voting figures, these activities are political. On the other side, political marginals such as Yippies, the Weathermen, the Situationists, and the Black Panthers are creating new styles of political activity based on strategies traditionally considered criminal.

We have been slow to take cognizance of these changes—for example, the political significance of the hippie movement in the United States was initially totally underplayed by activists and observers[5]—and I want to briefly note the reactions to these changes. Looking simply, for example, at recent deviance and social problem textbooks, one can immediately see a blurring that was not at all evident even a decade ago. Alongside crime and delinquency, there are chapters on the ghetto, political dissent, the black revolution, black power, hippies, and so on. Some of these juxtapositions are odd, and where there is no explanation of *why* they are, they are often inappropriate. Two recent readers included material not only on delinquency, prostitution, drug addiction, and the like but also on Whitaker Chambers entering and leaving communism, a Students for a Democratic Society statement, and extracts from Lenny Bruce's autobiography. Such texts are just being self-consciously "hip," and there is no conceptual clarification about what if anything justifies lumping such diverse material together.

In political science and political sociology the problem is that these developments have hardly percolated through at all. Political activists, too, have retained their traditional reluctance to admit to any interest in crime and delinquency. The extreme Right has always been simply punitive toward such behavior, and eager, even when using paramilitary techniques itself, to denounce violence.[6] The Left has taken a "softer" line, but in following liberal rhetoric it has consigned deviants to the welfare category. Orthodox Marxism certainly had little positive role to award to the delinquent. Phenomena such as the early waves of recreational drug use among the young were seen by the "old Left" as being devoid of political signficance and indeed counterrevolutionary. Instead, of course, the drug laws in the United States have been, alongside the civil rights and antiwar movements, a major issue in facilitating dissent and focusing attention on the elements of politics, power, and repression in the criminal law.[7]

This is all changing, but there is still resistance in the traditional Left to broadening its conception of what is and what is not politically significant. This is evidenced by the response of a prominent English left-wing ideologist to various articles by a colleague on crime and deviance. He was told that he was wasting his energies on such subjects; delinquents were of little political interest, though of course they should be treated as humanely as possible.

A Sociology of Violence?

Such positions are hardly tenable in regard to violence. Somewhere in between organized warfare, insurgency, and violent revolution on the one side and the slum violence that has been the stuff of criminological theory on the other, something has emerged. Official government commissions and inquiries,[8] public discussion, mass media coverage, and collections of papers[9] under such rubrics as "law and order," "violence on the streets," "civil disorder," and "the problems of violence" and the very organization and composition of this international symposium[10] are all indicative of the convergences I am pointing to. Increasingly political scientists and historians are becoming interested in such matters as the criminal statistics and the organization of the police.[11]

For the first time, groups outside the criminology-social welfare axis are taking an interest in such theories as status frustration and blocked opportunity that were developed with reference to subcultural delinquency and applying them (often indiscriminately) to participants in urban riots, student militants, Black Panther-like groups (in whatever country), and situations such as those current in Northern Ireland. There is much talk of alienation, dropping out, disaffiliation, and youth on the street. There is confusion about the line beyond which "stealing" becomes "looting," "hooliganism" becomes "rioting," "vandalism" becomes "sabotage." When do "reckless maniacs" become "freedom fighters"? Are the everyday encounters between police and urban slum youth throughout the world somehow stripped of their political significance if what is happening is not defined as a "riot" or "disturbance"?

I have expressed these questions in a highly simplified and rhetorical tone, but in whatever sophisticated form they appear, it is clear that we have few clear guidelines for answering them. Even official reports and governmental commissions themselves, where one would expect to find some ideological if not conceptual clarity, have admitted to this blurring. They have found it difficult even to distinguish between legitimate and illegitimate violence.

In regard to causal questions, it is evident that when members of the public or policymakers turn to criminological theories of violence for the answer to the question "Why do they do it?" they will find only limited help. It is not that such theories, which reached their apotheosis in Wolfgang and Ferracutti's notion of a "subculture of violence,"[12] are implausible or unsophisticated. The theory posits the existence of a system of norms and values standing apart from the dominant or parent culture. This system designates that in some types of social interaction a violent and physically aggressive response is either expected or required. Carrying a weapon, for example, becomes a common symbol of willingness to participate in violence, to expect it, and to be prepared for it. These themes are localized and concentrated in certain subgroups of the population. Although such theories are less helpful on the origins than on the distribution and nature of subcultures, clearly they are of considerably greater potential than the earlier psychopathological accounts and make sense in terms of the distribution of officially recorded violent crime in most societies.

What they do not make sense of is ideological violence. Wolfgang himself is, of course, aware of the need to deal with what he calls "collective" as well as "individual" violence — race riots, labor riots, etc. — [13] and has recently devoted a major part of a lecture entitled *Violent Behaviour* to talking about ghetto and student violence.[14] He has stated that the "sociology of violence still needs to be written," and, significantly, names Sorel's *Reflections on Violence* as one of the starting points for such a task.

Part of this task involves thinking about definitions. This does not mean indulging in exercises to find the "essence" of violence or debating whether only *physical* violence should be included, whether aggression and violence are the same things, whether car accidents are part of the same problem, and so on. Beck notes the real problem of such exercises:

> Formal definitions commonly do not express our tacit understandings, which remain inaccessible. Wherever there is a discrepancy between a formal definition and our commonsense understandings, the definitions will be sacrificed in substantive discussions. No one will forsake a topic he is interested in discussing merely because the formal definition has not been properly made to include it.[15]

The same applies to formal definitions in the whole area. I do not expect anyone in this symposium to give up discussing anything because it is not included in the definition of *youth unrest* that someone else formulates.

The more fruitful starting point is to examine the definitions used by others and the bases on which they are formulated. The very invocation of a term such as *violence*, whether in realistic or metaphorical descriptions, carries multidimensional moral, practical, and political implications. It can be crucial to the outcome of a social situation if certain actions are labeled violent or excused from this label. Responses by either side in a conflict relationship are legitimated on the basis of such labels. As Skolnick expressed it:

> Violence is an ambiguous term whose meaning is established through political processes. The kinds of acts that become classified as "violent" and, equally important, those which do not become so classified, vary according to who provides the definition and who has superior resources for disseminating and enforcing his decision.[16]

In the rest of this paper I want to consider, at a fairly abstract level and giving hardly any of the substantive and illustrative material necessary, some of the problems raised by the convergences so far introduced. I look first at labels or images and then, more briefly, at behavior.

Reversible Images

From Criminal to Political

Many forms of "ordinary" crime and delinquency, particularly when associated with violence, large-scale organization, or mass violation (e.g. black market offenses) have frequently been seen as presenting a political problem in the sense of threatening the stability of society. Phrases such as "law and order breaking down," "the war against crime," "menaces to society," and "public enemies" are part of the rhetoric of crime control. In the heyday of organized crime in the United States, the operation of large-scale rackets, the activities of Mafia-style syndicates, and groups such as "Murder Inc." made this rhetoric and phrases such as "the invisible government" (used to describe the Mafia) real enough. What is surprising, given contemporary revelations about the extent of such operations, is that they should not be seen in more threatening terms. Where there is little organization or serious violence involved and where the offenders are juveniles, most contemporary societies do not see crime in very menacing terms; it is merely a social nuisance, to be controlled either by harsher punishments or innovatory treatment techniques derived from a medical model. Occasionally, one does find the extension of political images to less organized forms of delinquent street violence. J. Edgar Hoover once complained that the term *juvenile delinquency* is too apologetic; he would prefer the description *teenage brigands*.

Historically, anarchists have been the most likely group to seize upon such analogies as the basis of *attacking* rather than *defending* the state. Although this is perhaps less consciously articulated than outsiders might think, with anarchists' image as bomb-throwing terrorists, there is a clear current of anarchist thought that welcomes the political potential of criminals. One such current could be found in the ideas among Blanquists of professional revolutionists supplementing their funds with armed robbery. More important, because of their influences on some contemporary European groups, are figures such as Ravochol, Durutti, and Emile Henry. A weaker version of this tradition is to be found among the minority of orthodox socialists who have questioned the welfare state ideology toward crime and delinquency. They might see deviance such as industrial sabotage as some sort of revolutionary consciousness and would certainly be concerned at politicizing delinquent working-class youth, such as football hooligans, rather than writing them off as being merely troublesome.

More significant, of course, than these European developments has been the emerging political context of ghetto delinquency in the United States. The point here is not that the participants are becoming "politicized" nor that their actions are becoming transformed from ordinary delinquency to unrest or protest but that these political attributions are being noticed by outside observers. Even in a psychiatric journal one recently found an analogy drawn between police juvenile encounters in the ghetto and guerilla warfare.[17]

From Political to Criminal

What is perhaps a more interesting problem is the reverse of all this, namely, the application to recognized areas of ideological conflict of the language and imagery derived from traditional understandings of deviance, crime, and delinquency. Increasingly, such conflicts are being conceptualized within a framework derived from deviance control, and the participants are referred to in terms of labels originally applied to subcultural delinquency or criminal violence: thugs, hooligans, hoodlums, vandals, gangs.

Such labeling is, of course, neither new nor restricted to recent forms of dissent, disaffiliation, or protest. Acts directed against the state itself raise certain questions of legitimacy and are easily discredited by being seen as forms of criminal lawlessness. The revolutionary crowd in European history was identified with the frenzied criminal mob; movements such as Luddism have been stripped of their political significance; and popular uprisings in the Third World have invariably suffered the same fate. The current disturbances in Northern Ireland have gone through the familiar transition from first being ascribed to unemployed youths who had nothing better to do than throw stones about and then (when this explanation was manifestly inadequate) to being the work of a small, tightly knit, conspiratorial band of fanatics.

This sort of labeling process, though, is familiar to any student of politics. What perhaps is new is that an increasing number of political minority groups have emerged, bypassing the established processes and occupying a no-man's-land between political marginality and privatized deviance or ordinary crime.[18] Political (or racial or religious) minorities and marginals are allowed to dissent, even though they might be stigmatized with such terms as *fanatics* or *extremists*. But when previously privatized forms of deviance such as drug taking or homosexuality cross over into *public* protest and militancy, then the right to dissent becomes problematic and might be eventually denied. The same might happen if previously tolerated forms of dissent are articulated with tactics such as sit-ins, disruptive street demonstrations, property destruction, squatting, and so on. And when a new political minority comes into existence, it is critical whether it is publicly legitimized or simply lumped with the marginal and less respectable forms of unrest. (One might note that the functions of, say, labeling demonstrations or protests as delinquent, are often contradictory. On the one hand, emotive terms such as *thugs* or *hooligans* increase the threat by conjuring a screaming horde of atavistic beings. On the other, the delinquent definition is reassuring: the threat can be contained within the familiar limits of the penal and social services.) Elsewhere I have examined some of these issues in the case of vandalism and suggested the various contexts in which the term is used and the secondary images it evokes.[19]

In looking at these problems, there are four related lines to work on: (1) How does the reversibility of images occur and enter the accepted rhetoric of politics? (2) When are such reversals and mergings appropriate (for example, in drawing attention to common processes such as the role of the mass media in amplifying deviance) or inappropriate (for example, in obscuring different patterns of motivation)? (3) What are the societal consequences of reversing the images, for example, in terms of the moral judgments and social control policies resorted to? (4) What are the consequences for the individual or group so labeled?

These questions should be looked at in specific cases, for example, radical student groups, various urban fringe-revolutionary movements, and militant religious groups. Cross-national comparisons are also exremely relevant: one would need to examine cases such as South Africa, where *overt* political unrest and protest is low, and "ordinary" crime and delinquency, especially violence, extremely high (e.g. one of the world's highest homicide and execution rates), but the public definition presents exactly the opposite balance.

The Lunatic Fringe and Criminal Riffraff Theories

An image that deserves separate attention is that contained in the lunatic fringe or criminal riffraff theory of political behavior. Time and time again we are told about a disturbance or protest that there are ringleaders or activists who are not really sincere about the cause but merely thugs, riffraff, or a lunatic fringe exploiting the situation or using it as a cover for their own (unstated but usually implied criminal) motivation. Take the following statement from a coroner's report on the 1919 Chicago race riot:

Race feeling and distrust reaches far back into the history of the past. While new perhaps to Chicago, other cities and communities have tasted of its frightfulness, and yet, race antagonism itself rarely gets beyond bound and control. The real danger lies with the criminal and hoodlum element, white and coloured, who are quick to take advantage of any incipient race riot conditions to spread firebrands of disorder, thieving, arson loss, and murder and under cover of large numbers to give full sway to cowardly animal and criminal instincts.[20]

It should be noted that this theory and its variants such as the "pool-of-deviants" concept, (which posits a floating number of all-purpose deviants ready to take part in whatever form of disturbance is going) is given credibility by all three witnesses to a conflict situation. Not just the outside observer (coroner, official inquiry, newspaper editor) but each party to the conflict uses the same conception; the one to denounce the other for being largely made up of "bad" elements and each responding by dissociating itself from this element and asserting the respectability of its own "genuine" supporters.

I am not sure on what basis one is supposed to distinguish the "genuine" from the "fake" participants. Certainly such images make little sense in many forms of contemporary protest. Sociological research on the last five years of major urban riots in the United States has made it abundantly clear that the criminal riffraff theory is untenable. Data from such projects as the Los Angeles Riot Study[21] point to an interpretation of the events as broad group responses to shared grievances with wide local support and participation, and not the expression of an unrepresentative lawless minority of shiftless young people urged on by outside agitators and unsupported by fellow residents. Of course, it is more comfortable to believe the opposite, which is congruent with a view of society that sees the deviant as a small, distinctive group whose actions define the boundaries of what is right, tolerable, or legitimate. Defining the group in lunatic-fringe terms serves to exaggerate its badness (its atypicality) in comparison to a hypothetically overnormal population.[22]

The Sick Label

An increasingly common form of spurious attribution to both political marginals and deviant groups is that of the sick label: the assumption that the actors are mentally disturbed in some way, and as a corollary are not fully responsible for their acts. Such an attribution is, of course, not new in politics, and the whole medicolegal debate about concepts such as diminished responsibility arose partly in response to cases of political assassination. Recent dramatic controversies of this sort in the West may be found in the cases of Oswald and Sirhan; in Soviet Russia the use of the mental illness label to discredit political opponents has a long history.

But the sick label is being extended to further areas of action. In many countries, defendants in obscenity, drug, and violence cases are being remanded for psychiatric reports and later finding themselves the astonished and unwilling recipients of psychotherapeutic ministrations and ideology. Student militants have been described as "clinical cases" or as having "essentially abnormal character structures," and evidence is accumulating about the increasing influence of "psychiatric channeling" as a way of dealing with various troublemakers in settings of higher education.[23] A weaker form of this labeling attributes various forms of unrest among adolescents as being due to such vague constellations as "unresolved authority problems."

The sick label can be a way of denying the legitimacy of certain forms of deviance and dissent. Jock Young has described some of the ways in which this occurs.[24] There is the *denial of authenticity*: the meaning that deviants give to their acts is ignored and they are told that the acts are due to wrong chromosomes, faulty socialization, or a weak superego; the *denial of freedom*: deviants are impelled by forces beyond their control that can be properly comprehended only by experts (the activities of normal people, on the other hand, are seen as rational and based on free choice — unlike us, deviants cannot help what they do); and the *denial of cognizance*: deviants are unable to realize the real reasons that they act the way they do, and need the superior recognizance of an expert such as a psychiatrist to root out these hidden forces.

We should be wary of the increasing permeation of psychiatric ideologies into everyday understandings of the world. This permeation is not necessarily liberal or progressive; when it results in annihilation of the expressed meaning of deviance or dissent, it does not lead to any sort of explanation either.

Action and Motivation

Despite the elements it contains of fantasy, selective perception, and deliberate distortion, the labeling of deviants is not a process entirely divorced from reality. The spectre of the violent urban guerrilla is not a psychogenic hallucination nor wholly the creation of a right-wing conspiracy or a left-wing wish fulfillment. I have concentrated on the question of labels because this is the more neglected side of the problem. Whether the convergences I have been discussing are matched by similar transition in the motivation and action of various groups, and if so, what these matching patterns might mean, is beyond my scope here. I will merely draw attention to a number of cases and research problems in this area.

1. Although these are few, there are a number of unambiguous historical cases of political groups self-consciously adopting traditionally criminal strategies and styles, particularly in regard to violence. One important such constellation took place in France at the beginning of the century with the wave

of "illegalism" — mainly bombing, sabotage and theft — on the fringes of the anarcho-syndicalist movement. The best-known example is probably the Bonnot Gang.[25] Allied historical types can be found in the study of bandits and rebels pioneered by Hobsbawm.[26] Contemporary examples include groups such as the "Black Mask" in the United States and various offshoots of Situationists and Anarchist movements. These movements and types constitute a potentially rich source of material, although for obvious reasons access tends to be limited to the study of various documentary ephemera[27] rather than any closer participation.

2. It could be argued that the marginal nature of many of the above groups, in terms of their actural political influence, makes their consideration a somewhat esoteric occupation. This argument is not wholly acceptable, if only because of the fact that the societal attitude toward such groups and their eventual location on the deviance-politics spectrum influences the whole continuum of politics. The question particulary arises of how the self-conceptions and actions of more orthodox movements are going to develop in response to being labeled in delinquent terms. The possibilities range from wholesale incorporation of the new identity proffered (an unlikely development), to highly conscious attempts to counteract such labeling.

3. The obverse of all this has already been hinted at: the degree to which political strategies and styles might influence traditional delinquent or criminal groupings. In adult crime we find that the more organized groupings (who always looked upon themselves as part of the ongoing political structure, which through corruption and infiltration they greatly influenced) adopt civil-rights-type rhetoric to defend themselves. Another highly significant development, the first manifestations of which are just beginning to appear in the events of San Quentin and Attica, is the growing politicization of some prisoners. The transformation of George Jackson from thief to revolutionary is only a microcosm of this change.[28] At a less dramatic level there is the use by street gangs of well-recognized political tactics, such as entering into negotiations with the police and bargaining over the use of weapons.

Conclusion

In calling for attention to be given to these various convergences and permutations, I am doing no more than picking out one facet of a collective self-doubt that exists in the social sciences today. The erosion of interdisciplinary boundaries is, in itself, quite insignificant; one is not particularly interested in *who* tries to explain unrest, protest, or delinquency. Such erosions are significant only in pointing to a confusion beyond the academic community with the current paradigms of explanation.

Notes

1. See, for example, G. Rudé, *The Crowd in History* (London: Wiley, 1964); H.D. Graham and T.R. Gurr, eds. *The History of Violence in America*, (New York: Bantam Books, 1969).
2. N. Polsky, "Research Method, Morality and Criminology," in *Hustlers, Beats and Others* (Chicago: Aldine, 1967).
3. I. L. Horowitz and M. Liebowitz, "Social Deviance and Political Marginality: Towards a Redefinition of the Relationship between Sociology and Politics," *Social Problems* 15 (1968): 280–96.
4. L. Bramson, *The Political Context of Sociology* (Princeton: Princeton University Press, 1961).
5. For an analysis that does not make this error, see S. Hall, "The Hippies: An American 'Moment,'" in *Student Power*, ed. J. Nagel (London: Merlin Press, 1969).
6. For the case of the British Fascist movement, see R. Benewick, *Political Violence and Public Order* (London: Allen Lane, 1969).
7. One of the best summaries of these changes is to be found in J. Skolnick, *The Politics of Protest* (New York: Simon & Schuster, 1969).
8. The best examples are to be found in the work of the National Commission on the Causes and Prevention of Violence. See the *Progress Report* (Washington, D.C.: Government Printing Office, January 1969) and the various task force reporters, especially those on the media, historical and comparative perspectives (in Graham and Gurr, *The History of Violence in America*) and on group violence (in Skolnick, *The Politics of Protest*).
9. For example, S. Endleman, ed., *Violence in the Streets* (London: Duckworth, 1969); L. Masotti and D. Bower, *Riots and Rebellion: Civil Violence in the Urban Community* (Beverly Hills, Calif.: Sage Publications, 1968); M. Oppenheim, *Urban Guerrilla* (London: Penguin, 1970); and so on.
10. This paper was originally given at an International Symposium on Youth Unrest.
11. A. Schlesinger, *Violence: America in the Sixties* (New York: Signet Books, 1968).
12. M. E. Wolfgang and F. Ferracuti, *The Subculture of Violence* (London: Tavistock, 1967).
13. M. E. Wolfgang, "A Preface to Violence," *Annals* 364 (March 1966): 1–7.
14. M. E. Wolfgang, *Violent Behaviour*, Churchill College Overseas Fellowship Lecture (Cambridge: Heffer & Son, 1969).
15. B. Beck, "Talking Violence Blues," in *Dialogue on Violence*, ed. G. Vickers (1969).
16. Skolnick, *The Politics of Protest*, p. 4.
17. H. Black and M. J. Labes, "Guerrilla Warfare: An Analogy to Police Criminal Interaction," *American Journal of Orthopsychiatry* 37 (July 1967).
18. See Stuart Hall, "Deviance, Politics and the Media," in *Deviance and Social Control*, ed. P. Rock and M. McIntosh (London: Tavistock, 1974), pp. 261–305.
19. S. Cohen, "Who Are the Vandals?" *New Society* 12 (December 1968): 872–78.
20. Quoted in J. Landesco, *Organized Crime in Chicago*, new ed. (Chicago: University of Chicago Press, 1969).
21. A. Oberschall, "The Los Angeles Riot of August 1965," *Social Problems* 15 (1968): 322–41.
22. This is an extension on a societal level of the conditions for successful status degra-

dation: H. Garfinkel, "Conditions of Successful Status Degradation Ceremonies," *American Journal of Sociology* 61 (March 1956): 420–24.

23. See T. Szasz, "The Psychiatrist as Double Agent," in *Where Medicine Fails*, ed. A. L. Strauss (Chicago: Aldine, 1970).

24. J. Young, "The Zookeepers of Deviancy," *Catalyst* (1970): 38–46. See also the same author's argument about the denial of legitimacy in the case of drug taking: *The Drug Takers: The Social Meaning of Drug Use* (London: Macgibbon & Kee, 1971).

25. For a somewhat romantic account of its exploits, see R. E. Mell, *The Truth about the Bonnot Gang* (London: Coptic Press, 1969). Almost no worthwhile sociohistorical account of this period exists.

26. E. J. Hobsbawm, *Primitive Rebels* (New York: Norton, 1959) and *Bandits* (London: Weidenfeld & Nicholson, 1969).

27. A recent anthology of such documents is P. Stansill and D.Z. Marowitz, eds., *BAMN: Outlaw Manifestoes and Ephemera, 1965-1970* (Harmondsworth: Penguin, 1971).

28. G. Jackson, *Soledad Brother: The Prison Letters of George Jackson* (Harmondsworth: Penguin, 1971).

6

Footprints in the Sand: A Further Report on Criminology and the Sociology of Deviance in Britain*

The development of social scientific theory and knowledge takes place not just within the heads of individuals but within particular institutional domains. These domains, in turn, are shaped by their surroundings: how academic institutions are organized, how disciplines are divided and subdivided, how disputes emerge, how research is funded, and how findings are published and used. In criminology an understanding of these institutional domains is especially important, for our knowledge is situated not just, or not even primarily, in the "pure" academic world but in the applied domain of the state's crime control apparatus.

Indeed, if we are to follow Foucault, the *whole content* of criminology — with its "garrulous discourse" and "endless repetitions" — is to be explained with reference to its application by the powerful: "Have you ever read any criminology texts?" he asks. "They are staggering. And I say this out of astonishment, not aggressiveness, because I fail to comprehend how the discourse of criminology has been able to go on at this level. One has the impression that it is of such utility, is needed so urgently and rendered so vital for the working of the system, that it does not even need to seek a theoretical, justification for itself, or even simply a coherent framework. It is entirely utilitarian."[1]

To judge whether this is an accurate intellectual picture or a piece of inflated rhetoric requires a careful study of the combined history of criminological theory and crime control. This is not such a study. It is, rather, a report on a brief interlude in the history of the criminological enterprise in Britain: the state

* From M. Fitzgerald et al (eds) *Crime and Society: Readings in History and Theory* (London: Routledge: 1981) pp. 220–267. This paper was written for an Open University Criminology Course.

of "mainstream criminology" at the end of the 1960s, the evolution at that point of the "new deviancy" school, and some of the consequent developments in the next decade. My aim is confined to mapping the places in which the more interesting ideas of this period have been produced and disputed. The enterprise is thus complementary, and must be read in conjunction with, Jock Young's overview of the ideas themselves and with other similar projects.[2]

The first and longer part of the paper is an edited and abbreviated version of a report prepared for the annual conference of the British Sociological Conference in 1971.[3] The second part, more a guide to reading than a substantive report, brings that chronicle up to date by listing some later developments.

Part One: At the End of the 1960s

In 1968 the ineptly named National Deviancy Conference (NDC), the major institutional vehicle through which new deviancy theory was developed and diffused in Britain, was founded. Its major ideas, as formulated initially through its own internal discussion and soon a series of publications,[4] were largely programmatic. They took the form, that is, of placing on the agenda a number of items self-consciously different from those that appeared on the agenda of mainstream British criminology at the time. These included (1) a reconstitution of criminology as part of the "sociology of deviance" and its reintegration into mainstream sociology; (2) an elevation of social control (or "societal reaction") as a question of central concern and a consequent adoption of a structurally and politically informed version of labeling theory; (3) a determination to "appreciate" deviance in the senses of granting recognition to the deviant's own subjective meaning and of not taking for granted the control system's aim of eradicating deviance; and (4) an emphasis on the political nature of defining and studying crime and deviance.

These ideas served to demarcate significantly one set of collective self-definitions from another. They were not so much novel in abstract as in their determined insertion into, and opposition toward, the existing criminological discourse. This type of negative construction is, of course, typical in the history of ideas,[5] and to understand its form, we must reconstruct the main features of established criminology at the time. This established paradigm was fairly secure, with an integrity of its own, a certain impressive weight, and an umbrella-like quality that was able to absorb all sorts of ideas, even those potentially threatening. I argued at the time that this paradigm would be difficult to reform: the new sociology of deviance would have to develop a critique of a structure on which it would also be partially parasitic. A rough analogy was the relationship between the sociology of industry on one hand and industrial relations on the other.

The three headings from the following summary of my original B.S.A. report (Mainstream British Criminology; The Response from Sociology; The Evolution of the National Deviancy Conference) will be used again in Part Two of this paper to categorize the post-1970s developments.

Mainstream British Criminology

The main institutions I reviewed in 1971 were (1) the Home Office and particularly the Home Office Research Unit, set up in 1957 to carry out a long-term research program mainly concerned with the treatment of offenders and to act as a "centre of discussion with universities and other interested organisations"; (2) the Institute for the Study and Treatment of Delinquency (ISTD), set up in 1931, and crucial in that it directly produced the British Society of Criminology (BSC) and the only criminological journal in the country, the *British Journal of Criminology (BJC)*; (3) the Institute of Criminology at Cambridge, set up under Home Office sponsorship in 1958; and (4) the teaching of criminology in London, particularly the work of Hermann Mannheim. These institutions and individuals by no means represented a monolithic establishment, and there were many cross-links, for example, the Cambridge Institute of Criminology had close links with the Home Office (but not until recently with the *British Journal of Criminology* group). Four characteristics common to these institutions — pragmatism, the interdisciplinary conception, correctionalism, and positivism — were identified.

Pragmatism. The pragmatic approach had become an indisputable feature of British criminology. This was not a characterization made in retrospect by current observers[6] but one that had been proudly proclaimed by the leading representatives of the indigenous British criminological tradition. Thus, Radzinowicz after surveying what he calls the "liberal" and "deterministic" theories of crime, ends up by endorsing what he himself terms the "pragmatic position." This he sees as a "new realism": there is no single purpose of punishment, there is no single causal theory of crime, therefore any or all perspectives, from Burt to Merton, have something to recommend them and in this "lies the strength and promise of the pragmatic position."[7]

The pragmatic frame of reference was the one that shaped the few general text-book-type works produced by British criminologists,[8] as well as the organization of research and teaching. There is an overall distrust of theory or of any master conception into which various subjects can be fitted. The impediments to a theoretical criminology are easier to find than account for. One major reason is alluded to at several points by Radzinowicz: the fact that the whole idea of "schools" of criminal law and criminology in the Continental sense is quite alien to the British legal tradition.[9] On the Continent major schools of criminal law — liberal, classical, determinist, positivist, social defense — flourished for decades, partly because of the powerful position of professors of criminal law in the legal system. In England such positions of influence were the prerogative of the judiciary, the makers and interpreters of the law; "to them the formulation of an all-embracing doctrine and the emergence of a school was something quite alien."[10] Criminology had to take root in this pragmatic legal tradition.

In the United States, by contrast, although an autonomous criminology also developed, it was much more firmly located among the social sciences. As Radzinowicz, among others, has suggested, this location was partly due to the American ideology of optimism, in which crime could be seen as the product of remediable social forces.[11] Legal training had also been different: lawyers had for a long time been exposed to the social sciences in their undergraduate training; the strong U.S. sociolegal tradition was virtually absent in Britain. There was, thus, little opportunity for either a legally or sociologically based theoretical criminology to emerge.

In a much wider sense the pragmatic tradition could be seen as part of the national culture: the amateur, muddling-along ethos of British life combined with the Fabian type of pragmatism in which disciplines with obvious practical implication like criminology are located. Behind many enterprises in such fields the attitude is find out the right facts, then let those well-meaning chaps (for example, in the Home Office) make the obvious inferences and do the rest. Contrast, for example, the highly professional and research-based collection of information for policy-making in a U.S. official commission with the typical Royal Commission—with its motley collection of peers, bishops, judges, very part-time experts, and "informed laymen," and its unbelievably slow rate of productivity.

Although I did not accept the drift of this whole argument, these points need to be put into a broader context, such as the one suggested by Anderson.[12] His argument is that there was not just an absence of a tradition of revolutionary thought in Britain but an absence of major intellectual traditions at all. Thus, the weakness of sociology (which he overstates) is diagnosed in terms of its failure to produce any classical tradition and its historical dependence on charity, social work, and Fabian institutions. Significantly (for the point of this report), Anderson finds one reason for the absence of a separate intelligentsia in a factor I have already mentioned: the absence of Roman law in England and the blocking of an intelligentsia based on legal faculties teaching abstract principles of jurisprudence. Another, somewhat less secure, plank of his argument is the influence of European emigres (Popper, Wittgenstein, Berlin, Eysenck, and others). These were "intellectuals with an elective affinity to English modes of thought and political outlook" who found British empiricism and conservatism—the way it shunned theories and systems even in its rejection of them—quite congenial.[13]

It is appealing (aesthetically at least) to apply much of this analysis to British criminology. To give a specific parallel, the careers of the major founders of contemporary British criminology — Mannheim, Radzinowicz, Grunhut — were not too far removed from those of the emigres Anderson considers. Mannheim, for example, after a distinguished judicial career in Germany, came to London in 1934, where — according to all his biographers and former students — his natural empiricism and tendency to relate his teaching to practical work in the courts found an affinity in "the ideas of English social reformers, the work of the probation service and expedients in the after care of prisoners."[14] To point to this pragmatic frame of mind does not, of course, detract from the contributions that such figures made to teaching or penal reform. Indeed, this might be their strength. But it does provide a necessary lens through which to view their work.

The interdisciplinary conception. Pragmatism and empiricism are perspectives that often go hand in hand with the interdisciplinary ideology. Criminology cannot be other than interdisciplinary in the sense that it has to draw on the findings of what Morris refers to as the "strange motley of investigators who have, at some time or another, borne the title of criminologist":[15] doctors, lawyers, statisticians, psychiatrists, clinical psychologists, and others more bizarre than these. It would be a waste of time, then, to belabor this point, if not for two additional turns this feature took in British criminology. The first was to make a religion out of the necessity of drawing on different disciplines, and the second was to play down the sociological contribution to this pantheon, pushing criminology either in the legalistic direction or (more frequently and more unfortunately) toward the clinical-psychological-forensic ideology.

Again, let me start with an assertion from Radzinowicz to the effect that progress in criminology can be made only by the interdisciplinary approach: "A psychiatrist, a social psychologist, a penologist, a lawyer, a statistician joining together on a combined research operation."[16] In the British context the fact that a sociologist is not even mentioned was predictable. By the end of the 1950s the major figures in teaching and research were Radzinowicz (legal), Grunhut (legal), and Mannheim (legal training and later psychiatric and sociological interest). The major institutions directly or marginally contributing — the Maudsley Hospital, the Tavistock Institute, the ISTD, the BSC, and the *BJC* — heavily weighted the field toward psychology and psychiatry. This weighting remained despite the later contribution by sociologists such as Mays, Morris, and later Downes.

The multidisciplinary image was reflected at a number of levels. It was part of the criminologists' presentation of self to the public.[17] It could be found in the criminological conferences, in textbooks, and in lecture courses. Thus, in Walker's textbook, out of the fifty-seven pages devoted to the topic of explaining crime, seven are given to "constitutional theories," fifteen to "mental subnormality and illness," twenty to psychological theories of "maladjustment, the normal offender, and psychopathy," and fifteen to "environmental theories" (including "economic theories," "topographical aspects," and the "human environment"). Mannheim's work is more difficult to characterize in this way because, although he clearly sees criminology as multidisciplinary and his own training was legal, he made significant sociological contributions in such books as *Social Aspects of Crime in England between the Wars*, and his treatment of most sociological theories is as comprehensive as the rest of this 1965 text.

A clear statement of the interdisciplinary commitment was provided by another leading British criminologist, Gibbens, at a Council of Europe Criminological Conference:

> Most of the important ideas and research hypotheses in criminology still come from the parent disciplines of law, social science, psychology and psychiatry . . . major contributions to criminology continue to come from studies which are not originally designed to come within its scope. Geneticists stumbled upon the significance of the XYY syndrome, the Danish twin study was a by-product of medical study, the English study of a sample of the population born on the same day was originally designed to study midwifery and infant mortality.[18]

Other institutions revealed much the same, with an even more striking weighting toward the legal or clinical disciplines. The twelve research reports published then by the Home Office Research Unit contain mainly topics of a statistical, social administrative type, together with highly technical psychological research.

The character of British criminology is seen very distinctively in the ISTD-BSC-*BJC* axis. The Institute for the Scientific Treatment of Delinquency, set up in 1931, was the only one of its kind until establishment of the Cambridge Institute of Criminology. Its original aims included "to initiate and promote scientific research into the causes and prevention of crime," to provide educational and training facilities, and "to establish observation centres or other auxilliary services for the study and treatment of delinquency." The essentially clinical nature of the Institute's approach was not altogether removed after its Psychopathic Clinic was taken over by the National Health Service in 1948 and the term "Scientific Treatment" in its name was replaced by "Study and Treatment."

Thus, in the Institute's 1957–58 annual report the case was stated against handling crime from the penal end of the system and just using outside scientific information. One should rather move toward "extending the principle of treating offences whenever possible as behaviour disorders calling for appropriate psycho-social measures." Clinical positivism was stressed as the scientific ideal. In the following year's report the phrase "the root problem of delinquency, viz. the condition of 'pre-delinquency'" appeared. The possibility of predicting delinquency, an obsession in British criminology, was always stressed. The 1960–61 report complained that there were still resistances to dealing with crime as a "behaviour problem with characteristic antecedents. . . . Judging by comparative study of *other* forms of mental disorder, it is in the highest degree probable that in all cases the existence of a 'predelinquent' stage can be established." (emphasis added).

It is of course true that ISTD was uniquely dominated by psychiatrists (Edward Glover and Emmanuel Miller being the most notable) but Mannheim was a leading member from the outset, and scrutiny of the annual reports from 1950 onward shows that virtually every leading British criminologist (with the exception of Radzinowicz) held some office in it. The parent organization had considerable import, through its educational activities and also through its offshoots: the *BJC*, started in July 1950 as the *British Journal of Delinquency*, with Glover, Miller, and Mannheim as its editors (the name was changed in July 1960), and the BSC, which started life within the ISTD in 1953 as the Scientific Group for the Discussion of Delinquency Problems. The contents of the *BJC* over its twenty years reflected fairly accurately the discipline's concerns. A detailed classification of these contents[19] and a closer textual reading show a very wide interdisciplinary spread, considerable attention given to clinical and applied penological matters (classification, prediction, treatment, etc.), concern with penal and legal reform, and a representation of nonacademic correctional interests (e.g. reprinting a Metropolitan Police Commissioner's talk). Despite what looked to an outsider like a fair proportion of space given to clinical material, an editor complained in 1970, "Where we may ask, are the brave, resourceful, and imaginative clinical papers of yesterday?"[20]

An examination of the British Society of Criminology revealed a similar pattern. The backgrounds of both the Organizing Committee and the guest speakers over twenty years show a commitment to the interdisciplinary spread, with a heavy bias in the clinical direction.[21]

This type of analysis of the disciplinary content and the preoccupations of British criminology's main institutions at the end of the sixties was not meant to imply that sociologists were excluded for conspiratorial professional reasons. The imbalance was there partly because sociological criminology had not demonstrated any practical potential, and also — more simply — because there was so little of it. As the editors of a collection on the sociology of crime and delinquency put it at the time:

> Our reliance upon theories developed in other countries and particularly in the United States is sometimes so pronounced in the teaching context, that students gain the impression of an almost complete hiatus in British research. Erroneous as such an impression may be the fact remains that the heavy traffic in ideas about delinquency has tended to flow almost exclusively in one direction.[22]

As I will show in the next section, the impression of a hiatus in sociological attention to crime is not all that erroneous. With the notable exceptions of

Morris's ecological study and its predecessors, the Morrises' sociological studies of prison, and some work on sentencing, there was virtually nothing before the post-1965 wave following Downes's *The Delinquent Solution*. Two of the most frequently cited works of sociological relevance before the 1960s, Sainsbury's study of the ecological patterns of suicide in London and Scott's description of delinquent gangs, were in fact both done by psychiatrists.

Although it is difficult altogether to blame British sociology for paying so little attention to indigenous work, it cannot be exonerated easily from two further charges: a certain parochialism that willfully excluded U.S. sociology of crime and deviance for so long, and, then, a clear misunderstanding as to what sociology is about. Mannheim was partly guilty on the first charge, with his apparent policy of selecting U.S. work for his textbook only when British or European work could not be found; and the work of West was a clear example on both these counts. Curious notions about sociology's being concerned with "area" or "environmental" factors appear, sociology is identified with statistics, and concepts such as anomie, subculture, or deprivation are distorted.

In summary, the objectionable features of the interdisciplinary commitment appeared as (1) the rigidity with which it was defended; (2) the way it was skewed to exclude sociology and to lean in the clinical direction; (3) its parochialism; and (4) its actual misunderstanding of sociology.

Correction, reform, and the problem of values. British criminology has always been tied to two explicit interests: first, the managerial interest in making the correctional system more efficient; second, the humanitarian interest in reforming the system. These interests are often incompatible, but they might not be so when they are rationalized jointly in terms of the medical or psychiatric model, or its softer version, the rehabilitative ethic. "Treatment" can be seen both as more efficient and more humanitarian.

These relationships are complex enough in the day-to-day functioning of the system. What is more at issue here is the way in which British criminology had compromised itself by an unreflexive espousal of both these interests. There was a certain unawareness that this was even a matter to worry about. The dominant position simply took correctional aims for granted:

> Criminology, in its narrow sense, is concerned with the study of the phenomenon of crime and of the factors or circumstances . . . which may have an influence on or be associated with criminal behaviour and the state of crime in general. But this does not and should not exhaust the whole subject matter of criminology. There remains the vitally important problem of combating crime. . . . To rob it of this practical function, is to divorce criminology from reality and render it sterile.[23]

Alternatively, attempts were made to divorce criminology from such "practical functions." Walker, for example, states that "perhaps the hardest impression to eradicate is that the criminologist is a penal reformer," and concedes that although criminological findings might form the basis of reform campaigns, such campaigns are humanitarian not scientific in nature:

> It is no more his [the criminologist's] function to attack or defend the death penalty than it is the function of the political scientist to take part in an election campaign. The confusion, however, between criminologists and penal reformers has been encouraged by criminologists themselves, many of whom have also been penal reformers. Strictly speaking, penal reform is a spare time occupation for criminologists just as canvassing for votes would be for political scientists. The difference is that the criminologists' spare time occupation is more likely to take this form, and when it does so it is more likely to interfere with what should be purely criminological thoughts.[24]

It was to Walker's credit that he stated his resolution of the problem so clearly. In contrast, the major institutions of British criminology apparently quite unselfconsciously accepted the official system's aims and took up, within these limits, various correctional ("hard") or reformative ("soft") stances. Most criminological contributions were made by those who were actually employed by the system (e.g. as prison doctors or psychologists) and those who were sponsored by the system (e.g. doing research financed by the Home Office) or through the numerous institutions that organize cooperation between so-called scientific and so-called practical objectives.

The stances appeared in differing guises among the institutions under review, ranging from a bland dominance of correctional interests and personnel, to a sophisticated attempt to involve "practitioners" with the academic enterprise. At the more sophisticated end of this spectrum, clearly there must have been some awareness of the potential tensions and conflicts of interest, but this awareness was seldom expressed in any public way. And if Walker's solution was clear, it was also oversimplified and untenable. What had been problematic to generations of social scientists — the question of values and commitment — could hardly be resolved by asserting that there could be such things as "purely criminological thoughts." The constraints that operate in the very selection of certain subjects as being worthy of research; the methods chosen by the investigator; the way the project is funded and sponsored; the question of access to confidential data; whether findings have to be vetted before publication; how results will be used — all these and related matters could not be ignored.

This is not, of course, a problem peculiar to criminology. The 1960s saw a growing questioning of traditional positions across the range of the social sciences. And on matters about crime and deviance, where the hierarchies of moral credibility are normally so taken for granted, the issues took on a dramatic form. Becker's partly rhetorical but justly celebrated 1967 question, "Whose side are we on?"[25] was to become a major focus of debate. But within the institutions of British criminology and the official or quasi-official grant-giving bodies on which individual researchers were dependent, the question was simply not on the agenda.

The positivist trap. The heavy and anachronistic dominance of clinical interests under the interdisciplinary rubric of British criminology ensured a total acceptance of the positivist paradigm. Because my report is concerned not with the content of the theories themselves, readers are referred to the standard accounts of positivist thought (such as Matza's) in order to understand this dominant paradigm. At the level of abstract ideas it was certainly the perceived (or caricatured) features of criminological positivism (the search for clinical or statistical proof of causation, the commitment to scientific determinism, the denial of authenticity and meaning to deviance) that were inverted in the embryonic countertheories of the time.

In my original report I used one example to epitomize the characteristics of British criminology at the time. This was West's first Report of the Cambridge Study of Delinquent Development.[26] At the time, 1969, this was one of the largest single pieces of criminological research ever carried out in Britain, financed by the Home Office with an eminent Consultative and Advisory Committee (including only two persons out of eleven with more or less sociological backgrounds). In his preface to the report Radzinowicz hailed the research as being "in the great tradition of explorations of the springs of delinquency. Although on a smaller scale it will ultimately claim a place alongside such classics as the work of Robins, the Gluecks and the McCords. All too little of this sort has been attempted in England."

Radzinowicz's assertion was correct: in methodology and conception this research went no further than the extraordinary jumble of eclectic positivism that had already rendered the work of the Gluecks such an anachronism. Sociologists could hardly be expected to be impressed with a study that states that although it is more concerned with individual characteristics, it is also interested in the "demonstration" of the extent to which troublesome boys and other family problems are concentrated among the very poorest: "It may be that the next stage of the inquiry will go some way to answering the question of whether these problems spring from poverty or whether poverty itself merely reflects an underlying individual inadequacy."

The design involved an eight-year follow-up of some 400 boys selected at the age of eight or nine. Did some overall conception inform the selection of dimensions to be studied? West answers: "The aim was to collect information on a large number of items, all of them said to have relevance to the development of juvenile delinquency and to see in the event which items or which combination of items would prove to be the clearest determinants of future delinquency."

Social factors such as television were excluded because these were too "universal" and, of course, neighborhood influences could be excluded because these were "constant." Besides such indices as teachers' ratings and psychological dimensions of the family, items used included ones such as height, weight, body-type, and various tests of psychomotor habits.[27] The preliminary findings suggested that the social level of the family was the most important single factor in discriminating poorly behaved boys from the rest. From an actuarial point of view, the most efficient prediction might be based on a few easily registered and objective social facts. The index "family income inadequate" was "remarkably effective" in identifying the "problem prone minority." If this is so (and of course such a finding had long been the basis of criticizing similar psychological research), then what was the point of a study like this? Why use the opportunities provided by a long-scale longitudinal design in such a way? Any theoretical payoff (which the researchers might want to say did not concern them) aside, the practical advantages of such individualistic prediction studies, as numerous critics have shown, are highly dubious.

This, then, was the sort of research that appeared typical of mainstream British criminology at the time. Besides the "internal" critique to which projects like this were open, they clearly could not have been expected to command much sociological credibility or interest. To talk of "mainstream" criminology in this way is, of course, to ignore the numerous sidestreams that were yielding interesting work at the time. Morris, Downes, and Trasler had all produced books connecting criminological interest to core social science theories (ecology, subculture, behaviorism); Tony Parker had begun publishing his series of vivid life histories of offenders; and in related areas such as the study of legal institutions, the police, and the mass media, work had already begun that implicitly rather than programmatically was very different from established criminology as I have characterized it. We need now to consider how sociology as a whole had responded to the insulation of criminology.

The Response from Sociology

In 1966 Morris argued that even if British criminology had *not* moved in its neo-Lombrosian direction away from the concerns of such amateur Victorian sociologists as Mayhew, it "would still not have been able to gain much from association with the social sciences in British Universities."[28] Without pioneers such as Mannheim, he suggested, criminology would still have been where it was in the thirties. But what were sociologists doing during all this time? This question is important because new deviancy theory was a response to a lack of sociological belonging nearly as much as it was to perceived defects of criminology.

Sociologists of the period were clearly not particularly interested in the subject matter and preoccupations of criminology. Few would have shown (or admitted) a comparable unfamiliarity with other areas, such as education or industry. For the most part — given the nature of British criminology at the time — this indifference was quite justified, but this does not account for the absence of interest in the actual "stuff" of crime and deviance. On the surface this was surprising, for the study of deviance was rooted in the classic sociological tradition. As Becker, among others, had pointed out, to theorists like Durkheim, "problems of deviance were problems of general sociology."[29]

The reasons for severing these connections are complex and beyond my scope in this report. On the side of sociology they include a sophisticated version of the sort of philistine distrust that greets, say, Durkheim's *Suicide* and the whole work of Freud. How can looking at suicide explain how societies work "normally"? How can the intrapsychic conflicts of a few middle-class Viennese Jews explain how the "normal" mind works? Studying deviance is seen as an esoteric and marginal occupation. Crucial, too, had been the development of consensual theories in sociology, in the more mechanistic versions of which crime and deviance are simply the results of the machine's going wrong. It was precisely this sort of conception that new deviancy theory reacted against. The major barriers, though, had been created on the other side: the moralistic, nonabstract ways in which deviance was studied and the early identification of this field with social work, reformative, or correctional concerns.[30] As Polsky noted, criminology was the least successful of all subfields of sociology in freeing itself from these concerns. He comments on Merton's condemnation of the "slum-encouraged provincialism of thinking that the primary subject matter of sociology was centered on such peripheral problems of social life as divorce and delinquency": "Given the perspectives within which delinquency and crime are always studied, it is obvious why Merton might regard them as peripheral problems of social life rather than fundamental processes of central concern to sociology."[31] Polsky might be caricaturing criminology and is wrong if the old Chicago School studies of crime and deviance are considered. But clearly the development of criminology had little to recommend itself to sociology.

Returning to the institutional level, would one not expect the reverse in Britain, that the pragmatic Fabian stream in sociology would find criminology and related fields highly congruent with its self-image? To some extent this was true, but this stream had already started running in different directions. On the one hand, sociology developed scientific, academic, or professional self-images into which certain topics were not responsible enough to be fitted. On the other, soft, liberal attitudes became anathema to the hard radicals of sociology to whom deviants were not really politically interesting. Both these developments, but particularly the first, which was the more dominant, led to those sniggerings about "girls who want to do sociology because they like people."

Elsewhere, in trying to describe the sort of attitudes that were prevalent in the profession, I wrote:

In terms of having congenial people to discuss our work with, we found some of our sociological colleagues equally unhelpful. They were either mandarins who were hostile towards a committed sociology and found subjects such as delinquency nasty, distasteful or simply boring, or else they were self-proclaimed radicals, whose political interests went only as far as their own definition of "political" and were happy to consign deviants to social welfare or psychiatry. For different reasons, both groups found our subject matter too messy and devoid of significance. They shared with official criminology a depersonalized, dehumanized picture of the deviant: he was simply part of the waste products of the system, the reject from the conveyor belt.[32]

For such reasons, then, the institutional domain of British sociology found little room for crime and deviance. The major journals (compared, say, to the U.S. ones over the same period) contained a very low proportion of articles even remotely connected to the subject. Whole substantive areas — such as sexual deviance, drug taking, and mental illness — were virtually completely missing and there were no specialist journals (like the U.S. *Social Problems*) to cover these areas. Until the 1971 conference, at which this report was presented, the British Sociological Association had shown very little interest in the area. Various professional surveys at the time confirmed that despite the sociological explosion in Britain (one university chair before the war; over forty in 1967) sociological interest in crime and deviance was insignificant and well below most other specialist fields.

Sociology at the time seemed to show a basic divide between those who, to use Horowitz's terms, thought that the discipline should be "impeccable" and those who thought it should be "important": "The aesthetic vision of the impeccable sociologist . . . preserves him from the worst infections of 'helping people'". This gap is more than a matter of aesthetic styles, though: "It demands a specific decision on the part of scholars and researchers as to where they will place their intellectual bets: on scientific autonomy or on social relevance."[33]

Although the search for impeccability might have shut deviance out of sociology, the obvious political question remains as to what is "important" and "socially relevant" — and to whom? In left-liberal thought as a whole, the potential relevance of crime and deviance was not yet recognized. In liberal rhetoric, deviants were consigned to the nonpolitical categories of welfare and reform, and for orthodox Marxists, criminals were part of the lumpen proletariat and of little political importance. Of radical political theories, only anarchism — later of indirect influence on the new deviancy movement — had room on its agenda for the question of crime.

By the end of the sixties, though, all these walls insulating crime and deviance from academic sociology and from left or radical political thought were beginning to crack.

The Evolution of the National Deviancy Conference

By the middle of the 1960s there were a number of young sociologists in Britain attracted to the then wholly U.S. field of the sociology of deviance. The ideas of such works as Becker's *Outsiders* and Matza's *Delinquency and Drift* seemed to make sense across a whole range of teaching and research interests, particularly in "marginal" areas such as drugs, sexual deviance, youth culture, and mental illness. Official criminology was regarded with attitudes ranging from ideological condemnation to a certain measure of boredom. But being a sociologist — often isolated in a small department — was not enough to get away from criminology; some sort of separate subculture had to be carved out within the sociological world. So, ostensibly for these reasons (though this account sounds suspiciously like color-supplement history), seven of us met in 1968, fittingly enough in Cambridge in the middle of a Institute of Criminology conference opened by the Home Secretary. We decided to form a group to provide some sort of intellectual support for one another and to cope with collective problems of identity.

Before picking up the group's subsequent development, it is important to speculate on the less than purely academic reasons for its formation and rapid growth.[34] The first is that we all sensed something in the skeptical, labeling, and societal reaction perspectives, the anti-psychiatry school, and similar currents, that struck a responsive political chord. The stress on labeling, injustice, scapegoating, stigmatizing, the implicit underdog sympathy, the whole "central irony" (as Matza called it) of the neo-Chicago School and its recognition of Leviathan, the implications of Laing's work — these were all sympathetic ideas.

Later the perceived limitations of these common ideas (being sympathetic to outsiders and being critical of social control institutions) were to be the basis for division within the group. But at the time such interests were appealing for reasons strongly related to the personal background of the group's original members and the overall political climate. A degree of involvement with left and radical political movements (anarchist, socialist, Campaign for Nuclear Disarmament) had been followed by a certain disillusionment with such "conventional" political activity. Contemporary commentators like Jeff Nuttall[35] captured well this generational experience. Talking or doing something about deviance seemed to offer a form of commitment, a way of staying in without on the one hand selling out, or on the other playing the drab game of orthodox politics.

Such commitment was easier because the historical period was one of growing and visible militancy of deviant groups working outside the political structure. The hope for real social change (or in any event, where the action was) seemed to be with the hippies, druggies, squatters, and above all, everything that was happening on the U.S. campuses and in ghettos. These identifications were facilitated by personal involvement in some of these marginal groups. Some of the original members and even more of the later members of the NDC were on the fringes of what Jock Young nicely called, "the Middle Underground." Involved as participants, we could not resist the lure to be observers also—and make a decent living from it. The romantic, voyeur-like appeal of the subject matter was thus important; one doubts whether a similar group could have sprung up around, say, industrial sociology, educational sociology, or community studies.

I have speculated on this sort of reason because it seems implausible to suggest that only some sort of disinterested quest for knowledge drew people to the field. As in all such causal stories, the matter is overdetermined, and from its early years onward the organization began to mean many things to its members at different stages of their involvement. Although these real differences and incipient tensions were noted in my 1971 report, the story nonetheless was one of some success. The original group kept growing; social workers and other groups outside academic sociology were actively recruited; social activists and commentators were drawn in as speakers. A forum and support (financial and moral) were given to radical groups such as tenant associations, claimant unions, Case Con (the militant social work organization), and RAP (Radical Alternatives to Prison). Plans were discussed to formalize contact with such groups and allow them to shelter under the NDC umbrella.

The actual substantive papers at the conferences could be grouped into four categories: ethnographies of deviant groups and activities; studies of social control agencies; critiques of existing criminology or deviancy theory; attempted connections with fields such as social work, psychiatry, and the mass media. The discussions in these early years reflected with reasonable fit the original agenda items: developing an alternative or counter-criminology; applying the new U.S. sociology of deviance ideas to the British scene; establishing a critical and committed sociology. As the group expanded, alternative (and, somewhat later, potentially divisive) directions began to appear: academic versus activist; liberal, libertarian, and Marxist; hard and soft. I ended my 1971 report by listing some differences manifest at that point:

1. Should the group just drift along, amplifying and if need be changing, or should some attempt be made at tightening up?
2. Should the tightening up be in the direction of demanding greater commitment to social action?
3. Should the tightening up be in the direction of demanding greater theoretical sophistication, making everything more impeccable? As a corollary, does this mean excluding or limiting the numbers of nonsociologists?
4. To what extent should the perceived limitations of the theories, which originally looked so attractive, lead to an immersion in "harder" and ostensibly more political theories?

Such differences were, indeed, to become important later. So, too, were some other problems that I raised in trying to make a provisional comparison between the positions of mainstream criminology and the deviancy group at the beginning of the seventies. One was the strength that criminology could draw from concentrating on areas most likely to be defined as "relevant" and "important." In contrast, sociologists of deviance often dealt with catchy, esoteric, and "hip" areas that seemed of less public relevance. This was due partly to personal preference, but more to the fact that the interactionist approach seemed better suited to forms of deviance such as drug taking, homosexuality, and mental illness, which are ambiguous, marginal, and already subject to widespread normative dissensus. An allied problem was the value commitment being developed in opposition to criminology's compromised identification with the official system. There was a danger here of self-indulgent romanticism, a tendency to oversimplify matters by simply "changing sides." But whatever these internal tensions and potential problems, the lines of confrontation between the rival discourses seemed well defined. The next decade promised some interesting movements.

Part Two: At the End of the 1970s

The ten years since my original report was compiled have been extraordinarily rich and interesting ones, both in the study of crime and deviance, and in sociology as a whole. It was as if the explosions in the wider cultural and intellectual world of the late sixties had left behind all sorts of mutations and fallouts that now had to be contemplated and classified. To a large extent, especially in the social sciences, the center did not hold, and fission, diversity, and crisis talk became the commonplaces of the decade. For this reason the more or less clear patterns of ten years ago are now much harder to find. And for the same reason there is some danger in attributing causal significance to one force — say, the growth of the National Deviancy Conference — when the developments in question would have occurred anyway under the influence of this wider movement. Nonetheless, the visible influence of the new deviancy theories, both within the field (centripetal) and spreading outward (centrifugal), was remarkable. Let me report briefly on some of these developments, following the same headings used in Part One of this paper.

Mainstream Criminology

There are more corners and cavities than ten years ago, but for the most part the institutional foundations of British criminology remain intact and unaltered. As I originally suggested, the establishment saw the new theories as simply a fashion that would eventually pass or as a few interesting ideas that could be swallowed up without changing the existing paradigms at all. If we are talking about the center of Foucault's "power-knowledge spiral," the point where the utilitarian connection between ideas and policy is most transparent, this is hardly surprising. Indeed, this decade has seen a *reinforcement* of this connection: the Home Office Research Unit, the research branches of the Prison Department, the Metropolitan Police, and allied state agencies have all expanded and become more professional and productive. This is particularly notable, given the overall decline of government support for social science research. In line with what happened in the United States over this decade, the content of this type of criminology has switched (and is likely to switch even more) in the direction of "criminal justice", that is to say, an exclusive concern with the operation of the system. Research deals mainly with matters of decision making, staffing, evaluation and classification.

As we move to those institutions on the periphery of power — those ostensibly concerned, that is, with knowledge — the picture is a little more diverse. The various quasi-academic bodies reviewed in Part One of this paper (such as the ISTD, the BSC, and the BJC) have become more catholic and a little more receptive to the newer sociological currents. The uneven nature of this receptivity, though, is shown nicely in the pages of the *British Journal of Criminology* between 1970 and 1980. The papers themselves reflect only a slight change from the previous decade, while the book review section (under a series of sociologically minded review editors) became fully tuned in to the whole range of "new" and "radical" theory.

Moving even further from the power-knowledge center and toward the more unambiguously academic settings, the decade's fallout is much more visible. Even in 1971 I reviewed a textbook in my original report — Hood and Spark's *Key Issues in Criminology*,[36] — which was already perceptibly different from its predecessors: more sociological, more theoretically aware, and more questioning of correctional interests. Over the decade changes such as these became taken for granted in official criminological circles, although more, I suspect, in teaching than in research and policy-making. A 1979 textbook such as Bottomley's,[37] while emerging from well within the mainstream criminological consensus, gave explicit and coherent recognition to potentially threatening ideas. And in the mild boom in postgraduate criminology studies, the old and new were shuffled around together in curricula, examination papers, and reading lists.

Let me take the 1977 inaugural lecture by A.E. Bottoms, the director of the newly established Centre for Criminological Studies at Sheffield, to illustrate this accommodation.[38] His subject matter, the dangerous offender, derives clearly from the agenda of the old criminology. It conjures up images of the traditional obsessions of positivism and social defense, it seems clearly "correctional," it raises the spectre of clinical prediction. But although Bottoms certainly addresses himself to these issues, the paper is informed by a skeptical and theoretically minded attempt to understand the current revival of interest in the *concept* of dangerousness itself. The question is not simply whether or not dangerousness can be predicted and legislated about but how the idea relates to current changes in penal thought, such as the emergence of neoclassicism. Yet other examples might be found within criminology of influence and accommodation of this sort. Policy debates in such areas as parole have thrown up much more fundamental controversies than would have been possible in the older liberal reform consensus.[39] Consideration of such matters as sentencing and the aims of punishment are more theoretically informed and less insular. And while longitudinal studies such as West's still continued, they were sometimes presented in a framework that took cognizance of such views as labeling theory.[40]

At the center of criminological enterprise thought, it is business as usual. At the academic edges, those more sensitive to changing currents (in thinking, publication, conference papers, student interests), a pattern of accommodation is taking place. What clearly has not happened is any sort of collective crisis of self-confidence. In allied fields elsewhere, such shifts have indeed taken place in response to the power of ideas,[41] but there is no reason to suppose that the institutions of British (or any other) criminology will crumble in the face of any ideas — let alone the vague, inconsistent, and incomplete alternative offered by the new theories. As I suggest elsewhere, the reluctance of the new theories to inhabit the same areas as the old, has left behind an ambiguous no-man's-land, on either side of which the protagonists can still carry on with their private preoccupations.[42]

The Response from Sociology

The centrifugal forces dispersed by the new deviancy theories and their later Marxist versions have undoubtedly had more effect on sociology than on criminology. This, of course, is predictable, given sociology's largely academic and nonpolitical base, and also its intrinsic and pathetic vulnerability to intellectual fashions, blackmailings, and hijackings of one sort or another. In any event these have been exciting years in what is still seriously called the "discipline." And while most of this excitement was in response to the more sweeping cultural changes of the last two decades, the NDC can justifiably claim some share of the fallout in Britain. The inhospitable terrain I described at the end of the sixties has changed dramatically. The sociological landscape has been fenced off into separate territories, and whether due to an indirect stimulation from the new deviancy work or to an actual migration of the group members to these territories, a whole range of sociological connections has now appeared for students of crime and deviance. I can do little more than list the more interesting ones:

- *Education.* These years have seen a major interest in the control functions of the educational system. The equation "education equals social control" has usually been extremely crude, but the byproducts of this work have been of considerable intrinsic interest as well as relevance to the sociology of deviance. These include studies of the control element in the historical development of state educational systems; the ideology of the curriculum; the microdynamics of deviance and control in the classroom;[43] and perhaps most important, a focus on the opppositional relationship between working-class culture and the school.[44]
- *Mass media.* Sociologists associated with the NDC were interested from the outset in the selection, presentation, and effects of images of deviance in the media.[45] This interest has since been pursued on a large and productive scale by individuals and by institutions like the Centre for Mass Communication Research at Leicester. A substantial body of work now exists on the social production of news and on media portrayals of crime, deviance, and other social problems, such as race and industrial conflict.[46]
- *Cultural Studies.* Two prominent elements in the new deviancy theory's critique of concepts such as the delinquent subculture were an insistence on seeing cultural forms as meaningful in their own right and on locating these forms structurally and historically. These two ideas, combined with cross-currents from European Marxist and structuralist thinking, found their most fertile ground in the work of the Centre for Contemporary Cultural Studies at the University of Birmingham. This work on popular culture, working-class culture, and various deviant youth subcultures has been of major intellectual importance.[47]
- *Medicine and psychiatry.* At the end of the sixties, the sociology of medicine had only just begun developing in Britain. Psychiatry and mental illness had received virtually no sociological attention. During the decade, though, a number of interests voiced in the early years of NDC meetings were soon to be found in the various institutional homes in which medical sociology developed, including specialist research centers. New journals in the field were started, and courses in "medicine and society" organized. Disability and handicap were studied as forms of deviance;[48] the notion of medicine as social control (again!) and allied ideas about the "medicalization of life" and the "therapeutic state" became common, and so did a sociological version of anti-psychiatry and a transfer of Scheff's type of labeling theory of mental illness.
- *Law.* My original report noted promising developments in the sociology of law, which were of obvious interest to students of crime and deviance. These have now been greatly extended, both through the institutionalization of empirically based "sociolegal studies" and by a theoretical interest in the sociology of law. A flourishing new journal was started (*British Journal of Law and Society*); an older one was republished (the *International Journal for the Sociology of Law*); and a substantially funded research center (Centre for Socio-Legal Studies) was set up. The study of law as a social institution

has moved both in a micro direction (e.g. research on the language and inter-action of the courtroom[49]) or toward more macro concerns (e.g. historical and theoretical work on law and the state[50]). In comparison with the United States, though (see, for example, the journal *Law and Society* over the past ten years), the study of law as a social institution has barely begun.

- *Social policy and welfare.* It is extremely difficult to determine whether the new theories have had much effect on the actual *practice* of social welfare in Britain — on the welfare state level, on individual agencies, or on profes-sional social work. There is little doubt, however, that the decade has seen a major revision in the way social policy has been conceptualized at all these levels. There has been a growing disillusionment with the achievements of state welfare in advanced capitalist societies. This disillusionment has taken a conservative form in the discrediting of humanitarianism, benevolence, and state intervention, but it has also led to a popularization of the more radical (including feminist) view of "welfare as control." This takes the form of a debunking of the pretensions of the welfare apparatus or (in combina-tion with Marxist type analysis of state expenditure) theorizing about wel-fare as part of the state's program of legitimation and pacification. As one recent observer notes, this social control view of social policy is of partic-ular interest not in areas like crime and deviance, where the control function is obvious, legitimate, and open, but in areas seen as more covert, mystifying, and illegitimate.[51]

The Evolution of the National Deviancy Conference

As we have just seen, various core ideas from the new deviancy paradigm found their way into already-established subfields of sociology. Certain institu-tional areas in particular — education, medicine, mass media, welfare — provided hospitable ground for reanalysis in terms of the master conception (vague and woolly as it is) of social control. In yet other areas, such as youth cultures, the master conceptions of meaning and authenticity become dominant. And actual substantive areas of deviance not initially given much attention were absorbed into the new paradigm.[52]

As to the original group's own internal trajectory, the most remarkable thing, perhaps, is its continued existence. Despite schisms, defections, recriminations, collective boredom, chronic illnesses, and premature burials, the organization survived. And despite migration to the academic subfields described earlier and to more political groupings (especially on the Left, in civil liberties, the women's movement, radical social work, the prison movement), the member-ship number remains respectable and there is a regular attendance at the an-nual or biannual conferences that remain the group's main intellectual and so-cial activity. Perhaps the most notable institutional achievement was the NDC's role in creating (in 1974) the European Group for the Study of Deviance and

Social Control, which became an influential force in bringing together like-minded sociologists and activists in Western Europe.[53]

The group's current concerns reflect the changing cultural and political mythology through which its dominant members choose to understand themselves. The loose cultural relativism of the euphoric late sixties gives way to the more brutal economic realities and diminished expectations of the late seventies. A large measure of the diversity and eccentricity that were so characteristic of the group's early years, has now been exported out, and the hard core of the remaining group consequently has become more orthodox and homogeneous.

In line with the master theoretical move from interactionism to Marxism signaled by the publication in 1973 of *The New Criminology*, a number of consequent changes have been apparent in the type of papers given, encouraged, and published under the group's official sponsorship. For example, a move away from ethnographies (of deviant types, life-styles, subcultures) and toward structural or historical work; a similar move away from empirical studies of control agencies toward macroanalysis of overall political tendencies; a disinheritance of the wider "sociology of deviance" rubric in favor of a concentration on "crime, law, and the state"; and the beginnings of real interest in problems of women and crime.

These tendencies can be observed in the two most recent NDC publications.[54] They have not, of course, gone uncriticized, and recent years have seen more or less clear divisions appearing between the orthodox Marxist vanguard, an older liberal tradition (still interested, for example, in labeling theory), and a maverick libertarian group. Current doubts about the new orthodoxy, coming from unconvinced insiders or sympathetic outsiders, take the form of accusation of closure: a premature burial of problems inherited from 1960s deviancy theory and a premature dismissal of the agenda of mainstream criminology.[55]

The existence of such interesting disputes and divisions aside, it is clear that the new perspective overall has now become established and institutionalized. In the same way that initially outrageous movements (such as Dada and surrealism) eventually become respectable, so too have the new deviancy and criminology become part of the accepted order of things. Its practitioners are ensconced in orthodox academic departments, journals, examining boards, and publishing companies. No booklist would be complete without one.

Finally, what about the world outside the university—the crime control system, welfare agencies, professional social work? Here the patterns of influence are much harder to detect. Making an impact of this sort was very high on the group's original agenda, though this commitment was, I think, eventually compromised by a certain ambiguity about whether any short-term or reformist objectives were worth supporting in the face of known structural obstacles toward any change of the existing social order. There have been "interventions" (to use the code word) in various policy debates over the last decade, but I doubt whether many direct lines of influence can be traced. This is not to say that some key ideas have not percolated through and informed important institutional changes. It is clear, for example, that early theories of stigma, secondary deviation, amplification, and the like were taken up in the various movements over the past decade against closed institutions, such as mental hospitals and prisons. It is equally clear, though, as some writing on decarceration and community control is beginning to suggest, that these policies often originated for quite different reasons and, moreover, are producing results not always in line with the theory from which they are supposedly derived.[56] The exact lines of influence in areas like this have yet to be understood.

The same could be said for the connections with social work practice. Here, though, after some early warnings about the ambiguity of new deviancy theory's practical implications,[57] the direct interest in establishing an "alternative" or "radical" social work has been considerable. And much of this interest has been consonant with, if not directly influenced by, the type of perspective on social work common in the ranks of the NDC. There has been a great deal of work, initially programmatic[58] or theoretical [59] but increasingly descriptive,[60] about the prospects for radical social work in Britain. In addition, specific social work settings, such as probation and the juvenile court, have been analyzed in quite new terms. A number of papers in a recent collection on social work and the courts, for example,[61] reproduce quite exactly the directions suggested by new deviancy theory. One paper demystifies the court process by analyzing the micropolitics of its flow ("exposing . . . the underbelly of the magistrates courts," as the editor claims);[62] another examines the construction of "practice theory" by probation officers;[63] and another looks at the clients' own perceptions of the court routine.[64]

There are a number of other sectors of the control and welfare system in Britain—notably prisons, police, juvenile institutions—where an equivalent list could be produced of work directly carried out or influenced by the new deviancy theorists.

In some cases this work has been mainly analytic; in others it has been sponsored by explicit policy interests, for example, civil liberties or prison abolition. Certain current tendencies in the new criminology, especially the interest in abstract and historical issues, do not lend themselves to such immediate policy connections. There is little doubt, however, that the global fallout from the past decade's ideas have profoundly influenced the ways in which middle-level control and welfare institutions are being conceptualized. Whether this has, or will, change their practice is another story.

Conclusion

At the end of my original B.S.A. paper I queried the whole purpose of this type of exercise in collective self-consciousness. What is the point of all the historical and institutional reflection embodied in reports of this sort? The dangers of obsessive self-reflection are even more apparent now than they were ten years ago. A great deal of thinking in the social sciences, mirroring the whole intellectual culture's narcissistic contemplation of itself, has been devoted to an examination of its own origins, crises, and reasons for existence.

Much of this thinking is patently unproductive. A reader might well wonder why, in a course about crime—a subject so obviously grounded in the real world—so much effort has been expended in mapping out the histories and present contexts in which knowledge is produced rather than in getting along with the real business. The answer is paradoxical: some measure of self-consciousness about how knowledge is produced and diffused is needed to assess what proportion of this knowledge speaks only to itself. This is true even for the natural world; as the astronomer Sir Arthur Eddington tells his scientific colleagues: "We have found a strange footprint on the shores of the unknown. We have devised profound theories, one after another, to account for its origins. At last, we have succeeded in reconstructing the creation that made the footprint. And lo! it is our own."[65]

Notes

1. M. Foucault, "Prison Talk," in *Power/Knowledge: Selected Interviews and Other Writings, Michel Foucault, 1972–1977* (Brighton: Harvester Press, 1980), pp. 47–48.
2. Jock Young, "Thinking Seriously about Crime: Some Models of Criminology," in *Crime and Society*, ed. M. Fitzgerald et al. (London: Routledge & Kegan Paul, 1981), pp. 248–309; and most notably David Matza's analysis of criminological positivism in *Delinquency and Drift* (New York: Wiley, 1964) and his definitive sociology of knowledge in *Becoming Deviant* (Englewood Cliffs, N.J.: Prentice-Hall, 1969). A great deal of the "new" criminology and sociology of deviance of the 1970s has been marked by such self-reflexive theory; for one of the most interesting attempts to relate theory to its policy implications, see G. Pearson, *The Deviant Imagination* (London: Macmillan, 1975).
3. Subsequently published as "Criminology and the Sociology of Deviance in Britain: A Recent History and a Current Report," in *Deviance and Social Control*, ed. P. Rock and M. McIntosh (London: Tavistock, 1974), pp. 1–40.
4. S. Cohen, ed., *Images of Deviance* (Harmondsworth: Penguin, 1971), and *Folk Devils and Moral Panics* (London: Macgibbon & Kee, 1972); J. Young, *The Drugtakers: The Social Meaning of Drug Use* (London: Macgibbon & Kee, 1971).
5. And accounts for the point of Jock Young's subsequent autocritique: the new theories were largely an idealist inversion of the old. "Working Class Criminology,": in Young, *Critical Criminology* (London: Routledge & Kegan Paul, 1975).

6. For example, W. G. Carson and P. Wiles, eds., *Crime and Delinquency in Britain: Sociological Readings* (London: Martin Robertson, 1971), p. 7.
7. L. Radzinowicz, *Ideology and Crime: A Study of Crime in Its Social and Historical Context* (London: Heinemann, 1966), p. 128.
8. The standard examples at that time being N. Walker, *Crime and Punishment* (Edinburgh: Edinburgh University Press, 1965); H. Jones, *Crime and the Penal System* (London: University Tutorial Press, 1965); H. Mannheim, *Comparative Criminology* (London: Routledge & Kegan Paul, 1965); D. West, *The Young Offender* (Harmondsworth: Penguin, 1967).
9. L. Radzinowicz, *Ideology and Crime*, and *In Search of Criminology* (London: Heinemann, 1961).
10. Radzinowicz, *Ideology and Crime*, p. 21.
11. Ibid.
12. P. Anderson, "Components of the National Culture," *New Left Review* 50 (1968): 3–57.
13. Ibid., pp. 18–19.
14. J. Croft, "Herman Mannheim: A Biographical Note," in *Criminology in Transition: Essays in Honour of Herman Mannheim*, ed. T. Grygier et al. (London: Tavistock, 1965), p. xvi. For further accounts of Mannheim's work, see Lord Chorley, "Hermann Mannheim: A Biographical Appreciation," *British Journal of Criminology* 10 (1970): 324–47; T. P. Morris, "Comparative Criminology: A Text Book," *Howard Journal* 12 (1966): 61–64.
15. Morris, "Comparative Criminology," p. 62.
16. Radzinowicz, *In Search of Criminology*, p. 177.
17. See, for example, the collections of papers published to mark the centenary of the Howard League of Penal Reform: H. J. Klare, ed., *Changing Concepts of Crime and Its Treatment* (Oxford: Pergamon Press, 1966); H. J. Klare and D. Haxby, eds., *Frontiers of Criminology* (Oxford: Pergamon Press, 1967).
18. T.C.N. Gibbens, *Identification of Key Problems of Criminological Research* (Strasbourg: Council of Europe, 1970), p. 5.
19. M. Wright, "Twenty Years of the *British Journal of Delinquency/Criminology*," *British Journal of Criminology* 10 (1970): 372–82.
20. E. Glover, "1950–1970: Retrospects and Reflections," *British Journal of Criminology* 10 (1970): 315.
21. Here, as elsewhere, see my original B.S.A. paper for more details.
22. Carson and Wiles, *Crime and Delinquency in Britain*, p. 48.
23. Radzinowicz, *In Search of Criminology*, p. 168.
24. Walker, *Crime and Punishment*, preface.
25. H. S. Becker, "Whose Side Are We On?" *Social Problems* 14 (1967): 239–47.
26. D. J. West, *Present Conduct and Future Delinquency* (London: Heinemann, 1969).
27. Such as the Gibson Maze Test; the Body Sway Test (most of the boys apparently hardly swayed at all; others found this test unpleasant and anxiety provoking); and the Tapping Test (tapping a pencil on a blank piece of paper for ten seconds; this apparently reveals extrapunitive personality types, and it could be expected that "boys with delinquent personalities would tend to scatter their dots more widely." Skeptics will note that the scores did reveal a slight but significant positive correlation with bad conduct as rated by teachers: $r = 0.17$).
28. Morris, "Comparative Criminology: A Text Book," *Howard Journal* XII (1966), p. 61.
29. H. S. Becker, ed., *The Other Side: Perspectives on Deviance* (New York: Macmillan, 1964), p. 4.

30. The classic demonstration of this remains C. Wright Mills, "The Professional Ideology of Social Pathologists," *American Journal of Sociology* 49 (1945): 165–80.
31. H. Polsky, "Research Method, Morality and Criminology," in *Hustlers, Beats and Others* (Chicago: Aldine, 1967), p. 142.
32. See chapter 3.
33. I. L. Horowitz, *Professing Sociology: Studies in the Life Cycle of Social Science* (Chicago: Aldine, 1969), p. 99.
34. See G. Pearson, *The Deviant Imagination* (London: Macmillan, 1975), for a complementary account of these wider reasons.
35. J. Nuttall, *Bomb Culture* (London: Macgibbon & Kee, 1968).
36. R. Hood and R. Sparks, *Key Issues in Criminology* (London: Hutchinson, 1971).
37. A. K. Bottomley, *Criminology in Focus* (Oxford: Martin Robertson, 1979).
38. A. E. Bottoms, "Reflections on the Renaissance of Dangerousness," *Howard Journal of Penology and Crime Prevention* 16, no. 2 (1977): 70–96.
39. For example, R. Hood, "Tolerance and the Tariff" (London: NACRO, 1974).
40. D. Farington, "Longitudinal Research on Crime and Delinquency," in *Crime and Justice: An Annual Review*, vol. 1, ed. N. Morris and M. Tonry (Chicago: University of Chicago, 1979).
41. For a model account of just such a crisis of confidence in the "law and development" movement, see D. M. Trubek and M. Galanter, "Scholars in Self-Estrangement: Some Reflections on the Crisis of Law and Development Studies in the United States," *Wisconsin Law Review*, no. 4 (1975): 1062–1102.
42. See chapter 8.
43. For example, D. Hargreaves, *Deviance in Classrooms* (London: Routledge & Kegan Paul, 1975).
44. Especially P. Corrigan, *Schooling the Smash Street Kids* (London: Macmillan, 1979); P. Willis, *Learning to Labour: How Working Class Kids Get Working Class Jobs* (London: Saxon House, 1978).
45. S. Cohen and Y. Young, eds., *The Manufacture of News: Deviance, Social Problems and the Mass Media* (London: Constable, 1973).
46. For a recent review and bibliographical guides, see ibid., 2d ed. (London: Constable, 1980); G. Murdock, "Misrepresenting Media Sociology," *Sociology* 17, no. 3 (August 1980).
47. The initial work was collected in S. Hall and T. Jefferson, eds., *Resistance through Rituals: Youth Subcultures in Post-War Britain* (London: Hutchinson, 1976). For a later review see chapter 9.
48. For example, M. Voysey, *A Constant Burden: The Reconstitution of Family Life* (London: Routledge & Kegan Paul, 1975).
49. Most notably, P. Carlen, *Magistrates Justice* (London: Martin Robertson, 1976).
50. An allied development (from history rather than sociology) has been the massive interest, associated with the work of E. P. Thompson, in law, crime and the state in seventeenth-century to nineteenth-century England. This work has been of major stimulus to some contemporary criminologists. See also G. Pearson, "Goths and Vandals: Crime in History," *Contemporary Crises* 2, no. 2 (April 1978): 119–39.
51. J. Higgins, "Social Control Theories of Social Policy," *Journal of Social Policy* 9, no. 1 (January 1980).
52. For a notable example in the area of sexual deviance, see the papers and bibliographical guides in K. Plummer, ed., *The Making of the Modern Homosexual* (London: Hutchinson, 1980).

53. For a selection of papers from the first European Group conference, see H. Bianchi et al., eds., *Deviance and Control in Europe* (London: Wiley, 1975).
54. *Permissiveness and Control* (London: Macmillan, 1979) and *Discipline and the Rule of Law* (London: Hutchinson, 1979).
55. See the papers in D. Downes and P. Rock, eds., *Deviant Interpretations* (Oxford: Martin Robertson, 1979).
56. A. Scull, *Decarceration: Community Treatment and the Deviant* (Englewood Cliffs, N.J.: Prentice-Hall, 1977); S. Cohen, "The Punitive City: Notes on the Dispersal of Social Control," *Contemporary Crises* 3 (1979): 339–63.
57. See chapter 7.
58. R. Bailey and M. Brake, eds., *Radical Social Work* (London: Edward Arnold, 1975).
59. P. Corrigan and P. Leonard, *Social Work Practice Under Capitalism* (London: Macmillan, 1978).
60. For example, M. Brake and R. Bailey, *Radical Social Work and Practice* (London: Edward Arnold, 1980).
61. H. Parker, ed., *Social Work and the Courts* (London: Edward Arnold, 1979).
62. P. Carlen and M. Powell, "Professionals in the Magistrates Courts: The Courtroom Lore of Probation Officers and Social Workers," ibid., pp. 97–117.
63. P. Hardiker, "The Role of the Probation Officer in Sentencing," ibid., pp. 117–34. See also her paper "Social Work Ideologies in the Probation Service," *British Journal of Social Work* 7, no. 2 (1977): 131–54.
64. H. Parker, "Client/Defendant Perceptions of Juvenile and Criminal Justice," in *Social Work and the Courts*, ed. H. Parker (London: Edward Arnold, 1979), pp. 135–52.
65. A. Eddington, *Space, Time and Gravitation* (New York: Harper, 1959), p. 201.

Part Three

The Twists of the Discourse

7

It's All Right for You to Talk: Political and Sociological Manifestos for Social Work Action*

I would like in this essay to deal with certain aspects of the relationship between sociology (the sociology of deviance in particular) and social work practice. The aspects I have chosen have been suggested quite specifically by my personal experience and that of my colleagues in our contacts with various groups of social workers, especially those in probation, community work, youth work, and residential institutions. In these contacts—as we trail around the country, serving on study groups, examining on training courses, or simply talking to captive audiences at the inevitable weekend conference by the sea— the most familiar reaction we encounter is encapsulated in the phrase (often quite explicitly used) "It's all right for you to talk." The implication is that, however interesting, amusing, correct, and even morally uplifting our message might be, it is ultimately a self-indulgent intellectual exercise, a luxury that cannot be afforded by anyone tied down by the day-to-day demands of a social work job. This reaction is especially pronounced when our message is supposed to be "radical" and our audience includes self-professed "radical social workers."

I am still surprised, even on occasions hurt, by this reaction because I continue to think that those areas of sociology that interest me should be relevant to social workers, and also because I self-consciously avoid presenting ideas in a style that could be pejoratively termed "academic." Yet, the negative reaction still comes up either in an extreme form that is accompanied by manifest hostility and defensiveness ("We've got to do your dirty work"; "What right

* "It's All Right for You to Talk: Political and Sociological Manifestos for Social Work Action" from R. Bailey and M. Brake (eds.), *Radical Social Work* (London: Edward Arnold, 1975), 76–95.

have you got to stand up there and judge us?"; "You've got no idea about our problems"), or in a weaker version that allows the validity of the sociologist's claims but is genuinely perplexed about their practical implications. Our responses to such attacks or queries are invariably feeble. We resort either to a simpleminded role theory (poor social workers are trapped in their professional roles and cannot detach themselves enough to see what is to be done) or the only slightly less simpleminded political variants of this theory couched in the rhetoric of "working in the system," "tools of the state," and "bourgeois individualism." Such responses are not only patronizing and not only intellectually inadequate but also downright useless to most social workers. They serve only as self-fulfilling prophecies for the "it's-all-right-for-you-to-talk" position and further reinforce the social workers' feelings that we do not take their problems seriously.

I want here to take the social worker's reaction to us at its face value, and to examine some of the models for action that we appear to be offering. For present purposes this means taking for granted the familiar sociological and political critiques about the limitations of social work as an agent for radical social change. I do not question the validity of such critiques, which continue to stress the macrosocietal contexts of race, class, inequality, and power in which social work practice in contemporary industrial societies must be located. But such critiques, as social workers correctly perceive, might have marginal, contradictory, or ambiguous implications for day-to-day work. In this sense social workers are correct in saying that it's all right for us to talk, we don't have to do the dirty work.

And this perception is becoming increasingly urgent as social workers themselves become swept along in their own self-generated rhetoric (that is, unaided by the platitudes of sociological tracts) that demands radical changes in the professional role. This revolt from being the "agents of social control" or "morality enforcers" (to use the by now familiar labels) might of course come from a right-wing rather than the more obviously left-wing political position. Witness the power, for example, of prison guards who refuse to go along with liberalizing changes in penal policy. But more importantly it comes from the whole cohort of radicalized social workers who are increasingly resisting definitions of themselves as functionaries of the social control apparatus. Such definitions are especially painful in settings not like the prison or the courtroom but in mental hospitals, community organizations, child-care agencies, and other institutions officially designed to further well being but increasingly perceived by workers and clients alike as disguised forms of punishment or repression. As Rainwater nicely puts it, "The dirty workers are increasingly caught between the silent middle class which wants them to do the work and keep quiet about it and the objects of that work who refuse to continue to take it lying down."[1]

These new cohorts of dirty workers are now looking for some theoretical reference point outside their immediate work situation that would legitimate the sense of activism and commitment they have brought to their profession.[2] If Freudianism is the god that has to be seen to have failed, then Marxism became the correct and only god, but unfortunately it seemed a god a little too far away and a little too harsh in its judgments. It was bad enough for an ordinary bourgeois individualist to fight the good fight, but it was so much worse if one were actually employed as an agent of social control, a tool of the welfare state, a weapon of pacification. What was needed was a middle-range theory that would make these judgments less severe, that would bridge the gap from mundane work to a revolutionary theory of society and allow one not to sell out. This need was met in some perfectly justifiable but also in some perverse ways by the new deviancy theory. This, and the more orthodox Marxism, are the major radical models being offered.

The Promise of Deviancy Theory

In the past decade or so a liberal view of deviancy percolated through social work under such rubrics as interactionism or labeling theory. The basic premises of this perspective are simple enough and involve little more than recognizing the deviants' right to present their own definition of the situation, a humanization of their supposed process of becoming deviant, and a sensitivity to the undesirable and stigmatizing effects of intervention by control agents. Much heavy weather has been made by some sociologists about the higher theoretical intricacies of this view,[3] and these critics have been particularly insistent in pressing the charge that interactionism presents a picture of deviants as innocuous creatures clumsily mismanaged by middle-level caretakers. Deviants, this by now familiar critique argues, are portrayed as passive victims of circumstances beyond their control, creations not of the old pathologies of positivist criminology but of intervention by control agents. This tends to deny intentionality and consciousness, particularly of a political variety.

This is not the place to engage with these critiques, which to say the least are overstated. The main point is that in pushing their particular political and epistemological line, such critics had to downgrade the possible implications of deviancy theory. They argued correctly that the endless series of ethnographies of deviant groups and control agencies are dead ends in themselves, but surely social workers can—and have—derived considerable benefit from this sort of work, simply in sensitizing them to such matters as the deviants' own accounts of the world. And if one does not take too doctrinaire a line about the desirability of short-scale reform (an issue to which I will return), then the policy implications are also not to be dismissed too easily. It is of course true that labeling theory does not get directly at the roots of inequality and human misery, but it seems absurd to write off all the many reforms that are consequent on its position. We find the following in *Case Con*, the "revolutionary magazine for social workers" that has enjoyed such a wide success and that I will take as representing the radical position in the United Kingdom: "This means that labelling theory really goes no further than being able to reform the ways we deal with deviance, so that we don't create deviant 'careers' and don't amplify social problems."[4] As radicals, we would obviously want to go much further, but would it really not be a significant social change if we could reform the "ways we deal with deviance"? The indictment of labeling theory is not so much that it goes "no further" than this, but that it has not been too clear about how to get this far.

Later in the same article Canaan talks about how the rapid absorption of labeling theory into radical social workers' critique of the welfare state will change only the state's methods and not the whole power structure. No doubt. But where, five years after this article was written, are the signs of this rapid absorption? And again, the self-styled radical social workers (and the sociologists and criminologists who feed them their theories) need to be reminded that there are some clients, deviants, and dependents who are indeed victims. They have, objectively, been exploited and victimized, railroaded and stigmatized, punished and excluded — and they see themselves like this. Most of them would prefer the "methods" with which they were handled to be changed and would presumably not want to hang around until the power structure shifts for this to happen. More later about the revolutionary solution.

To repeat: the indictment is not that the solutions have been only at the middle level, without an explicitly political program, but that these changes have not been made clear enough. The worker in a residential institution who reads Goffman wants to know how institutionalization can be dealt with; the community worker hearing about deviancy amplification is interested in how this spiral can be checked; case workers want to operate without further stigmatizing their clients. The reasons that these matters have not been spelled out (and here I agree with the radical critique of interactionism) is because of the laissez-faire, hands-off attitude behind the new theories. As Young correctly states, "New deviancy theorists have been stridently non-interventionist."[5] They have often done little more than ask the middle-level managers of the control apparatus to leave deviants alone. That this defect is not simply an oversight that will eventually be dealt with is shown by the recent attempt by Edwin Schur, a successful apologist for the theory, to dignify non-interventionism as a preferred solution to certain policy matters.[6] I want to consider in some detail his recommendation of non-interventionism in the delinquency field, because this solution points to both the appeal and some of the weaknesses of this particular strategy.

Radical Non-intervention: The Liberal Answer?

What Schur does is construct three ideal types to cover the dominant societal reactions to the delinquency problem. These are: *individual treatment, liberal reform*, and *radical non-intervention*, the first two accounting between them for most current research and policy in delinquency. The *individual treatment* model is based on psychological theories assuming the differentness of offenders: delinquency is attributable to the special personal characteristics of delinquents. It favors clinical types of research and treatment, directs preventive measures toward identifying "pre-delinquents" or at individualized casework and counseling programs, and favors the individualized justice approach to the juvenile court. The orthodox stream of casework and social reform in Britain would probably lean toward this model, directing efforts, for example as it has in recent years, toward a welfare type of juvenile court and the introduction of more school counseling services. The *liberal reform* model is the more sociological variant on the treatment theme, focusing as it does on factors at the social-class and community level. It sees the immediate sources of delinquency in structural or subcultural terms; uses such theories as anomie and status frustration; directs prevention to the street-gang or community level; advocates piecemeal social reform such as the increase of educational opportunities for the underprivileged; and directs juvenile courts and correctional institutions to be more socially aware. One could identify this model with the more sociologically rather then psychologically trained generation of probation officers and with such movements as group work and community work.

Schur then proceeds, plausibly enough for the most part, to show the many problems that have arisen in implementing both the treatment and reform models. The treatment model lacks anything like a sound empirical basis in the demonstration that delinquency can be accounted for by psychological differences; its favored methods of intervention, such as prediction and early treatment, are theoretically and empirically suspect; the results of various traditional counseling and community treatment programs have been uniformly disappointing, and new programs such as behavior modification raise uncomfortable ethical problems. Juvenile institutions, which have yet to resolve the conflict between treatment and custody, have not been notably successful.

Schur's critique of the reform model is somewhat less convincing. It is no argument against class-based theories, such as anomie, status frustration and blocked opportunity, to show that a few neighborhood street projects, community organization schemes, and programs to widen educational and employment opportunities, have not worked particularly well in actually reducing delinquency rates. Nor are the theories necessarily undermined by the ritualistic repetition of the unrecorded delinquency studies that suggest that rates are more widespread throughout the class structure than the official statistics suggest.

There is no way of knowing that the liberal prescriptions for reduction of socioeconomic inequality and racism are "correct" or not simply because they have not really been implemented in the United States (or anywhere else). Where the argument against the liberal reform model is most telling is in showing the relative failure of the reformed juvenile court and of probation and juvenile correctional institutions in materially affecting the delinquency problem.

Schur then spells out the third alternative, *radical non-intervention*. Its assumptions are clearly based on the new deviancy theory, incorporating concepts derived from labeling and interactionism. The stress is on stigma, stereotyping, and societal reaction, together with a somewhat more radical reformist position than in the older liberal version. Delinquents are seen not as having special personality characteristics or even being subject to socioeconomic constraints. They suffer, rather, from contingencies; they are the ones who have been processed by the juvenile justice system. Delinquency is widespread throughout society; some juveniles drift into clearly disapproved behavior and are processed. This drift allows slightly more free choice than the constrained picture of the first two models, a position termed clumsily by Schur as "neo-antideterminist."

The focal point of attention thus switches from the individual delinquent to his interaction with the social control system, and policy is directed toward changing the system: there should be voluntary treatment, decriminalization (particularly in regard to crimes without victims), and a narrowing of the scope of juvenile court jurisdiction and its increased formalization rather than relaxation toward a welfare model. There should also be an unmasking of euphemism: an end to the use of rhetoric of treatment and rehabilitation in juvenile courts and correctional institutions to negate or disguise the reality of punishment. The differences between the models can be seen in the example of the school: the treatment model might advocate early identification of the delinquency prone and suitable counseling programs; the reform model would suggest the widening of educational opportunity for school leavers; the nonintervention model would advocate an end to policies that label and stream troublemakers.

Behind such specific reforms, the nonintervention model implies a policy to increase societal accommodation to youthful diversity. The basic injunction is leave the kids alone wherever possible. Even further in the background, lies a vague commitment to radical social change in structure and values rather than piecemeal social reform. It must be said that the model is very appealing, even without Schur's concession that he is not completely rejecting some policies stemming from the other two. Social workers should endorse any program that would take them away from the seductive powers of the treatment model. They would also be well advised to support non-interventionist tactics particularly in those areas where the legal system has extended too far and, conversely, where the legal model has been eroded by moralistic busybodies under the banner of welfare. They should certainly take up Schur's call for an end to euphemism, and should stop trying to resolve the contradictions between their dual commitment to welfare and control by pretending that the control element does not exist. But beyond this, the non-interventionist argument peters out: it is painfully weak theoretically, and it offers very few prescriptions to resolve day-to-day problems. Specifically:

1. Schur correctly notes how the sociological model has undermined the notion of individual pathology, but he suggests an alternative that rejects all notions of constraint. He complains, for example, that "the reform outlook to a large extent rests on the notion of structured variations in the freedom of individuals to shape their own destinies."[7] Now, no social worker can get through an hour of his or her rounds without being aware of precisely such "structured variations," and it would be absurd to expect social workers to be convinced of a policy that suggests otherwise. This applies to problems of mental health, housing, and child care as much as to delinquency. But, again, the defect of "neo-antideterminism" is not so much that it is incorrect — it has been a crucial antidote to the overdeterminist legacy of positivist criminology — but that its implications for practice have not been spelled out. It matters a great deal theoretically to show, say, that a female shoplifter acted intentionally and with some degree of choice rather than from some obscure condition called kleptomania or menopausal depression, but *how* this may matter to the probation officer dealing with her is not at all apparent.
2. When it comes to the argument about the overreach of criminal law the non-interventionist case rests primarily on the pragmatic grounds of the law's sheer inefficiency in controlling certain areas of undesirable behavior.[8] When principles are cited, they tend to be little more than a restatement of traditional Wolfenden-report rhetoric about the existence of realms of private morality that are not the business of the law. Now, both pragmatic and principled arguments are all very well in areas of normative dissensus and crimes without victims. It is clearly desirable for any self-respecting radical social worker to devote energy — through pressure-group politics and campaigns — to change certain laws in such areas as drugs, abortion, homosexuality, and prostitution rather than simply to mop up the casualties of the law. But there are two inbuilt limitations to the decriminalization argument. The first is a self-admitted one, that only a small proportion of offenses are suitable candidates for this treatment. The vast bulk of offenses (property crime) plus other obvious areas such as personal violence will remain criminal. This is not to say anything of the other areas of social work activity — in regard to poverty, homelessness, mental health — where the criminal law has little significance.

The second limitation is less often admitted. Once an area of deviance stops being criminalized, it still has to be policed by some other form of social control. And more often than not, this form derives from the individual treatment or the liberal reform model. Now, it might be preferable for all sorts of reasons to treat, say, drug taking within a medical or welfare rather than a criminal model, but someone still has to run the control machine.

3. This leads to the third problem with non-interventionism from a social worker's point of view. The stress on the control system — how the raw material of rule breaking is fed into the machine, processed, and recycled — is valuable. It may be quite in order to talk of organizations' producing deviants and to say that "from an organizational standpoint the problem of delinquency is to some extent one of management."⁹ Statements such as these might justifiably give rise to sociologists' concern that the deviant is forgotten as the whole problem is transformed into one of mismanagement. But for the moment my concern is that the preferred system of management — and as long as social workers exist, management is where they will be — remains obscure.

4. Finally, there is a more disturbing aspect of the non-interventionist case to be considered: its argument against treatment and reform rests quite correctly on a fundamental questioning of the taken-for-granted assumption that delinquency is a problem about which something must be done. But to combine this question with the actual evidence that current delinquency policies are unworkable and even harmful, in order to justify a theory of accommodation to diversity, is empty without some guidelines for establishing just how this accommodation is to take place. Moreover, although some aspects of the delinquency problem — and indeed many other social problems as defined by the powerful for social workers to deal with — can wither away, the structural features of society that both create real problems for certain members and then exacerbate these problems by dealing with them unfairly will not. Non-intervention can become a euphemism for benign neglect, for simply doing nothing.

At this point we can return to the critiques of the new deviancy theory itself. Some of the problems in non-interventionism can indeed be traced back to the peculiar mixture of liberalism and romanticism inherent in the original theory, for what was sometimes implied — although not perhaps as unambiguously as some critics suggest — was an image of the naturally good person who was interfered with by state busybodies. If he was left alone, the problems would disappear. Philosophical speculations about the nature of human beings aside (where they should be left by sociologists), clearly this picture cannot be held against the day-to-day experience of social workers. The parent threatening to drop a baby from a window ledge, the alcoholic suffering withdrawal symptoms, the pregnant schoolgirl kicked out of her home are all doing things that call for help. The help (or "social control" as this came to be classified) has not yet come to interfere with them or change their natures. This, of course, has always been recognized by the more sophisticated deviancy theorists, most notably Matza in his warnings against romanticism and sentimentality; he is quite clear about the deviant being something more than the product of control apparatus.

But another type of romanticism was to emerge. With the rise of militant and aggressive deviant groups, some of the new theorists — particularly those of us in the United Kingdom associated with the National Deviancy Conference — started (and some have never stopped) celebrating such deviance and claiming it as evidence of a newfound political consciousness. Virtually any antisocial activity became elevated in this way. Young correctly detects the contradiction in this version of the theory: "Now the message of the deviancy theorist to official society was 'hands off you'll only make matters worse' but *at the same time* the implicit ideology was 'believe and hope that the new deviant constituencies do represent a genuine threat to the social order.'"[10]

Those (like Young) who became disenchanted with this position, because of the idealism that advocated alliances with deviant groups and the unmasking of conservative control ideologists as the only two tactics to adopt, moved in a position somewhat different to mine. They argued for a social base, specifically in Marxism, that would somehow resolve the weakness of the idealist position. But when their solution appears as a set of guidelines for social workers, it looks either notably ambiguous itself or else suspiciously like the romanticism from which they are so eager to dissociate themselves.

Client Co-optation: A Revolutionary Manifesto?

Social workers themselves were correct in suspecting that uncomfortably mixed up with the liberalism of deviancy theory was a degree of romanticism. They saw the deviant co-opted as hero in a series of revolutionary struggles as deviancy theorists rushed around to find in the actions and — with greater difficulty — the words of football hooligans, vandals, rapists, bank robbers, and kidnappers signs of militancy and class consciousness. In some quarters prisoners were seen as being in the vanguard of the revolutionary struggle, homosexuals as precursors of the destruction of the bourgeois capitalist family, and schizophrenics as visionary prophets of human beings' alienation. In retrospect it is not difficult to see why such attributions were made: from the middle of the 1960s onward, various of the previously despised and pathetic groups among the deprived and the deviant did become more organized, vocal, and likely to build up collective defenses against the stigmatized positions that the powerful had cast them in. Gay liberation, ideological drug users, tenants' associations, squatters, prisoners' unions, and more recently mental patients' unions were calling the tunes. In a real sense these groups were becoming politicized, and it was (and still is) impossible for any sociologist to avoid trying to make sense of these developments.

Equally impossible, however, is to accept the way in which the brand of deviancy theory evolved by contemporary "hip Marxists" seized upon these groups and elevated them to the status of political without any clear thought about the conceptual problems involved. Having rejected the legacy of positivism, having conveniently (so they thought) disposed of the notion of deviant as victim, they now urged sociologists to join hands with their subjects, and social workers with their clients, in a joyous storming of the Bastille of social control. The hip Marxists could sit in their universities and conferences while the social workers (and the occasional activist involved in a tenants' association) would spread the message to the people. Deviants of the world unite, you have nothing to lose but your stigmas.

Unfortunately, not only was this approach excessively romantic in conception but—like the radical nonintervention model—it carried remarkably few prescriptions that could actually be followed by social workers in any practical sense. Indeed, this supposed radical alternative to traditional social work was often extremely evasive about what sort of gains the client could expect from their new workers. I rely again on journals such as *Case Con* and personal contacts over the past five years with many of these social workers and sociologists to try to analyze what alternative models of action were actually being offered.

In examining the programs of such radical social work movements, I am interested less in matters of internal consistency or ideological "correctness" than in what sort of help the radical social worker might get from absorbing the message. The *Case Con* type of program seems to consist of three separate strands that I will call *theory, self-help*, and *client-co-optation*. The first strand stresses the need for a total sociopolitical theory (obviously Marxism, but some are a little coy about the label) that would inform action. It is continually emphasized that part of being a radical social worker is to have such an ongoing analysis to provide a critique of the welfare state and a guard against not being conned by the system. To quote an early statement of aims, "We believe that the first step to the solution of many of the problem facing social workers' clients—such as poverty, inadequate housing, inadequate welfare services, isolation and alienation—lies in the replacement through working-class struggle of capitalism by socialism." This strand of the program—in the *Case Con* version at least—is backed up by the standard polemics about a world in which international capitalism is always on the edge of crisis and in which every government measure, down to obscure clauses in the Mental Health or Childrens Acts, is an attack on the working class.

The second strand in the program stresses the social workers' own internal organization. To be radical, training courses and the profession itself must be democratically organized. This means the forging of alliances with other unions, rank-and-file involvement in local government unions, militancy about pay and conditions, and protecting victimized colleagues.

The third strand, the one most relevant to this discussion, is to find a work role for the social worker as something other than an agent of control buttressing the system. A *Case Con* statement of aims arrives at this alternative: "We support the attempts of social workers to engage in community action and encourage the activities of grass roots organizations such as claimants' unions and tenants' associations." This forging of links with various militant groups of deviants and dependents, together with general support for anything identified as the "working-class struggle," is the main basis of radical social work activity.

Given acceptance of the Marxist model, each of these elements makes some sense. Working outward from what most social workers actually do, though, one finds the elements represent something less than a guideline for action. Not only do they leave out those very groups that because of their lack of organization, grass-roots activity, and militancy make up the bulk of social workers' clients but, in the case of the first and last strands (the second is largely irrelevant to this discussion) they can be incompatible. Before going on to this, let me take a case from personal experience that was instrumental in leading me away from a career in psychiatric social work into the safe world of sociology.

Mrs. X was the mother of a five-year-old boy who had been referred for gross "behavior problems" to the child guidance clinic in which I was working. The child was clearly unmanageable at home and school. The mother was a middle-aged Cypriot woman. She had married the father of the child, a British soldier, and he had left her soon after the child was born. She followed her husband to England but could not persuade him to return to her. She was now living with the child in one room, and had been joined there by her blind mother, a semi-invalid who could not speak any English. It was a nightmare: the poor woman, her blind mother, and a hyperactive five-year-old living in one room. On reporting my first so-called diagnostic interview to my supervisor, I concluded that there was nothing the clinic could do until we badgered the housing department to get somewhere else for the family to live. My supervisor thought otherwise, and I was queried about whether I had gone into the psychodynamics of the woman's relationship with her former husband (was she perhaps punishing herself for something?), and had I noticed the obsessional way she had been holding her handbag?

Then, as now, one could not but see the futility of a purely individualistic casework approach. But then, as now, one could also see some role for the social worker to help the distressed, the powerless, the helpless. Now, although it would be wholly unfair to argue that revolutionaries are inhuman monsters wholly obsessed with Marxist dogma, it seems to me an inescapable conclusion from this literature, that in cases like these (or perhaps ones a little less obvious) radical social workers not only will be able to derive very little from their theory but in fact also will encounter a line of argument that mere practical help is in fact undesirable. They will end up—like the Freudian caseworker—doing very little in the way of immediate help or more long-term community action. Such help, by improving the client's material condition, is seen as dangerous because it blunts the contradictions in the system. In practice, of course, most revolutionary or any other social workers would probably have helped Mrs. X in the obvious ways. It must be remembered, however, that her plight is not made any more helpfully understandable to her by reference to contradictions in the system and the crisis in late capitalism than it is by talking about masochistic personality traits and identity crises.

Let me deal more fully with these practical and theoretical problems. On the practical level it must be said that with the two notable exceptions of housing and welfare rights, through tenants' associations and claimants' unions respectively, there is very little indication in *Case Con* circles of how revolutionary social workers would operate very differently from their nonrevolutionary colleagues. Having satisfied yourself that your clients' struggles are actually part of the working-class movement—and this is somewhat unlikely in most cases of the disabled, the old, the unhappy, the sick—what would support for this struggle actually look like? As in the non-intervention model, there is very little attempt to spell out what the alternative support or control system would look like, unless of course we are sustained by the thought that, come the revolution, there will be no casualties, miseries, or distress. There are only rare attempts in the pages of *Case Con* itself actually to recognize what social workers, radical or otherwise, are really doing—that is, such tasks as mopping up casualties and offering patronage to clients unable to get resources themselves. I found only one brave attempt to spell out a concrete alternative strategy, one that makes no bones about transforming client help into client co-optation.[11]

What Taylor suggests is that the social worker should refuse to accept the client as a client—in terms of a symptom, or a case—but rather "should accept the new 'cases' continually being thrown up by the crisis in the system as political allies 'in need of protection and care' only in the sense that the system has them pinpointed for processing through the courts, through the SS [Social Security] through the hands of City Hall and so on." The notion that the social workers' clients—Taylor gives such examples as the unemployed and the mother on probation for stealing children's clothes—are "thrown up by the crisis in the system" (whatever this may mean) leads to the suggestion that social workers must look after their clients' political as well as other interests. The argument is that social workers should *defend* their clients by acting as lawyers, organizers, and information providers in helping the clients fight the system that has created their problems. In this defender role social workers refuse to accept clients as clients but rather sees them as allies against the system. Thus—on an analogous ground to my refusal to deal with Mrs. X in casework terms — one refuses to spend hours with soccer hooligans discussing their emotional problems but rather ensures that they receive the right material help. But you must demonstrate that this is all being done on political grounds. This will expose the division that exists between the master institutions (the probation officer is not always in league with the police officer), and this knowledge will eventually politicize the street-corner kids. Taylor sees "striking alliances" developing out of the politicization of the social work relationship, and suggests that these various defense strategies (for example, seeing not just the delinquent but the whole of working-class culture on trial in the courtroom) "throws up for question the very ideological basis of social control under capitalism. If such a strategy were to mushroom, at a time when courts are full to bursting at any case, the working of the machinery itself could also be thrown into doubt."[12]

Skepticism aside about whether most or even many clients are "thrown up by the crisis in the system" and are likely allies in any working-class struggle, real or potential, what if these clients refuse to see themselves in this way? What Taylor implies is that if the clients refuse to accept the social workers' refusal to accept them as clients, then they should get no help at all. Indeed, Taylor is quite explicit about this, noting in passing that the client-refusal strategy provides radical social workers a basis for discriminating within their caseloads! Not only are we back to the elitism of psychoanalytically derived casework — whatever you say, we really know best what your problem is — but we end up with another form of non-intervention or benign neglect, only this time one reserved for the unfortunate few who refuse to see themselves as the social workers' political allies. What if the client actually wants something looking like casework? A case of false consciousness, no doubt. One can only hope that social workers who take this strategy literally will also respect clients' refusal to have anything to do with them.

To return to the more theoretical obstacle: the existence in some Marxist social work theory of a strand of thought suspicious of *any* attempt (and this presumably includes the client-refusal strategy) to support clients. The first problem is one of which most activists are well aware: social workers and their clients, because of their respective class positions, might be quite marginal to the working-class struggle. Social workers themselves are part of the welfare apparatus that protects ruling-class interests, while the clients are the powerless, being unemployed, old, disabled, ill, institutionalized. Typically, this paradox is avoided in revolutionary social work circles, and after some rather diffuse talk about repression and the crisis in late capitalism, eventually the client (or consumer) organization is often completely rejected in the belief that such groups cannot after all be slotted into the history of the working-class movement. (Some groups such as gay liberation, hippies, and druggies have always been an embarrassment to the organized Left, who have yet to decide whether to disown them or to co-opt them.)

A problem less clearly recognized by outsiders, because it depends on an extremely orthodox adherence indeed to the doctrine, is that even the likeliest candidates for co-optation can be refused support on the grounds that this would be counterrevolutionary. The argument is that the working class is not yet equipped to lead a radical movement, and although it should be given guidance, simply "organizing people around poverty, although effective in terms of improving the material existence of the poor, is generally not in the interests of the total working class."[13] Working with tenants and claimants (and one shudders to think what this orthodoxy makes of the freaks, the lonely, the misfits), so the line goes, is alienated from the needs of the genuine working class. Are than *any* genuine community organizations that can be co-opted into the struggle? Yes, those that have "a solid theoretical framework, an ongoing socialist analysis and an in-depth understanding of the working class situation."[14] Otherwise, and it is worth quoting the catechism at length:

> Issues concerning consumer community services are essentially peripheral to the basic contradictions in capitalist society, to the class struggle between the working and ruling classes. Organizing around such issues is therefore very much secondary to organizing around productive relations in the work place and can be misleading and diversionary, siphoning off radical energy and obscuring the real nature of capitalism. . . . On a simple level, community action aims to improve the material condition of the working class and hence tends to blunt the basic contradictions in our society. Its value as a revolutionary tool is therefore doubtful to say the least.[15]

This is not the place to discuss this particular view of society. All I am concerned to show is that it has some peculiar implications indeed for social work practice. These implications differ, depending on whether one is dealing with this orthodox view, which virtually negates all social work, or with the revisionist view (clearly the one influenced by the new deviancy theory), which is selective about which clients or organizations to co-opt. In either case—and I use this extreme judgment with great reluctance—social workers are asked to develop an exploitative relationship with their clients. Clients' problems are not interesting in themselves but as signs of something else, such as the crisis in the system; the solutions are not important in themselves unless they help something else, that is, the working-class struggle.

In a highly schematic way, which is not meant to depict any one individual's position that I know of but to distill the message that might be received by a social work audience, let me summarize the problems so far before considering briefly a more positive strategy. A social worker is involved in running an imaginative adventure playground in a deprived working-class area. What do our models tell the social worker?

1. *Weak deviancy theory/non-interventionism*
   Be careful of possible stigmatizing and stereotyping.
2. *Strong deviancy theory/non-interventionism*
   Perhaps you should not be doing this at all; there is no hard evidence that adventure playgrounds decrease delinquency rates.
3. *Revisionist Marxism/revolutionary social work*
   Politicize the kids; they are your allies in the struggle.
4. *Orthodox Marxism/revolutionary social work*
   Perhaps you should not be doing this at all; it simply prevents the kids and their parents from realizing how the system exploits them.

"The Unfinished"

The least that one can say for the first as opposed to the other three solutions is that it does not ignore the present problem and that it does not prematurely close the debate. What it does lack, of course, compared with the other three, is a clear positive strategy and not just a set of recommendations about what to avoid. It should be apparent that the strategy I want to suggest is one that does not (like authoritarian Marxism) make people expendable and that does not write off all short-scale intervention. The long-term versus short-term view of exploitation, power, and inequality should not carry the prescription of abandoning all else. A possible way out of this impasse has been suggested by the Norwegian sociologist Thomas Mathiesen,[16] and I want to take his account of his involvement with the prisoners' union there and its fight against the prison system as a paradigm for change in some other parts of the welfare and control system.

"The unfinished" is a program based on what does not yet exist. From the beginning Mathiesen is quite clear about the dangers of going for short term goals only; taking up reformist positions in the system — as a humane prison governor, an advocate of inmate councils — cannot but lead to absorption and an abandonment of the long-range goals of changing the system totally. As every social worker well knows, absorption eventually takes place through all sorts of subtle ways of incorporation, initiation into the agency's secrets, compromising for too long. On the other hand, there are some very effective short-term possibilities, not just through humanitarian work but in conscious policies of raiding the establishment for resources, contributing to its crises, unmasking and embarrassing its ideologies and pretensions. Any such effectiveness can be lost by finishing. One must be able to live with ambiguity and refuse to accept what the others, the authorities, demand: a choice between revolution and reform.

It was correct, Mathiesen suggests, for the Norwegian prison union, KROM, after a long struggle about going to either extreme, to have kept open the relation between revolution and reform. To make this choice is really "the choice between being "defined out" as irrelevant and "defined in" as undangerous.[17] Only an authoritarian political program cannot tolerate this ambiguity and is constantly looking (like the revolutionary social work movement) for clarity about the "way ahead." The point is to remain open and capable of growth, to see some ambiguities as irrelevant, never to let oneself be placed. KROM realized that to be revolutionary was to lose the power of competition, but that to be exclusively reformist it would lose its character of contradicting the establishment. In either case it would be neutralized. The old system is not threatened by a counterorganization that becomes incorporated, but it is threatened by counterorganizing. As long as one is in transition, there are no normative expectations to define one's behavior: "The adversary does not know where you are heading. The only thing that he knows is that you are heading somewhere, because you are organizing. At this moment, the power of the system is threatened, because you are yourself neither powerless nor fully incorporated in a fully developed positive contributing relationship."[18]

If one defines oneself as revolutionary, it becomes illicit to adopt near-at-hand pressing changes (as we saw in the *Case Con* line) and this must separate one from those one wants to work for. If one defines oneself as reformist, the danger is that anything really radical is seen as inadmissible, wild, irresponsible. The choice is not to let oneself be forced to make the choice; let the clients take as their points of departure reforms that are closest to them and will change their lives now. Only then can one move on to wider political questions when the clients become dissatisfied. This is not a simple plea for humanitarian work, for although Mathiesen is aware that there are greater pulls in this direction because results are more visible, this can lead to politically unsound short-term choices and to expedient changes that leave the overall structure intact. There are clear and well-documented examples of this in the prison reform area, where short-term humanizing reforms, particularly those that accepted the rhetoric of rehabilitation and the help of psychiatrists, have arguably led to changes that have made the system ever more repressive.[19]

Mathiesen sustains the idea of "the unfinished" throughout a complex analysis of how one may change the system and organize from below. To avoid working for short-term goals is politically impossible and paralyzes action, but reform alone will corrupt long-term work; to work within the system is to risk legitimating it, but to stay out would be wrong: "We did not wish to sacrifice the short-term interests of the prisoners on the altar of general system abolition."[20]

There is one other strand to his argument that provides a guide to which reforms to work for: this is the notion of the politics of abolition. One must always work at what is close at hand and always in the direction of abolition. Concentrate first on abolishing whatever gives legitimacy to a system one regards as wrong, whatever masks it uses to disguise its true nature. Again "the unfinished" applies: abolition cannot wait until the alternatives are established. Mathiesen uses the examples of the campaign to get rid of the Norwegian Vagrancy Act. An example I would cite from my own work is the attempt to abolish the forcible use of psychotropic drugs in prisons. When the establishment demands "alternatives" before contemplating any changes, it knows in advance that it can already lay down the framework for the discussion. The conservative aims remain taken for granted—in the one case, to get rid of vagrants; in the other, to control prisoners' behavior—and only the means are debated. The demand for alternatives, then, has a conserving effect. Real oppositional values because of their nature must be long-term and uncertain. So when opponents are presented with the choice of specifying alternatives, they find it difficult to avoid coming close to the prevailing order in what they suggest (reform) or emphasizing completely different values and thereby being defined away as irresponsible or unrealistic. The answer is to go always for abolition and actually to resist the pressure to make positive reforms.

I have suggested this as a paradigm for social work action. This is not to say it will fit every case, but it seems to me that the notion of "the unfinished" is the most appropriate one for radical social workers to adopt in welfare-state or social-democratic systems. It has the critical advantage of not exploiting or selling out one's clients. As a footnote to Mathiesen's strategy, I would also commend the notion of "the unfinished" as relevant to the image we transmit of our "subjects." Clients and deviants should not be too easily placed on such continua as "sick" and "normal," "militant" or "passive." The new deviancy theory has, quite rightly, been systematically hacking away at the positivist picture of deviants as pathologically constrained by forces beyond their control. And the treatment ideology that follows from this is correctly seen as the most insidious enemy to radical social change. But alternative images of deviants— either in the feeble version of the unconstrained delinquent in Schur's "neo-antideterminism" or the excessively romantic version in the new-criminology, hip-Marxist, radical-social-work version of the rebel against the system—are beyond credibility. I believe that they must discredit in advance any radical policy.

Here, cryptically, would be some of my suggestions for a radical social work program:

1. Tell those sociologists who urge you to be theoretically more sophisticated to get off your backs. (They are the same sociologists who want to turn their own subject into matters of epistemology and philosophy.)
2. Refuse the ideology of casework, but always think of cases: your constituency is not just claimants' unions and tenants' associations but also mothers

of autistic children, suicidal housewives in council tower blocks, derelict old vagrants, and so on. You do not have to be sentimental about these people but neither should you write them off.

3. Take seriously the insights of deviancy theory, however low level they may sound to your superior academic sages. Think very concretely about how to avoid stigmatizing your clients, unwittingly facilitating their drift into further troubles, trapping them in cycles of rejection.

4. Stay in your agency or organization, but do not let it seduce you. Take every opportunity to unmask its pretensions and euphemisms, use its resources in a defensive way for your clients, work for abolition.

5. In practice and in theory stay "unfinished." Do not be ashamed of working for short-term humanitarian or libertarian goals, but always keep in mind the long-term political prospects. This might mean living with the uncomfortable ambiguity that your most radical work will be outside your day-to-day job.

6. Most important: do not sell out your clients' interests for the sake of ideological purity or theoretical neatness.

And keep telling sociologists and political theorists, "It's all right for you to talk."

Notes

1. L. Rainwater, *Social Problems and Public Policy* (Chicago: Aldine, 1974), p. 335.
2. See Geoffrey Pearson, "Social Work as a Privatized Solution to Public Ills," *British Journal of Social Work* 3, no. 2 (1973): 209–23; and "The Politics of Uncertainty: A Study in the Socialization of the Social Worker," in *Towards a New Social Work*, ed. H. Jones (London: Routledge & Kegan Paul, 1974).
3. See especially, Ian Taylor et al., *The New Criminology* (London: Routledge & Kegan Paul, 1973).
4. C. Cannan, "Deviants—Victims or Rebels?" *Case Con* 1 (January 1970).
5. Jock Young, "Working Class Criminology," in *Critical Criminology*, ed. I. Taylor et al. (London: Routledge & Kegan Paul, 1975).
6. Edwin Schur, *Radical Non-Intervention: Rethinking the Delinquency Problem* (Englewood Cliffs, N.J.: Prentice-Hall, 1973).
7. Ibid., p. 83.
8. The liberal-pragmatic position here is presented by Edwin Schur, *Crimes without Victims: Deviant Behavior and Public Policy* (Englewood Cliffs, N.J.: Prentice-Hall, 1965); N. Morris and G. Hawkins, *The Honest Politician's Guide to Crime Control* (Chicago: University of Chicago Press, 1970).
9. Schur, *Radical Non-Intervention*, p. 130.
10. Young, "Working Class Criminology."
11. Ian Taylor, "Client Refusal: A Political Strategy for Radical Social Work," *Case Con* 7 (1972): 5–10.
12. Ibid., p. 9.

13. G. Hague, "Community Work: A Carrot for Radicals," *Case Con* 10 (January 1973): 8.
14. Ibid.
15. Ibid.
16. Thomas Mathiesen, *The Politics of Abolition* (London: Martin Robertson, 1974).
17. Ibid., p. 23.
18. Ibid., p. 119.
19. Stanley Cohen, "Prisons and the Future of Control Systems," in *Welfare in Action* ed. M. Fitzgerald et al. (London: Routledge & Kegan Paul, 1977).
20. Mathiesen, *The Politics of Abolition*, p. 115.

8

Guilt, Justice, and Tolerance: Some Old Concepts for a New Criminology*

> *It is not the business of writers to accuse or prosecute, but to take the part even of guilty men once they have been condemned and are undergoing punishment. You will say: what about politics? what about the interests of the State? But great writers and artists must engage in politics only so far as it is necessary to defend oneself against it. There are plenty of accusers, prosecutors and gendarmes without them; and anyway the role of Paul suits them better than the role of Saul.*
>
> —Anton Chekov

If by "writers" we are to understand novelists, poets, or dramatists, then perhaps Chekov had some sort of point. Substitute, though, "sociologists of deviance" or "criminologists" for "writers" and we find that different parts of his statement lead us into quite opposite directions. The recommendation not to accuse or prosecute looks acceptable enough, but the warning against politics is obviously less so. It is the split between these two directions that I want to examine in this paper.

The new sociologies of deviance of the sixties and the emergent radical, new, critical, and Marxist criminologies of the seventies, certainly followed the injunction not to accuse or prosecute — or (as we would have put it) not to "side with the agents of social control." And the specific injunction "to take the part even of guilty men" was exactly the principle articulated by the writers who

* "Guilt, Justice and Tolerance: Some Old Concepts for a New Criminology" from D. Downes and P. Rock (eds.), *Deviant Interpretations* (Oxford: Martin Robertson, 1979), 17–51.

I am grateful to David Downes, Paul Rock, Ken Plummer, Geoff Pearson and Jock Young for comments on an earlier draft.

shaped our ideas in the sixties and whose quotations littered our lectures and publications: Polsky on the need to suspend conventional moral judgments; Becker's "Whose Side Are We On?"; and — most eloquently and imaginatively — Matza's advocacy of appreciation as against correctionalism. Any comparisons of sociological naturalism with naturalism in the novel (or "social realism" in another tradition) were quite deliberate and indeed most sociologists working in this vein began to see themselves as novelists manqué. Sociology of deviance booklists were (and still are) full of those works of fiction that we told our students would give a more realistic view of the world than our own research: *Last Exit to Brooklyn, Junkie, Our Lady of the Flowers, One Flew over the Cuckoo's Nest* — these would tell it like it is. (Curiously, we forgot that most such "realistic" works were also profoundly moralistic in intent.)

The methodological and theoretical problems in this position have been pursued relentlessly enough, and most of the warnings against the drift toward an ahistorical subjectivism are surely justified. But one set of problems, the moral ones to which this paper is addressed, was brushed aside. It is not that we were unaware of them; intellectual autobiographies always made us sound dumber in the past than we really were in order to give the illusion of continual cerebral progression. In fact, few were dumb enough to think that naturalism and appreciation were without certain moral inconsistencies — to say the least. Matza, with his usual sense of irony, covered himself: "To appreciate the variety of deviant enterprises requires a temporary or permanent suspension of conventional morality and thus by usual standards inescapable elements of irresponsibility and absurdity are implicit in the appreciative stance."[1]

Both in this early naturalistic phase and its later more romantic deviations such irresponsibility and absurdity were obvious enough in the heady world of seminar rooms — but they could not be readily translated into the public world of social policy. Indeed, their existence there could not easily even be admitted. If — so one of the public's questions ran — deviants were not pathological beings driven by forces beyond their control, then surely as rational, responsible beings should they not be punished *more* severely? Ah no, that is not *quite* what we meant. And when we talked about being on the side of the deviant, did this mean we were actually in favor of what he did? Here, our answers were really tortuous. Faced with behavior like vandalism or football hooliganism, which we could not openly approve of (in the sense of advocating tolerance or non-punishment), then our main message was that actually there was much *less* of this than the public thought (because of moral panics, selective perception, stereotyping, scapegoating, and the like). Simultaneously, of course, to other audiences, we welcomed such behavior and pointed to the evidence that showed that if society did not Radically Change, then indeed the public's fears would materialize and more of the behavior occur. With other forms of deviance easier to support openly within the liberal consensus —

abortion, the gay movement, smoking dope — we happily advocated tolerance, even in public. And this time we would say that there was not less but far, far *more* of such behavior than anyone could imagine through their stereotypes. Confusion indeed.

Already apparent in these stances was the vacillation between the image of the deviant as mismanaged and the deviant as cultural hero, images that Young later correctly identified as associated with laissez-faire liberalism and a more full-blown ideological romanticism.[2] The moral mixture persisted. Toward most forms of deviance, an exceedingly low-minded moral nihilism seemed the order of the day, but this stance was hardly consistent. Toward other forms of deviance, a high-minded moral absolutism prevailed; crimes of the powerful were condemned with puritanical zeal. Appreciative studies of polluters, exploiters, and manipulators (all highly morally loaded works) were not, to my knowledge, advocated. And who today would dare to embark on an appreciative study of rapists in the face of the consensus between radicals of both sexes that these offenders must be immediately and strictly punished? But appreciation is not the same as *conversion*. A suspended morality operated all along in choosing which subjects and which groups were suitable candidates for the new theories. It was less a question of consistent moral nihilism — which is at least an established philosophical position — than of selective morality. Refusing to support conservative values, we operated only just a fraction outside the liberal consensus. "Radicalism" was liberalism with a loud mouth — and on subjects like pedophilia, not a very loud mouth either.

The further we got drawn into the world of criminal justice policy (where this paper focuses) the more evident these confusions became.[3] Correctly, I believe, the solution to this was seen as the need to move more macropolitical theory and strategy. The precise direction that this move took (toward developing a political economy of law and crime and worrying about metatheoretical issues) might be defensible in its own terms. It does not, however, really answer the confusions left behind by the faltering attempts to translate an earlier unstated morality into policy.[4] It was as if we had drafted the blueprint for a new bomb, even constructed bits of it, left it lying around and then ran rapidly in other directions. The running has now stopped, and in a number of important statements such as Young's "Working Class Criminology" paper, we are at least back to the scene of the intended crime.

"What about politics? What about the interests of the State?" Now, while there might be something to be said in favor of Chekov's injunction simply to defend oneself against the interests of the state, this was obviously not the direction the new criminologies took. Libertarian and Marxist principles, though unarticulated, unseparated, and usually submerged under simpler underdog sympathy, were always there. When the Marxist elements became more explicit, the problem was not that criminology became too politicized (whatever that may mean) but that the crucial political question about the interest of the state — the question central to libertarian and anarchist writing — was never properly asked. Matza made a beginning with his baroque philosophical contemplation of Leviathan, but the preoccupations of Marxist criminology with the political economy of law and the theory of capitalism as criminogenic never came to grips with the concrete political and moral dimensions to which I think Chekov refers. The interests of the state lie in prohibiting certain action and punishing those responsible for this action. The questions these interests raise (and always have) about justice, tolerance, morality, guilt, and responsibility are only now being considered in the new criminologies. I believe that it is only by putting them firmly on the agenda that the connections with criminal justice politics can be made.

In suggesting this agenda, I am not really concerned whether anyone has got Marx right or with the bridge between these theories and the rest of sociology. It is the bridge to criminal justice policy that is the more precarious. Beyond filling in the picture of the system as being repressive, the impact of the new theories has been slight. And although it would be politically naive to assume that our writings in themselves could have much power, it is important to construct an agenda that does not leave the debate to the Right.

On Rediscovering Moral Judgments

In classical criminology the moral fit between the image of the criminal and the nature of criminal policy was reasonably close. And the moral judgments in the debates about what the law should prohibit and how individual offenders should be punished were open and transparent. With the positivist introduction of determinism, and its consequent inversion of the notion of personal responsibility, the potential for a new fit between image and policy began. All historians have exaggerated the impact of the positivist revolution, not so much in the world of academic theory, where it was profound, but in criminal policy, where it was extremely uneven. The gap between image and policy never closed. As *The New Criminology* correctly pointed out, the conflict between the free will classical legal model and the deterministic scientific paradigm of positivism was resolved by the extremely awkward compromise of neo-classicism: "A qualitative distinction is made between the majority who are seen as capable of free choice and the minority of deviants who are determined."[5] It is not clear whether this "minority of deviants" refers to *all* the deviants compared with the conformists, or a minority *within* the deviant population. In either case, although the compromise might have been theoretically clumsy, it was quite sound ideologically.

In some areas, most notably juvenile justice, the fit looked a bit closer, though even here the classical model was undermined more in theory than in practice.

Instead of one policy's replacing another, the rhetoric of treatment and the rhetoric of punishment were used simultaneously in the same courts and the same custodial institutions. But the impression of a genuine fit between theory and policy was sustained in public. Hence, it is more obviously in regard to juveniles that the current attack from radicals (in the name of justice) and conservatives (in the name of law and order) is the most aggressive. In adult criminal policy it has been more transparently business as usual, and to blame the failures of the criminal justice system on the doctrine of positivism is much like blaming structural inequality on the doctrine of functionalism. In retrospect, our attacks on positivism should have been more discriminating and should have identified more clearly the special ways in which "positivism" appeared under such guises as "extenuating circumstances," "diminished responsibility," probation, the indeterminate sentence or parole — all within a neoclassical system. And all these developments (even comparing just England with the United States, let alone the rest of the world) were extremely uneven from one society to another. Positivism was indeed a massive theoretical con trick — the separation of crime from the state — but we were also conned into thinking that the change had happened in criminal policy as well. The separation indeed went along — but so did the state.

At this point — the assault on positivism — there was some potential for the moral position of neo-classicism (some should be punished, others should not) to be positively confronted. But in its initial stages, the assault was only a job of demystification. As Pearson describes it well, it was medicine and technology defrocked. The effect of the new sociologies was to dereify the technical and professional screen behind which welfare and medicine operated. This was supposedly to lay bare the morality underneath, to reveal that deviance is a moral matter, a matter about what sort of society we are to live in.

The defrocking and undermining were not nearly as effective as Pearson and others suggest, partly because the original sin of mystification had never been committed in the first place. More important, the effect was lost because the implicit substitute, the emperor underneath the tacky clothes of positivism, was revealed not in his full moral nakedness but in his new underwear of naturalism and appreciation — with the absurdities I earlier suggested. Our first glimpse into the dressing room was of the mismanaged, stigmatized underdog, or so it looked to some. This was quickly deemed inadequate, not a "fully social" picture of man. But once again, instead of a glimpse of moral nakedness, a new (albeit short-lived) disguise was tried on: the "fully social," rational, cryptopolitical deviant.

Here, with so many outfits being tried on before so many fitting room mirrors, is where our problem starts. Though few were irresponsible or silly enough to promote these disguises in their pure forms, these two new images remained in the mirrors: the underdog and the hero. And whatever the differences between them, the images suggested a common suspension of conventional morality. Deviants are troublesome or disruptive, but we should still try to appreciate them. This could and did lead to a giddy irresponsibility, and although these successive images were always accompanied by careful qualifications and later were repudiated altogether, their reflections remained in the mirror. In the texts of this period, delinquents are busy redistributing private property and schizophrenics are attacking the double-bind concentration camp of the nuclear family.

I want to repeat that these images were both qualified at the time and rejected later. The rejection was most explicit in Young's argument that the new theories merely inverted positivist images: either man's possibilities were pictured as being infinite or he was naturally good and being interfered with by the state busybodies, or (in the voyeuristic version) he was the existentially superior deviant poised on society's margins.[6] So while deviancy theory was applauded for demystifying positivism, it was condemned for doing so at the expense of erecting "a rational Frankenstein constructed out of the inverted conceptual debris of its positivist opponents."[7]

Unfortunately, these rejections came too late and, as I will suggest, they still need filling out with some sort of alternative. To vary my earlier metaphor: we flashed around the plans for a new bomb, and then said, "That's not what we really meant; back to the drawing board." In the meantime despite the dire warnings, the old images remained. The new sociologies were stranded in positions that lack credibility. The solution to this—which, as Pearson suggests,[8] was partly an embarrassed reaction to the excesses of the counterculture—has been interesting enough, but it bears on a different set of questions. The emerging political critique of criminology, right or wrong, simply did not address itself to the criminal policy questions raised by the initial defrocking.

Such a critique was understandable in the light of the harder political realities of the seventies compared with the softer subjectivism of the heady sixties. Worries about the subjective idealism, irresponsible hipsterism, moral voyeurism, zookeeping, liberal cop-outs—though by now surely sounding a little tired and hysterical—are understandable. It must be right to correct a theory that suggests (to the theoretically unsophisticated at least) that people make their own history in conditions of their own choosing. But my complaint remains. This critique leaves us either contemplating people who have no motives, no subjective lives, or with the vacuous rhetoric in which, as forty earnest students tell me each year, "Matza's view of man" (or something like that) is "inadequate" and has to be replaced by a "fully social" picture. Either way we remain frozen in the old gestures of demystification. And either way moral nihilism is close at hand. We are locked in the same stances that Matza warned us would result from the temporary suspension of correctionalist interests and of the commonsense view that criminals should be punished.

These stances, as we are now realizing to our cost, are extremely difficult to emerge from. The current justice debate (which I will later examine) is a major breakthrough, and there are two other roads within critical criminology now that offer routes back to the moral dimensions of criminal politics (though the authors of these routes might not agree with my signposting them this way). The one lies in the view more prominent in the North American strand of critical criminology:[9] to extend the definition of crime. To me, this has always seemed little more than a muckraking and moralistic exercise, in the best senses. This position attacks the state definition of crime and tries to redefine and extend criminology's subject matter in terms of violations of politically defined human rights (such as food, shelter, dignity). Thus, imperialism, racism, sexism, colonialism, capitalism, and exploitation all are to fall within the rubric of criminology. This is, of course, no mere plea for demarcating new academic subject lines, drawing up new book lists, and asking different exam questions (though, curiously from such a group of radicals, it usually looks to be just this). It announces a moral stance: not just that we should "study" (and certainly not "appreciate") all these evils but that we should *condemn* them, condemn them as if they were like or worse than the crimes that fill our current textbooks and our criminal justice system. It is not always too clear whether we are being asked to condemn these evils *instead of* conventionally defined crimes or *in addition* to these crimes, but in either case the moral element is right in the open. Indeed, this element appears with such naive and evangelical fervor in some American adherents of radical criminology that one wonders what they were doing in the sixties and what sort of sociology they have ever read. For them, the debate is cast as a Quixotic onslaught against Value Freedom and is not only openly moralistic but also extravagantly partisan. Here is Quinney:

> I find it difficult to support the position that the criminal law can be stripped of its moral judgements. To the contrary the very stuff of the criminal law is moral. The criminal law is moralistic if for no other reason than it takes the position that any human action should be limited. The assumption that either society or the individual should be regulated is a moral one. And certainly the decision to regulate specific substantive actions is moralistic. A moral decision is taken when it is decided to protect others by means of criminal law. Legal reform or even legal revolutions cannot be achieved by taking morality out of the law.[10]

The embarrassing possibility that such statements could be interpreted as saying anything "radical" aside, it would be difficult to find anyone who has thought about the criminal law for more than two minutes who could disagree with a word. The importance of all this is that it carries the simple recognition that the regulation of human behavior is on the radical agenda and involves moral judgments. Hardly a startling insight, but an important one to emerge from the radical camp that sometimes (as I will discuss later) comes close to the assertion that in the good society the eventual regulation of human behavior through the criminal law will become an irrelevant matter. This utopia is a crime-free society, where apparently the troublesome and difficult business of making judgments about regulating and limiting behavior, will not take up too much time.

The other route back to what I see as the relevant debate about the state is potentially more fruitful than the concern with changing the definition of crime. This lies in the recognition of two simple matters.[11] (1) On the public side, the existence of some moral consensus, however much the product of bourgeois ideology, that condemns certain crimes. The working class also suffers from crime and its objective class interests here coincide with certain features of bourgeois ideology, for example, the demand for justice. (2) On the criminal side, there are internal contradictions, and problems of guilt and irrationality. There is no monolithic criminal consciousness.

I am not sure that all of Young's analysis of these matters helps, particularly the circular reference back to the content of bourgeois ideology to "explain" working-class politics and crime. The notion, though, that the effect of brutalization by the system might make people into determined creatures is important in developing what is in effect a new typology of crime. Crime *could* be the brutalization by the system, it *could* arise from voluntaristic action within an ethos of competitive individualism, it *could* indicate a primitive political consciousness. Whether we accept such a typology or not (and this one is more illuminating than most), the mere recognition of such possibilities must, as Young sees, change the game and in just the directions I think it should change: "If we confuse these categories we are unable to discriminate in our attitudes to crime—i.e. we either condemn it out of hand or we romanticise it. Either way, we accept the legal categories at face value and neglect to study criminal phenomena from the perspective of class interests and socialist principles."[12] This particular recommendation seems to be unhelpful, but at least by discriminating between categories of crime and (like the American radical criminologists) talking about categories of antisocial behavior outside the criminal law, some ways are open to counter the conservative domination of the public debate on crime. This does not yet confront, though, the specific issue of punishment, which I believe has been obscured by a careless and tendentious reading of the fit between criminological theory and policy.

For it is punishment, in both its dimensions of ban and enforcement, which is at the core of criminal politics and always has been. It is fatal that until recently radicals have ignored or fudged this question. Alongside the tendency to pretend a suspension of morality, there was the assumption—implicit in *The New Criminology*—that any sort of correctionalism, however liberal, must depend upon theories of pathology. In fact, correctionalism in its classical version made no such judgment of pathology; this was its whole point. And when the new deviancy theory tried to expel pathology (by arguing against determinism and in favor of rationality), what this did was to open the route back to the older form of correctionalism. Responsible criminals were constructed whose responsibility lay precisely in their right to be punished, not treated.[13]

Even in Matza's weaker rejection of pathology—weaker in the sense that "deviance as diversity" is not as radical a break as "deviance as rational"—no necessary elimination of correctional interests is implied. Pathology is an *untenable* variant or change. Diversity may be tenable, but it is nonetheless a variant that is prescribed, regulated, and controlled. In the same way as common sense should lead us away from a romanticism that ignores pathos, dissatisfaction, and weakness, so it should remind us about punishment. Despite their having drawn attention to the compromised position of neo-classicism on precisely this point, the new criminologies assumed a fit between theory and policy that was never present.

The other fit they assumed, is, as I have suggested, closer to the mark: the tendency for appreciation and subjectivism to lapse into moral relativism. But again this tendency was one that should have contained an inbuilt self-correcting mechanism:

> The appreciation of shift, ambiguity and pluralism need hardly imply the wholescale repudiation of the idea of common morality. Such an inference is the mistake of a rampant and mindless relativism. Plural evaluation, shifting standards and moral ambiguity may and do co-exist with a phenomenal realm that is commonly sensed as deviant.[14]

Correctionalism interferes with appreciation, but it is hardly an absurd goal in itself: "The correctional perspective is reasonable enough, perhaps even commendable, except that it makes empathy and understanding difficult and even impossible."[15]

In fact, appreciation is not intrinsically connected with moral nihilism any more than (in a completely opposite version of the radical attack) it is simply a more liberal version of correctionalism. It was something recommended and adopted as a tactic, a temporary methodological stance. Criminologists no doubt *looked* as if they were transcending what Matza refers to as their earlier "incapacity to separate standards of morality from actual description."[16] And we might have *said*, with Chekov, "There are plenty of accusers, prosecutors and gendarmes" without us. But all this shrill moral innocence struck a false note. Most of the time we were saying to "our" deviants (who knew this quite well): we will study you *as if* we had no moral judgments whatsoever about your actions. That we could get away with such dishonesty was no doubt a tribute to the prevailing intellectual climate, but sometimes it really was the product of innocence rather than bad faith. In our waking hours we were innocent; we simply never raised the question, Did these people deserve to be punished in this way?

The connection between appreciation and relativism, thus, was and is no more an organic one than the connection between pathology and correctionalism. In any event my earlier problem remains: If pathology goes out the window, and so does the underdog, the drifter, and the rebel, then what is left? Young's "typology" offers a way out, an unexpected one: the rediscovery of another sort of pathology, perhaps the kind Lukacs had in mind when repudiating the romantic view of psychopathology:

> Life under capitalism is often rightly presented as a distortion (a petrification or paralysis) of the human substance. But to present psychopathology as a way of escape from this distortion, is itself a distortion. We are invited to measure one type of distortion against another and arrive, necessarily at universal distortion.[17]

This is another version of Young's admission that the unreflexive attribution of rationality to all forms of deviance could lead to a denial of any consensual reality in the external world. His plaintive, not to say poignant, tone marks the possibility of emerging from the frozen moral positions left behind in the attack on positivism:

> There is some standard somewhere, whereby one is able to talk of appropriate and, most importantly, of inappropriate responses to problem situations. The spectre of normality and pathology, once exorcised, re-emerges. Only by holding to some standard of normality is it possible, indeed, to talk of lapses in rationality on the part of an individual, a group or even on the part of a total society.[18]

The reemergence of the spectres of normality and pathology, of appropriate and inappropriate behavior, of standards and of rationality, all open the way to a more plausible criminology. As theorists such as Jaccoby have commented, positivism is often at least nearer the *appearance* of reality than pure idealism.

Guilt and Responsibility

"It is a failure of sociological theory that it has rarely examined concepts such as guilt and conscience."[19] Indeed. Words like *guilt, conscience,* and *evil* (especially *evil*) are not ones with which sociologists have ever been comfortable. A course in the sociology of evil would be laughed away in most departments, though it is no less respectable than many and more so than some (for example, a course on analyzing telephone conversations).

In criminology the fuzziness of the attack on positivism left the problem of guilt unresolved. Appreciation, as we saw, should not have implied conversion or the impossibility of condemnation. It should also allow that what might have to be appreciated is whether and how the subject feels guilty. The commonsense conception of guilt—implied in Chekov's reference to "guilty men"—refers probably to *legal* guilt: the simple judgment of whether the subject was responsible for the supposed offense. But determinism also allows for judgments of *moral* guilt: whether the action was caused by factors for which the subject was not responsible.

At its extreme—in the novelist's resolve to "take the part of guilty men once they have been condemned and punished"—the appreciative stance appears to urge a suspension of judgments of either sort of guilt. This is indeed the whole point of appreciation: one must try to understand the crime even if it was the actor's fault. There is no point in making such a fuss if the crime was not the actor's fault; *anyone* could "appreciate" it then.

But to move from all this to policy is another matter. It calls for making connections with the obvious literature in law, moral philosophy, and jurisprudence that deals with the question of moral and legal guilt, the relationship between deterministic theories and the rationale of punishment. I would be the last to suggest that we abandon empirical sociology for philosophical speculation—we have already been colonized by philosophers—but in this case the connections between the pretensions of the new criminologies and standard philosophical concerns is absolutely intrinsic. The problem of individual responsibility is more relevant to the study of crime than it is to any other area of sociology, for the particular reason that our theories have unstated implications for the rationale of punishment.

We have only dimly realized that these theories (and the criminal's own accounts—more of this later) obscured the question at the heart of criminal justice politics: In what sense is the criminal *guilty*? It was never thought necessary even to enter this debate on blameworthiness. In the hermetically sealed world of theory, we performed elegant pirouettes around notions of freedom and determinism, and meantime let the state get on with its business of blaming and prosecuting. The quicksands to which such political irresponsibility leads might best be illustrated in the extreme but instructive case of war crimes. Even the most cursory examination of this subject shows how problematic are the connections between theories ("they were just obeying orders," "they were part of the system") and assessments of responsibility, culpability, blameworthiness, or guilt.[20] One of the best recent examples of the mess that radicals can get into because of not thinking through these problems, is the reaction on the part of the U.S. Left to the series of trials of Calley, Medina, and others for their alleged part in the My Lai massacres.

Mary McCarthy's superb account of Medina's trial should be required reading for criminologists.[21] Her argument is that the deliberate massacre of over a hundred villagers at My Lai was morally different—and seen to be so—from on the one hand the "ordinary" prosecution of war and on the other the haphazard rapes and killings practiced by ordinary soldiers.[22] The earlier attempts by Nixon and the Right to whitewash Calley coincided with attempts by the Left to denounce the Calley prosecutions as "scapegoating" (Calley was innocent; the army was the real criminal). Though by most accounts Medina (Calley's company commander) knew pretty well what was happening in the village, it was argued that it was liberal hypocrisy to blame such figures. But as McCarthy comments:

> Medina was a transition figure between the war makers and the "animals" (as the airmen in Vietnam called the infantry) and his acquittal halted a process that might have gone up the ladder of responsibility. If Medina had been in jail, it would have been harder to acquit Colonel Henderson. With Henderson in jail . . . the finger would steadily have pointed upward. Had public pressure been maintained, it might not have been left to the Army to decide when enough was enough. If there was a conspiracy, it was a great nationwide breathing together of left, right and much of the middle to frustrate punishment of the guilty.[23]

McCarthy's point is that from the North Vietnamese and Viet Cong positions it did not follow that if Johnson and General Westmoreland were war criminals, then Calley, Medina, and others directly responsible for the massacre were "choiceless victims of the war machine." The North Vietnamese could draw a distinction between the ordinary soldier's shooting at troops and an infantry company's butchering women, old men, and children. Some of the Left and the counterculture in the United States not only would not concede this distinction but seemed to hold to a theory that denied all freedom of action. The notion was that those like Calley were pawns moved around from birth by "the system." But if Calley's social conditioning left him no option as to whether to "open up" or not on the people of My Lai, how did other (presumably similarly conditioned) ordinary soldiers keep their rifles to the ground? And how did others express disbelief and shock about what was happening and eventually denounce the massacre to the authorities? Without some notion of individual responsibility, no credit or blame could be assigned to anybody. Masochistic indictments of the whole culture of being "guilty" — everyone is a war criminal — sound virtuous but are politically sterile. And they helped in producing a visibly devastating result:

> Medina and Henderson off the hook, Calley's sentence reduced, others not tried, several identified and unidentified mass murderers welcomed back into the population. Now any member of the armed forces in Indo-China can, if he so desires, slaughter a reasonable number of babies, confident that the public will acquit him, a) because they support the war, or b) because they don't.[24]

The position is perhaps more complicated than McCarthy allows, in that it should be possible to theorize about the "ultimate" or "real" cause of the massacre—and still hold that individual participants exercised some real choices at a particular moment. I have, nevertheless, spent so much time on this case because—without putting too fine a point on it—there are some parallels between the dissidents who championed Calley and Medina against the army and criminologists who champion "their" criminals against society. It was not just that we did not think too much (if at all) about the problem of legal guilt, but that the more we talked about the problems of determinism and individual responsibility, the cloudier we made the whole issue. One constant sociological impulse has been to shift accountability for crime onto higher and higher levels of the social structure. Not just family, neighborhood, and social-class position but the whole system—capitalism in all its ways—was to blame. And final irony: the very system of social control itself was fatefully implicated in the causal path to crime. Each successive theory harbored its own particular implications for the question of guilt but these never surfaced.

In regard to juveniles, as I suggested earlier, the fit looked more transparent: the move to welfare, treatment, and rehabilitation seemed to have happened. But even here, the specific implications for policy of theories of shifting accountability are open to dispute. Finestone's ambitious recent attempt to relate changes in the image of the delinquent—from "potential pauper" to "disaffiliated" to "frustrated social climber" to "aggrieved citizen"—to changes in U.S. society and its juvenile justice system raises interesting problems here. Note, for example, his comment on labeling theory: "Labeling theory fundamentally represents a crisis in the legitimacy of authority, a crisis that is quite inconsistent with the acceptance of legitimate authority in any form, even under the guise of professionally trained experts, for it attributes delinquency precisely to professionals and experts."[25] Such statements vulgarize labeling theory and surely exaggerate its radical thrust.[26] But this aside, even if the theory hardly implied a "crisis in the legitimacy of authority," some political consequences surely followed from the more sentimental (and I believe largely correct) thrust of the theory that most official criminals have been pushed around, railroaded, and generally had a raw deal. We were elusive about these consequences. Nor did we stop to analyze the fundamentally morally compromised position into which we had cast agents of social control. We were asking them to uphold a system whose very basis rested upon the notion of individual responsibility and at the same time to subscribe to theories that cast them as partially responsible for this delinquency.

As the My Lai case illustrates, causal theories, however aesthetically pleasing or even morally worthy, have to be translated into the real social settings where blame is allocated. At least this is a well-charted intellectual enterprise and we could have taken note of (though we choose not to) the massive standard philosophical literature, for example, about the extent to which determinism is compatible with talk of legal guilt and responsibility. Aside from this intellectual parochialism, we made matters worse; just when the constant sociological impulse to shift accountability upward was gathering momentum, the new deviancy theory suddenly shifted ground and mounted what looked like a massive critique of determinism in any form. Even more bewildering, accountability was shifted upward and determinism attacked by the very same theorists. Just when the startling implications of anti-determinism were being digested, Marxist criminology appeared on the scene to announce an even more deterministic edifice than ever contemplated.

The initial thrust of the new theories was indisputably against determinism in any form. In its earlier naturalist version (Matza's formula: "*anyone* can become a marijuana user and *no one* has to") and the later more "radical" strands, the attack on determinism was accompanied by an implicit exercise of decoding. A new semiology of meaning was constructed within the conceptual debris of positivism. If the deviant had previously been denied legitimacy, meaning, rationality, intentionality, and authenticity, then — but by implication only — a correct decoding would restore these properties. Yet, not only was this new semiology never made very explicit but, as I have stressed repeatedly, its implications for policy were never made clear.

Such implications should have been even more obvious at a historical point where a self-conscious conflict was being staged between two rival conceptual discourses trying to establish hegemonic control over meanings. When at the beginning of the nineteenth century, an earlier such conflict took place — precisely the one that established the psychiatric version of positivism in the first place — it was clear enough what sort of policy consequences would follow. Foucault has used the startling case of Pierre Riviere to show how dramatic the alternatives were.[27] Was Riviere's crime to be coded as rational and hence grounds for executing him, or was he to be diagnosed as mad and hence shut up for life in a mental hospital? The issue was clear: clumsy psychiatry, with its new epistemology and causal theories, was trying to *cheat* Riviere of his death.

Was this in fact the allegation against positivism that was being made some hundred fifty years later — that it was trying to cheat deviants? But cheat them of what? From being punished properly as responsible free human beings? Or from being seen as critics of society? Or was there, after all, in the attack on determinism, the equivalent sophistry that Pearson detects in the liberal treatment model, "The misfit must at one and the same time be held accountable for his actions, which are judged wrong *and* treated with compassion"?[28]

Such questions not only were never posed but were rendered surrealistic by the simultaneous presence of strident attacks on determinism *as well as* statements denouncing elements of voluntarism in everyone else's theories for being idealistic and individualistic. (It might, of course, be quite right to attack the extremes of both total voluntarism and total determinism, but not — in criminology at least — unless some credible and not wholly rhetorical alternative is sketched out.) Anyway, just when readers were beginning to make sense of this dizzy double bind, we were informed not that the original attack on positivism was to be recanted but that because of romantic and Fanonist excesses, the new criminal man had been a mistaken creation. All criminals were not, after all, Weathermen. A creature of Frankenstein had been constructed.

But in truth, the new criminal was less a creature of Frankenstein than a Jekyll and Hyde: rational in the morning, drifting in the afternoon, and brutalized in the evening. How could all this confusion arise? My answer is breathtakingly simple and will doubtless be seen as simplistic: it lies in the nature of the sociological worldview. What was being attacked all the time was not "determinism" at all but its psychological and psychiatric versions. The fight was against nasties like Lombroso and Eysenck. Accepted social facts, the brute Marxist and Durkheimian contingencies of life — history, structure, inequality, power — were never questioned. How could anyone question them and remain a sociologist?

To repeat, it was not that the new semiology had merely inverted the positivist image by replacing determinism with freedom. Only *some* forms of determinism were attacked; sociological determinism remained alive and well, the taken-for-granted backdrop against which the whole play was being enacted. This backdrop has now come alive by being filled out with a specifically Marxist appearance. *Both* the determinism of psychological positivism *and* the supposed voluntarism of new deviancy theory have been banished by a powerful new set of forces: material circumstances, the persuasiveness of bourgeois ideology, the potential for biography to be ossified by the control apparatus. All this, together with Young's form of typology, resolved the double bind by a compromise parallel to that of neo-classicism. The crypto-political criminal is allowed *more* free choice, the brutalized criminal *less*, though the area of choice for everyone is whittled down. In one sense our single Jekyll and Hyde monster disappears; there are, after all, different criminals, with different degrees of choice. But a tension remains, precisely the tension within Marxism between subjective choice and the forces of history. And because of its moral implications, criminology has registered this tension perhaps more sensitively than any other social science. On the one hand, it was assumed to be "radical" to uncover those deterministic forces structually most remote from the actor; on the other, the influence of the early Marx and the residue of 1960s cultural voluntarism left behind the potentially free actor, struggling heroically against structure and the mystifications of bourgeois ideology:

> The biographical characteristics that lead to psychic conflicts and resistance are ossified by the ongoing institutions of the social control apparatus and by the lack of any real moral or material alternatives. Choice occurs within a cage, whose bars are ob-

scured and glimpsed with certainty only at the terminal points of the social control process. It is the role of the radical criminologists to demystify control and to join with those movements which seek to provide tangible alternatives and areas of choice.[29]

Internal problems in this view of determinism aside, it still leaves us with the old policy questions. If people have no "moral and material alternatives" (to crime?), how can anybody be held responsible or punished for personal action at all? And what follows from seeing the "cage" as more solid for some people than for others? Radical criminology cannot evade these questions by labeling them pejoratively as "correctional" or "moralistic." Its own stance, even when it denies the value of expose criminology, is both correctional and moralistic; openly so in regard to crimes of the powerful, and tacitly so elsewhere. It might not look "correctional" to call for ending the system that allows the powerful to exploit and damage others, but in the meantime must they be left unpunished? And how about rapists? Or female criminals, whom we are being urged to see not as pathological but to be taken as seriously as we do male criminals—in other words, not to *cheat* them of their punishment?

There is one familiar criminological debate that might be used to open up the question of guilt and responsibility to such policy considerations: the theory of "techniques of neutralization."[30] A standard question is this: Does the presence of certain motivational accounts really indicate a sense of guilt that has to be neutralized, or are these statements merely surface gestures behind which may lie the shadow of an alternative value system or at least more self-consciousness than Sykes and Matza allow? This is, of course, an important question in itself to resolve, from the point of view of the competing causal theories of delinquency. Let us, though, express the issue in a slightly different way: What degree of guilt has to be present or admitted by the criminal in order to fit a just and fair punishment for the offense?

Such a question raises the part of the Sykes and Matza argument that is usually ignored: the extent to which causally neutralizing statements (moral guilt) actually rest upon or are coincidental with statements about legal guilt. An account such as "I didn't know what came over me" is at one and the same time a subscription to a deterministic theory of causation *and* also (if honored) not merely an extenuating circumstance but a method of evading legal guilt. My suggestion is that criminologists at all concerned with the consequences of their theories might begin to consider seriously the effects of the motivational accounts they accept or construct. There have been only a few speculations along these lines, such as Taylor's suggestion that if we are as skeptical as we claim to be about the total involuntarism common in sexual offenders' motivational accounts, then we should confront such offenders with their own responsibility.[31] This might be psychologically more desirable as well as more honest (though Taylor does not ask what consequences this strategy might have in achieving goals of social justice). Following this track, criminologists should be analyzing such accounting systems as probation officer records and social inquiry reports to determine what sort of accounts might have particular consequences for the client. Probation officers are familiar enough with a model of social intervention that reverses the positivist sequence of diagnosis then treatment. One decides first on the best (by this I mean the most just) "treatment" and then constructs the images accordingly.

If such programs look too pragmatic and individualistic, there is a quite different line of analysis about guilt and responsibility that criminologists might follow: a comparison of crime and its control in different societies. When we examine other control systems, particularly those labeled as socialist, we might find that the systems often held up as desirable models (such as the Chinese) are precisely those in which the most massive sense of individual responsibility and guilt is engendered and built into the rationale of punishment. We need a typology of social control that relates dominant ideology and structure on the one hand to modes of allocating blame and responsibility to individual offenders on the other.

Justice or Social Justice

The moral question, which positivism threatened to bury but only managed to disguise, and radical theory rendered so confusing, has reappeared with startling force in criminal justice politics over the past few years. From the Right, the law-and-order lobby is saying more stridently and less apologetically what is has always been saying: the liberal treatment model is mistaken and we must go back to a hard-line punitive approach based on strict classical lines. From the Liberal Left, there is much heart searching and breast beating; the ideals of treatment and rehabilitation have, alas, gone sour and we must go back to some sort of neoclassical position that stresses justice and fair play. And from the Marxist-Left, the debates about social justice and bourgeois legality versus socialist legality are beginning (at last) to mark out some position in this spectrum. I want to examine here some aspects of this debate, which I believe is the most promising possible one to rescue radical theory from some of its political stalemates and to find new answers to the old question: Is it just to treat this offender this way?

The conservative position needs no exegesis, though it certainly needs more sustained attention than we have given it. The increasing plausibility of the law-and-order lobby and the resonant political chords it strikes have sometimes to be confronted in their own terms instead of always shifting ground by looking for ideological roots. If indeed, as radical criminologists now concede, such working-class interests as those for justice are real and not the product of false consciousness, then the coincidence of such interests with those of bourgeois ideology need exploration, not to say exploitation.

I would like to look, though, not at the conservative position but at one extremely radical version of the justice model. The Report of the Committee for the Study of Incarceration is radical not so much for its intrinsic content (which is hardly new) but its emergence from the Left-liberal disillusionment in the United States with the treatment ideology.[32] Together with allied statements, such as *Struggle for Justice*, this report seems to me to announce an extraordinary landmark in criminal justice policy — again for its context rather than its content.

Starting with the question of incarceration (and eventually suggesting some worthwhile policies to reduce incarceration) the Committee found itself arguing for a new rationale for punishment. Disenchantment is the dominant note: rehabilitation has failed and attempts to change people have been abused. Only a minimalist position is defensible, not just about prisons but the whole criminal justice system. The state has to do less rather than more. This means "a crucial shift in perspective from a commitment to do good to a commitment to do as little mischief as possible." What little should be done is guided not by the positivist notion of individuation but by the principles of justice, equity, fairness, and above all *just deserts*, a more palatable version of traditional retributivist principles. This marks a departure not just from the pure treatment ideal but from any guiding utilitarian rationale. Intervention is not justified by prevention, deterrence, or protection but by the notion that "certain things are simply wrong and ought to be punished." The report is all too aware of the ironies in liberal humanists arriving at this position today and finding themselves so close to the conservatives. They abandon the therapeutic model with reluctance and despair but it has not worked; it has often turned out more cruel and punitive than an overtly punitive system; it is hypocritical and unjust, especially in sentencing people guilty of similar crimes to different dispositions because of their "background." And finally, the treatment model has hardly furthered the goal of a more equal distribution of power and property (as if anyone thought it could!).

Many details of the Committee's argument — against treatment, against attempts to predict dangerousness, and against both individualism and utilitarian deterrence — are extremely persuasive and need sustained attention. I want to pay more attention, though, to their alternative, the key notion of commensurate deserts, which invokes the quite explicit moral and commonsense rationale for punishment: people are punished because they deserve it , and the seriousness of the offense (and the number and seriousness of prior offenses) should determine the seriousness of the penalty.[33] Critically, *past* action and not predicted *future* action (as in the rehabilitation, deterrence, or incapacitation models) is the criterion. More specifically, seriousness depends on the amount of *harm* done and the degree of the actor's *culpability* (in terms of the strict legal categories of intent, seriousness, and negligence). Such considerations should have priority over all other overriding aims of punishment, such as crime control, deterrence, prevention, or rehabilitation—and these need not all be juggled to achieve some hypothetical balance.

Let us begin consideration of the scheme by looking at some limitations acknowledged in the report itself. It recognizes, for example, that there might be problems in calculating the seriousness of offenses, but then quotes public opinion surveys that suggest that some consensus on ratings can be found (with little race, occupational, or educational variation). This suggests that some commonsense notion of seriousness exists, which sounds plausible enough, especially if we are thinking in such terms as a five- or six-point scale of judgment. But such measurements might be reflecting only a reified public opinion that is the product of the dominant ideology. And if the basis of this is unjust, then public opinion surveys will hardly guarantee the objective of justice. An allied problem that the Committee acknowledges is that of harm—harm to whose interests? In an unequal society not all interests are comparable; simply taking into account what the report refers to as the "particular moral traditions of the culture" might again lead to an unjust result in trying to assess harm.

These, of course, are serious problems and not just examples of operational difficulties in putting the just deserts model into practice. They are related to the more fundamental flaws in the Kantian-derived argument on punishment, which are conceded (in a footnote):

> The Kantian argument presupposes that what violators are being punished for is the infringement of the rules that safeguard the rights of *all* members of a society including the violators own right. This raises a question . . . whether a desert-based justification of punishment, such as Kant's, can hold in a society whose penal system helps maintain a less than just social system.[34]

It is precisely when this flaw is explored—in the "Lingering Questions" raised in the report's last chapter, "Just Deserts in an Unjust Society"—that we come to the criticisms from radical criminology of such versions of the justice model. For while it might be true that Marxism itself would suggest that the only morally acceptable grounds for punishment is that it is deserved,[35] this principle holds only if the laws are fair and the society is equal. Yet, if the laws (or even some of them) serve particular class or power interests, then it is not self-evident that all violations are moral wrongs that deserve to be condemned and punished along the lines of just deserts.

The Comittee members recognize this problem but try not to let it disturb them too much. They concede that there might be social injustice, but there is also at least a partial acceptance of legal norms which allows violators to be considered deserving of punishment. The Committee will not accept that society (American society?) and its rules are fundamentally and irretrievably unjust. On the question of how *much* punishment is deserved, it concedes only that the "impoverished defendant" poses "dilemmas" for the theory. If social deprivation is seen as a mitigating factor (thus allowing a plea of diminished culpability), this goes against the principled objection to the whole notion of individuation. It may not be feasible, anyway, to treat social deprivation like this:"The sentencing system may simply not be capable of compensating for the social ills of the wider society."[36]

There is obviously no question of "may"; clearly, no sentencing system can possibly do this. The report trivializes all these issues by referring simply to "social ills" or "impoverished defendants." These are no mere isolated social pathologies; there are whole societies (such as South Africa) where the laws are fundamentally and irretrievably unjust, where the inequalities of privilege and power are so gross that even to suggest that the law can be fair or just is absurd.

The Committee must recognize something of this in its final, somewhat despairing concession: "As long as a substantial segment of the population is denied adequate opportunities for a livelihood, any system of punishment will be morally flawed."[37] This is only a partial recognition of the problem, but even to allow a "moral flaw" in an argument that rests so self-consciously on moral principles is almost to give the game away. Despite the obvious flaws in this version of the justice model, though, it confronts directly the hidden moral agenda of criminology and should be taken very seriously. In a reference to a paper by Greenberg advocating the justice model (if not the specific deserts version), Taylor and Young deride his "collapse into the justice lobby," and they appear to be quite hostile to any radical sympathy with the back-to-justice movement on the grounds that this does not take into account the movement's origins and convergence with conservative interests.[38]

It seems to me more productive to confront the model in its own terms rather than mount only this sociology of knowledge critique. It might be true that the justice lobby is dominated by embittered liberals and is shaped by the strains on corporate liberal reformism, and that any liberal influence can be easily absorbed into the most reactionary aims — but these are not sufficient reasons for rejecting the model. It has enough problems in its own terms. As Marxist theory itself has always pointed out, it is the essence of bourgeois ideology that it will absorb contradictory elements. Where the radical critique is surely correct is in its showing that the justice model is inadequate unless located in a broader critique and program.

Such a critique is now beginning to emerge, though the program is more opaque. Quinney and Wildeman, for example, despite their zeal to accept the moral elements of the law, argue,

To accept the principle of the rule of law, however, is to also run the risk of uncritically accepting the legal system and the political economy upon which the entire legal system rests. Therefore if we are to understand law and crime in the state we have to be aware of the ideological foundations of the legal order.[39]

This seems reasonably unobjectionable as a theoretical statement. It would be a pity, though, if the strategic implication of an awareness of the ideological foundations of the legal order was abandonment of the struggle for justice to conservative interests. Taylor and Young's warnings about the danger of the struggle being co-opted into conservative goals might open up this risk: "Greenberg's plea that radical criminology in America should work for justice is in danger of accommodation to the attempts made to restore order and legitimacy to American capitalist order in the midst of a crisis of hegemony."[40] This is a legitimate political worry: the danger of lending oneself to struggles that make the social arrangements of capitalism appear to be just, when patently they are not. This is precisely the "moral flaw" in the *Doing Justice* position. All this comes close, though, to the same potential problem that some of us found in the Marxist critique of social work: a theoretical critique, plausible or not, freezes the possibility of any sort of action at all.

Most radical criminologists seem aware of this problem and of the central strategic importance of the justice debate. As Foucault's argument about the historical evolution of penal and judicial system shows, crime control is intimately related to questions of social control in other settings, such as family, school, and work. Far from being either a suitable target for piecemeal reform or a residual problem to be dealt with after the revolution, the question of justice must be near the top of the revolutionary agenda.

At the moment the task of socialist criminologists has been seen as "to work at the point of contradictions of law and justice." As I understand it, this implies pushing the justice model to its more political ramifications, showing, for example, that strict conformity to standards of justice would require massive structural change. (It would also point to an intermediate program in which prison would be abolished for property offenses and more upper-class criminals would be prosecuted).

Two levels are distinguished in this Marxist version of the struggle for justice. At the first level, one exposes the discrepancies between the ideals of the bourgeois legal code and the actual exercise of power in the penal system and in civil society generally. A real implementation of justice, it is argued, would raise political consciousness and reveal the class bias in the legal process. At the second level, once society has realized the connection between bourgeois legal standards and the creation of a just, classless society, the progression to socialist legality begins: "The task is not merely to implement bourgeois legality nor either to ignore it . . . the task is to transcend the struggle for individual justice and to usher in a socialist legality."[41] At this second level the program envisages such policies as the democratization of the legal profession and the police force, and the demand that the punishment for crime should be made proportionate to the amount of general harm caused to the community.

This program leaves a fair amount to the imagination, particularly the notion of moving from one "level" to the other and the question of how exactly these new standards of justice and legality are to be implemented. How, for example, are assessments of "general harm" and the "context" of individual responsibility to be made? And who is to make them? Bland categories such as crimes "against the state" or the "general good" or whatever will not necessarily cover particular forms of harm or victimization. And in the transitional phase at least — where strict legality, we are told, will be ensured — how will such measures as the democratization of the police force and legal profession actually guarantee the legal protection of the deprived and powerless? I would also insist, at the risk of sounding sentimental, that both the new liberal version and this Marxist version of the justice model are too determined to sound tough-minded and oh-so-*principled*. They forget that by the time many offenders get to this wonderful justice system, the damage has already been done. To set the standards of justice in terms of the principle of "proportionate harm" is no less problematic than talking about "commensurate deserts." In both cases we lose sight of the humane and compassionate vision that positivism (and common sense) has allowed. Certainly the positivist ideal of reform and rehabilitation as being the *aim* of the criminal justice is fatal. But it is obvious also to anyone who has spent five minutes in a court or prison that it would be blatantly *unjust* to return, even as an intermediate tactic, to an undiluted classicism. The much maligned humanitarianism that has accompanied the otherwise unjustifiable positivist goal of "treating" criminals should not itself be obliterated. Once upon a time it was "radical" to attack law, then it became "radical" to attack psychiatry. As we now rush back to the bewildered embrace of lawyers who always thought we were against them,[42] we should remind ourselves just what a tyranny the literal rule of law could turn out to be.

Socialist legality, we are assured, is another matter, and I turn to some aspects of this ideal in the next section. I would like to repeat, though, that however incomplete the "two-level" radical program might appear, the concentration on the question of justice is, from all perspectives, a welcome one.

Tolerance and Diversity

One of the more remarkable claims in the new criminologies, one that is now sometimes played down for being too utopian, was that it is possible to envisage and work toward a crime-free society. This claim needs stating in full:

Albeit by implication, the insistence in *The New Criminology* was that insofar as the crime producing features of contemporary capitalism are bound up with the inequities and divisions in material production and ownership, then it must be possible via social transformations to create social and productive arrangements that would abolish crime. Critically we would assert that it is possible to envisage societies free from any material necessity to criminalise deviance. Other controls on "anti-social behavior" (and other definitions of what that might constitute) can be imagined and from the point of view of a socialist diversity would be essential.
. . . Additionally there are forms of human diversity which, under capitalism, are labelled and processed as criminal but which should not be subject to control in societies that proclaimed themselves to be socialist. In other words we were asserting that the "withering away of the State" identified in orthodox Left discussions as a feature of thorough-going socialist societies has to feature in the discussion of a socialist criminology.[43]

The meaning is unambiguous: it is the structure of capitalist society that produces crime, and a socially heterogenous society is possible in which the powerful will not and need not criminalize human diversity. I said that this claim is remarkable; it also seems to be a most vulnerable and (at least as now stated) implausible plank in the new criminology's program. At the risk of being elliptical, let me briefly state some problems.

1. The idea of a society that is free of crime but that does contain human diversity is so vague as to defy imagination. Particularly vague is the notion of "diversity" and whether or not this is the same as "deviance." What would be examples of "human diversity," and would there not be antisocial behavior that might appear in any system that could not be tolerated in the name of diversity and might have to be criminalized?
2. A crime-free society, we are sometimes told, is one in which social control would be abolished. This makes complete sociological nonsense. A society implies rules, and rules imply social control. One can certainly say that X type of society is more criminogenic then Y society, but one cannot talk about abolishing social control. And, as we are told at other times, if controls other than the criminal law are both imaginable and essential, just what forms will such controls take?
3. When such claims are made so unambiguously, the onus is surely on those who make them to refer, even occasionally, to the known human societies that at least "proclaim themselves to be socialist" in order to show how they are approaching the stated goal of being free of crime. The most cursory examination of societies that "proclaim themselves to be socialist" — Russia, China, Cuba, Eastern European satellites, Cambodia in its current transition to "socialist legality" — can hardly be said to lend credibility to many theoretical claims about the possibility of a crime-free society. And even if such an examination were inconclusive, on the ground that the theorist does not regard such societies as being truly socialist, it is disingenuous to refuse to embark on it at all.

4. The struggle, we are told, is not for bourgeois legality but socialist legality. Whatever socialist legality might be — and some very well known and extremely unappealing policies have appeared under this name — it is not at all clear why a crime-free society should require *any* form of legality. A crime-free society is one thing; a society with a legal system different from that of capitalist social democracies is another. One cannot argue for both at the same time. Any attempts to do so should be seen as nonsense — unless, that is (and this is by no means clear in the literature), "socialist legality" is seen as merely the organizing feature of the transitional rather than eventual regime.

5. Finally, and this is the level with which I am really most concerned here, it is not clear whether the immediate political strategy is either or both: (a) producing an intellectual critique by which materialist criminology creates a political economy of crime and law — this would carry an implicit "after-the-revolution" perspective about the actual policies of the transitional or eventual good society — or (b) as is suggested in the "struggle for justice" program, identifying a recognizable set of policy objectives in the current social world.

Let us examine more closely the ideal of "diversity" and the ways a society might attain this goal. In a sense, though this sense is not usually acknowledged, the argument here goes back to one of the oldest debates in political philosophy: What are the desirable limits of the state's intervention? The vision of diversity in earlier deviancy theory embodied an implicit laissez-faire position: the state should pull out and let deviants do their thing. Of course, this stance was largely bogus, but reading it as a properly thought out theory of the state rather than a well-meaning set of gestures about tolerance, radicalized criminology pointed to its obvious shortcomings. Some of the polemics about the culture of civility, zookeeping, and normative ghettos were, I think, unfair, but it was quite right to criticize the "moralistic view of 'tolerance' as a kind of free floating sentiment to be mobilised irrespective of social context."[44] What *The New Criminology* proposed instead, most promisingly, was to "substitute a conception of socialist diversity for the pluralism of the idealist tradition." This substitute is spelled out as follows: "a socialist culture which is diverse and expressive — that is, a culture which takes up the progressive elements in pluralism, whilst rejecting those activities which are directly the product of the brutalisations of existing society (however diverse, expressive or idiosyncratic their manifestations)."[45]

At this point, I hope not unfairly, we have to ask for a certain concreteness. Critically, What does the word *rejecting* mean? If it means punish or control (and I cannot see any other conceivable meaning), then we are certainly not talking about a "crime-free society" or the "abolition of social control." Nor is it clear just what action will be tolerated in the name of "socialist diversity" rather than "idealist pluralism," or on what grounds certain elements will be judged as "progressive" and who will make such judgments. At the risk of offending their liberal friends (surely a familiar occupational hazard), Marxists should come clean about these matters. If they would like to see an alternative model of social control in which offenders wearing sandwich boards listing their crimes kneel before a crowd that shouts, "Down with the counterrevolutionaries," and are then led away to be publicly shot, then let such alternatives be discussed. For it is something like this that socialist legality means to millions of people today. Its dubious history has been one of secret trials, the abandonment of the right to defense, and criminalization by analogy. And if different parameters of tolerance from those in traditionally valued bourgeois liberalism are envisaged, then let such criteria be made explit. The issue is too important to be clouded by vague references to "diversity."

Clearly, it is some advance to acknowledge that even after the revolution, some forms of behavior will need to be "rejected." And the reemergence of the "spectres of normality and pathology" gives us some basis for identifying what these forms might be. Indeed, it seems immanent in the notion of a truly socialist society that crime would not occur except for biological and psychological reasons. Paradoxically, then, correctionalist ideologies will be reproduced, buttressed by fully blown pathology theories that will look *more* rather than less tenable because the overarching cause of structural inequality has been removed. The psychiatric labeling of political dissidents in the Soviet Union is the obvious perversion of this ideology.

Socialists will obviously want to dissociate themselves from such perversions. But in some form or another a move is envisaged beyond the indiscriminate blame of pure classicism and the apparent amorality of early deviancy theory to distinguish between actions that are antisocial (and antisocialist?), those that are justifiable (though primitive in conception), and others that are the products of brutalization. To use Young's own example in applying these distinctions,[46] however, it is not clear what might follow from simply *distinguishing* between "the positive and negative moments" in deviant sexuality. If, shall we say, the rape and murder of a small child is identified as one such "negative moment," how can this "moment" be rejected without being criminalized?

The history of power has taught us one clear lesson here: what appears in intellectual circles as a new sensibility or a paradigmatic change in the modality of social control (to make it more rational or more just) is invariably transformed into a base for exercising more power.[47] Despite the references in the debate about crime-free societies to the withering away of the state, there is little evidence to suggest that "socialist legality" as we know it will do anything other than increase the power of the state.

Actually radical criminology has been a lot more specific in its favored models of control than I have so far allowed. One model that has correctly attracted much interest and support (both as an intermediate reform and a model to be eventually incorporated into the good society) is the notion of decentralized self-control systems, organized by the working-class community itself (when talking about "community" it is sometimes forgotten that a middle class exists). Young's version:

> We have to argue therefore, strategically for the exercise of social control but also to argue that such control must be exercised within the working class community and not by external policing agents. The control of crime on the streets, like the control of rate busting on the factory floor, can only be achieved effectively by the community actually involved.[48]

This is an attractive suggestion, though it is probably true that such visions can be traced to what Pearson calls the "sociological pastoral." It is assumed that the deviant question can be resolved only in the idealized *gemeinschaft* village, in which people happily tolerate diversity and deal with their deviants through face-to-face social control.

Much of the current radical preference for decentralized control comes from the standard critique about the dehumanizing effects of urban life. In one criminological version:

> Urban America as we know it has become outmoded and like the dinosaur, is threatened with extinction unless we radically restructure our urban institutions along truly humanitarian and socialist lines, free from alienation, competition, hierarchy and exploitation. Such restructuring, for example, would accord priority to decentralised power structures of community control over massive dehumanised and centralised power structures.[49]

Some elements in the critiques of mass society are shared by conservatives and radicals alike. As anyone who has listened to magistrates or policemen will know, their vision of perfect social control is not a Nazi dictatorship but a collection of simple rural communities in which the heroic village bobby deals with trouble by friendly cuffs on the ear and cozy chats with mum and dad. To point to certain similarities of interest between conservatives and radicals is not — as I said myself about the back-to-justice movement — to argue against these proposals. We should be wary, though, of some versions of the decentralization arguments (for example, those of Oscar Newman) that under the banner of neighborhood control provide blueprints for paranoid fortress communities being patroled by local vigilante squads. And on the whole I tend to be more suspicious than Marxist criminologists of putting such touching faith in the natural instincts of the working-class community on the streets and the factory floor to allow much human diversity. This might admittedly not be the most ideal of experiments to cite, but the contemporary example of self-policing in the "no-go" areas of Belfast is hardly encouraging.

The more constructive criticisms I would like to make about these decentralization proposals, and the overall program for social change in which they are cast, are of very different kinds. In one sense these proposals need to be more concrete and empirical; in another, they need to be more theoretical and utopian. Concreteness is to be gained by looking at the levels of current systems at which changes might take place. There is a certain impetus now *within* the criminal justice system itself that is entirely expedient in its support for decentralization. The argument is that the system has become too bureaucratic, too remote, too inhuman to deal with the current volume of crime and that greater efficiency could be achieved by breaking up parts of the system. The "community court" in particular is seen as a way of reducing the social distance between judge and those who are judged, supposedly facilitating a sense of local involvement.

The interests behind such proposals are unashamedly and naively correctional — crime will be reduced by increasing personal responsibility, justice, efficiency, and a respect for authority — but the empirical models that are cited are worth examining. These include informal work-group controls over such offenses as pilfering; more formal factory courts and arbitration procedures; dispute and conciliation mechanisms used in non-Western societies; and adaptations of procedures used in civil rather than criminal law. Most important for the argument about socialist legality, the models referred to include the various forms of community courts used in socialist countries: comrades courts in the Soviet Union, peoples courts in China, popular tribunals in Cuba, and workers courts in Poland. Despite the relative inaccessibility of the literature on these experiments, something at least is known about their philosophy (particularly the stress on the court's educational role) and operation to warrant serious examination by anyone advocating decentralized or community control.

A recent version of this argument, but one that is idealistic in the sense that it explicitly does not claim that this model of control will necessarily reduce recidivism, is to be found in Christie's call for conflict to be removed from the courts and the experts, and given back to the community.[50] Advancing this position from an Illich-inspired attack on professionals and specialists, Christie argues that models along neighborhood court lines (such as the Tanzanian village court) give better opportunities for norm clarification and the staging of what are effectively political debates. Questions that relate judgments of blameworthiness to such factors as the status and power of the victims, and the offender's status and background can be asked in direct, personal terms. "Decisions on relevance and on the weight of what is found relevant ought to be taken away from legal scholars, the chief idealogues of crime control systems, and brought back for free decision in the court room."[51] Thus, guilt-neutralizing statements such as "They won't miss it" can be confronted in concrete moral and political terms. In conventional systems, the loss of this personal confrontation through expert and professional controls means that the offender does not have the opportunity to be confronted with the type of blame that would be difficult to neutralize.

Besides the need to examine those experiments aimed specifically at creating new forms of social control, there is another valuable empirical reference point in looking at the more ambitious attempts to create whole new microsocieties. Communes, kibbutzim, and other utopian communities have been founded with the explicit purpose of creating just and tolerant social orders. Some of the evaluative literature on these experiments has concerned itself explicitly with questions of tolerance, diversity, and rule enforcement.[52] It is extraordinary that criminologists and sociologists of deviance have made so little reference to these experiments, which contain crucial sociological lessons about rules and boundary lines. Despite the obvious objection that such communities are but imperfect realizations of their original vision and that they are invariably parasitic on the surrounding social order, these experiments are no less relevant than the macropolitical attempts in this century at creating new societies. In both cases we might have as much to learn from the flaws as from the original vision.

But the debate on tolerance and diversity needs also to be extended in more thoretical and utopian directions. Since Wilkins's early formulations about tolerance levels,[53] few criminologists have even speculated about what the concept of "tolerating" deviance actually means. It is by no means clear, for example, that tolerance would necessarily go along with greater decentralization. And are trade-offs necessarily involved, more tolerance in one sphere of life resulting in more restrictions elsewhere? One matter is certain: the opposition between "crime" on the one hand and "socialist diversity" on the other, is entirely unreal. Somewhere in the middle lies the much-abused concept of deviance (and derivative formulations about rule breaking, normalization, and so on). The current attempt to return from deviance to crime as an organizing framework means giving up many theoretical gains.

Finally, there is the need for more "utopian" theory construction. All the loose talk about legality, morality, justice, and tolerance needs to be related to classic and current attempts (most notably those identified with Rawls) to specify the abstract properties of a just system. In addition, there is the vast anarchist and libertarian tradition of writing about the state that addresses problems of tolerance more directly than does Marxist literature. Nozick's *Anarchy, State and Utopia* brings together many of these separate strands and is a compelling attempt to spell out what a minimalist state position would look like. It is precisely such formulations that are needed to rescue the concept of tolerance from its purely subjectivist meaning.

Strategies and Agendas

Two lines of objection would suggest that much of my argument has been entirely unfair. In the first place, the demand for policy blueprints to be constructed or alternatives to be spelled out, clarified, and made explicit can hardly be expected from *any* body of sociological theory, least of all the new deviancy theories that have had to establish themselves against an antitheoretical, pragmatic tradition. Second, when one strand of this new theory adopts an avowedly revolutionary program, it hardly seems appropriate to expect it to concern itself with the details of reformist policies. (Marxists would also presumably object to any separate examination of parts or derivatives of the theory without looking at the whole package, for example, the particular view about the nature of science or historical materialism.)

The first objection is justified in the sense that the relationship between theory and practice in the social sciences is obviously not one that easily allows the precise spelling out of strategies and tactics for social policy. I am asking less for such step-by-step strategies, though, than suggesting that the new criminologies have maneuvered themselves too tightly into theoretical positions whose immediate moral and political implications are not even on the agenda. This is irresponsible, precisely because of the way these theories have evolved. At first, and understandably, the battle with mainstream criminology was fought against not just conservative correctional interests but any sort of policy interests at all. Particularly in the United States rather than Britain, the pretensions of the new deviancy school to be accepted into the sociological fold meant shaking off all identification with social work, correctional, or social policy traditions. In Britain this was never quite the case, and from the beginning of the National Deviancy Conference and its later more Marxist strands, it was patently obvious that the older policy interests were not to be replaced by pure naturalism (if that were possible) but by the construction of *new* policy interests. The struggle was to be on behalf of others — the deviants — and practical people like social workers were to be in the front line. If we were at all honest in this stance, then it seems to me disingenuous to imply that the consideration of policy, and an active involvement in current policy debates is not our business.

As to the question of revolution and reform, it is tempting to do little more than recognize this as being the perennial question on the political agenda. In the specific context of radical criminology, Mathiesen's analysis has had a powerful effect in opening up this debate. The central argument against reformist politics remains: the danger not just of co-optation but of pushing for reforms that would allow a society to present itself as more just and legitimate than it is. And similarly, the dangers of utopianism remain: in the meantime there are victims and sufferers, and their plight is not relieved by suspending help till the revolution comes.

It should be possible — by using, for example, the current "struggle for justice" debate — to develop middle-range policy alternatives that do not compromise any overall design for fundamental social change. This does not mean simply employing this overall design to develop a theoretical critique of the justice program but actually being brave enough to speculate on some policy alternatives, however unfinished and unworkable they might appear. Christie's vision of using the courtroom as a stage for acting out real social conflict and for deciding the question of individual responsibility without the aid of experts is the type of example I have in mind.

The "purer" theoretical tasks still remain on the agenda: to reconcile the twists of classical and positivist philosophies with a sociological conception of individual responsibility; to apply an abstract theory of justice to the brute facts of the social order and the possibilities of a different order; to understand what the notions of diversity and tolerance would look like in the good society. But these tasks must be performed with at least one eye on the day-to-day world of crime and criminal justice politics. When this world goes out of frame, as it has tended to do in the past, we lose the chance of influencing it. Conservative interests have always kept this world in focus, for they are part of the frame. A critical criminology has to combat not just knowledge, but the power of knowledge.

Notes

1. David Matza, *Becoming Deviant* (Englewood Cliffs, N.J.: Prentice-Hall, 1969), p. 17.
2. Jock Young, "Working Class Criminology," in *Critical Criminology*, ed. I. Taylor et al. (London: Routledge & Kegan Paul, 1975).
3. This was also true the further we ventured into the world of social work, and these worries prompted me to write a paper (chapter 7) that was interpreted as a polemic against *The New Criminology*. It was intended, rather, to show how inadequate both the interactionist and Marxist versions of the new deviancy theories were when translated into social work practice. The Marxist versions were treated more harshly because their claims and pretensions were, and are, more ambitious.
4. Only Pearson's account of this period deals with criminology's hidden moral agenda in the way I understand it in this paper; G. Pearson, *The Deviant Imagination* (London: Macmillan, 1975).
5. I. Taylor et al., *The New Criminology* (London: Routledge & Kegan Paul, 1973), p. 37.
6. Young, "Working Class Criminology," pp. 68–71. Though this critique is very much to the point, there is some confusion in the standard argument that *simultaneously* attacks interactionist-inspired theory for seeing the deviant as being free (subjectivism) and also as being the passive "person on his back" (determinism).
7. Ibid., p. 71.
8. Pearson, *The Deviant Imagination*, p. 105.

9. See, for example, Tony Platt, "Prospects for a Radical Criminology in the U.S.A.," and H. and J. Schwendinger, "Defenders of Order or Guardians of Human Rights," in *Critical Criminology*, ed. I. Taylor et al. (London: Routledge & Kegan Paul, 1975).

10. Richard Quinney, "The Ideology of Law: Notes for a Radical Alternative to Legal Repression," *Issues in Criminology* 7 (1972): 24. See also Richard Quinney and John Wildeman, *The Problem of Crime: A Critical Introduction to Criminology* (New York: Harper & Row, 1977).

11. Young, "Working Class Criminology," pp. 71–75.

12. Ibid., p. 79.

13. One of the most revealing possible lessons from this period is to be derived from David Matza's story of receiving enthusiastic letters from police chiefs after his publication of *Delinquency and Drift*, his critique of positivism in the juvenile court. At last, they said, someone is coming out clearly in favor of punishment against soft liberal treatment. Fatally, we have never understood the implications of such stories.

14. Matza, *Becoming Deviant*, p. 12.

15. Ibid., p. 17.

16. Ibid.

17. Georgy Lukacs, *The Meaning of Contemporary Realism* (London: Merlin Press, 1963), p. 33.

18. Young, "Working Class Criminology," p. 75.

19. Taylor et al., *The New Criminology*, p. 52.

20. I am thinking particularly of the massive literature on the Nuremberg trials and such specific arguments as Hannah Arendt's famous account of the Eichmann trial.

21. Mary McCarthy, *Medina* (London: Wildwood House, 1972).

22. Her argument about this moral difference is, of course, not conclusive, though persuasive enough:

> Though it would have changed nothing for the victims, most of us would prefer to think that those women and babies and old men had died in a raid rather than been singled out, one by one, for slaughter. Logic here is unpersuasive: the deliberate individual killing of unresisting people is more repugnant than the same result effected by mechanical means deployed at a distance and without clear perception of who or what is below. Even those who profess to see no distinction in Vietnam between the crime of war and single acts of homicide would be hard put to deny that distance does not seem to count in diminishing responsibility. Demonstrators shouting 'Hey, hey LBJ how many kids did you kill today?' were logically right in viewing Johnson as the final cause, insofar as that could be targetted in one person, but humanly they failed to convince, since he was not the proximate cause and could not even be said to have intended the slaughter of Vietnamese children in the same sense that Hitler intended the annihilation of Jews in the gas ovens.

Ibid., p. 42.

23. Ibid., p. 168.

24. Ibid., p. 87.

25. Harold Finestone, *Victims of Change: Juvenile Delinquents in American Society* (London: Greenwood Press, 1977), p. 215.

26. See Ken Plummer, "Misunderstanding Labelling Perspectives," in *Deviant Interpretations*, ed. D. Downes and P. Rock (Oxford: Martin Robertson, 1979).

27. M. Foucault, ed., *I. Pierre Riviere, Having Slaughtered My Mother, My Sister and My Brother . . . A Case of Homicide in the Nineteenth Century* (New York: Random House, 1975).

28. Pearson, *The Deviant Imagination*, p. 25.

29. Young, "Working Class Criminology," p. 90.

30. Gresham Sykes and David Matza, "Techniques of Neutralization: A Theory of Delinquency," *American Sociological Review* 22 (December 1957): 664–70.

31. Laurie Taylor, "The Significance and Interpretation of Replies to Motivational Questions: The Case of Sex Offenders," *Sociology* 6 (1972): 23–39.

32. Andrew von Hirsch, *Doing Justice: The Choice of Punishments* (New York: Hill & Wang, 1976).

33. In support of the just deserts position here, the report cites such arguments as J. Feinberg's in *Doing and Deserving* (Princeton: Princeton University Press, 1970). For a more critical view, see Ted Honderich, *Punishment: The Supposed Justifications* (Harmondsworth: Penguin, 1976), ch. 2.

34. von Hirsch, *Doing Justice*, p. 47.

35. J. G. Murphy, "Marxism and Retribution," *Philosophy and Public Affairs* 2 (1972).

36. von Hirsch, *Doing Justice*, p. 147.

37. Ibid., p. 149.

38. Taylor and Young, unpublished paper, 5th Conference of European Group for the Study of Deviance and Social Control, Barcelona, 1977. The paper they criticize was later published as David Greenberg, "Reflections on the Justice Model Debate," *Contemporary Crises* 7 (November 1983): 313–27.

39. Quinney and Wildeman, *The Problem of Crime*, p. 29.

40. Taylor and Young, unpublished paper, p. 27.

41. Ibid., p. 43.

42. This slightly opportunistic element in the justice debate is paralleled in the shifting stances toward the welfare state. In the late 1960s the welfare state was attacked as the most repressive branch of the apparatus, most repressive because its control functions were disguised. Then, with the economic crisis, radicals jumped to the other foot, forgot their previous critique of the welfare soft machine, and started defending welfare against the cuts. The underdog sympathy remained, but now the underdogs had to be defended against new threats. Some of the older positions in deviancy theory and anti-psychiatry (for example, the analysis of stigma) became regarded as irrelevant or even reactionary. It remains to be seen, as in the justice debate, how these different types of attack can be reconciled.

43. Taylor et al., *Critical Criminology*, p. 20.

44. Young, "Working Class Criminology," p. 71.

45. Taylor et al., *Critical Criminology*, p. 90.

46. Young, "Working Class Criminology," p. 91.

47. Michel Foucault, *Discipline and Punish* (London: Allen Lane, 1977).

48. Young, "Working Class Criminology," p. 89.

49. Quinney and Wildeman, *The Problem of Crime*, pp. 149–50.

50. Nils Christie, "Conflicts as Property," *British Journal of Criminology* 17 (1977): 1–15.

51. Ibid., p. 15.

52. Philip Abrams and Andrew McCulloch, *Communes, Sociology and Society* (Cambridge: Cambridge University Press, 1978).

53. Leslie Wilkins, *Social Deviance* (London: Tavistock, 1961).

9

Symbols of Trouble*

Taken as an instant pop sociological response to the immediate and newsworthy problems of the day, this book was "out of date" even when it originally appeared in 1972: Such an enterprise is anyway best left to good journalists who know far better than sociologists about reacting to the contemporary and, moreover, about meeting deadlines. But then, as now, I would want to justify this piece of historical reconstruction as having implications somewhat beyond the immediate and topical. It matters neither here not there that there is now (1980) a major Mod revival, spinning its way through music, fashion, color-supplement journalism, and even two full-length movies from The Who, trying the recreate the spirit of the Brighton beaches.

We need to look beyond these ephemera. Admittedly, the assertion in my original preface that the processes by which moral panics and folk devils are generated do not date was a little brash in implying that I had cleverly succeeded in uncovering these processes. But I doubt that later developments have changed this picture. My pessimistic concluding words have, alas, also been justified: "More moral panics will be generated and other, as yet nameless folk devils will be created. This is not because such developments have an inexorable inner logic, but because our society as present structured will continue to generate problems for some of its members—like working class adolescents—and then condemn whatever solution these groups find."

One cannot let things rest at this point, though. Indeed, a defect of the book was the impression it sometimes might have conveyed of a certain timelessness, an unveiling of a set of consequences insulated from history and politics. This is what Barthes calls the "miraculous evaporation of history from events." While having to leave the actual text intact for this edition, I want to use this introduction to comment on recent theoretical developments in the study of

* "Symbols of Trouble", Introduction to New Edition of *Folk Devils and Moral Panics: The Creation of the Mods and Rockers* (Oxford: Martin Robertson, 1980).

delinquency and subcultures, which are very much concerned with reinserting the historical and the political. Given my limited space, I can do little more than give a critical guide to this literature and also (more than the original text) address issues within the sociological debate rather than looking to a more general audience.

I refer to theoretical developments rather than actual historical occurrences because I do not believe that anything that has actually happened or has been "discovered" (about youth, popular culture, delinquency, mass media reporting) in the decade since the research was completed needs extended reconstruction here. True, the substance of this period has been continually interesting: the Skinhead years, the brief glamrock interlude, the punk explosion, the revival of both the Teds and the Mods, the continued noise of football hooliganism. But to reexamine the subject of postwar British youth subcultures is not quite the same as constructing, say, a revised historiography of World War II; there are no new archives to be opened, no secret documents to be discovered, no pacts of silence to be broken. There are just the same (rather poor) sources of information from the same (often inarticulate) informants. The question is what new sense can be made of these "same" data.

This decade has been one of quite phenomenal growth in relevant "making sense" fields such as deviancy theory and cultural studies. These years saw the novelty of the labeling perspective in the sociology of deviance being challenged by Marxism, which at the same time (in combination with various branches of structuralism and semiotics) established virtual hegemony over the cultural studies field. And in the theorizing about delinquent subcultures there was a leap straight from the functionalism of the original American theory to various types of neo-Marxism. The interactionist/labeling intervention hardly registered here. *Folk Devils and Moral Panics* certainly relied heavily on labeling theory but never suggested that the origins of the behavior itself could be explained by anything other than a slightly tougher version of original subcultural theory. Despite my pains to avoid this, the book was still misinterpreted (together with most labeling studies) as implying that there is no need for a structural explanation of the subculture in its own right.

It is quite true, of course, that the book was more a study of moral panics than of folk devils. Influenced by labeling theory, I wanted to study reaction; the actors themselves just flitted across the screen. Now, to redress this balance but also because this is where the most creative and challenging work has been done during this decade, I want to concentrate more on action. Accordingly — still following this rather abstract distinction between actor and audience, action and reaction, behavior and labeling — I will reverse the book's sequence and consider action first.

Action

Traditional subcultural theory of delinquency is too well known to have to be expounded here.[1] The intellectual offspring of two oddly matched but conventional strands of American sociology — functionalist anomie theory and the Chicago school — and the political offspring of the end-of-ideology era, it has shaped sociological visions of delinquency for twenty-five years. Like all intellectual departures, particularly those influenced by political considerations and particularly those in the deviancy field,[2] when new subcultural theory appeared in Britain at the beginning of the seventies,[3] it was concerned to show how radically it differed from tradition. And it could hardly have *looked* more different.

It was not just the switch from functionalist to Marxist language but the sense conveyed of why this switch "had" to take place. The context was light years away from the United States in the mid-fifties: a sour, post-welfare-state Britain that had patently not delivered the goods; the cracking of all those interdependent myths of classlessness, embourgeoisement, consumerism, and pluralism; the early warnings of economic recession and high (particularly juvenile) unemployment; the relative weakness of recognizably political resistance.

No tortuous sociology of knowledge is needed to see how this context "influenced" the theories; the context was explicitly woven into the theories' very substance. History and political economy became open rather than hidden; the "problem" of the working-class adolescent was seen not in terms of adjustment or of being provided more opportunities to buy a larger share of the cake but of bitter conflict, resistance, and strife. The delinquent changed from "frustrated social climber"[4] to cultural innovator and critic. What was really happening on the beaches of Brighton and Clacton, as well as earlier at the Teddy Boy dance halls and later on the football terraces and punk concerts, was a drama of profound symbolic resonance. Subculture was, no less, a political battleground between the classes.

I will come back in more detail to this framework. It is worth noting, though, that for all its obvious novelty and achievement — it is now simply not possible to talk about delinquent subcultures in the same way — the new theory shares a great deal more with the old than it cared to admit. Both work with the same "problematic" (to use the fashionable term): growing up in a class society. Both identify the same vulnerable group: the urban, male, working-class adolescent. Both see delinquency as a collective solution to a structurally imposed problem. For example, although its tone and political agenda are distinctive enough, Willis's statement of what has to be explained is not too far away from the original theories: "the experience and cultural processes of being male, white, working class, unqualified, disaffected and moving into manual work in contemporary capitalism."[5] These assumptions must be emphasized precisely because they do *not* appear in the rhetoric of moral panics or in conventional criminology or in the official control culture.

Beyond this, of course, there are the novelties and differences to which I will now turn. These lie primarily in the levels of sophistication and complexity that the new theories have added, in the location of delinquency in the whole repertoire of class-based negotiations, and in the rescuing of traditional subcultural theory from its historical flatness by placing both the structural "problem" and its subcultural "solution" in a recognizable time and place. Of course, as I will point out again, most delinquency is numbingly the same and has never had much to do with those historical "moments" and "conjunctures" that today's students of working-class youth cultures are so ingeniously trying to find. But whatever the object of attention — "expressive fringe delinquency" (as I originally called it) or ordinary mainstream delinquency — the new theories distinguish three general levels of analysis: *structure, culture,* and *biography.* I will adopt (and adapt) these headings to organize my review.

(i) *Structure* refers to those aspects of society that appear beyond individual control, especially those deriving from the distribution of power, wealth, and differential location in the labor market. These are the structural "constraints," "conditions," "contingencies," or "imperatives" that the new theory identifies in general terms, and then applies to the group most vulnerable to them, that is, working-class youth. In old subcultural theory, these conditions constitute the "problem" to which (ii) the *culture* is the solution. More broadly, *culture* refers to the traditions, maps of meanings, and ideologies that are patterned responses to structural conditions; more narrowly *sub*culture is the specific, especially symbolic form through which the subordinate group negotiates its position. Then (iii) there is *biography*: broadly, the pattern and sequence of personal circumstance through which the culture and structure are experienced; more narrowly, what the subculture means and how it is actually lived out by its carriers.

Much of the new work on British postwar youth cultures is a teasing out of the relationship between these three levels. And all of this work is more or less informed by the Marxist categorization of structure, culture, and biography as the determinate conditions ("being born into a world not of your own choosing") to which the subculture is one of the possible working-class responses ("making your own history").[6]

Structure/History/Problem

In the more one-dimensional world of original theories, working-class kids somehow hit the system — as represented variously by school, work, or leisure. To use the common metaphor: the theories explained how and why kids would kick a machine that did not pay; no one asked how the machine was rigged in the first place. The new theories are very much concerned with how the machine got there. From a general analysis of postwar British capitalism, specific features, particularly the pervasiveness of class, are extracted and historicized. Their impact on the working class — and more particularly its community and its most vulnerable members, adolescents — is then identified as a series of pressures or contradictions stemming from domination and subordination.

To determine what the old theories would classify as the "problem" to which delinquency is the "solution," one must "situate youth in the dialectic between a 'hegemonic' dominant culture and the subordinate working-class 'parent'" culture of which youth is a fraction."[7] The conventional assumptions of the old theories are thus politically (and alas, linguistically) retranslated. In this retranslation the individualistic bias of those theories (the assumption that status frustration, alienation, or whatever somehow had to be psychologically recognized) is removed. By stating the problem in historical or structural terms there is no necessary assumption that it has to be present in a realized conscious form. Ethnographic support (in the form of statements about the "system," the "authorities," the "fucking bosses") is occasionally cited, but clearly the theories would not be embarrassed without this support. (I will return later to the question of consciousness.)

Let me list three representative such attempts to find the structural problem; each is a Marxist revision of the liberal or social-democratic assumptions behind the equivalent traditional theories.

Phil Cohen's influential work is thus a radicalized and historically specific rendering of traditional accounts of working-class culture and community.[8] He uses a particular delinquent youth culture, the Skinheads, and a particular place, the East End of London, to analyze the destruction of the working-class community and the erosion of its traditional culture. Kinship network, neighborhood ecology, local occupational structure, depopulation, the destruction of communal space, immigration, postwar development and housing, the stress on the privatized space of the family unit — all these vectors of life so commonly ignored in standard delinquency theory are assembled into a model of the internal conflicts in the parent (i.e. adult) culture that come to be worked out in terms of generational conflict. These conflicts (or contradictions) register most acutely on the young and might appear at all sorts of levels: at the ideological, between the traditional working-class puritanism and the new hedonism of consumption; at the economic, between the future as part of the socially mobile elite (the future "explored" by the Mods) and the future as part of the new lumpen (represented by the Skinhead inversion of the glossy element in Mod style). The latent function of the subculture is "to express and resolve, albeit magically, the contradictions which remain hidden or unresolved in the parent culture."[9] Delinquent cultures retrieve social cohesive elements destroyed in the parent culture.

My next example is Corrigan — and this time the target is the social democratic view of educational disadvantage. The persistent theme in his ethnography of fourteen-to-fifteen-year-old boys in two Sunderland working-class schools is power and subordination. Far from being a public sports track in which the earnest working-class youth's striving for status and mobility is thwarted by his deprived background, the school is a hidden political battleground, a setting in which the historical role of compulsory state education in attacking working-class culture is reenacted each day. Bougeois morality, values, discipline, and surveillance on the one hand; the continuous "guerrilla warfare" of truancy, mucking about, "dolling off," and getting into trouble on the other. The kids simply do not see the world in the same way as the school; their "problem" is how to resist and protect themselves from an alien imposition, not how to attain its values.

Then there is Willis — whose target is also liberal ideologies about education, opportunity, and work (and who provides the most sophisticated theory of the interplay between structure, culture, and biography). His ethnographic picture — based on two years' work with boys in a Midlands comprehensive school, "Hammertown," and then another year as they moved into work — is similar to Corrigan's but even bleaker and darker. Again, there is the metaphor of a "permanent guerrilla war," and the bland sociological notion of a "counterculture" is replaced by "caged resentment which always stops just short of outright confrontation."[10] The boys' class culture is devoted to subverting the institution's main aim: making them work. But also — and here lies the subtlety and originality of Willis's thesis — this culture, with its values of chauvinism, solidarity, masculinity, and toughness, contains also the seeds of the boys' defeat. The same transcendance of the school system, the refusal to collude in the elaborate pretense of qualifications, useless certificates, vocational guidance, and career advice, signals insertion into a system of exploitation through the acceptance of manual labor. (Willis's view of culture, — "not simply layers of padding between human beings and unpleasantness,"[11] — as a creative appropriation in its own right, in fact, undermines the whole solution/problem framework. The solution, ironically, is the problem: the boys eventually collude in their own domination.)

Each of these formulations — and other allied work — needs, and no doubt will receive, separate criticism. I want to mention here just one general problem: the overfacile drift to historicism. There are too many points at which the sociological enterprise of understanding the present is assumed to have been solved by an appeal to the past. No doubt it is important to see today's school in terms of the development of state education in the nineteenth century; to specify the exact historical transformations in the working-class neighborhood; to define football hooliganism in terms of the erosion of the sport's traditions by bourgeois entertainment values;[12] or to explain an episode of "Paki-bashing" by Skinheads not in terms of a timeless concept of racial prejudice but by the

place of migrant workers in the long historical drama of the collapse and transformation of local industry.[13] In each case the connections sound plausible,
but in each case a single and one-directional historical trend is picked out—
commercialization, repression, bourgeoisification, destruction of community,
erosion of leisure values—and then projected onto a present that (often by the
same sociologists's own admission) is much more complicated, contradictory,
or ambiguous.

The recent enthusiasm with which criminologists have taken up the new "history from below" derives from a common spirit.[14] The enterprise of bestowing
meaning to certain contemporary forms of deviance was identical to the rescuing of groups like Luddites from (in E.P. Thompson's famous ringing phrase)
"the enormous condescension of posterity." The appeal to history, though, is
a hazardous business, especially in the form I will later discuss of trying to
find actual continuities in resistance. I am less than convinced that any essen-
tialist version of history, such as the dominant one of a free working class interfered with since the eighteenth century by the bourgeois state apparatus,
is either necessary or sufficient to make sense of delinquency or youth culture
today. It also leads to such nonsense as the assertion that *because* of this historical transformation, each working-class adolescent generation has to learn
anew that its innocent actions constitute delinquency in the eyes of the state.

Culture/Style/Solution

Above all else the new theories about British postwar youth cultures are massive exercises of decoding, reading, deciphering, and interrogating. These
phenomena *must* be saying something to us, if only we could know exactly
what. So the whole assembly of cultural artifacts, down to the Punks' last safety
pin, have been scrutinized, taken apart, contextualized, and recontextualized.
The conceptual tools of Marxism, structuralism and semiotics, a Left-Bank
pantheon of Genet, Lévi-Strauss, Barthes, and Althusser have all been wheeled
in to aid this hunt for the hidden code.[15] The result has been an ingenious and,
more often than not, plausible reading of subcultural style as a process of generating, appropriating, and reordering to communicate new and subversive
meanings.

Whether the objects for decoding are Teddy Boys, Mods and Rockers, Skinheads, or Punks, two dominant themes are suggested: first, that style, whatever
else it is, is essentially a type of *resistance* to subordination; second, that the
form taken by this resistance is somehow *symbolic or magical*, in the sense
of not being an actual, successful solution to whatever is the problem. The
phrase *resistance through ritual* clearly announces these two themes.

The notion of resistance conveys, and is usually intended to convey, something more active, radical, and political than the equivalent phrases in old subcultural theory. It is not a question anymore of passive adaption or desperate

lashing out in the face of frustrated aspirations but of a collective (and, we are sometimes asked to believe) historically informed response, mediated by the class-culture of the oppressed. The following is a list of the terms actually used in the literature to convey this reaction:

- *in relationship to dominant values*
  either: *resistance*: attack, subversion, overturning, undermining, struggle, opposition, defiance, violation, challenge, refusal, contempt
  or: *transformation*: transcendance, reworking, adaption, negotiation, resolution, realization
- *in relationship to traditional working-class values*
  either: *defend*: safeguard, protect, preserve, conserve
  or: *recapture*: reappropriate, retrieve, reassert, reaffirm, reclaim, recover

Clearly, the nuances of these words convey somewhat different meanings but there are common threads, particularly in the recurrent theme of *winning space*. Territoriality, solidarity, aggressive masculinity, stylistic innovation — these are all attempts by working-class youth to reclaim community and reassert traditional values.

Sociologically more opaque than this notion of resistance is the reciprocal[16] idea that this process (whether conceived as defense, reworking, reassertion, or whatever) is somehow a symbolic one.[17] Again, it is instructive to list the actual words used to convey this meaning: ritualistic; imaginary; mythical; fantastic; metaphorical; magical; allegorical; ideological; suppressed; displaced; dislocated. There appear to be three contexts in which such concepts are invoked:

1. When the target for attack is inappropriate, irrational, or simply wrong in the sense that it is not logically or actually connected with the source of the problem. Thus Teddy Boys attacking Cypriot cafe owners, Mods and Rockers attacking each other, Skinheads beating up Pakistanis and gays, or football hooligans smashing up trains are all really (though they might not know it) reacting to other things, for example, threats to community homogeneity or traditional stereotypes of masculinity. To quote Cohen and Robins on the Arsenal youth end, "It's as if for these youngsters, the space they share on the North Bank is a way of magically retrieving the sense of group solidarity and identification that once went along with living in a traditional working-class neighbourhood."[18]
2. The second (and allied) meaning is that the solution is "always and only" magical in that it does not confront the real material bases of subordination and hence lacks the organization and consequences of a genuinely political response. Such attempts to deal with contradictions and subordination "crucially do not mount their solutions on the real terrain where the contradictions themselves arise and . . . thus fail to pose an alternative, potentially counter hegemonic solution."[19] The gestures are as effective as sticking

pins into kewpie dolls or as neurotic defense mechanisms like displacement or suppression. The bosses, educational disadvantage, unemployment, the police, remain where they were. Relations with the state are conducted at an imaginary level, "not in the sense that they are illusory, but in that they enfold the human beings who find themselves in confrontation in a common misrecognition of the real mechanisms which have distributed them to their respective positions."[20] It is a staged shadowboxing, a very bad case indeed of false consciousness.

3. The final (and more conventional) meaning of *symbolic* is simply that the subcultural style stands for, signifies, points to, or denotes something beyond its surface appearance. The Mods' scooters, the Skinheads' working boots, the Punks' facial makeup are all making oblique, coded statements about relationshiops, real or imaginary, to a particular past or present. Objects are borrowed from the world of consumer commodities and their meanings transferred by being reworked into a new ensemble that expresses its opposition obliquely or ironically.

Hebdige captures all these three meanings: "These 'humble objects' can be magically appropriated: 'stolen' by subordinate groups and made to carry 'secret' meanings which express, in code a form of resistance to the order which guarantee their continued subordination."[21]

The themes of *resistance* and *symbols* are rich and suggestive. I have the space to mention, somewhat cryptically, only a few of the problems they raise. The first arises from the constant impulse to decode the style in terms *only* of opposition and resistance. This means that instances are sometimes missed when the style is conservative or supportive; in other words, not reworked or reassembled but taken over intact from dominant commercial culture. Such instances are conceded but then brushed aside because — as we all know — the style is a *bricolage* of inconsistencies, and anyway things are not what they seem and so the apparently conservative meaning really hides just the opposite.

There is also a tendency in some of this work to see the historical development of a style as being wholly internal to the group, with commercialization and co-optation as something that just happens afterward. In the understandable zeal to depict the kids as creative agents rather than manipulated dummies, this often plays down the extent to which changes in youth culture are manufactured changes, dictated by consumer society.[22] I am not aware of much evidence, for example, that the major components in punk originated too far away from that distinctive London cultural monopoly carved up between commercial entrepreneurs and the lumpen intellectuals from art schools and rock journals. An allied problem is the often exaggerated status given to the internal circuit of English working-class history. The spell cast on the young by American cultural imperialism[23] is sometimes downgraded. Instead of being given a sense of the interplay between borrowed and native traditions,[24] we are directed exclusively to the experiences of nineteenth-century Lancashire cotton weavers. This is inevitable if the subculture is taken to denote some form of cumulative historical resistance. Where we are really being directed is toward the "profound line of historical continuity" between today's delinquents and their "equivalents" in the past. To find this line, we have to ask questions like "How would 'our' hooligans appear if they were afforded the same possibilities of rationality and intelligibility, say, as those of Edward Thompson?"[25]

To afford them these possibilities, what these theorists have to do is subscribe to what Ditton nicely calls the dinosaur theory of history.[26] A recent zoological argument apparently proposes that dinosaurs did not after all die out; one group still lives on, known as—birds! Similarly, historical evidence is cited to prove that mass proletarian resistance to the imposition of bourgeois control did not after all die out. It lives on in certain forms of delinquency which though more symbolic and individualistic than their progenitors, must still be read as rudimentary forms of political action, as versions of the same working-class struggle which has occurred since the defeat of Chartism. What is going on in the streets and terraces is not only not what it appears to be but, moreover, is really the same as what went on before. To justify this claim a double leap of imagination is required. In Pearson's example, the "proof" that something like Paki-bashing is a "primitive form of political and economic struggle" lies not in the kids' understanding of what it is they are resisting (they would probably only say something like "When you get some long stick in your hand and you are bashing some Paki's face in, you don't think about it") but in the fact that the machine smashers of 1826 would *also* not have been aware of the real political significance of their action.[27] This seems to me a very peculiar sort of proof indeed. If ever Tolstoy's remark applied, it might be here: "History is like a deaf man replying to questions which nobody puts to him."[28]

This leads on to the vexing issue of consciousness and intent, a problem present even when the appeal is to symbols rather than history. Now, it would be as absurd to demand here that all bearers of symbols walk around with structuralist theory in their heads as it would be to expect the oppressed to have a detailed knowledge of dialectical materialism. It seems to me, though, that *somewhere* along the line symbolic language implies a knowing subject, a subject at least dimly aware of what the symbols are supposed to mean. To be really tough-minded about this, our criterion for whether or not to go along with a particular symbolic interpretation should be Beckett's famous warning to his critics: "No symbols where none intended."

At times the new theories seem to accept such a tough criterion. Clark, for example, insists at one point "that the group self-consciousness is sufficiently developed for its members to be concerned to recognize themselves in the range of symbolic objects available."[29] More often than not, though, this tough criterion of a fit, consonance, or homology between self-consciousness and symbolism is totally ignored and the theory is content to find theoretical meanings (magic, recovery of community, resistance, or whatever) quite independent of intent or awareness. Indeed Hebdige, who is more sensitive than most to this problem, ends up by conceding, "It is highly unlikely . . . that the members of any subcultures described in this book would recognize themselves reflected here."[30]

Some inconsistencies arise, I think, from a too-literal application of certain strands in structuralism and semiotics. Hebdige, for example, uses Barthes's contrast between the obviously intentional signification of advertisements and the apparently innocent signification of news photos to suggest that subcultural style bears the same relationship to conventional culture as the advertising image bears to the less consciously constructed news photo. In other words, subcultural symbols are, obviously and conspicuously, fabricated and displayed. This is precisely how and why they are subversive and against the grain of mainstream culture, which is unreflexive and "natural." But in the same breath, Hebdige repeats the semiotic article of faith that signification need not be intentional, that Eco's "semiotic guerrilla warfare" can be conducted at a level beneath the consciousness of the individual members of a spectacular subculture— though to confuse things further, "the subculture is still at another level an intentional communication."[31]

This leaves me puzzled about the question of intent. I doubt whether these theories take seriously enough their own question about how the subculture makes sense to its members. If indeed not all Punks "were equally aware of the disjunction between experience and signification upon which the whole style was ultimately based" or if the style made sense for the first wave of self-conscious innovators from the arts schools "at a level which remained inaccessible to those who became punks after the subculture had surfaced and been publicized"[32] — and surely all this must be the case—then why proceed as if such questions were only incidental? It is hard to say which is the more sociologically incredible: a theory that postulates cultural dummies who give homologous meanings to all artifacts surrounding them or a theory that suggests that individual meanings do not matter at all.

Even if this problem of differential meaning and intent is set aside, we are left with the perennial sociological question of how to know whether one set of symbolic interpretations is better than another, or indeed if it is appropriate to invoke the notion of symbols *at all*. Here, my feeling is that the symbolic baggage the kids are being asked to carry is just too heavy, that the interrogations are just a little forced. This is especially so when appearances are, to say the least, ambiguous or (alternatively) when they are simple but taken to point to just their opposite. The exercise of decoding can then only become as arcane, esoteric, and mysterious as such terms as Hebdige's imply: "insidious significance," "the invisible seam," "secret language," "double meaning," "second order system," "opaque sign," "secret identity," "double life," "mimes of imagined conditions," "oblique expression," "magical elisions," "sleight of hand," "present absence," "frozen dialectic," "fractured circuitry," "elliptic coherence," "coded exchanges," "submerged possibilities," etc.

This is, to be sure, an imaginative way of reading the style, but how can we be sure that it is also not imaginary? When the code is embedded in a meaning system already rich in conscious symbolism, then there are fewer problems. For example, when Hebdige is writing about black rasta culture, the connections flow smoothly, the homology between symbols and life could hardly be closer.[33] The conditions in the original Jamaican society, Rastafarian beliefs, the translation of reggae music to Britain—all these elements cohere. A transposed religion, language, and style create a simultaneously marginal and magical system that provides a subtle and indirect language of rebellion. Symbols are *necessary*; if a more direct language had been chosen, it would have been more easily dealt with by the group against which it was directed. Not only does the system display a high degree of internal consistency—particularly in its references to the historical experience of slavery—but it refers directly to patterns of thought that are *actually* hermetic, arcane, syncretic, and associative.

If such patterns have to be forced out of the subject matter, though, the end result is often equally forced. When any apparent inconsistencies loom up, the notion of *bricolage* comes to the rescue: the magic ensemble is only *implicitly* coherent, the connections can be infinitely extended and improvised. And even this sort of rescue is too "traditional" and "simple" we are now told; instead of a reading being a revelation of a fixed number of concealed meanings, it is really a matter of polysemy: each text is seen to generate a potentially infinite range of meanings. Style fits together precisely because it does not fit; it coheres "elliptically through a chain of conspicuous absenses."[34]

This is an aesthetics that may work for art but not equally well for life. The danger is of getting lost in "the forest of symbols,"[35] and we should take heed of the warnings given by those, like anthropologists, who have searched more carefully in these same forests than most students of youth culture. Thus, in trying to interpret what he calls those "enigmatic formations," Turner is aware of certain frontiers to the anthropologist's explanatory competence.[36] Some method or rules of guidance are needed. It would do no harm, for example, to follow his distinction between the three levels of data involved in trying to infer the structure and property of symbols and rituals: first, the actual observable external form, the "thing"; second, the indigenous exegetics offered either by ritual specialists like priests (esoteric interpretations) or by laymen (exoteric interpretations); and finally, the attempt by the social scientist to contextualize all this, particularly by reference to the field: the structure and composition of the group that handles the symbol or performs mimetic acts with reference to it.

Once a simple enough distinction like this is made, it is then possible to proceed to the interesting complications: the problem of intent; of polysemy (a single symbol standing for many things); how people's interpretations of what they are doing might contradict how they actually behave; under what conditions observers must go beyond indigenous interpretations because of what they know of the context. All this requires great care. Much decoding of youth cultures simply does not make the effort, and often does foolish things like taking a priestly exegesis (for example, by a rock journalist) at its face value or, alternatively, offering a contextualization that is wholly gratuitous.

Let me conclude this section by giving an example of the dangers of searching the forest of symbols without such a method, or indeed any method. This is the example often used by Hebdige and other theorists of punk: the wearing of the swastika emblem. Time and time again, we are assured that although this symbol is "on one level" intended to outrage and shock, it is *really* being employed in a metalanguage: the wearers are ironically distancing themselves from the very message that the symbol is usually intended to convey. Displaying a swastika (or singing lyrics like "Belsen was a gas") shows how symbols are stripped from their natural context, exploited for empty effect, displayed through mockery, distancing, irony, parody, inversion.

But how are we to know this? We are never told much about the "thing": when, how, where, by whom or in what context it is worn. We do not know what, if any, differences exists between indigenous and sociological explanations. We are given no clue about how these particular actors manage the complicated business of distancing and irony. In the end there is no basis whatsoever for choosing between this particular sort of interpretation and any others, say, that for many or most of the kids walking around with swastikas on their jackets, the dominant context is simple conformity, blind ignorance, or knee-jerk racism.

Something more of an answer is needed to such questions than simply quoting Genet or Breton. Nor does it help much to have Hebdige's admission (about a similar equation) that such interpretations are not open to being tested by standard sociological procedures: "Though it is undeniably there in the social structure, it is there as an immanence, as a submerged possibility, as an existential option; and one cannot verify an existential option scientifically — you either see it or you don't."[37]

Well, in the swastika example, I don't. And, moreover, when Hebdige does defend this particular interpretation of punk, he does it not by any existential leap but by a good old-fashioned positivist appeal to evidence: Punks, we are told, "were not generally sympathetic to the parties of the extreme right" and showed "widespread support for the anti-Fascist movement."[38] These statements certainly constitute evidence, not immanence, though not particularly good evidence, and go right against widespread findings about the racism and support for restrictive immigration policies among substantial sections of working-class youth.

I do not want to judge one reading against the other nor to detract from the considerable interest and value of this new decoding work. We need to be more skeptical, though, of the exquisite aesthetics that tell us about things being fictional and real, absent and present, caricatures and reassertions. This language might indeed help by framing a meaning to the otherwise meaningless, but this help seems limited when we are drawn to saying about Skinheads' attacks on Pakistani immigrants: "Every time the boot went in, a contradiction was concealed, glossed over or made to disappear."[39] It seems to me, to borrow from the language of contradictions, that both a lot more and a lot less was going on. Time indeed to leave the forest of symbols and "shudder back thankfully into the light of the social day."[40]

Biography/Phenomenology/Living Through

In one way or another most of the problems in the "resistance-through-rituals" framework are to be found at the theory's third level: how the subculture is actually lived out by its bearers. The nagging sense here is that these lives, selves, and identities do not always coincide with what they are supposed to stand for.

What must be remembered first is that the troubles associated with stylistic innovation are not all representative of all delinquency (let alone of all postwar British youth). Mundane day-to-day delinquency is and always has been predominantly property crime and has little to do with magic, codes, or rituals. I doubt that many of the intricate preoccupations of these theorists impinge much on the lives, say, of that large (and increasing) number of juveniles in today's custodial institutions in Britain: the 11,638 sent to detention centers; 7,067 to Borstals; 7,519 to prisons in 1978.

I fear that the obvious fascination with these subcultures will draw attention away from these more enduring numbers, as well as lead to quite inappropriate criticisms of other modes of explanation. This, of course, will not be entirely the fault of the theorists themselves; the Birmingham group, for example, makes it absolutely clear that it is concerned only with subcultures that have reasonably tight boundaries and distinctive shapes, and that cohere around specific actions or places. As the group is very careful to point out, the majority of working-class youth never enter such subcultures at all: "Individuals may in their personal careers move into one and out of one, or indeed, several subcultures. There relations to the existing subcultures may be fleeting or permanent, marginal or central."[41]

Despite these disavowals, the *method* used in most of this work detracts us from answering the more traditional but surely not altogether trivial sociological questions about these different patterns of involvement. Why should some individuals exposed to the same pressures respond one way rather than another or with different degrees of commitment? As one sympathetic criticism suggests, the problem arises from *starting* with groups that are already card-carrying members of a subculture and then working backward to uncover their class base.[42] If the procedure is reversed and one starts from the class base rather than the cultural responses, it becomes obvious that an identical location generates a very wide range of responses and modes of accommodation.

Thus, time and time again studies that start in a particular biographical location — school, neighborhood, work — come up with a much looser relationship between class and style. They show, for example, the sheer ordinariness and passivity of much working-class adolescent accommodation and its similarities to, rather then dramatic breaks with, the respectable parent culture.[43] In the cultural repertoire of responses to subordination — learning how to get by, how to make the best of a bad job, how to make things thoroughly unpleasant for "them" — symbolic innovation may not be very important.

Such studies are also needed to give a sense of the concrete, some feeling of time and space; when and how the styles and symbols fit into the daily round of home, work or school, friendship.[44] Without this, it becomes difficult, for example, to meet the same standard objection leveled against traditional subcultural theory: the assumption of overcommitment and the fact that apart from the code itself these young people may be models of conventionality elsewhere. The intellectual pyrotechnics behind many of these theories are also too cerebral, in the sense that a remote, historically derived motivational account (such as "recapturing community") hardly conveys the immediate emotional tone and satisfaction of the actions themselves. Indeed, the action (for example, fighting or vandalism) is often completely ignored except when historicism is temporarily abandoned. A good example of this might be Corrigan's wholly believable account of the context and sequence in which trouble emerges among kids in the street corner of Sunderland: how "doing nothing" leads to "weird ideas" which leads to trouble. Another example would be the Cohen and Roberts's account of growing upon a council estate. The sense of imprisonment running through the different biographies they collect (under the heading "We Gotta Get Out of This Place") relates closely with their theoretical explanation of what the street groups are actually doing.

Willis stands alone in showing how that (now) abused sociological task of linking history to subjective experience can be attempted. Structure is not left floating on its own, but a commitment to ethnography need not produce a series of disembodied phenomenological snapshots. He can retain the Marxist insistence that not everything is lived out at the level of practical consciousness — a level that is a poor guide to contradictions — and refuse "to impute to the lads individually any critique or analytic motive" but still try to show what the "giving of labour power" actually means subjectively. The struggle against subordination is lived out in the daily round of school life, in the rituals about dress, discipline, smoking, drinking, rules.

A footnote to this section on biography should draw attention to two sets of lives that have been hidden from cultural studies and delinquency theory, old and new, over these twenty-five years: girls and blacks.

For neither of these groups, of course, should this be a footnote and in the case of girls, particularly, this is just to perpetuate the very tendency that needs combating: "It is as if everything that relates only to us comes out in footnotes to the main text, as worthy of the odd reference. We encounter ourselves in men's cultures as by the way and peripheral." As one analysis (which starts with these words of Rowbotham's) says, the absence of girls from the subcultural literature is striking and demands explanation.[45] The past few years have seen the beginning of such an explanation,[46] and it certainly does not simply lie in any physical invisibility of girls from these subcultures. As I originally pointed out in *Folk Devils*, "In many ways Mod was a more female than male phenomenon": and much more serious attention needs to be paid to this presence as well as the more general problems of applying the subculture model to girls

In the case of black youth, the "physical invisibility" explanation is more plausible, at least before the beginning of the 1960s. Up till then blacks appeared mainly as the victims of Teddy Boy attacks. From about the birth of the Mods onwards, though, the presence of youth of West Indian and then later Asian origin, both new immigrant and first generation, could hardly be ignored. Their significance has now been variously acknowledged: as historical agents in their own right and objects for the 1972–73 moral panic about mugging; in Willis's argument that much of the exclusiveness of working-class culture is defined *against* ethnic minorities (and women); and in Hebdige's far-reaching suggestion that the whole of white working-class youth subcultures, from Teddy Boys to Punks, can be understood as a series of mediated responses to black (American) culture and then the presence of a sizeable black community in Britain.

From a more empirical direction, Pryce's detailed ethnography of black corner kids in Bristol between 1969 and 1974 not only provides information about the previously invisible but contributes to a general understanding of the experience of subordination.[47] His hustlers show less a cerebral and symbolic rejection of work "values" than a direct rejection of menial work itself; an abhorrence of having to take orders from the cheeky white boss, a resentment of such affronts to their pride as men. *Slave labor* and *shit work* are terms used interchangeably to mean monotonous work, white people's work. Ironically, the very prop out of which Willis's white "lads" build up their attachment to work — masculinity — is used by these black boys to reject the low-paid subproletarian work they are offered.

Their situation is more precarious than that of their white counterparts: they are not only given equivalent or lower roles in the labor market but have the additional "endless pressure" caused by a fragmented family life, parents with high educational aspirations for their children, a lack of community roots, and being the objects of continuing racism and discrimination. Pryce describes this endless pressure — as well as the very different responses to it. The complicated overlaps between reggae, rasta, and rude-boy ideologies are used by both the delinquent teeny-bopper group and the nondelinquent politicals to give their lives some sense of purpose. It is painfully clear that future developments, such as the vulnerability of ethnic minorities to structural unemployment, will add to these "endless pressures," creating the potential for both a greater rage and a greater social condemnation of it.

Reaction

Following my stated intention of giving more space to "action," I can do little more here than mention in passing the relevant recent work on societal reaction. This is hardly because I am satisfied with the way this topic was treated in my book. Certainly, I gave a lot of information about how the moral panic around the Mods and Rockers was created, transmitted, and sustained, but the theory behind this process was somewhat undeveloped. I described the reaction in detail but my attempt to suggest *why* moral panics occur, not just "now and then" but at particular times and in particular forms, hardly gave much basis for further generalization.

Subsequent contributions to what can be said about moral panics and the like have come from a number of sources. First, the intervening years have seen much interest in the major promoters of moral panics, the mass media, and in analyzing the relationships between deviance and the media. This interest initially took the form of pulling together various disparate contributions about how the mass media select and present news about deviance, what models of society are revealed in this presentation, and what effects they might have, particularly in shaping the control culture.[48] There have since been a number of empirical studies in Britain on media coverage of industrial conflict,[49] on the 1972–73 mugging panic,[50] and on crime reporting[51] — each of which has contributed to building up media theory.[52] The mugging study — to which I will return — is particulary important in locating the media's broader ideological role in shaping and reflecting a consensual view of the world.

From a quite different direction, and in a category of its own because no one else has seriously taken up this model, there is Ditton's ingenious refinement of deviancy amplification theory.[53] What he has done is to push the "control-leads-to-deviance" formula to its logical extreme, and in so doing, to separate out the various forms of feedback in Wilkins's original model.

Then, and most important, there is *Policing the Crisis,* also the product of Birmingham Centre and also devoted to inserting history and politics into the discourse about crime. The book stands as an important substantive contribution to charting the moral panic about mugging in 1972–73, but also makes a number of important theoretical connections and claims.

The level for explaining labeling, societal reaction, or moral panic is shifted from social control agencies or cultures – or vague allusions to the "wider society" – to the specific operation of the state. This means relating the working of the moral panic – the mobilization of public opinion, the orchestration by the media and public figures of an otherwise inchoate sense of unease – to overall political shifts. In the same way that I picked out certain features of the Mods and Rockers events as touching very deep social tensions and ambiguities, this work shows how the themes of race, crime, and youth were condensed into the image of the mugger – the violent black youth – and used to articulate major shifts in British political and economic life since the war.

The center's work here can be understood only as part of its overall project on Gramsci's concept of hegemony. Hegemony denotes the moment when the ruling class is able not merely to coerce its subordinates to conform but to exercise the sort of power that wins and shapes consent, that frames alternatives and structures agendas in such a way as to appear natural. The thesis is that by the 1960s, and then more openly by the 1970s, the consent that might have previously been won was undermined. Though the dominant class retained power, its repertoire of control was weakened. Concomitantly, there occurred a shift to a more coercive rather than dominantly consensual mode of control. This shift signaled the birth of a law-and-order society and was evidenced in the development of a preemptive escalation of social control. Instead of discrete moral panics of the Mods and Rockers type, with their familiar sequence of dramatic event, public disquiet, moral enterprise, and mobilization of control culture, the sequence is (in the late 60s) speeded up by creating a general disquiet and then, by the time of the 1970s mugging campaign, radically altered. The control culture is mobilized in advance, real events being anticipated and taken to confirm and justify the need for gradual ideological repression.

It is impossible to give proper critical attention here to this formidable argument.[54] All I can do is express similar reservations as applied to the "resistance-through-ritual" framework. At too many points, it seems to me, the Center's determination to find ideological closure leads it to a premature theoretical closure. The actual material selected as proof of the slide into the crisis (newspaper editorials, statements by M.P.'s and police chiefs) does not always add up to something of such monumental proportions. The diffuse normative concern about delinquency is, I think, more diffuse and less political than is suggested. And the assumption of a monolithic drift to repression gives little room for understanding why some objects are repressed more severely than others. This, paradoxically, is the same criticism that applied to vulgar labeling theory.

Taking Stock

To read the literature on subcultural delinquency, old and new, is a depressing business. Depressing for the same reasons given in the original rather fatalistic concluding paragraph of *Folk Devils*, but also for the sense of repetition and continuity.

I do not want to suppress the considerable theoretical differences within this literature; in no way can the language and concepts of functionalism, interactionism, Marxism, structuralism, cybernetics, and semiotics simply be jumbled together. But at no important point in this heterogeneous material is there much doubt about what delinquent and troublesome youth subcultures signify: a reaction (with greater or lesser degrees of commitment, consciousness, and symbolic weight) to growing up in a class society. The rest is just commentary, a little baroque and far-fetched for some tastes, but not an arena for major dispute.

The "tone" of the literature, though—its implied value judgments and its implied policy implications—is more diverse and more difficult to capture. In the original subcultural theories the delinquents were neither admired nor condemned. They were the rejects of a machine that had gone wrong; with careful repair work (better schools, housing, job opportunities) the kids could be incorporated into a smoothly running nonideological, postindustrial society. The version of liberalism that emerged in labeling theory was somewhat more skeptical of the benevolent pretensions of social democracy. The social order was more obviously up for criticism, and a consequent note of suppressed admiration for the delinquents crept in. The Who's tribute to the Mods—"The Kids Are All Right"—became echoed in a type of sociology which nearly implied that everything would be all right if only the kids were left alone.

When the fully blown "new criminology" emerged, these hidden moral and political agendas became a bit more ambiguous.[55] The revolution would produce a classless society in which, by definition, problems of subordination and domination would disapear. In the meantime one could only admire the kids even when (and perhaps especially when) they patently were *not* all right. Thus, even the "Refusal" that punk subculture signified, its gestures of defiance and contempt, its smiles and sneers, was something to celebrate: "I would like to think that this Refusal is worth making, that these gestures have a meaning, that the smiles and sneers have some subversive value," and further, "I have sought, in Sartre's words, to acknowledge the right of the subordinate class [the young, the black, the working class] to 'make something of what is made of [them]' — to embellish, decorate, parody and wherever possible to recognize and rise above a subordinate position which was never of their own choosing."[56]

I find myself in sympathy with such an acknowledgment and do not think it far removed from what is recorded in *Folk Devils*. The dangers of romanticism, though, are always present, particularly in the political form that seeks to elevate delinquents into the vanguard of the revolution. Now, virtually every theorist I have mentioned takes considerable care to avoid this premature elevation. The creative and in the short run often very successful nature of the resistance is welcomed, but at the same time its limits clearly recognized. Either the kids' consciousness of their position is subordinate and "negotiated" rather than being truly oppositional and political; or opposition is expressed in only one limited area, leisure, which is anyway the inappropriate one; or the dominant culture can recuperate itself from whatever is subversive or potentially subversive; or the implicit politics of these groups is nihilist and confused, making them open, if anything, to reactionary and fascist appeals. Here is a typical recognition of these limitations: "In the long run no one 'magically' can appropriate what in reality does not belong to them by virture of their working place in society. The pathos and futility of fighting among rival groups of socially dispossessed youth is the best demonstration of the extent of the victory of those who really do hold the class power over them."[57]

But — and this is perhaps a credit to political faith — there is still a strong commitment to seek and to defend any signs of inarticulate criticism or historical resistance. And consequently there is a note of regret: if only the kids could see the real enemy, if only they could be awakened to their true class interests, then they would be liberated.

And, as Pearson so honestly puts it, "Of course it would be easier to defend hooligans if they were not so badly behaved."[58] Such candor is rare, and too much of the theory masks a curious value distortion. The subculture is observed and decoded, its creativity celebrated, its political limitations acknowledged and then the critique of the social order is constructed. But while this critique stems form a moral absolutism, the subculture itself is treated in the language of cultural relativism. Those same values of racism, sexism, chauvinism, compulsive masculinity, and anti-intellectualism, the slightest traces of which are condemned in bourgeois culture, are treated with a deferential care, an exaggerated contextualization, when they appear in the subculture.

This is by no means a problem unique to this literature. Lévi-Strauss has dealt in a most moving and sympathetic way with the equivalent contradictions faced by the anthropologist who is a stern cultural critic at home but a conformist abroad. The value that he attaches to "foreign societies" (read: subcultures) " is a function of his disdain for and occasionally hostility towards the customs prevailing in his own native setting. While often inclined to subversion among his own people and in revolt against traditional behaviour, the anthropologist appears respectful to the point of conservatism as soon as he is dealing with a society different from his own."[59]

As Lévi-Strauss makes clear, all this is not a simple question of bias. It raises more fundamental contradictions about what social scientists are doing. To say that each group has made choices within the range of human possibilities and that all are equally valid rescues us from a blindness to everything different (from viewing, say, working-class culture wholly in terms of bourgeois norms). But it might also lead to an eclecticism that prevents us from deploring any features of a culture. Cannibalism is the anthropologist's obvious example. The dilemma is profound, though it need not necessarily lead us into abandoning sociology altogether: "After peering into the abyss which yawns in front of us, we may be allowed to look for a way of avoiding it."[60]

The ways Lévi-Strauss recommends include moderation, honesty, and self-awareness, qualities not always present in the *much too respectful* enterprise of picking on the subcultural detritus of musical notes, hairstyles, safety pins, zips, and boots. We might not have to go so far in the other direction as Hunter Thompson's famous epitaph to his appreciation of the California Hell's Angels ("There was no escaping the echo of Mistah Kurtz' comment from the heart of darkness; 'The horror, The horror. . . . Exterminate all the brutes.'"[61]) to see that we can understand without being too respectful. Much of this respect, anyway, strikes some false and condescending notes. I sometimes have a sense of working-class kids suffering an awful triple fate. First, their actual current prospects are grim enough; then their predicament is used, shaped, and turned to financial profit by the same interests that created it; and then—the final irony—they find themselves patronized in the latest vocabulary imported from the Left Bank.[62]

Ultimately, because of its simplicity and its translation of the obvious truths at the core of subcultural theory into a recognizable and dignified language, I would prefer to lean on Paul Goodman's classic diatribe against American society in the fifties.[63] What he saw then was just the same waste of human potential, worthlessness of jobs, emptiness of education, cynicism, and lack of opportunity for worthwhile experience that the latter theories identified.

The social critique comes first: what it is to grow up in a society where there is nothing worthwhile. Then comes the identification (again, in exactly the same way as today's theories) of "poor youth" as the group among whom the contradictions and absurdities of industrial society show up "first and worst." These kids constituted for Goodman the same surplus population later theorized about in more sophisticated ways. Their plight was also the same: the pathos of being compelled to go to school in order to receive an education for a society that does not need them. School was a waste, jobs were dull, and when you were questioned on the street (like Corrigan's boys twenty years later) about what you wanted to do, there was the same terrible answer: "Nothing."

Goodman also saw social revolution as the only solution to all this, but he did not lapse into the patronizing cultural relativism that would analyze the working-class adolescent response only in its own terms and dismiss usefulness, honor, and satisfaction as mere bourgeois values. The same middle-class intellectuals who spend so much time agonizing over their own alienation, the need for meaning, commitment, and self-fulfillment in their own work, suddenly find these values bourgeois and beneath contempt. Naturally, the working classes are right to reject them, for has history not decreed that their jobs will never be satisfying?

This specious logic can be avoided by confronting these responses more honestly; as Goodman says, "The so-called delinquent subculture has a few flashing and charming traits, but nothing in it is viable or inimitable. . . . Their choices and inventions are rarely charming, usually stupid and often disastrous; we cannot expect average kids to deviate with genius."[64] Sociologists do not like making their aesthetics and morals as open and disingenuously simple as this. But the complications of current theory share the same message as Goodman's: although the kids' behavior might not look too good, it speaks clearly enough; it asks for what we cannot give. When the last fake safety pin is sold on the Kings Road and the first juvenile unemployment figures for the 1980s appear, the message will be just the same:

"It is better to adopt the simplest explanation, even if it is not simple, even if it does not explain very much."[65]

Notes

1. The key texts remain A. K. Cohen, *Delinquent Boys: The Culture of the Gang* (Chicago: Free Press, 1955); R. Cloward and L. Ohlin, *Delinquency and Opportunity: A Theory of Delinquent Groups* (Chicago: Free Press, 1960); and the original application to England, D.M. Downes, *The Delinquent Solution* (London: Routledge & Kegan Paul, 1966).

2. For some interesting comments on the uneven development of theories of crime and delinquency, see P. Rock, "The Sociology of Crime, Symbolic Interactionism and Some Problematic Qualities of Radical Criminology," in *Deviant Interpretations*, ed. D. Downes and P. Rock (Oxford: Martin Robertson, 1979), pp. 52–84.

3. In the absence of a better classification, I shall use the term *new subcultural theory* to cover the work emerging in Britain from about 1972 and associated primarily with the Centre for Contemporary Studies at the University of Birmingham. These are the main sources on which I have based my review; they have been produced either directly from the Center or by those working on parallel lines: S. Hall and T. Jefferson, eds., *Resistance through Rituals: Youth Subcultures in Post-War Britain* (London: Hutchinson, 1976); G. Mungham and G. Pearson, *Working Class Youth Culture* (London: Routledge & Kegan Paul, 1976); P. Willis *Learning to Labour: How Working Class Kids Get Working Class Jobs* (London: Saxon House, 1978); D. Robins and P. Cohen, *Knuckle Sandwich: Growing up in the Working Class City* (Harmondsworth: Penguin, 1978); P. Corrigan, *Schooling the Smash Street Kids* (London: Macmillan, 1979); D. Hebdige, *Subculture: The Meaning of Style*

(London: Methuen, 1979). See also the journal *Working Papers in Cultural Studies* (from 1972 to 1979) and the regular series of Stencilled Papers produced by the Center since 1972. It is impossible in this short review to do justice to the considerable diversity within this literature, but unless I single out individual voices, I will take the term *new subcultural theory* to cover some common ground.

4. Finestone's caricature of the original American theories: H. Finestone, *Victims of Change: Juvenile Delinquents in American Society* (London: Greenwood Press, 1976).

5. Willis, *Learning to Labour*, p. 119. Though less explicitly concerned with delinquency or style than the other new subcultural writings, this study, I believe, will make the most enduring contribution.

6. This version of the social formation is used most explicitly in J. Clarke and T. Jefferson, "Working Class Youth Cultures," in *Working Class Youth Culture*, ed. G. Mungham and G. Pearson (London: Routledge & Kegan Paul, 1976), pp. 138–58.

7. J. Clark et al., "Subcultures, Cultures and Classes," in *Resistance through Ritual*, ed. S. Hall and T. Jefferson (London: Hutchinson, 1976), p. 38.

8. P. Cohen, "Subcultural Conflict and Working Class Community," *Working Papers in Cultural Studies* 2 (Spring 1972): 5–52. In Cohen's later work with Robins (*Knuckle Sandwich*) there is an even more solid location of the chains of cultural transmission, internal division, and conflict in a tough inner-city area—a working-class London estate—between 1972 and 1977.

9. Cohen, "Subcultural Conflict and Working Class Community," p. 23.

10. Willis, *Learning to Labour*, pp. 12–13.

11. Ibid., p. 52.

12. I. Taylor, "'Football Mad': A speculative Sociology of Soccer Hooliganism," in *The Sociology of Sport*, ed. E. Dunning (London: Cass, 1971); and "Spectacular Violence around Football: The Rise and Fall of the Working Class Weekend," *Research Papers in Physical Education* 3, no. 2 (1976): 4–9. See also J. Clarke, "Football and Working Class Fans: Tradition and Change," in *Football Hooliganism: The Wider Context*, ed. R. Ingham et al. (London: Interaction Imprint, 1978).

13. G. Pearson, "'Paki-bashing' in a North East Lancashire Cotton Town: A Case Study and Its History," in *Working Class Youth Culture*, ed. G. Mungham and G. Pearson (London: Routledge & Kegan Paul, 1976), pp. 48–81; and "In Defense of Hooliganism: Social Theory and Violence," in *Violence*, ed. N. Tutt (London: HMSO, 1976).

14. For a good summary of how contemporary criminologists have taken up this historical work, see G. Pearson, "Goths and Vandals: Crime in History," *Contemporary Crises* 2, no. 2 (April 1978): 119–39.

15. Hebdige, *Subculture*, provides the most recent and ambitious version of this whole enterprise.

16. Not equally reciprocal in all the new writing. Willis and Corrigan, for example, hardly ever see resistance as "symbolic," while Pearson is more ambivalent: he appears to accept (in relation to "Paki-bashing") a displacement or scapegoating theory but also insists that the response is real and rational.

17. An idea hardly as original as is claimed. In Albert Cohen's original theory, the process he called "reaction formation" was clearly symbolic. What could be more magical than "solving" the frustration at being unable to reach a goal by inverting the ideology associated with it? This is one of the many instances of the new theories' tendency toward "social amnesia": the repression of previous insights in order to appear new and radical. On this general tendency, see R. Jacoby *Social Amnesia* (London: Harvester Press, 1977) esp. ch. 1. Thus the whole of symbolic interactionism has been repressed in this way and its potential for dealing with at least

some problems of meaning and symbol has been lost just because its overall politics and sociology is judged to be wrong.

18. Cohen and Robins, *Knuckle Sandwich*, p. 137.

19. J. Clarke, "'Style,'" in *Resistance through Ritual* ed. S. Hall and T. Jefferson (London: Hutchinson, 1976), p. 189.

20. Cohen and Robins, *Knuckle Sandwich*, p. 113.

21. Hebdige, *Subculture*, p. 18.

22. One contribution that does stress "manufactured change" is I. Taylor and D. Wall, "Beyond the Skinheads: Comments on the Emergence and Significance of the Glamrock Cult," in *Working Class Youth Culture*, ed. G. Mungham and G. Pearson (London: Routledge & Kegan Paul, 1976), 105-24.

23. A brilliant evocation of this spell is to be found in the bleak Wimpies and shopping arcades of Stephen Poliakoff's plays. As John Lahr comments about Poliakoff's adolescents: "Their roots are in England, but their dreams are somewhere between the Mississippi delta and the Hollywood hills. From junk food to rock and roll they are weighted down with borrowed cultural baggage." Lahr, "The Psychopath as Hero," *New Society* 28 (June 1979): 780-81.

24. Hebdige, of course, does do just this, and advances the rather extreme argument that the whole shape of postwar British youth culture emerges as a dialogue with black culture. See also the fine analysis in Cohen and Robins (*Knuckle Sandwich*, pp. 96-103) of the appeal of Bruce Lee and Kung Fu mythology to the kids on the estate.

25. Pearson, "Goths and Vandals," p. 134.

26. J. Ditton, "The Dinosaur Theory of History" (Paper given at the British Sociological Association Annual Conference, April 1980).

27. Pearson, "'Paki-bashing.'"

28. Quoted by Isaiah Berlin, *Russian Thinkers* (London: Hogarth Press, 1978), p. 242.

29. Clarke, "'Style,'" p. 179.

30. Hebdige, *Subculture*, p. 139.

31. Ibid., pp. 101, 105.

32. Ibid., p. 122.

33. Ibid., and also "Reggae, Rastas and Rudies," in *Resistance through Ritual*, ed. S. Hall and T. Jefferson (London: Hutchinson, 1976), pp. 135-54; and C.C.S. Stencilled Papers, Nos. 20, 21, 24, 25.

34. Hebdige, *Subculture*, pp. 117-20.

35. The famous words from Baudelaire's poem "Correspondences." That great literary symbolizer Malcolm Lowry thought that he knew exactly where he was going here but used Baudelaire's phrase to project himself into the suffering of his hero in *Under the Volcano*, a man who saw portents and symbols everywhere, his life wracked by a symbolizing frenzy, trying to find an occult and total correspondence between all things material and spiritual. See D. Day, *Malcolm Lowry: A Biography* (London: Oxford University Press, 1974), pp. 273-74, 317-50.

36. I have selected Victor Turner's work from the standard literature not just because of his clarity of method here but, of course, because he, too, uses the Baudelaire reference: Turner, *The Forest of Symbols: Aspects of Ndembu Ritual* (London: Cornell University Press, 1967). See especially the first essay, "Symbols in Ndembu Ritual," pp. 19-47.

37. Hebdige, *Subculture*, p. 131.

38. Ibid., p. 116.

39. Ibid., p. 58.

40. Turner, *The Forest of Symbols*, p. 46.
41. Hall and Jefferson, *Resistance through Rituals*, p. 16.
42. G. Murdock and R. McCron, "Consciousness of Class and Consciousness of Generation," in *Resistance through Rituals*, ed. S. Hall and T. Jefferson (London: Hutchinson, 1976), p. 205; and "Youth and Class: The Career of a Confusion," in *Working Class Youth Culture*, ed. G. Mungham and G. Pearson (London: Routledge & Kegan Paul, 1976), p. 25.
43. See, for example, Mungham's ethnography of commercial dance hall culture, "Youth in Pursuit of Itself," in *Working Class Youth Culture*, ed. G. Mungham and G. Pearson (London: Routledge & Kegan Paul, 1976), pp. 82–104. And, from outside sociology, the snapshots of youth in a Northern England cotton town in J. Seabrook, *City Close-Up* (Harmondsworth: Penguin, 1973).
44. Parker's ethnography of "the Boys" in the Roundhouse area of Liverpool is an excellent example of how this can be done: H. Parker, *The View from the Boys* (Newton Abbott: David & Charles, 1974); and "Boys Will Be Men: Brief Adolescence in a Down Town Neighbourhood," in *Working Class Youth Culture*, ed. G. Mungham and G. Pearson (London: Routledge & Kegan Paul, 1976), pp. 27–47. This is one of the few studies that gives any sense of the passage of time.
45. A. McRobbie and J. Garber, "Girls and Subcultures: An Exploration," in *Resistance through Ritual*, ed. S. Hall and T. Jefferson (London: Hutchinson, 1976), pp. 223–30.
46. For example, in C. Smart, *Women, Crime and Criminology* (London: Routledge & Kegan Paul, 1976), and M. Millman, "She Did It All for Love" in *Another Voice*, ed. M. Millman and R. Kanter (New York: Anchor Books, 1975).
47. K. Pryce, *Endless Pressure: A Study of West Indian Life Styles in Bristol* (Harmondsworth: Penguin, 1979).
48. S. Cohen and J. Young, eds., *The Manufacture of News: Deviance, Social Problems and Mass Media* (London: Constable, 1973).
49. Glasgow University Media Group, *Bad News* (London: Routledge & Kegan Paul, 1976).
50. S. Hall et al., *Policing the Crisis: Mugging, the State and Law and Order* (London: Macmillan, 1978).
51. S. Chibnall, *Law and Order News* (London: Tavistock, 1977).
52. See, for example, S. Hall, "Culture, the Media and the 'Ideological Effect,'" in *Mass Communication and Society*, ed. J. Curson et al. (London: Arnold, 1977).
53. J. Ditton, *Controlology: Beyond the New Criminology* (London: Macmillan, 1979).
54. Or to the rest of what is really three books: a substantive analysis of the mugging panic, an interpretation of the connections between politics and delinquency among black youth in Britain, and the first serious attempt to relate ideologies of crime control to a theory of the state.
55. See chapter 8.
56. Hebdige, *Subculture*, pp. 3, 138–39.
57. Cohen and Robins, *Knuckle Sandwich*, p. 151.
58. Pearson, "'Paki-bashing,'" p. 216.
59. C. Levi Strauss, *Tristes Tropiques* (Harmondsworth: Penguin, 1976) p. 502. I cannot do justice here to his wonderful chapter 'A Little Glass of Rum,' pp. 501–15.
60. Ibid., p. 506.
61. H. S. Thompson, *Hell's Angels* (Harmondsworth: Penguin, 1967), p. 284.
62. Which is then repulped for the cultural supermarket; note, for example, this review (of Hebdige's book) in *Time Out* (31 August 1979): "He dissects the nihilism ex-

pressed in the zips and buckles of a Sex jacket, and digs deep into the subversive commodity fetishism of the original mods who turned their short hair and suits against the straight culture from which they had appropriated them" p. 59. There might be nothing "wrong" with these words, but why do they leave one with such a heavy heart?

63. P. Goodman, *Growing Up Absurd: Problems of Youth in the Organized Society* (New York: Random House, 1960).
64. Ibid., pp. 191, 13.
65. S. Beckett, *Malone Dies* (Paris: Olympia Press, 1959), p. 248.

10

Western Crime Control Models in the Third World: Benign or Malignant?*

> *Comrades, have we not other work to do than to create a third Europe?*
> —Frantz Fanon, *The Wretched of the Earth*

My aim in this paper is relatively limited and modest: to classify and discuss the various models that have been and could be used to signify the relevance of the Western crime-control experience for the Third World. While the implicitly relevant literature, for example, on the anthropology of law or on the nature of development, is vast and complex, the explicit literature on crime in the Third World is sparse and poor. Criminologists have either ignored the Third World completely or treated it in a most theoretically primitive fashion, and the general literature on development and colonialism is remarkably silent about crime.

For anyone like me whose primary sociological interest lies in the history, ideologies, and systems of crime control in such advanced capitalist societies as Britain and the United States, an initial exposure to the equivalent subjects in this Third World literature leaves a recurrent sense of irony and paradox,

* "Western Crime Control Models in the Third World: Benign or Malignant?" from S. Spitzer and R. Simon (eds.), *Research in Law, Deviance and Social Control*, Vol. 4 (Greenwich: JAI Press, 1982), pp. 85–119.

An original draft of this paper was read at the Conference on "Crime and Crime Control in Developing Countries," organized by the Research Committee on Deviance and Social Control, International Sociological Association, University of Ibadan, Nigeria, July 9–12, 1980. I am grateful to Maxine Molyneux and Harold Wolpe for initial suggestions and then to many colleagues and friends at the Ibadan Conference, as well as Richard Abel, Nils Christie, Robin Cohen, and Marc Galanter for helpful comments on the original version.

a sense, indeed, that could have been used to organize this whole paper. The irony can be expressed, with considerable simplification, in this three-part sequence:

1. Current systems of crime and deviance control in Western industrialized societies originated in those three great historical transformations that took place from the end of the eighteenth century to the beginning of the nineteenth century: first, the development of a centralized state apparatus for the control of crime and the care of dependency; second, the increasing differentiation of the deviant and dependent into separate types, each with its own attendant body of "scientific" knowledge and accredited experts; and, finally, the increased segregation of deviants and dependents into "asylums": mental hospitals, prisons, reformatories, and other such closed, purpose-built institutions for treatment, punishment, and custody.

2. In the past decade or so, each of these transformations has been subject to sustained attack in the West. Certain well-defined social movements (each with varying degrees of actual impact) have mounted abolitionist critiques of those original three structures: first, under such slogans as "decentralization," "deformalization," "diversion," and "decriminalization," there has been a call to dismantle or bypass the central state apparatus; then under "delegalization" or "deprofessionalization," a widespread distrust of professionals and experts; and — most notably — "decarceration" and "community control," a move against traditional custodial institutions and toward the dispersal of social control into the "community."

3. This "new," "radical" critique, though, embodies and appeals to those very features that are (or were) the most traditional and accepted in many Third World or developing countries. The irony, then, is that the type of crime-control models (and the criminological theories that sometimes inform them) being exported by criminologists, crime-control officials, international agencies, and various other "experts," are the very ones that are now being discredited in the West. For example, just at the time when treatment and psychotherapy in prisons is under attack in North America and Britain (for being ineffective as well as potentially inhumane), countries in Africa and Latin America are being urged to expand the use of therapy in their prisons. Just when Western crime-control rhetoric is talking about "community" and extolling the virtues of mediation, conciliation, and informal dispute resolution, the Third World appears to be abandoning such methods and moving toward centralized, bureaucratized, and professional criminal justice systems.

Now, obviously the irony and paradox are not quite as uncomplicated as this three-part sequence suggests. Not the least of the complications is the fact that the actual translation of this apparently radical ideological switch in the West has not been quite what it appears. Far from leading to decreased state control, classification, and professionalization, it has led to more; far from marking a radical break with previous models, these developments have been continuous with the great transformations of the early nineteenth century. And the experience of the Third World has been far more diverse and uneven than the third statement implies; traditional forms of control and conflict resolution have long survived alongside Western systems or are actually being revived.

Nonetheless, the irony is striking and remains a genuine one: most "advanced thinking" about social control in the West and at least *some* practice draws its inspiration from the myth of the idyllic *gemeinschaft* community. And if this perfect form of social control has already been destroyed in our own (romantic) past, it is about to be destroyed in the (equally romantic) present elsewhere — sacrificed to the inexorable process of "modernization" or (depending on the preferred theory) "neocolonialism."

The full sense of this irony can, perhaps, best be captured by looking at areas of discourse about the Third World quite unconnected with crime control. Consider, for example, the case of tobacco production and cigarette smoking. Just when the obviously harmful effects of smoking are being widely disseminated in the West, together with the introduction of advertising codes and other restrictions, so the multinational tobacco companies are expanding massively in the Third World, their sales efforts unhindered by restraints, controls, or health warnings. Not only is tobacco consumption growing fastest in the poorest and hungriest parts of the world but their inhabitants will often be smoking (without any warning) dangerous high-tar tobacco containing twice the cancer-causing agents allowed in the rich world. And they will be using valuable land and resources to grow this tobacco.[1]

Striking as this example is — the same epidemic of preventable disease being promoted in one part of the world and condemned in another — it is not a particularly good one for our case. The motives and intentions of multinational tobacco companies are grossly and unashamedly commercial and exploitative; there is little pretense otherwise. But crime-control models contain an elaborate ideology justifying them on various criteria of "doing good" for society and/or the individual offender. A more appropriate parallel than the tobacco case might be the export of drugs to the Third World. Here there is an obvious ideology of benevolence and cure, yet considerable evidence that harm is being done and in precisely the ways already warned about in the West.[2] Intentionally or not, the multinational drug companies are creating a dependency on curative technical treatment rather than primary protection, and clearly intentionally are using deceptive hard-sell techniques to dump drugs on the Third World that are out of date, ineffective, or even banned in the West because of toxic side effects.

A more specific example from the health field (and a better one because of the even wider presence or pretense of good intentions) is the case of manufactured baby milk. This is not just a commercial product of the multinationals but is widely distributed as aid. The dangers here have been well documented.[3] The massive exportation of baby milk to the Third World has fostered dependence on an expensive manufactured product and decreased reliance on the perfectly adequate traditional solution of breast feeding. Moreover, under the conditions prevalent in most Third World countries, bottle feeding is not only unnecessary and expensive but actually exacerbates the link between malnutrition and infection. Little access to running water, no proper cooking facilities, poorly understood mixing instructions, overdilution because of high cost, and so on, are all factors that increase the chances of sickness or death among bottle-fed babies. Traditional methods of feeding are superior, especially in protecting against infection, and cost less. Yet, they are being undermined by the promotional techniques of the multinationals, including the bombardment of professional health workers by unethical stunts such as offers of free gifts, equipment, and sponsorship.

The ironies here are too painful for comment: mothers in the rich world are being encouraged to breast feed because it is "natural"; mothers in the poor world are being told that synthetic bottle feeding is a sign of "progress." Before considering potential parallels with crime control, let me cite a more general and more complex example: the whole area of food production and technology. Recent critical writing here has uncovered even more subtle layers of dependency and irony than the baby food case. Thus, production technology and consumption "needs" are being exported to the Third World that are not only inappropriate but lead to the possible impoverishment of natural resources and diets. At the same time "advanced" Western nutritional theory has swung back to high-fiber, unrefined food, though Western centralized production and capital investment can only *simulate* these original "natural" goods. As one observer comments in regard to a U.S. bakery's producing "high-fiber bread" by adding purified wood pulp to refined flour, "With a little more technology, they might be able to imitate unrefined wheat flour almost exactly."[4]

But the irony — the equivalent of which, remember, is the technology of simulated community control in the West — does not stop here. The exported models of food production and consumption have *also* registered (unevenly) the current revisionist theories. So the technology of ersatz high protein supplements is also being exported. Third World countries that have traditionally made extensive use of beans and other pulses and, of necessity, less use of meat, are importing ersatz products that actually decrease the natural nutritional value of pulses. "To suggest that it is better to use an expensive imitation of something they have never had in great quantity, rather than using the something in its original form as they have done for thousands of years, seems merely perverse."[5]

Bearing in mind the possible ironies and perversities suggested by this series of examples (tobacco, drugs, bottle feeding, food technology), we now return to the problem of crime control. I will offer three models for signifying the possible relevance of the Western crime-control experience for the Third World. Each accords a somewhat different role to ideology and this requires some initial comment.

Any social control system can be seen as ideological in two senses. First, its planning and structure are based on certain principles, ideas, beliefs, justifications, philosophies, or theories. And second, a quite different sense, these stated justifications conceal the real interests, intentions, and motives behind the system. The official, surface appearance is merely a mask or camouflage to make acceptable the exercise of otherwise unacceptable power, domination, or class interest. In this second sense the stated ideology is important only insofar as it succeeds in passing off repression as being fair, natural, or even just. Theories or statements of intent, therefore, are not to be taken at their face value (as the first view is assumed to imply) but as epiphenomena behind which more serious and important forces are at work.

This is not the place for a comparison of these views in the abstract, though as we shall see, the contrasting models about criminology in the Third World are informed by just this debate. Let me insist only that although ideas and ideologies do not, of course, exist as autonomous forces of social change, they nevertheless are important in shaping social control systems. Even when they are only justifications, they still constitute sociological data, whether they rationalize what already has been done or justify and theorize about what might be done. The history of crime control in the West and in the Third World is a history not only of changing modes of production but also of ideas and ideologies.

To sidestep this complex debate about ideology, I will use the term *model* as a way of at least describing, if not explaining, these relationships. By *model* I mean something like the symbolic, ideological, or theoretical way in which the control system might make sense of what it has done, is doing, and intends to do. Such models will, of course, contain contradictions; they will often not be altogether sure (to say the least) of what they are doing. But all this is in the nature of power and ideology.

Any exercise, historical or comparative, of trying to uncover models of control is something like trying to make sense of an archeological excavation. Successive "digs" reveal different ideological layers. More generally, Berger has recently used a similar metaphor to suggest the importance of political ideas in explaining social change in the Third World. The great pyramid at Chalula in Mexico reveals a vision of centuries of power: theoretical schemes and ideologies constructed by the priests (intellectuals) and embodied in stone by the wielders of power who dominated the generations of silent peasants, those who provided the labor and sacrifice. The great pyramid is a "metaphorical paradigm for the relations among theory and power and the 'victims of both.'"[6]

The following typology of theory and power perhaps exaggerates certain tendencies and groups together otherwise disparate ones but conveys, I hope, most of the range of possibilities. Note that each type embodies in turn three different areas of discourse: two master models, one about the general history of crime control and the other about the nature of "underdevelopment," and then a third, derivative model of the relevance of the Western crime-control experience for the Third World. Combining these dimensions yields my three types: (1) benign transfer, (2) malignant colonialism, and (3) paradoxical damage. I will deal with each separately, though in an obvious sense the last two emerge as critiques of the first.

Benign Transfer

The first model is the most popular and, on the surface at least, the simplest. The history of crime control is seen as a record of inexorable progress: a triumph of enlightened humanism over barbarity, and of rationality and scientific knowledge over irrationality and prejudice. This is not always an entirely complacent vision. Prisons, the police, the criminal justice apparatus are heavily criticized as both morally flawed and ineffective, but the system is seen as capable of being humanized by good liberal intentions and made more effective by scientific advances in such disciplines as criminology.

The second master theory explains the nature of the Third World in terms of such concepts as growth, development, modernization, social change, progress, and economic takeoff. The assumption is that the economic growth of these countries has somehow been retarded (has not yet achieved "takeoff point") and has reached a stage roughly equivalent to the industrialized world at the beginning of the nineteenth century. That is to say, developing countries will have to replicate the phases through which the West has already passed. This view is sometimes complacent ("do more or less what we did") but more often gives dire warnings about the "mistakes" and "problems" that marked the West's experience of industrialization.

Now applying these master theories to the question of crime control in the Third World, we arrive at the model of benign transfer. This suggests (and like the theories from which it derives, with varying degrees of qualification and sophistication) that crime is one of the many problems associated with "development," an invariable by-product of modernization and progress. Further, crime in the Third World today is more or less the same as crime in industrialized countries over a century ago. These theories contain an explicit Durkheimian underpinning: industrialization releases people from traditional social controls, but this rapid social change (modernization) is not matched by an equal development of new regulations. Social change, then, is inevitably brutal and disruptive; the market economy, industrial production, universal education, urbanization, and new political ideals all create problems. Aspirations remain unfulfilled, opportunities are blocked, new strains are generated, rural depopulation creates the overcrowded demoralized urban slum. Crime is the price to be paid for change.

Because this paper is concerned not with causation but with control, this is not the place for a critique of these theories.[7] Suffice to say that they consist of a textbook transfer (often a very literal and insensitive one) of standard Western sociological theories, especially of the anomie variety. In Clinard and Abbott's popular version, for example, the causes of Third World crime are to be found in a "universal process that crosses cultural lines." Findings about crime in Africa, Asia, and Latin America can simply be "brought together" within "a framework of a number of theoretical constructs derived from criminological research in the United States and Europe."[8]

The control implications of this causal theory are seen as relatively straightforward: we have seen it all before, and with our sophisticated knowledge we can help you try to avoid most of the mistakes we made. The essential working assumption of the benign transfer model is that crime is an *inevitable* by-product of development and modernization; it cannot be altogether prevented, though it can be ameliorated or kept in check by some combination of benevolent social reform and a rational, professional, and efficient criminal justice system.

Different variants of the model weight this working assumption with more or less optimistic overtones. The more pessimistic versions not only assume the total inevitability of high crime rates in developing societies but suggest an almost exact linear relationship between the extent of development and the sophistication of crime.[9] The standard cynical formula is that crime is not just the *price* for progress but an *index* of progress. Thus Radzinowicz and King quote (approvingly?) the minister of justice of an unnamed "developing country" as not being embarrassed by a particular armed robbery: "It simply means that we are becoming at last a civilized country."[10] Or: "It's *our* turn to pollute now," apparently a Brazilian politician's reply to a question about the ecological implications of industrialization.[11] A tragic Oedipal story then, with the Third World doomed to go through the same mistakes to discover the awful truth. The well-intentioned Western expert can only mitigate the worst effects of the tragedy.

In another variant, though, the tone is somewhat more confident and less cynical. The institutional origins of the benign transfer model lie in the International Congresses at the end of the nineteenth century. In these early organizations and their later counterparts, particularly through the United Nations and the Social Defense movement,[12] there is little questioning or self-doubt. It is all a question of scientific progress and the transfer of knowledge. An international criminological syndicate has been created (key figures include Clifford, Ancel, Lopez-Rey, Szabo, Radzinowicz, and Pinatel) that bestows patronage and prestige in the form of scholarships, certificates, conferences, and research grants. Clifford has recently described, apparently seriously, the importance of the five yearly UN Crime Conferences: "The host country has usually used the occasion to demonstrate internationally its advancement in criminal justice."[13] A kind of Olympic Games of crime control is set up, with competitions in different events, such as "Reliability of Statistics," "Lowest Delinquency Rates," "Numbers of Psychiatrists," "Proportions of Trained Prison Staff."

The most strident note of self-confidence in this institutional network could be found from the late 1960s, the heyday of the ideology of developmentalism. Crime control experts became part of what Illich was later to call "the rise and fall of a multinational consortium for the export of optimism to the Third World."[14] A useful example of an institution emerging from this period is the Montreal-based International Center for Comparative Criminology (ICCC).

The ICCC's dominant note was not only optimistic but — at least in the voice of its director, Denis Szabo — evangelical in its zeal.[15] The aim of criminology is "contributing to man's progress" and the application of criminology on a world scale is part of "a quest to improve the human condition."[16] The appeal is to enlightened Third World countries to turn aside from punitive and irrational methods of control and to satisfy their aspirations for justice, progress, and security by building a scientific crime-control program into their development plans. Protection from crime should be seen as a basic human right, like education, improved health, and a higher standard of living.

Leaving the flowery rhetoric aside, it should be said that the ICCC's actual diagnosis of Third World crime is much more sophisticated, acute, and well argued than that of most other international experts. And although the rhetoric is quite unselfconscious about the enterprise itself, it is not insensitive or chauvinist about local conditions, or blind to the limits of developmentalism. The enigma constantly expressed in this sort of literature is, how, despite "growth," is there still crime? The answer is the familiar one about the criminogenic effects of rapid and unregulated social change. The solution to the consequent crime problem follows directly from the model and is again more modest and realistic than the evangelical rhetoric implies. As the Western experience is supposed to have shown, a sheer improvement in social and material conditions will not lead to less crime. And the failure of the fight against crime in advanced societies is due to the wrong use of resources. Under the conditions of accelerated social change, anomie, and disorganization in the Third World, the need for crime-control planning is urgent. If measures for social defense are not included in development planning, crime will get worse and its social costs eventually escalate. The key planning objective is to limit the crime increase to unavoidable bounds and assure development and growth at lower costs.

To implement this program, an infrastructure of conferences, grants, courses, exchanges, and collaborative research was set up by the ICCC in different regions of the world.[17] A panel of experts is recycled to pass on the message, particularly at regular "scientific conferences." Such conferences typically begin with taking an inventory of national crime statistics and resources and end with recommended improvements. What counts as an "improvement" follows from a relatively unproblematic reading of criminological history — from classicism, to positivism, to an eventual victory for social defense. Thus, "the research and experiments carried out in Europe and America should help the African states avoid the errors and failures which had to be surmounted in other countries."[18]

All versions of the benign transfer model — whether cynical or evangelical, ethnocentric or sensitively culturally relativist — share a fundamental commitment to more of the same. The "same" means the positivist paradigm of causation, centralized planning, specialized control and prevention systems, and increased state expenditure. To Clinard and Abbott, for example, the "failure" of crime control in the West (i.e. the failure to deal with the regrettable side effects of industrialization) should not at all be discouraging. The West made three "mistakes," all now avoidable: (1) relegating crime-control planning to a secondary place; (2) not reaching consensus about causes; and, above all, (3) persistently and foolishly believing that improvement in socioeconomic conditions prevents crime.[19] The lessons are clear and urgent: "Because of the increase of crime in developing countries, urgently needed developmental resources must be diverted into crime control. Additional manpower, transportation, special equipment and building must be provided for police, court and prisons."[20] The dual assumptions of an expanding criminal justice system and an exploding criminal justice budget are never questioned, nor are the motives and intentions of the helping experts.

More of the same, then: more control; a more serious location of crime on the political agenda (understandably now relegated to secondary importance compared with health, education, and welfare, but developing countries cannot afford to wait until they are prosperous enough to afford more crime control); and, naturally, more criminologists and more research. The literature is replete with sad tales about the resistance to criminology from reactionary judges and civil servants or an emotional and prejudiced public.

Any proper criticism of the benign transfer model — well beyond my scope here — must avoid the danger of caricaturing its proponents either as knaves or as fools being manipulated by abstract historical forces beyond their comprehension. And whatever we might conceive as the real interests at stake, clearly surface intentions are genuinely benevolent, even if tinged with neocolonial paternalism and Cold War mentality. The context of these intentions is almost identical to the law-and-development movement, as chronicled by Trubek and Galanter in a model case study about the transfer of knowledge, which is directly relevant to the question of Third World crime control.[21]

The law-and-development movement consisted of a group of American scholars who developed over the 1960s a particular paradigm and research agenda for legal development in the Third World. The paradigm was *liberal legalism*: law and the courts as the central embodiments of the pluralist state and the major instruments for progressive social change. The research agenda (under the auspices of U.S. government development assistance programs, international agencies, and private foundations) applied this paradigm to the ills of the Third World, and then prescribed remedies, whose effectiveness and moral worth was unquestioned, in line with the American model. "Development" was good and law was a major instrument toward furthering the goals of development, such as equality, well-being, rationality, individual freedom, and citizen participation. Projects for legal reform, access, assistance, education, and professionalization were all developed and supported.

As with the benevolent transfer model (which, of course, derives from a similar paradigm and set of interests), these beliefs were sincerely held. As Trubek and Galanter stress, although these projects might well have set up a benevolent rhetoric that cloaked and served the ends of U.S. foreign policy, their supporters were neither charlatans nor cynical schemers: "These views were held honestly and unreflectively: liberal legalism may have been ingenuous, but it was not insincere."[22] It was indeed *because* of this sincerity that the movement could later experience such a crisis of self-confidence when its theoretical paradigm was threatened. These same scholars began to doubt the moral worth of their own enterprise. They came to see that legal change had little or no potency in changing the socioeconomic conditions of the Third World. To the contrary: they saw that many legal reforms can increase inequality, reduce citizen participation, restrict individual freedoms, and retard certain efforts to increase material well-being. The liberal legalistic model appeared to them as naive, unreal, and ethnocentric. In their resulting "crisis of self-estrangement," they began to attack the very things they helped create, the very ideology that supported them.

Although similar intellectual conditions are present, it does not seem to me that anything like this crisis of self-confidence has developed among supporters of the benign transfer model of crime control. Nonetheless, some cracks are noticeable and at least some of these experts have (belatedly) become more self-conscious and skeptical of their roles. Clifford, for example, in a recent adulatory text about the Japanese crime-control system acknowledges, "One of the absurdities of modern times has been the flow of 'experts' from countries with more crime to countries with less to show them how to organise the police courts and correctional services."[23] And even in his 1974 textbook, the statement "If Africa could provide itself with the elaborate crime control and prevention services common to affluent nations, then it could keep its crime rates at a lower level than they are and so reduce the undesirable by-products of its struggle to advance materially" was qualified by a footnote: "This assumes, of course, that such services are really effective preventatives in the developed countries — an assumption that rising crime rates may not support."[24]

The optimism of the international crime-control syndicate has somewhat mellowed since the heady years of "growthism." Influenced by the Illich-type critiques I will consider later and by cultural currents about "zero growth" and "small is beautiful," and always skeptical about material progress as such, the experts themselves, I suspect, might become even more disaffected with their own solutions. They have, in any event, always been more sympathetic than might first appear to indigenous solutions, either on the pragmatic grounds of cost effectiveness or out of some sense of cultural relativism that questions the sacred civilizing mission of the colonial power to destroy traditional laws and customs. For these reasons, such criminologists have often found themselves trying to protect "their" natives from the worst effects of colonial domination. In this respect at least, they are roughly equivalent to the anthropologists whom James calls, in only a slightly different context, "reluctant imperialists."[25] These anthropologists, though working within the overall context of colonialism, did try to appreciate traditional values and structures (including, of course, those of social control). They contributed to and were part of the structure of colonial power, but in their liberal defense of the weak they were not a simple unreflexive tool of domination.

Such sociology of knowledge considerations aside, the benign transfer model must be confronted in its own terms, a task beyond my scope here. The model's irremediable flaws stem from its parent theories themselves rather than its pragmatic derivatives. The notion of Western crime-control history as being a record of progress is too simpleminded to deserve much inspection. The modernization thesis, of course, raises more complex and controversial objections. Leaving aside the massive general onslaught by Marxist theories of colonialism and imperialism (the basis of my next model), the particular thesis about the parallels between crime in the Third World now and during early industrialization, although not entirely implausible, rests on some tenuous foundations. Third World societies are in a historically unique position, which differs in fundamental ways from early-nineteenth-century Europe. Such patterns as population growth and urbanization are quite different, but above all "growth" (or lack of growth, more often) is occurring under conditions of dependency, a prolonged process of industrial accumulation that is neither constant nor assured.

Underdevelopment simply cannot be understood without understanding the nature of dependency. The fact that development is taking place not in a vacuum but in relationship to an already powerful international capitalist system should be obvious. The consequences of penetration and dependency have been well documented: the economic polarization between the rich and poor countries, and the rich and poor populations within developing countries; the growing economic dependency and vulnerability of the poor countries; and the extent of hunger, disease, unemployment, and marginalization. Faith in "trickle-down" or "spread" effects has little justification. And the notion of crime being the price paid for prosperity is both laughable and cruel in countries that have much crime but no sign of prosperity.

All this, of course — whether or not we accept the full implications of Marxist theories of imperialism — is old news to Marxists and non-Marxists alike. But the tidings from decades of theory and research do not seem to have reached the ranks of these criminologists, who continue quite uncritically to reproduce the simplistic theory of "growth" and "historical stages." This invariably leads to the derivative flaw of assuming the nature and extent of crime in the Third World to be inevitable. As such examples as tobacco, drugs, baby foods, diet, pollution, and disease show, many problems facing (or about to face) the Third World are not at all "inevitable." To use the tobacco analogy: this would be like waiting for twenty years and millions of deaths, during which scientific papers are written once again to demonstrate that tobacco is dangerous. Neither in rich nor poor countries is death by lung cancer just an unfortunate side effect of industrialization; it is a product of traceable political and economic priorities.

It is analogously mistaken to suggest that unsuitable crime-control methods, particularly those that destroy perfectably workable traditional methods, are just regrettable accidents. All modes of colonization — whether from missionary zeal; military, economic, or political imperatives; or liberal idealism — consciously *intended* to destroy or manipulate previous systems. And the creation of new offenses — take such obvious examples as the effects, still present, of slave law in the Caribbean[26] — were intrinsic to colonialism. Legal control was built into the process from the outset, not tagged on afterward, and law was a chosen mechanism to achieve particular social changes.[27]

When it comes to criticizing not these theoretical assumptions but the actual preferred policies (for prevention, control, amelioration, "blunting the inevitable," or whatever), there is not much to say except to register incredulity at the continued and touching faith in the technical paradigm of positivist criminology. Despite a growing skepticism in the West about this paradigm, by no means confined to "radicals," the possibility of value-free technical solutions is still peddled in its made-for-export criminology.

As we will see when taking stock of each model, the use of much of this product is inevitable. And at its *best* (or perhaps, at its least harmful), the results have been benign. At its worst, it leads to the advocacy of policies that are chauvinistic, patronizing, and totally inappropriate. No doubt such exports as prison psychiatry, psychological predictions of predelinquency, or wasteful and silly replication research are not as harmful as high-tar tobacco, out-of-date drugs, and baby food, but the analogy stands. What is especially pernicious is the advocated transfer of technical policies taken out of their original ideological context. A grotesque example of this is Clinard and Abbott's suggestion of how to decrease crime rates by slowing down the rate of urbanization and migration.[28] For such measures to be effective, they argue, a pass system or some other enforceable control over population movements is necessary. The example they cite *approvingly* is the control of black peoples' residence and movement by the pass system in South Africa. Such policy directives defy critical comment.

Malignant Colonialism

A consistent reversal of assumptions behind the benign transfer model leads to its diametrical opposite in the model of malignant colonialism. The history of crime control, far from being a record of progress and benevolence, is the story of sham, hypocrisy, and ideological mystification. From its initial connection with the emergence of industrial capitalism and the modern state, the crime-control system has evolved in an increasingly repressive fashion. It arose as part of the relations of capitalist domination and is either the same as (but disguised) or supplements other systems used by the state to maintain order, stability, and class inequality. Liberal ideologies both mystify and legitimize this apparatus of repression, while bourgeois criminologists are merely hired hands, part of the apparatus.[29]

As to the nature of the Third World, the terminology and conceptual baggage associated with "developmentalism" are replaced by such terms as *colonialism, neocolonialism, dependency, imperialism, exploitation,* and *marginalization*. Far from being bland about the prospects for "growth," the picture is uniformly bleak: through intensified penetration, dependency, and exploitation, Third World countries are destined not only to become poorer in relationship to the capitalist world but to reproduce massive internal inequalities. Neocolonialism must result in increasing impoverishment and "the development of underdevelopment." The problem is not a lack of resources, knowledge, or technology—not a matter of retarded takeoff—but systematic exploitation by a worldwide capitalist system. And far from this being a regrettable historical accident, this process, in terms of Leninist theories of imperialism, is systemic, a necessary consequence of the present stage of late corporate capitalism.

Unlike its polar opposites in the benign transfer model, these assumptions have not really been worked through in the case of Third World crime. The failure to do this by criminologists is hardly surprising, but the neglect of crime in the vast literature of colonialism and dependency certainly is, given (1) the centrality of law, police, courts, punishment, and imprisonment to the apparatus of colonial repression; (2) the high and expanding costs of crime in national budgets, approaching or exceeding those of education and health, which have received so much attention; (3) the real or potential political significance of crime, for example, in the debate about the revolutionary potential of the lumpen proletariate; and (4) the importance of Marxist theories about the role of the state in protecting the institution of private property.

Future attempts to apply the theory of imperialism to Third World crime control, however, would no doubt be able to draw on parallels from other areas, such as health[30] and education.[31] More obviously relevant sources would be the anthropological literature (Marxist and non-Marxist) on law and social control; historical studies of legal systems as agencies of colonial control; and the increasing literature on crime control in such noncapitalist societies as Cuba, China, and Tanzania.

In any event, by drawing on such literature and by combining the parent models, the argument would be that both colonialism in general and the cultural colonialism of imposed crime-control policy in particular are, in essence, ideological masks for subordination and the extraction of labor.The stated rationale of crime-control policy, its benevolent pretensions, and what passes for criminological theory are not to be taken at their face value. Of course, as in education or health, colonialism might have had some benign consequences, but this is only like conceding that slaves were sometimes well fed.

This position is to be found in its pure and extreme form in writings of Fanon. Decolonization is the project of stripping away the whole apparatus that has violently destroyed the traditional social system. The humanistic, liberal intentions behind the transfer of knowledge and technology are a mask. Sometimes the appearance is direct and brutal—the police, the military. At other times it is more subtle. Even those forms of knowledge like medicine that offer such ostensible benefits as health, even humane values themselves, are to be distrusted: "As soon as the native begins to pull on his moorings, and to cause anxiety to the settler, he is handed over to the well-meaning souls who in cultural congresses point out to him the specificity and wealth of Western values."[32]

It takes little imagination to see how such remarks could be applied to the "well-meaning souls" who have peddled their values about reform and rehabilitation. Fanon's essay, "Medicine and Colonialism," remains the classic statement of how, despite the acceptance of benefits from more technically advanced societies, all the colonizers' contributions are appraised in a negative or ambivalent way.[33] In the "tragic labyrinth" of distrust at the heart of colonialism, the occupier's values, even if objectively worth choosing, must be rejected. Nothing can be shared. If even the fight against illness is an aspect of the colonial presence, how much more so is the "fight against crime"?

The same example of medicine has been developed recently in more systematic (and conventionally Marxist) formulations. Doyal, for example, sets out to show that even the more obvious advantages of Western medicine in the

Third World are illusory.³⁴ Not only has imperialism failed to solve problems of hunger, malnutrition, and infectious disease but its failure is a direct consequence of particular forms of capitalist expansion. The continued prevalence of certain diseases, such as cholera, plague, typhoid, and smallpox, was not because they were somehow endemic to the tropics (they existed in the West and were eradicated there) but were tied up to particular patterns of dependency. New health problems were originally created by certain colonial regulations and continue to be created (as we have already seen in the examples of tobacco, baby milk, and food technology) by neocolonialism. Pollution, hazardous technology, and safety risks exported by multinationals, migrant labor, dangerous aid policies, export of unhealthy foods, and consumption patterns are all obvious examples.

All this is not just a rerun of the same unfortunate phase of the early Industrial Revolution but the result of the systematic undermining of health. Furthermore, current ameliorative techniques are simply obstacles to effective health care and have resulted in little more than the reproduction of inadequate and unsuitable Western technology and false values about training and professionalism. In particular, cultural colonialism led to the replication of a high-technology, hospital-based, individual curative mode of intervention as a substitute rather than a supplement for basic public health measures taken for granted in advanced industrial societies. The model transplanted by philanthropic foundations, foreign aid programs, and international health agencies leads to a caricature of the original. The ends of imperialism are served by this form of "modernization," and the resultant system benefits mainly the new urban elites with little or detrimental impact on the health of the vast bulk of the population. In the analogy used in a fascinating recent study (of the Rockefeller Foundation medical modernization programs in China from 1914, culminating in the Peking Union Medical College), Western medicine is "the Trojan Horse."³⁵

Whether or not one is convinced of the relevance of this sort of analysis to crime and whether or not one is committed to Fanonism in general, it is clear that the malignant colonialism model must place quite different questions on the traditional criminological agenda. Alternative causal theories, at present hardly spelled out, would obviously have to contend with the "same" facts of urbanization, consumerism, destruction of tradition, and marginalization of the labor force but (presumably) make something different of them. Clearly, the thesis of high crime rates as an inevitable by-product of industrialization would be replaced by a thesis locating crime as an intrinsic product of the patterns of dependency, exploitation, marginalization, and capitalist-intensive industrialization. In practice, though, despite their obviously differing *political* consequences, I doubt that theories about the inevitably criminogenic effects of capitalism will look very different from those about the inevitably criminogenic effects of industrialism. And the notion of the capitalist mode of production "needing" to create a certain number of marginals in its different phases looks remarkably similar to the Durkheimian notion of society's "needing" crime that appears in bourgeois functionalist theory.

In fact (as is true with Western Marxist criminology), the model is more explicit and distinctive about control than about causation. The analytic framework is that of "law and the state": legal and judicial systems emerge in colonial dependencies in order to control and direct labor.[36] They produce, legitimate, and reinforce a structure of inequality. This economic function is coupled with the more general role of law in legitimating the state. And both functions are perpetuated when indigenous political elites replace the European ruling class but continue using the same Western conceptions of legality imported to the colonies as part of the civilizing mission. Current regimes thus legitimate themselves by appeals not just to democracy, socialism, or nationalism but also to the "rule of law."

These themes have been explored in a substantial body of literature dealing with both the early period of pure, paternal colonialism and its later neocolonial, technicist variants dominated by multinationals and international agencies. The fact that this literature seldom refers to matters of standard criminological concern is probably due to the fact that colonial law was essentially directed toward establishing capitalist social and property relationships and seemed to be less concerned with traditional forms of conflict and dispute. The point, though, is that in operationalizing property and social relationships, colonial governments set up a framework of law on the one hand and crime on the other. To impose property rights, for example, patterns of traditional usage and allocation by community leaders are replaced by land ownership, and title by law. In the transition from communal to private land ownership, laws of vagrancy are established. Worker mobility is criminalized through such measures as pass laws, apprenticeships acts, and work certificates.

The immediate implications of this historical and political analysis for current control policy are not particularly well worked out, for the obvious and simple reason that a complete socialist revolution is seen as the only real solution. If the criminal justice system is being used to support and legitimate bourgeois domination, then short-term pragmatic and reformist policies are not worth much consideration and can only be co-opted into the system, thereby strengthening it. In one way or another the possibility is denied that a humane and just system is attainable under capitalist economic and political arrangements.

Contemporary radical criminologists in Latin America have provided the most explicit statements of these themes. Del Olmo, for example, has pointed to the particular way in which Latin American criminologists have colluded in the process of cultural dependency.[37] As consumers rather than producers of ideas, armed with outdated imported textbook and theories, they have allowed themselves to reproduce mimetically the shapes of Western criminology. She uses the particularly vivid example of the distortions produced by using individualistic theories of violence in the middle of a continent dominated by institutional violence of various sorts: terror, torture, genocide, and left, right, or militaristic political violence. And Riera, drawing on two recent books by Latin American criminologists, has more explicitly applied the general prospectus of Marxist criminology.[38] He argues for a demystification of bourgeois conceptions of crime and liberal reform, and for seeing the control system in international terms. "In short, crime can only be understood by looking at the position of Latin America in relation to the development of the capitalist mode of production and the corresponding class conflict."[39] The prospectus includes paying attention to the role of the national bourgeoisie in the evolution of justice systems and analyzing how the state brings coercive pressure on petty property offenders while neglecting the corporate crimes of the powerful.

As with the liberal models of benign transfer, so with the Marxist models of malignant colonialism, it is beyond my scope even to indicate what a proper critique would look like. My own view, cryptically, is that while the master theories of control and colonialism are essentially correct in their demystification of the myth of development and in their factual diagnosis of dependency, their alternative theories are overstated and tendentious in places. The importance of ideas and intentions is often obscured,[40] the malignancy of every capitalist enterprise in the Third World exaggerated, and the possibilities of short-term liberal reforms prematurely condemned. In addition, certain doctrinaire tendencies in Marxism have led to a curious reluctance to confront either the nature of crime and crime control in contemporary noncapitalist societies or their prospects in future societies after the socialist revolution.

The current wave of interest in crime control in China and Cuba, though, offers real potential for considering this last set of problems. Western criminologists have used the Chinese experience to speculate on how the "delegalization" model might be applied to the emerging postrevolutionary social order.[41] Taking the crucial questions of both legal form and substance, they have looked critically at such moves as procedural informalism and dispute resolution as transitional models in the struggle toward socialism.

The emerging literature on China is particularly interesting, if sometimes a little opaque, about the possibilities of various decentralized informal or extralegal mechanisms.[42] Such models, already strongly promoted by Confucianism and embodied in the culture and politics of imperial China, provided a flexible and familiar intrastructure upon which the "new" informalism (justice without law) was to be built. Unlike in the West, where ersatz versions of this model have strengthened the state and increased the sweep of formal control, the Chinese case seemed to offer genuine alternative forms of acceptable decentralized control congruent with existing institutions. On the other hand, the history of the new informalism in China has not been without its tensions, and has showed a continued oscillation between phases of Western-type formalism and informalism. Formalist episodes — centralization, professionalization, constitutionalism, rationalization — made comebacks after the initial postrevolutionary informalism, and again after these "gains" were reversed by the Great Leap Forward. The consensus on current developments (following the 1978 constitution, the rise of a new moderate leadership, the trial of the "Gang of Four") is that China can no longer be held up as a successful example of delegalization. Indeed, for erstwhile sympathetic observers, such as Brady, this "new conservatism" (the return of legal formalism, professionalism, centralization) is a tragic revisionism, indicating a "downhill path to modernization."

Whether or not these developments represent an ironic vindication of the modernization thesis is another matter. Just as interesting to note are parallel oscillations in Western capitalist societies between such episodes of substantive and formal justice, as well as the astonishing capacity of many Third World societies (whether influenced by capitalist or socialist ideologies) to retain both formal and informal systems at the same time. In any event, socialist transitions such as those in China and Cuba can hardly be said to have provided unequivocal policy implications in line with the malignant colonialism model.

Paradoxical Damage

My third model hardly exists as such. It has neither the powerful institutional base of benign transfer models nor the sophisticated theoretical tradition of malignant colonialism models. I offer it very tentatively as a way of framing certain short-term policy implications without losing the theoretical thrust of the colonialism critique. Again it incorporates different tendencies, some closer to one of the two more influential models, some to the other.

The parent view on the history of crime control in the West tends to a left liberalism rather than an orthodox Marxism. The story, though, is very clearly *not* seen as a record of progress. Influenced by a skeptical, sour, and ironic view about the working of social institutions in general, these theorists will always doubt the pretensions of social control agencies to be doing what they claim. On the other hand, intentions are not seen as wholly malevolent. To quote, for example, the conclusions of Rothman's well-known history of the prison: "Proposals that promise the most grandiose consequences often legitimate the most unsatisfactory development. And one also grows wary about taking reform programs at face value; arrangements designed for the best of motives may have disastrous results."[43] The malignant model of this same history, of course, explicitly rejects this conclusion: "To interpret the history of reform as a cycle of good intentions confounded by unintended consequences is to see it as a history of failure. But reform was a success."[44] Whichever side we take in this complex debate, it seems important to take ideology seriously while at the same time not merely reproducing it.

As to the parent view on the Third World, this model would share all the theory of colonialism's critique of the bland ideology of growth. Problems of poverty, illness, crime, and exploitation would be seen as immanent and intrinsic to the historical and current relationships between the poor and the rich countries. Although this model is skeptical about the myth of growth, it is also skeptical about some implications of the theory of imperialism. It is likely to talk about the malignancy of "postindustrialism" as well as that of "late capitalism"; it would take intentions seriously enough to be uncomfortable about assuming that abstract historical forces are responsible for making people sick or unhappy; it would support selected short-term reforms; it is likely to sympathize with certain libertarian political ideas.

The derivative application of these doubts and reservations to the discourse about Western crime control models in the Third World has yet to be made. The closest parallel lies in Illich's writings on education, medicine, and welfare.[45] His central obsession (for the rich and the poor worlds alike) is the power of these major institutions to subvert the purposes for which they were originally intended and that they still profess. As a general theory this indictment of the destructive effects of industrialized service agencies is obviously open to objections. On the one hand, as the colonialism model suggests, when intentions are so blatantly malevolent and exploitative from the outset, the notion of subsequent failure or subversion is quite misplaced. And on the other, as the transfer model suggests, these agencies sometimes do work.

But the strength of this argument lies not in its theoretical comprehensiveness but its sensitivity to certain middle-range issues that the other two models fail to pick up. Illich starts from an attack on the ideology of growth and the particular assumption, central to benign transfer models, that the destructive effects of industrialization can be solved by more planning. Quite the contrary: these efforts actually make things worse even if (especially if?) their intentions are benevolent. The supposedly enabling service professions like law, medicine, social work, and psychiatry are in fact "disabling professions," and the proper attitude to be taken toward such experts "especially when they presume to diagnose and prescribe" is "patronising and sceptical."[46] There are very few elements in the Illich polemic against these professionals that cannot be applied to Western crime-control experts and especially to their export efforts in the Third World: the development of radical monopolies; arcane claims to secret knowledge; a crusading and commandeering philanthropy; a moral enterprise aimed at creating the need for one's own services; the self-interested tendencies to develop more specialization and more research.

Illich adopts the medical concept of *iatrogenesis* to expand on the disabling nature of such professional intervention. Iatrogenesis is an instance of the destructive dominance of industry: the "paradoxical counterproductivity" of institutions. Such forms of damage or destruction are not just external costs that can be budgeted for, like pollution caused by cars or the crime "fallout" from economic progress. They are those far more dramatic and direct consequences of planning that actually take away from society whatever the institution was designed to promote. The causes lie neither in mistakes, bad theories, and inadequate resources nor in the nature of class exploitation but rather in the industrially induced paralysis that results from the systemic invasion and undermining of underdeveloped countries by instruments of production designed for capital efficiency that then create the need for a therapeutic solution to their own effects.

The three specific forms of medical iatrogenesis that Illich suggests all have their parallels in regard to crime. *Clinical iatrogenesis* refers to the ways in which hospitals, doctors, and modes of treatment are themselves the sickening agents: harmful side effects of drugs, doctor-inflicted pain, unnecessary surgery, and the like. Labeling and stigma theory, the demonstration of the ironic ways in which control agencies create and stabilize deviance, obviously point to the equivalent effects in crime control.

Social iatrogenesis refers to the expropriation of health through overmedicalization and the encouragement of people to become passive dependents: "All impairments to health that are due precisely to those socio-economic transformations which have been made attractive or necessary by the institutional shape health care has taken."[47] This has parallels in the increasing growth of social control networks, with finer gradations and classifications, each created by state professionals who then find deviants to fill these places. "Diagnostic imperialism" and "preventive stigma" in medical care, lifelong regimes of supervision and classification, the marketing of panaceas about risk and early identification have exact parallels in Western systems of control, welfare, and therapy.[48] And the medicalization of the budget is matched by the criminalization of other sectors of society. For example, the planning of crime prevention projects in streets, schools, and public housing.

Further, the technical and managerial devices rationalized as remedies for the unwanted by-products of clinical and social iatrogenesis themselves produce a new epidemic. An example of such a "self-reinforcing iatrogenic loop" in delinquency control would be so-called diversion policy: the juvenile court was set up at the end of the nineteenth century as a form of diversion from the adult court, but there are now diversion agencies from the juvenile courts, and these are generating further agencies to divert offenders from diversion agencies.

Finally, there is what Illich calls *cultural iatrogenesis*: the deeper destructive effects of medical imperialism on healthy, autonomous cultural responses to suffering. The new professions actually paralyze certain abilities to help, cope, and tolerate. In the case of deviance, the coercive powers of formal courts, for example, undermine the authority of traditional consensual forms of dispute settlement. Judicial access is restricted to the privileged few, most people just avoiding or giving up any active participation. Because ordinary people stop acting and reacting in traditional ways, the control system's loops can become further elaborated, thus creating even greater passivity. The formal system is countercultural[49] and monopolistic, creating deviance by creating the need for control agents. Old ways of learning to live with diversity, trouble, and conflict eventually disappear.

The central thrust of this critique is directed at the power of systems of diagnosis, nosology, and classification. In this model, if the analogy between the Third World and Western "stages" of development is to be of any use at all, it lies in seeing how these same systems are being reproduced and imposed again. These modes of power and discipline, the essense of what Foucault calls the "power-knowledge spiral," cannot be evaluated in terms of cost effectiveness or success. They are systems of regulation, supervision, and classification, and their point is simply *more* regulation, supervision, and classification. It is this discourse, this way of seeing and thinking about the world, that is being exported and that has to be resisted.

This precise strand of thought has not yet been consistently applied to Third World crime control. From a modestly pragmatic position, for example, Whetton has recently queried the need for the inflationary spiral (often unnoticed) of expanding criminal justice systems and exploding criminal justice budgets in the Third World.[50] Often borrowing directly from the West, the country lurches from one ad hoc response to another, neglecting possibilities less costly, more effective, and more in accordance with the community's ideas of justice. Under these conditions policies are informed by an abstract concept of crime that is totally unrelated to the finer distinctions already available to the community.

The solution is to encourage traditional systems of informal and community justice and to rely less on expert prescriptions and personnel. An analogy might be drawn from current work on "appropriate" or "intermediate" technology in areas such as ecology, food production, and energy. The point is not to encourage a Luddite-like rejection of all outside knowledge but to apply consistently such criteria as low capital investment, organizational simplicity, high adaptability, and absence of undesirable side effects.

Admirable as such programs are—as counters to both optimistic growthism and revolutionary despair—they need locating in what I see as the tougher version of the paradoxical damage model. "Tougher" in that the theoretical vision must go beyond either a left-liberal skepticism about the benevolence of professions or questions of cost effectiveness. A common and justified criticism of the Illich approach is that it places so much stress on the power of intellectuals and professionals. Social control officials, however, have only limited autonomy and operate within constraints set by the state and the economy. A tougher theory would emphasize such structural constraints; professionals can neither completely initiate nor completely reverse the ironies and paradoxes that the theory so elegantly uncovers. Indeed, Illich's stress on the power of professionals is contradicted by his own version of cynical conservatism: "medical nemesis" is a monster born from the industrial dream of progress, divine vengeance for tampering with nature.

Another quite different point can be made about any program that follows from this (or indeed any other) model: it should be supported only if regarded as politically worthwhile in itself and not as an adjunct to the "war against crime." This applies to all programs of so-called general prevention; the objective of lower crime rates is independent of and irrelevant to the struggle against poverty, inequality, and repression. And similarly, those policies that undermine traditional solutions and foster dependency on foreign expertise should be resisted out of principle rather than expediency. Quite the contrary to the benign transfer program, the point of the exercise is to put crime control *lower* rather than higher on the political agenda; to make criminologists *redundant* rather than create more jobs for them.

All such principles, in other words, need a more positive defense than a vague desire to "preserve" local traditions and an equally vague assumption that any policy containing the word *community* must be worth supporting. Christie, for example, has stated a strong case for reappropriating more conflict from the professionals who have monopolized it and for returning it to key participants such as victims and families.[51] There is no reason to assume, as these professionals do, that a conflict should have a "solution" or "resolution." Many traditional societies were used to high levels of conflict and emotion (insults, ritual fighting, gossip, public quarrels, politicking, competitive display, sorcery, witchcraft) that were handled or cared about without ever being "solved." The traditional occasions for staging these conflicts provide advantages for norm classification and resolution that are obscured by the professional endeavors of law, social work, and psychiatry. These advantages would be present even if official recidivism rates were unaffected. There is encouraging evidence of people's preferring these methods, even in the interstices of a well-developed Westernized system.[52]

The model of paradoxical damage, then — loose and eclectic as its theoretical bases might be — offers some productive routes into these middle-level policy considerations. In particular, it provides an informed basis for skepticism toward benign transfer ideologists. This should be equivalent to the skepticism now being shown about the claims of baby food manufacturers, with their photos of big, bouncing protein-fed babies, their propaganda about the need to abandon primitive practices, and their company representatives dressed as nurses who appear in clinics giving sales pitches in the guise of nutritional advice. No one aware of the history of crime control in the West can continue advocating "more of the same" in good faith.

Final Muddles

Models, when it comes to applying them, look more like muddles. Leaving aside their internal theoretical inconsistencies and contradictions, models of crime control are not simply "out there" to be selected like commodities in a supermarket and then somehow "applied." The powerful (who are supposed to make and implement these selections) and the intellectual priesthood (who theorize for or against them) are constrained by histories that are not of their own making. The choices are never free and are certainly far less rational and far more pragmatic than the concept of a "model" implies.

Nevertheless, preferences are visible and some choices can be made — and having indicated where my own sympathies lie, I must admit to their muddled elements. No one sensitive to the extraordinary mixture of benevolence and coercion, good intentions and disastrous consequences, which has been the history of progressive crime-control ideology, could not subject any set of intentions to profound self-criticism.

A major limitation of my typology, leaving aside my preference for some version of the third type, is its naivete in implying that it covers the range of political choices. For those large sectors of the Third World that are ruled by military dictatorships, feudal overlords, religious despots, or foreign masters, the choice is only between different variants of more or less brutal oppression. All three models under review — including (and perhaps especially) the liberal, progressive version — are right off the political spectrum. Torture, repression, and punishment without trial are the facts of political life, while for ordinary crime-control sectors, "progress" consists of the latest gadgetry imported via Interpol and televised in "Starsky and Hutch." This is a crucial point, for under these conditions policies that might look reactionary, problematic, or dangerous within the range of my three ideal types might now be worth supporting. Such decisions depend on the historical context. If the immediate need is for humanitarian reform (through welfare or even psychiatric ideology), then it would be politically absurd to oppose these reforms *solely* on the grounds that such humanizing impulses have produced undesirable consequences elsewhere.[53] This is the sort of agonizing choice that the paradoxical model creates, but it also creates some rather profound muddles that I now want to list:

1. The Illich-type critique clearly does contain some Luddite and romantic undertones; the danger lies in perpetuating another version of the noble

savage myth. Some proponents of intermediate technology and the like appear to suppose that peasants actually prefer hard work, subsistence diets, and disease; that patriarchy and feudalism should be preserved and customs like clitoral circumcision condoned; that people live without running water, medicine, or agricultural equipment because of an ideological attachment to self-sufficiency and the principles of ecologically sound calorie conservation. At their worst, these assumptions can lead to the sort of exoticism that Fanon rightly condemned: native intellectuals being urged to take up a caricatured version of local tradition, and what is more, local tradition that should not be supported.[54] Those who advocate an unselective traditionalism (in the name, perhaps, of cultural relativism) can find themselves supporting trial by gossip, the stoning of adulterers, and the mutilation of thieves.

In addition to the obvious moral problems of romanticism, there is the factual problem that these supposedly "traditional values" are simply not the traditional values at all. What the Western observer sees as the replication of traditional practices might be based on a completely false history and anthropology. A more careful reading of the nature of order and authority in traditional societies and a more careful dichotomization between the models of law used in "Western" and "tribal" societies show a range of complications that the paradoxical damage model simply ignores.[55] These distortions become manifest when the idealized tribal package is reexported to the West. The new version of the justice model, for example, is radically different from the simple version of justice to which it appeals. Tribal, village, or customary courts make use of particularistic and reputational criteria not all consistent with the abstract Kantian notions of just deserts now being advocated. Nor are traditional methods of reconciliation and reparation very often allocated according to some abstract tarriff system. Nor is it true that traditional systems were in a simple sense more "tolerant" of deviance, with the implication that such policies as decriminalization or radical nonintervention must be supported because they are somehow "natural."

It might also be noted that many interesting (and in many senses "successful") experiments with peoples' courts, popular justice, revolutionary courts, and the like reproduce practices very different from those found in existing and previous informal systems. Their force and sense of natural justice are owed more to the revolutionary upsurge itself (and foreign ideologies such as "socialist legality") than to any attempt to recapture the past.

2. The dangers of romanticism and exoticism suggest more serious obstacles to realizing humane and nonescalating crime control policies. The problem might be that it is simply too late to reverse existing directions, to put the brakes on a process begun inexorably by development or colonialism. The "reexport" of the most radical and advanced solutions from the West — remember the example of ersatz protein supplement — will arrive too late to undo the damage already done.

This is obviously a serious issue. Once modernization (or colonialism) has already taken root, there is a sense in which the simple choice between Western imposition and indigenous tradition is simply not possible. As the mass of literature on neocolonialism has shown, penetration — through the modes of production — has occurred too deeply for such a choice. And the old solutions are not the "same" when they are self-consciously readopted. Berger illustrates this point nicely with the image of a tribal dance in Tanzania. Previously, the dance took place at times designated by tradition; it was an inevitable ritual. Now it is staged on occasions chosen by the village council; a previously unreflective choice now becomes a good thing for morale. So, "even if the motions of the dance remained unaltered in every detail, they would no longer be the same dances."[56]

The problem is not just the irony of "radical" Westerners descending from their airplanes to recommend local solutions (we all have to live with such ironies!), but the fact that these solutions are now embedded in a different discourse. If people have to be *trained* to be informal and communities have to be *informed* by the state that they exist, then the point of the message is hardly the same. Illich himself, usually accused of a radical chic encouragement of self-help, warns us nicely what might happen when tradition becomes professionalized:

> In each of the seven U.N. defined world regions a new clergy is trained to preach the appropriate style of austerity drafted by the new need-designers. Consciousness raisers roam through local communities inciting people to meet the decentralised production goals that have been assigned to them. Milking the family goat was a liberty until more ruthless planning made it a duty to contribute the milk yield to the GNP.[57]

Applying this problem to the question of crime control,[58] it could be argued that the revival of, say, village courts destroyed by Western legal systems and indirect rule can never be entirely successful. Even when dual legal systems allow a choice, it might be only between a Western court and a local court with a caricatured nativist solution. And once it *is* a choice (whether stimulated by local intellectuals resisting cultural colonialism or avant-garde Western social scientists), it is not like the old system. Even changes that exclude choice by reviving custom must be seen in a particular historical context. The same conception of legality that was part of the colonial mission and was used to denounce tribal settlements as arbitrary and capricious is now used to support and encourage new systems of justice in populist and radical terms: "giving justice back to the people." The resulting forms, though, are often more adjudicative, coercive, formal, and distant than the original and run by new elites different from traditional leaders.[59] The question, then, is whether traditional forms of justice destroyed or caricatured under the impact of colonial law can ever regain their organic connections with the community.

3. Such difficulties should not, I believe, be used to justify a passive surrender to "progress." Some degree of professional zeal can be curbed and some

traditional methods (including those that had never really been suppressed) can be rejuvenated and adapted. But unfortunately many of these middle-level changes depend on the willingness of the new professional and intellectuals elites of the Third World to give up some of the very privileges that bind them to the Western system. To expect them to do this might be unrealistic and also—as I have already suggested—might attribute too much autonomous power to these professionals.

To look again at the analogy with medicine, it is obvious that experts alone cannot and will not solve these Third World health problems that have resulted from the inappropriate transfer of Western medicine. Take the specific example of breast versus bottle feeding. In the West the return to breast feeding was only *partly* a reaction to the expropriation of care by experts; it also required a mother who could stay at home, given the rarity of adequate facilities at work. And although breast feeding might make sense in rural Third World areas, educated women who want to pursue careers have little choice but artificial feeding. This is an issue in the politics of gender and not just of professional influence. And another reason for promoting bottle feeding is that it sidesteps the more intractable economic and structural problems of providing an adequate diet for mothers who wish to breast feed. The focus on babies allows the high rates of infant mortality to be wished away as a consequence of "underdevelopment." If one focuses the discussion on the *mother's* condition, though, one is drawn into questions of land tenure or the sexual division of labor, questions that many Third World governments would rather not raise too openly.

It takes little imagination to think of an equivalent range of issues in regard to Third World crime, where questions of "professional disablement," "transfer of knowledge," and the like are more or less irrelevant, and where the real issues can seldom be mentioned. Crimes of the powerful, such as political corruption, police brutality, government lawlessness, and exploitation by multinationals, are hardly matters of "paradoxical damage."

4. This leads to an even greater flaw in the model: the difficulties of reinforcing traditional methods aside, the problem is indeed (as both other models see in their different ways) that traditional methods are totally ill equipped to deal with some current Third World crime problems. Undesirable change at the periphery of the political economy can be modified by an appeal to tradition. But at the center—big business, the multinationals, the state itself—no such reversal or stoppage is possible through using traditional authority. And in dealing with such matters as baby food, tobacco, drugs, food consumption, and pollution, the question is no longer one of an *analogy* to crime but the actual creation of new forms of criminal victimization.

In areas like these there are few ways of controlling and regulating the powerful without strong centrally enforced legislation. "Delegalization" and "decriminalization" are unrealistic enough responses to the equivalent areas in advanced industrial societies; how much more so in the Third World, given the history of such damage and exploitation there. It would be difficult to visualize forms of mediation, arbitration, and conciliation as substitutes for formal adjudication and sanctioning. The conditions of equality and consensus, on which traditional methods depend, are simply not there. Moreover, as Abel points out in his extremely suggestive analysis of these and other drawbacks facing the delegalization movement, "Because delegalization assumes rough equality between social actors, it tends to deprive those who are weaker, poorer or of lower social status of whatever protection they had obtained from formal legal recognition of their rights."[60] Nonintervention, then, can hardly be an adequate response to the crimes of the powerful. Nor should such problems as bribery and corruption be normalized as "functional" to the system, mere extensions of traditional tribal and kinship ties.

These four problems are among those confronting any attempt to relate the Western crime-control experience to the Third World, whether or not informed by the paradoxical damage model. They are all permutations of the same fateful prediction at the root of colonialism: developing countries have to go through the same experiences, repeat the same mistakes as those of the advanced industrial world. Some Third World intellectuals have openly welcomed and facilitated this prediction; others have regarded it as a sad inevitability; yet others have raised Fanon's resounding call to resist creating a "Third Europe."

While the muddles might occasionally threaten the models, the crime-control case surely provides an important, and largely ignored, route into that wider debate.

Notes

1. M. Muller, *Tobacco and the Third World: Tomorrow's Epidemic* (London: War on Want, 1978).
2. T. Heller, *Poor Health, Rich Profits: Multinational Drug Companies and the Third World* (London: Spokesman Books, 1977); C. Medawar, *Insult or Injury: An Inquiry into the Marketing and Advertising of Food and Drug Products in the Third World* (London: Social Audit, 1979).
3. A. Chetley, *The Baby Killer Scandal: A War on Want Investigation into the Promotion and Sale of Powdered Baby Milk in the Third World* (London: War on Want, 1978).
4. C. Judge, *The Famine Business* (Harmondsworth: Penguin, 1979), p. 83.
5. Ibid., p. 126.
6. P. Berger, *Pyramids of Sacrifice: Political Ethics and Social Change* (London: Allen Lane, 1976).
7. For such a critique, see C. Summer, "Crime, Justice and Underdevelopment: Beyond Modernization Theory," in *Crime, Justice and Development*, ed. Summer (London: Heinemann, 1982). His two main examples of the orthodox approach to Third World crime ("Modernization Theory") also serve as examples of my Benign Transfer model: M. B. Clinard and D. J. Abbott, *Crime in Developing Countries: A Comparative Perspective* (London: Wiley, 1973); W. Clifford, *An Introduc-*

tion to African Criminology (Nairobi: Oxford University Press, 1974). For an earlier criticism of Clifford's, see G. Boehringer, "African Criminology: Towards the Necessary Dialogue," *East African Law Journal* 11 (1975): 81–106.

8. Clinard and Abbott, *Crime in Developing Countries*, pp. 1, 5.
9. Ibid., p. 357.
10. L. Radzinowicz and J. King, *The Growth of Crime: The International Experience* (London: Hamish Hamilton, 1977), p. 12.
11. Quoted in Berger, *Pyramids of Sacrifice*, p. 62.
12. The key institutions here are the annual UN Congress on the Prevention of Crime and Treatment of Offenders (a continuation of the International Penal and Penitentiary Commission started in 1870); the UN Social Defense Section, in New York, and Research Institute, in Rome; the UN Asia and Far East Institute for the Prevention of Crime, in Tokyo; various UN crime prevention and criminal justice programs; the International Society of Criminology and the International Center for Comparative Criminology (ICCC). The fascinating history of these institutions remains to be written. For an "insider's" view of the UN activity, see W. Clifford, "The Committee on Crime Prevention and Control," *International Review of Criminal Policy* 38 (1978): 11–18. For a description of how the UN assumed international leadership in crime control policy and a content analysis of the reports to the five UN Congresses on the Prevention of Crime and Treatment of Offenders held so far, see B. Hassenpusch, "The United Nations Congresses on the Prevention of Crime and the Treatment of Offenders: An Analysis of Trends in Content and Participation," *International Journal of Criminology* 6, no. 4 (1978): 339–62.
13. W. Clifford, "Directors Digest," *Reporter* (newsmagazine of the Australian Institute of Criminology) 1 (September 1979): 3.
14. I. Illich, *Limits to Medicine* (Harmondsworth: Penguin, 1977).
15. Szabo was hailed by Marcel Ette, the Director of the Abidjan Institute of Criminology, as "that untiring apostle of criminology" (opening address, Fourth West African Conference on Criminology, Abidjan, May 1974). The proceedings of this conference (published by the ICCC) and the previous three West African conferences (Abidjan, 1972, Lagos, 1973; Abidjan, 1973) are interesting and invaluable resources for Third World criminologists. A useful section of papers from the Second Conference is to be found in A. Adeyemi, ed., *Nigerian Criminal Process* (Lagos: University of Lagos Press, 1977). The collected papers from other conferences organized by the Center, particularly from Latin America, are also available from the ICCC.
16. D. Szabo, "Foreword," *Proceedings of First West African Conference in Comparative Criminology* (Abidjan and Montreal: International Centre for Comparative Criminology, 1972).
17. To anticipate accusations of ingratitude to hands that have fed me, I should record my own participation in two such conferences.
18. Ibid., p. 12.
19. Clinard and Abbott, *Crime in Developing Countries*, pp. 259–62.
20. Ibid., pp. 254–55.
21. D. M. Trubek and M. Galanter, "Scholars in Self-Estrangement: Some Reflections on the Crisis in Law and Development Studies in the United States," *Wisconsin Law Review*, no. 4 (1975): 1062–1102.
22. Ibid., p. 1088.
23. W. Clifford, *Crime Control in Japan* (London: Lexington Books, 1976), p. 174.
24. Clifford, *An Introduction to African Criminology*, p. ix.

25. W. James, "The Anthropologist as Reluctant Imperialist," in *Anthropology and the Colonial Encounter*, ed. T. Asad (London: Ithaca Press, 1973).

26. D. Dodds, "The Role of Law in Plantation Society: Reflections on the Development of a Caribbean Legal System," *International Journal and Society of Law* 7, no. 3 (1979): 275-96.

27. It should be pointed out here that, contrary to most Marxist theory, this process was hardly confined to capitalism. The Soviet assault on traditional Muslim societies in Southeast Asia, for example, was an equivalent form of legal repression: the deliberate undermining of prevailing patterns of traditional authority based on lineage, kinship, custom, gender, religion, and age. See G. Massell, "Law as an Instrument of Social Change in a Traditional Milieu: The Case of Soviet Central Asia," *Law and Society Review* 2, no. 2 (1968): 182-226.

28. Clifford and Abbott, *Crime in Developing Countries*, pp. 275-78.

29. With considerable internal disagreements beyond my scope to consider here, such a view would be associated with the early writings of Rusche and Kirchheimer, and the recent Marxist theorists such as Ignatieff, Melossi, Spitzer, Scull, and (more problematically and, for my purposes, more usefully) Foucault. See also B. Fine et al., eds., *Capitalism and the Rule of Law* (London: Hutchinson, 1979).

30. V. Navarro, *Medicine under Capitalism* (New York: Prodist, 1976); L. Doyal, *The Political Economy of Health* (London: Pluto Press, 1979).

31. M. Carnoy, *Education as Cultural Imperialism* (London: Longmans, 1978).

32. F. Fanon, *The Wretched of the Earth* (Harmondsworth: Penguin, 1967), p. 33.

33. F. Fanon, "Medicine and Colonialism," in *A Dying Colonialism* (New York: Monthly Review Press, 1965).

34. Doyal, *The Political Economy of Health*.

35. E. R. Brown, "Exporting Medical Education: Professionalization, Modernization and Imperialism," *Social Science and Medicine* 13 (November 1979): 585-600.

36. See, for example, R. Seidman, *The State, Law and Development* (New York: St. Martin's Press, 1978).

37. R. Del Olmo, "Limitations for the Prevention of Violence: The Latin American Reality and Its Criminological Theory," *Crime and Social Justice*, no. 13 (Summer 1975): 21-29.

38. A. Riera, "Latin American Radical Criminology," *Crime and Social Justice*, no. 11 (Spring 1979): 71-79.

39. Ibid., p. 72.

40. This does not happen inevitably. It is, of course, possible to take intentions seriously and at the same time (unlike in the benign transfer model) to understand other interests at stake. Thus, Brown argues that the Rockefeller philanthropists did not *intend* to create an inaccessible medical care system. They genuinely believed that their policies would serve China's health needs. Rather than lacking benevolence, "their humanitarianism was shaped by their ethnocentrism, their class interests and their support of the imperialist objectives of their own country. By the time their humanitarianism was expressed in programs, it was so intertwined with the interests of American capitalism as to be indistinguishable" (Brown, "Exporting Medical Education," p. 592).

41. S. Spitzer, "The Dialectics of Formal and Informal Control," in *The Politics of Informal Justice*, vol. 1, ed. R. Abel (New York: Academic Press, 1982).

42. See J. A. Cohen, "Reflections on the Criminal Process in China," *Journal of Criminal Law and Criminology* 68 (1977): 323-55; A. Wilson et al., eds., *Deviance and Social Control in Chinese Society* (New York: Praeger, 1977); and, especially, J. Brady,

Justice and Politics in People's China: Legal Order of Continuing Revolution (New York: Academic Press, 1984).

43. D. Rothman, *The Discovery of the Asylum* (Boston: Little, Brown, 1971), p. 295.

44. M. Ignatieff, *A Just Measure of Pain: The Penitentiary and the Industrial Revolution* (London: Macmillan, 1979), p. 209. For Foucault, the conventional notion of "success" and "failure" is also rejected but in a much more comprehensive way, a way that, despite his political affinity to the Marxist model, lends itself also to the paradoxical damage model's stress on systems of classification. The argument is that various projects of discipline, docility, and classification become ends in themselves; the question of success or failure is irrelevant. For an elaboration of this new model together with a comparison of the alternative models of changes in social control systems and ideologies, see S. Cohen, *Visions of Social Control: Crime, Punishment and Classification* (Cambridge: Polity Press, 1985).

45. Here I will be particularly drawing on his writings about medicine (*Limits to Medicine*); professions in general: *Disabling Professions* (London: Marion Boyars, 1977); and social policy: *Tools for Conviviality* (London: Calder and Boyars, 1973). Note also his suggestions in "Outwitting the 'Developed' Countries," in *Underdevelopment and Development: The Third World Today,* ed. H. Bernstein (Harmondsworth: Penguin, 1973).

46. Illich, *Disabling Professions,* p. 14.

47. Illich, *Limits to Medicine,* p. 45.

48. Ibid., pp. 85–104.

49. A banal example would be the standard countercultural laws that prohibit juveniles from wandering, begging, hawking, and trading at certain times or in certain places. This might not always be behavior that is encouraged, but it is not clear why it should be criminal. For this sort of analysis of African delinquency offenses, see Y. Brillon, *Crime, Justice and Culture in Black Africa* (Montreal: Centre International de Criminologie Comparee, University de Montreal, 1985). (Reviewed in chapter 12.)

50. J. Whetton, *Towards a Community Strategy for Criminal Justice,* Occasional Paper No. 7 (Centre for Development Studies, University College of Swansea, 1978).

51. N. Christie, "Conflicts as Property," *British Journal of Criminology,* 17 (January 1977): 1–15.

52. See Brillon, *Crime, Justice and Culture in Black Africa.* Ordinary people's loyalty to various systems of "tribal," indigenous, or customary justice is often in contrast to the professional classes, who find their interests best served in the Westernized system.

53. This argument needs stating in the West as well. There is considerable danger that the current onslaught against criminological positivism and the treatment ideal (under the banner of "back to justice" and "neoclassicism") will suppress the hidden humane agenda of positivism and lend unwitting support to the most reactionary and punitive crime control ideology. For some discussion of these problems, see chapter 8 and N. Christie, *Limits to Pain* (Oxford: Martin Robertson, 1981).

54. Fanon, *The Wretched of the Earth,* pp. 178–80.

55. For useful reviews of these areas, see R. L. Abel, "The Problem of Values in the Analysis of Political Order: Myths of Tribal Society and Liberal Democracy," *African Law Studies* 16 (1978): 132–65; and "Theories of Litigation in Society: Modern Dispute Settlements in 'Tribal' Society and 'Tribal' Dispute Settlements in 'Modern' Society," in *Alternative Rechsformen und Alternativen zun Recht. Jahrbuch fur*

Recchssoziolgie, and 6, ed. E. Blankenburg et al. (Opladen: Westdeutscher Verlag, 1979).

56. Berger, *Pyramids of Sacrifice*, p. 198.
57. Illich, *Limits to Medicine*, p. 36.
58. In the West, of course, the professionalization of lay crime control is well under way. As the criminal justice system gets more clogged, expensive, inflexible, and counterproductive, a new cadre of experts in self-help, conflict resolution, dispute mediation, arbitration facilitation, and conciliation are establishing themselves. There are an American Arbitration Association Community Dispute Services Department, an Institute for Mediation and Conflict Resolution, training courses in neighborhood conflict resolution financed by the Ford Foundation, and local justice centers financed by the Law Enforcement Assistance Administration. On the implications of these developments, see Abel's volumes, *The Politics of Informal Justice*, reviewed in chapter 11.
59. See P. Fitzpatrick, *Law and the State in Papua New Guinea* (New York: Academic Press, 1980).
60. R. L. Abel, "Delegalization: A Critical Review of Its Ideology, Manifestations and Social Consequences," in *Alternative Rechsformen udn Alternativen zun Recht. Jahrbuch fur Recchssoziolgie*, and 6, ed. E. Blankenburg, et al. (Opladen: Westdeutscher Verlag, 1979).

11

The Deeper Structures of the Law, or "Beware the Rulers Bearing Justice"*

Neither labeling theory of the sixties nor all the new, radical, critical, conflict, and Marxist criminologies of the seventies were false starts, dead ends, or gods that failed. They were simply staging points on the road back to rediscovering the buried — if tautological — truth of classical sociology and radical politics: the centrality of crime, law, and social control to any consideration of the social order. And both labeling theory (with its ironical worldview) and the new criminology (with its critical worldview) were but sophisticated variations on the old Chicago school's more gentle skepticism: society is not what the civics textbooks tell us it is.

In no other part of the crime, law, and social control terrain is this critical irony (ironical criticism?) more called for than in contemplating the supposed changes in the social control apparatus of Western liberal democracies over the past few decades. We appear to be at the peak of a profound destructuring impulse. Those deep structures of the late eighteenth century, so beautifully and (to my mind) convincingly exhumed by Foucault, are alleged to be fracturing. The rhetoric of reform became abolitionist. The slogans were literally destructive: deinstitutionalization, decarceration, deprofessionalization, delegalization, demedicalization, antipsychiatry, decentralization, deformalization, decriminalization, and so on. And when all those walls began to crumble, so new, looser, and so much *nicer* arrangements would be set up: community control, informalism, neighborhood justice, mediation, self-help, the culture of civility.

* "The Deeper Structures of the Law or 'Beware the Rulers Bearing Justice'" from *Contemporary Crises: Law, Crime and Social Policy*, Vol. 8 (April 1984), pp. 83–93. This was a review essay of: Richard Abel (ed.) *The Politics of Informal Justice, Volume One: The American Experience* and *Volume Two: Comparative Studies*, (New York: Academic Press, 1982).

Not much more than good, sensible sociology is needed to understand why and how things have not quite worked out like this. But for political radicals, the analytical problem is more complicated and more poignant. Committed to a worldview that (roughly speaking) believes that life in advanced captalist states must be getting worse and worse, their (our) analysis concludes that the destructuring promise not only has not been fulfilled but has led to insidious changes in the opposite direction. This conclusion is "poignant" because those changes were precisely the ones that seemed so appealing in the heady sixties, and even now would be difficult to repudiate. Who is *in favor* of a monopolistic legal profession, psychiatric imperialism, and increasing rates of long-term imprisonment?

The tasks, thus, for the inheritors of this skeptical intellectual tradition are fascinating and compelling: to reexamine the nature and causes of those original destructuring ideologies; to do careful empirical work on what is actually happening today; to explain what has "gone wrong"; and to rethink "what is to be done." Perhaps those original ideologies were too simple, perhaps they were never taken seriously, perhaps they were undermined by organizational or political imperatives, or perhaps ideology never matters much anyway.

These and many other analytical possibilities have already been explored, especially in areas such as decarceration and community control.[1] The area of delegalization and informal justice, though, is a much more difficult one to understand. The community-prison dichotomy is ideologically simple and the literature really quite primitive. But when we start talking about such matters as conflict resolution, dispute processing, and mediation and when we describe justice as "informal," "substantive," "socialist," or "popular," we are entering a much more ambiguous and difficult subject than that of criminology or "corrections." There is the whole of the anthropology of law; Marxist and non-Marxist formulations about law and the state; the special political role of legality in revolutionary politics; competing notions about the rule of law. A sharp eye and a steady hand are needed to guide us through these dark waters and we are fortunate to have such qualities in Richard Abel. His earlier sightings[2] have already been well used and he has now edited two exceptionally interesting volumes, with each of the twenty papers (grouped in volume 1 under *The American Experience* and in volume 2 under *Comparative Studies*) demanding separate attention.

In his introduction and his own chapter in volume 1 ("The Contradictions of Informal Justice"), Abel frames the three major projects for himself and his fellow contributors. First, to unravel the reasons behind "what may well be" this major transformation in our legal system: the apparent movement against formal legal institutions, rights, and processes and toward informal justice (that is, the declaration, modification, application, and negotiation of legal norms in ways that are supposed to be relatively nonbureaucratic, undifferentiated, decentralized, nonprofessional, and autonomous from the formal legal system). Second, to show that the contours of this change are uncertain and its significance ambiguous ("What is it that is really changing: ideology, substantive norms, processes or institutions? Is the ambit of state control contracting or expanding? What impact will these changes have on fundamental social, economic, and political structures? Or is it all a lot of talk, with minimal significance for anyone except those who manage the legal system?") And third, the sometimes unstated but always present agenda for most of the contributors, to suggest the implications of all this for the project of human liberation — variously conceived as "society without law," "socialist legality," or, in Spitzer's words ("The Dialectics of Formal and Informal Control," volume 1), "peeling away the legal integument, exploding the legal myths and dismantling the legal institutions that stand in the way of human emancipation."

I will provide a selective viewing of each of these three common issues.

Cycles and Crises

The competing explanations for the various movements in the West toward rejection of formal legal institutions can be easily distinguished if not evaluated. In Abel's classification, theories are *idealist* (stressing the growing disenchantment with state intervention; hostility toward bureaucracy; pragmatic demonstrations of system failure or inefficiency); *materialist* (stressing the changing exigencies of welfare capitalism; the fiscal crisis; the need for new measures to discipline labor and control surplus populations); *political* (stressing the legitimacy crisis, in which the state "regroups its forces," concentrating on areas of conflict where less coercive methods can be used); and *professional* (stressing the more or less autonomous role of welfare professionals in expanding their jurisdiction and fostering dependency on their services).

Alongside these theories is the model of "cycles" (of formalism and informalism), which Abel heavily relied upon in his earlier work but here dismisses — somewhat too casually, I believe — as being "idealist." One can avoid the idealist and Spenglerian overtones of this notion by using it as Spitzer does in his "dialectical" analysis of episodes of formalism and informalism in China since the revolution. Here we see clear reform cycles between "law as form" and "law as substance," each movement provoking reactions and counterreactions. It seems to me also a pity that the "professional-power" model, particularly the Illich-inspired critique of "radical monopolies," receives no attention at all from any of Abel's contributors.

In fact, most of them, whether in the American or comparative sections, rely on a somewhat-taken-for-granted political economy model to explain the dynamics of legal change. This works except when it is used rather heavy-handedly, as in Hofrichter's paper connecting the neighborhood justice movement with the "social control problems of American capitalism." *If* social control is simply "the material and ideological means by which the economic and political order is reproduced in capitalist society" and *if* the essence of American (why just American?) capitalism is the "unending effort" by the social class that owns and controls the apparatus of production to increase the rate of capital accumulation, then, of course, no other connections are possible.

But well within Marxism itself powerful objections have been raised to the one-dimensional, Mickey Mouse view of social control in which the class struggle somehow remains "constant" but its fluctuating forms and content call for the institutions of regulation, containment, and mediation to disguise their true functions. It may well be that the emergence of Neighborhood Justice Centers is associated with "transformations in the character of the class struggle, requirements for the reproduction of labour and systemic tendencies that propel advanced capitalism in the United States," but this is not at all the whole story, nor is the argument strengthened by the glib inclusion of "mental institutions" as one of these stage props of capitalism.[3]

But here, as elsewhere, there is valuable analysis both of historical antecedents and current developments. Note, for example, Garlock's account of the Knights of Labour courts at the end of the nineteenth century and Harrington's review of previous and current delegalization reform movements. In one way or another, all contributors address themselves to Abel's questions: Why do we find *these* changes? Why are they occurring now? Are they "real" changes? And if so, are they "progressive"? Given the contradictory role of law in advanced capitalism, the answers to all those questions remain "complex and qualified."

"Contradictory" as the ultimate status of informalism is judged to be, it clearly expresses ideals that are widely embraced and deeply resonant. This is the point most forcibly made in de Sousa Santos's paper. I am afraid that I got lost in his general thesis about the changing nature of state power in capitalism. His notions about power dislocations and the asymmetrical nature of the core and the periphery seemed helpful, but other images, such as the "dynamics of multiple structural articulations," were definitely less so. He is clear enough, though, in pointing to the error—made by some of his fellow contributors—of dismissing current reforms as "sheer manipulation and state conspiracy." The reform movements toward informalism and community justice evoke powerful symbols of participation, self-government, and real community. There are "utopian transcendental," even "potentially liberating" elements here, even if they are imprisoned and distorted in the overall state structure of social control.

Beware the Greeks

All the contributors sense this liberatory presence, although only in those "comparative" studies in volume 2 that deal with socialist-type transformations—Portugal, Chile, Mozambique—is it allowed credible expression. For the masses under late capitalism, the message is skeptical in the extreme: beware your rulers bearing gifts of justice.

Following Foucault—an omniscient if not always acknowledged presence—informalism must or already has or soon will expand the reach and power of the state. That is, the loosening of structures merely allows repressive power (in the standard hydraulic metaphor) to "spill over" the walls and "permeate" the social fabric. The liberatory element is illusory. Behind the comforting facade of informalism there is a hidden political mechanism "by which the state extends its control to manage capital accumulation and defuse the resistance this engenders" (Abel).

Ideology, then, is "Orwellian newspeak" (Abel), an Alice-in-Wonderland in which everything is its opposite. *Informal* means created and sustained by the formal state apparatus; *decentralized* means centrally controlled; *accessibility* means rendering justice more inaccessible; *noncoercive* means disguising coercion; *community* means nothing; *informalism* means undermining existing non state models of informal control; *benevolent* is beginning to mean malign. This is more or less the sad message from Scull's account of the community corrections movement ("Panacea, Progress or Pretense") and Lazerson's detailed case study of how referrals to the New York City Housing Court ("institutionalized legal informality") in fact eroded rather than improved the legal position of tenants.

In one way or another these analyses point to Spitzer's (surely correct) generalization: the dispersal and deformalization of control is not at all inconsistent with the functional expansion of the state. He does well to quote Adorno (the Frankfurt school understood a paradox when it saw one):

> Whatever raises from within itself a claim to be autonomous, critical and antithetical—while at the same time never being able to assert this claim with total legitimacy—must necessarily come to naught; this is particularly true when its impulses are integrated into something heteronomous to them which has been worked out previously from above—that is to say, when it is granted the space to draw breath immediately by that power against which it rebels.

But "come to naught" is a heavy sentence. E.P. Thompson's reminders about the liberatory potential of legal formalism, or at least the equivocal and ambiguous nature of the bourgeois legal form, must be extended to informalism as well. The flat picture of legal informalism as a mere "rhetorical device," a "comfortable facade," must be changed (as Spitzer and Abel eventually suggest) to a final evaluation that leaves its political and moral status as provisional or "confusing at best." Above all we must remember that movements toward formalism or informalism (or indeed any other type of legal change) take on different political meanings according to how and by whom they are created and used.[4]

What Is to Be done?

There can, of course, be no better way of understanding the meaning of informalism than by comparing the actual social contexts in which it has appeared. The ten comparative studies in volume 2 — on nonindustrial societies, fascist states, welfare capitalism, and socialist revolutionary transformations — all help us here as well as being of intrinsic interest. They are either cautious or enthusiastic, reflecting the dilemma of informalism itself.

Caution comes when contemplating the meaning of informalism in nonindustrial social formations where informal justice has provided the model or ideal. Merry's useful review of the anthropological literature on small-scale pastoral and agricultural societies where mediation is the dominant mode of settling disputes shows how much we have idealized and misunderstood the whole process. The focus on consensual and conciliatory qualities has ignored the important role of coercion and power. And further, the "transplant" of the model to complex heterogenous urban neighborhoods is uncritical and misplaced. Precapitalist legal informalism cannot simply be used as a "model"; it is embedded in and contingent upon a social structure incompatible with Western capitalism. As Abel nicely comments: "It is not surprising . . . that when informal legal institutions are introduced into Western capitalism societies they do not help to preserve relationships (though they are often justified by invoking this goal) but rather serve to celebrate their termination." And in their study of village courts in Uttar Pradesh, Meschievitz and Galanter show how a mixed system might manifest the worst attributes of traditional and more modern legal forms.

A far more dramatic and less academic note of caution appears in the three papers on societies at the edge of facism. The cases are the organization of legal advice for workers in pre-fascist Germany (a turgid and unilluminating paper); informal justice in Japan between 1942 and 1944; and summary justice in Argentina in 1977. The German and Japanese cases, in which for different political reasons informalism embodied an ideology of the "higher good" to which individual rights had to defer, show how the voluntary element becomes compelling and controlling. This, as Abel argues, serves as a discomforting parallel to contemporary informalism in capitalism.

But more discomforting (and to my mind more interesting) are the comparisons between Argentinian summary justice and the rhetoric or form of popular justice under socialism. Ietswaart's fascinating paper is based entirely on the linguistic characteristics of official communiques from the Argentinian military regime (between March and November 1977) as it began to eliminate all political opposition and subversion. These are narrative texts describing the day-to-day struggle with the enemy; this is not bland "social control" but instant execution on the streets. Her argument (after dissecting the paradigmatic difference between formal and popular justice) is that the deeper linguistic structures of the military communiques reveal, in fact, a cruel parody, a caricature of the ideology of popular justice. The point is not simply to demonstrate this distortion but to show how the form is "free" enough to allow such an application.

A linguistic feature of summary military justice is the judgment of deviants in terms of their conformity to general principles rather than their departure from a fixed and finite number of legal rules (positivism rather than classicism?). It is not behavior but *essence* that is being judged: the whole person. Being subversive is the crime, not doing anything. It is therefore not too important to establish exactly what happened or even the consequences of the behavior. Conventional notions of legal causality and responsibility are distorted. And always, as in the rhetoric of popular justice, the public is "linguistically present": being informed, behaving cooperatively, watching as approving witnesses—and then, in all the "arrogance" of this type of discourse, being asked ultimately to approve:

> The Zone 1 Command informs the public that another victory has been gained over Marxist subversion, thanks to the spontaneous and valuable collaboration of the neighbours of the house who informed the forces of the law about suspect happenings in a dwelling. . . .

> The Zone 1 Command wishes to point out that in this unremitting battle we are waging, delinquent subversives will continue to perish until their complete extermination, so as to restore peace and tranquility to the inhabitants of the Fatherland.

Note that Ietswaart is talking about the similarities between the *discourses* of popular and summary justice; she is not making any crude political point about the one "leading" to the other. But even this subtle analytical caution is missing in the evangelical enthusiasm that usually greets informalist and popular experiments during socialist legal transformations. Dialectical skills (not to mention common sense) are suspended and the most outrageous state propaganda is accepted without question.

In abstract terms (and it is by no means apparent that the three cases considered here, Mozambique, Chile, and Portugal, conform to this) the program is one of removing the coercive, constraining, and dehumanizing features of the law as a precondition of human liberation. This entails—as Spitzer reminds us — not just a stripping away (destructuring), not just a delegalization of social relations (freeing them from "the stranglehold of legal thought") but the creation of a model social order. Yet, here comes the problem: "It is only as the social order is re-invented that the student of law can fully understand the essential embeddedness of the legal order in everyday life" (Spitzer).

We have, then, two paradoxical warnings about the deeper structures of the law: one revealed by discourse analysis, one revealed by the dialectical study of remaking the legal order either in failed socialist revolutions (like Chile) or in the aftermath of more successful ones (such as Cuba and China). I would have preferred to find a greater sense of such paradoxes in Spence's otherwise very informative review of the experiments with neighborhood courts in Allende's Chile and, more particularly, in the Isaacsons' rather breathless guide to the making of a socialist legal system in postrevolutionary Mozambique. What they describe is a *formalization* of a system of popular justice, a dispersal of the practices improvised in Frelimo's liberated zones before it took over the state. We need not be cynical when viewing this transformation — but at the same time we should not be romantic. A certain measure of romanticism (and a lack of awareness of the deeper structures of such propaganda exercises in the capitalist state as well) informs their bland acceptance of the claims of juvenile penal institutions to be so busy reintegrating, reeducating, and rehabilitating.[5]

Of these three reports from the revolutary front, it is de Sousa Santo's now-well-known account of the experiments with popular justice in Portugal after April 1974 that is the most illuminating and subtle. He has a quite clear model of the differences between class justice and socialist legality and uses it consistently to argue that popular justice during a revolutionary crisis is a form of revolutionary law in action, but in this case an embryo of the new power structure rather than a stage toward it.

The argument is illustrated by two forms of legal struggles: for the redefinition of criminal justice, and for the right to decent housing. In the first form our "leading case" is Jose Diogo, a poor rural worker arrested by the G.N.R. for having stabbed a rich landowner. He is indicted for murder, expresses a political vocabulary of motives (the landowner is a "fascist beast," a "hangman," an "enemy of the people") and in a confused political context, with the legal system in crisis, he appears before a popular tribunal that determines that he has "committed no crime," even though his was an individual, not political act. Here (and in the housing example) de Sousa Santos gives a vivid sense of the confused struggle between the old and new forms of legality as the state bureaucracy began to regroup its forces.[6]

The struggle is the familiar one between "justice" and "social justice": the use of *individual* judgments to resolve structural contradictions. It is not clear, however, that the experiments described by de Sousa Santos actually correspond to Abel's characterization of informalism during a transitionary legal period: the anticipation and prevention of future problems rather than redress of past injustice. In a sense the opposite is true. Nor is it apparent that litigation is avoided as an individualist form of political action, a hangover from bourgeois justice. In the transitional period popular justice tries to repudiate the legitimacy of the state and pronounces its own verdicts that "often exculpate conduct that the bourgeois state had penalized and condemns behaviour that it had excused."

This suggests that both in the transitional and final phases of socialist legality we are simply talking about different systems of allocating punishment (or, as Nils Christie prefers, of deciding on levels of pain infliction). The implied contrast in these volumes between "informalism" under capitalism (bad) and under socialism (good) often circumvents this question. And in the absence of a comprehensive survey of what "socialist legality" has actually turned out to be for millions of people in our times (a survey these volumes were obviously not designed to provide), we must remain skeptical of some of its pretensions. And, what, I wonder, are we meant to make of these words of Otelo Saraiva de Carvalho (who, according to de Sousa Santos) "summarized the idea of revolutionary justice better than anyone else":

> There are no limits on revolutionary legality but those imposed by good sense and revolutionary coherence. . . . Experience tells us which are the good measures and which are the bad". Asked about the criterion for the distinction between good measures and bad, Otelo answered: "The benefit for the workers. If the working class accepts our measures that means we are on the right path."

The final fruits of this joyous pragmatism were, of course, not to be reached in Portugal. The transitional period was one of competing jurisdictions, each pronouncing its own verdicts. In the end, the state apparatus did not collapse; it suffered a paralysis during which "pockets of dual power" remained.

The lesson drawn is that informal justice plays an important but eventually limited and symbolic part in the revolutionary struggle; only a "foretaste" because the state can co-opt, ignore, or undermine this challenge to its authority. Even in historical cases (unlike, of course, Portugal and Chile) where informalism appears to triumph, formalism — the deeper structure of the law — retains an ambigous presence. Reformalization, argues Abel, is inevitable, the tension between informal popular justice and formal bureaucratized legality is never properly resolved: "The struggle for informal justice never ends."

And so the question "What is to be done?" remains, opaquely, on the agenda. The revolutionary crisis, de Sousa Santos maintains, gives us only negative knowledge. We learn what not to do. The day after starting this review, I participated in a discussion in a peace group in Israel about alternative strategies for resisting the military occupation of the West Bank. Part of the argument concerned legality. One side argued that because the government had been systematically evading or breaking the law, we were justified, indeed obliged, to do the same. By using illegal means, we could draw attention to an alternative notion of justice. The other side argued that as long as the rule of law was even nominally present, our greatest strength would be to remain scrupulously legal ourselves while exploiting the formal system to find loopholes or to expose and ridicule the authorities.

This sort of dilemma is, of course, hardly related to the macropolitics of informal justice and even less to the overall conflict between bourgeois and socialist legality. I mention it only to remind us of the obvious: at any particular moment the choice is moral and tactical, not theoretical. The poverty of theory is reflected in Abel's comparison of the E.P. Thompson argument about preserving the "rule of law" (as a rhetoric that at least inhibits power) with that of his critics (who point to the interdependence of law and order). The choice, he suggests, "will ultimately depend on whether we emphasize the hegemonic or instrumental function of the law in capitalist society."

But this does not help much; it merely restates the problem in different words. Such is sociology.

Notes

1. I review this in *Visions of Social Control* (New York: Basil Blackwell, 1985).
2. Notably, R. Abel, "Delegalization: A Critical Review of Its Ideology, Manifestations and Social Consequences," and "Theories of Litigation in Society: 'Modern' Dispute Settlements in 'Tribal' Society and 'Tribal' Dispute Settlements in 'Modern' Society," in *Alternative Rechsformen und Alternativen zun Recht. Jahrbuch fur Recchssoziologie* band 6, ed. E. Blankenburg et al. (Opladen: Westdeutscher Verlag, 1979).
3. A socialist attempt to expose the *conservative* undercurrents of various fashionable versions of the "psychiatry-equals-social-control" thesis is Peter Sedgewick's recent polemic *Psychopolitics* (London: Pluto Press, 1982).
4. In respect to crime control policy and the so-called justice movement, this point has been most eloquently made by Nils Christie; see his *Limits to Pain* (Oxford: Martin Robertson, 1981). For an even more concrete political setting of criminal justice policy (in postwar Britain), see Ian Taylor, *Law and Order* (London: Macmillan, 1982). Perhaps because of their largely North American origin, Abel and his contributors are strangely silent about matters that quite rightly occupy Taylor and other British or European commentators: the changing shape of the welfare state, social democracy, and (most important, and particularly ignored in these volumes) the concept of civil liberties.
5. And what measure of revolutionary chic will be needed in the future to describe public floggings and other such current legal innovations in Mozambique as examples of "informal justice"?
6. We are told that in June 1976 — after the military group in favor of popular power was defeated, the COPCON dissolved, and the legal apparatus reestablished itself — that Diogo was "hunted down" by the police after failing to come to court on the trial date. We do not learn of his eventual fate.

12

Taking Decentralization Seriously: Values, Visions, and Policies*

The decentralization of social control—What is it? Is it happening? Is it desirable? Is it possible?—must be understood as part of a complex package of ideologies, theories, and social movements that captured liberal and radical thinking about social control over the past two decades. My subject in this paper is not the social origins of this package nor the actual (or alleged) changes that have been caused by (or accompanied) it. I have given such an account elsewhere, setting out the two intellectual strategies that have been used to understand shifts in social control theory and policy.[1] The first is to locate specific changes (in rhetoric or practice) in terms of overall master patterns that are conceived in sociological, historical, or archeological terms (progress, rationalization, extension of discipline, legitimation crises, epistemological breaks, or whatever). The second is to conceive these changes as the product of particular reform movements (such as diversion, antipsychiatry, or decriminalization) and then to use the tools of social policy analysis to examine such matters as implementation, consequences, and evaluation.

These remain the most important subjects on the sociological agenda. We are still some way from knowing why the old system was challenged so radically, what the meaning of these challenges was, what changes (if any) have taken place, and how to account for the apparent gap between intentions and results. My paper, however, is less an addition to this analytic literature than a slightly distant reflection on it. In particular, I will be concerned with the stated or implied preferences—values, visions, and policies—to which this literature has been leading. My method will be to trace a Pilgram's Progress: from inspiration, then disillusionment, through to cautious reaffirmation.

* "Taking Decentralization Seriously: Values, Visions and Policies" from John Lowman et al. (eds.), *Transcarceration: Essays in the Sociology of Social Control* (London: Gower, 1987).

Inspired by Alternatives

There was something genuinely creative in the impulse that some twenty years ago in North America and Western Europe took hold of much liberal and radical thinking about crime and punishment, deviance and social control. Of course there were antecedents (labeling theory could be traced back to Durkheim, decentralization is the base of the classical anarchist tradition), and of course there were elements of confusion, romanticism, and downright silliness. But the creative edge of what Pearson called the "deviant imagination" was its sense that matters of deviance and social control were integral to the constitution of the good society. That is: the theory and practice of social control could not be resolved in technicist and positivist terms; these were political issues.

This impulse expressed itself in many diverse ways: in the formation of movements aimed to weaken, bypass, or even abolish conventional structures of legality, punishment, control, and treatment; in the advocacy and actual setting up of innovative and radical alternatives to the conventional system; in the struggles of various deviant, criminal, and other stigmatized groups against the institutions and ways of thinking that had imprisoned them; in the adaptation of various sociological theories and political ideologies (labeling, Marxist, libertarian, and others) to rationalize these movements; and in the development within criminology, law, social work, and psychiatry of various "radical," "critical," or "counter" cultures: intellectuals and activists dedicated to reconstituting their disciplines and professions.

These diverse streams of thought and practice can be classifed in a number of different ways. First, they varied in terms of their commitment to what I have called "destructuring" and what in Western Europe is known as "abolitionism." Sometimes the negative, destructive tone was muted ("Look, why don't you at least try this as an alternative to the old system"); sometimes it was moderately utopian ("Abolish first, then let's talk about alternatives"); sometimes abolitionism was proclaimed proudly as a value for its own sake. Second, they ranged from liberal, reformist movements that were continuous with Progressivist, Fabian, and other such middle-range accommodative tendencies to more genuinely radical and theoretically informed visions, glimpses of an alternative social order and not just different "methods of control." The one edge was pragmatic, the other visionary. And third, there was a different emphasis about just *what* should be abolished or destructured. Some stressed physical apparatuses and visible practices (prisons, criminal justice agencies, mental hospitals); others wanted to get rid of accepted thought processes and cognitive categories (positivist criminology, the very concept of crime, the medical model of mental illness). This corresponds more or less to Foucault's difference between nondiscursive and discursive practices.

Such variations—how abolitionist, how radical, and how idealist—appear in each of the various components of the destructuring package. These components are easily identified in the negative terminology of *de*, *anti*, and *non*:

- *Decarceration* (or deinstitutionalization, prison abolition): to close down or phase out the traditional closed institutions (prisons, asylums) and to locate control, treatment, and care in the open community.
- *Diversion*: to deflect various offenders from being processed by the official criminal justice apparatus and to direct them instead into innovative community-based agencies not formally a part of the official system.
- *Decategorization* (also delabeling, destigmatization): to break down the various discourses and cognitive systems that create categories of deviance. Thus, decriminalization tries to reduce the scope of the state's power to declare certain behavior criminal; abolitionism wants to dispense altogether with the concept of crime; anti-psychiatry questions the whole status of mental illness as an illness.
- *Delegalization* (and deformalization, informal justice): to find new forms and to cultivate traditional forms of justice, dispute resolution, and conflict mangement outside the formal criminal system.
- *Deprofessionalization*: in place of the structures of professional monopoly and power (in criminal justice, social work, or psychiatry), to set up networks of citizen control, public participation, self-help and mutual help, and informal care.

The common core of these overlapping (and sometimes incongruent) strategies lies in some notion of *decentralized community control*. In its less ambitious versions this is a project of traditional liberal reformism within the interstices of the social democratic state. In its more ambitious versions the very hegemonic systems of power and knowledge identified with the centralized state were to be broken up and returned to the people. Ideally, for pragmatists and visionaries alike, all this should take place at each of the three fateful stages through which deviants (notably delinquents and criminals) are processed, that is: identification (categorization, labeling, detection); adjudication (justice, sentencing, diagnosis, allocation); and disposal (deployment, punishment, treatment).

The inspiration behind the prosiac phrase "decentralized community control" can be understood in another way: a vision of *inclusion* rather than *exclusion* as the preferred mode of social control. The traditional exclusionary mode was the product of the original projects of rationalization associated with the birth of the modern state: centralization, criminalization, classification, segregation, professionalization. These projects created the great structures of knowledge and power that are known as the "criminal justice" and other such systems. Exclusion means physical separation (segregation, isolation, and incarceration behind walls) and also social separation, the allocation of individuals to categories of deviance via the process of what Foucault calls "normalization."

The destructuring and abolitionist movements, on the other hand, represent the moment when the inclusionary impulse dominated social control rhetoric. The structures of knowledge and power that allow for exclusion should now be weakened, bypassed, or eliminated altogether. Inclusion means incorporation, integration, and assimilation. Deviants are to be retained physically as long as possible within the boundaries of conventional institutions (family, school, neighborhood, workplace) and conceptually within the bounds of ordinary knowledge. This is "normalization" not in Foucault's definition (distribution according to the certified metrics or normality) but in Lemert's exactly opposite definition of the same term: accommodation to rule breaking before setting in motion the rituals of exclusion.

These, then, are some ways of visualizing the inspirations and alternatives of the sixties: reform movements, abolitionist attacks, destructuring ideologies, the vision of inclusion. The analytical task, as I have said, still remains: looking for historical roots, background assumptions, theoretical genealogies, and political strategies.

But the sociological pilgrim who moves straight from this visit into the past to contemplating the present "state of the art" about social control will encounter some rather strange problems. In the discourse of conventional criminology it looks as if nothing at all has changed. True, there are now courses and textbooks on "Community Corrections," and true, they tell of new agencies, professionals, and methods. But there is no sense of any visionary transformation. The reforms have been absorbed and integrated. Here, at the center of the discourse, it is business as usual. But in the critical literature on law, social control, justice, and the state—the literature that does not even like to call itself criminology[2]—all is not well.

Confronted by Reality

If the last half of the 1960s was the moment of the counterculture, the dawning of the Age of Aquarius—walls to be torn down, chains to be removed, experts to be defrocked, possibilities of another world to be revealed—so a decade later came the Age of Realism. Taking stock in the seventies became a bleak business. And also a sophisticated business: demystification not just of the old fossilized structures, always easy targets for criticism, but of the very alternatives and visions that radicals had themselves offered in the good years.

Conservative ideologists did not have to do very much of this hard work. Liberals, civil libertarians, and empirical social scientists had unintentionally helped them by showing that good intentions lead to bad consequences, benevolent treatment ends up as coercion, less harm is better than more good, everything costs too much, and anyway nothing works. The "new realists of crime control"[3] had little trouble establishing their hegemony.

The radical discourse took longer to find its consensus — radicals have never been strong on "evaluation" of their own intentions — but eventually a disturbing pattern of conclusions revealed itself. A new orthodoxy emerged. In the wider left-intellectual culture this took the form of a distancing from and discrediting of erstwhile mentors and their theories. So Marcuse, Laing, Illich, Fanon were dismissed for their idealism, utopianism, and romantic excesses. *New Left* became a term of contempt. A harder, grimmer, and more realistic form of theory and praxis was found, for example, in the structural Marxism of Althusser and (from an opposite direction but equally antagonistic to the New Left visionary politics) in the stern histories of E.P. Thompson.[4]

In the much narrower world of social control theory and "critical criminology" the disenchantment did not immediately take quite this portentous form. Still, echoes of the same themes began to emerge in critical thinking about decarceration and community control, delegalization and informal justice, and (most explicitly) anti-psychiatry. Cain's recent summary [5] of the radical critique of informal justice can be transposed to any one part or whole of the destructuring package:

- It is *unnecessary*: an elaborate new infrastructure of agencies has been set up to deal with conflicts that would have been handled and solved informally anyway (it only by "lumping it").
- It is a *failure in its own terms*: informal justice is not always cheap; it does not work like its supposed prototypes (moots, village courts); it deals with the wrong cases (only the trivia); it becomes a subsidiary rather than substitute form of justice; its practitioners and practices are not those of the "real" local community; it becomes professionalized, co-opted, and dependent on the official system for referrals; in short, it becomes reformalized.
- It is *sinister*: it solves the state's problems of legitimacy by deflecting potential criticism and opposition; it neutralizes and individualizes conflict; it disguises coercion; it extends the net of state social control.
- It is *impossible anyway*: the project of transferring models from one society or period to another is hopelessly idealist; justice is a state-organized, centralized system, and so the notion of informal justice is a contradiction in terms.

Cain's list could be reproduced almost identically from the late 1970s evaluations of decarceration, community control, and diversion. Thus:

- Reforms and alternatives are supported for the wrong reasons (fiscal crises, legitimation crises, or whatever).
- The old structures (prison, juvenile institutions, professional monopolies)

still remain and are even becoming stronger. Despite "community control," rates of incarceration increase, despite "decentralization," the reach of the centralized state widens.

- Alternatives are co-opted and absorbed. These reforms turn out to be not (in Mathiesen's terms) "abolitionist reforms" but "legitimating reforms"; the old regime is strengthened rather than weakened.
- The new structures are neither cheaper, nor more humane, nor more effective.
- All sorts of previously unimagined problems and dangers (Cain's "sinister" results) have now been created: the net of social control intensified and widened, and coercion disguised.

And here is yet another way of classifying the dismal message of the new evaluators, by looking at the supposed objects of social control:

- The weak, pathetic, and sick — they are subject to too little "control." Neglected and deprived of help, treatment, and services (under the libertarian, noninterventionist banners of decarceration and anti-psychiatry), they are left to suffer silently or be exploited by commercial interest. They should be looked after.
- The petty or "potential" delinquents — they are subject to more instrusive and disguised control (net widening) in the name of diversion or prevention. They should be left alone, as they were before all the new alternatives came along.
- The parties to minor conflicts and disputes — they too find themselves subject to new and ineffectual forms of intervention and conflict resolution that merely neutralize real social conflicts. They should be left to solve their problems naturally (as they always did) or alternatively be given proper access to the full power of the formal legal system.
- The hard core, serious criminals — they are subject to further degradation. As the soft end of the system appears more and more benign, so the hard core (chronics, recidivists) appear more helpless and become easy targets for such policies as selective incapacitation.
- The powerful — they are still left free to carry out their depredations. Their actions should be criminalized and subject to the full weight of the formal punishment system.
- The ordinary population — they are subjected to further and more subtle involvement in the business of social control. Everyday life becomes "controlized" by "Crime Prevention Through Environmental Design," secret agents and informers, new systems of surveillance of public space, data banks. Whole populations are made the object of preventive social control before any deviant act can take place.

A final way of summarizing the conclusion of the new evaluation would be to say that reforms motivated by the inclusionary impulse are misguided. They fail precisely because they lead to further forms of exclusion. Thus, the decision whom to include calls for an act of formal classification, and this means further separation; inclusionary agencies are dependent for their space and clientele on the state's exclusionary apparatus, which then absorbs them; inclusionary alternatives still remain staffed by state-accredited professionals; the dispersal of control through decentralization ends up drawing in new (that is, previously included) populations; even inclusion by tolerance leads to forms of ecological separation and the ghettoization of deviant populations.

These are all different ways of arriving at the same set of dismal conclusions. Things have not turned out the way they were supposed to; unintended consequences are always bad; things are worse than they seem, and they are getting even worse.

Now, of course, this a caricature. The new reflective literature is by no means uniform in its tone or direction. There is, especially, a great deal of difference between critics who feel that the original inspirations were misguided and those who still retain at least some of the vision and do not regard failure as inevitable. And the literature is full of internal inconsistencies. At times the emerging patterns are "sinister" because they are new and incomprehensible, at other times, because they are merely a replication of the same old story. Alternatives are simultaneously denounced for their proliferation and for the fact that they are not actually being implemented. (Abel, for example, after showing that informalism extends state control, neutralizes conflict, redistributes state resources to the privileged, advances professional interests, and legitimates state and capital, then notes, "Despite the current surge of enthusiasm for informalism, there are relatively few programs and these are underfunded and little used."[6]) Particular "success stories" — rape crisis centers, the gay movement — are lavishly praised but then ignored in the overall evaluations.

To be charitable to those of us who took part in this debunking, it must be said that the confusion was in the world and not just the observers' theories. The results of the destructuring movements were indeed complicated, ambiguous, contradictory, and dialectical. But it was only the dark side of the dialectic that was exposed. To travel from the radical social control literature of the mid-1960s to its equivalent in the mid-1980s is to sense not just confusion (which would be fine) but a different sense of the possible.

Stranded by Demystification

Various theories of different levels of sophistication and persuasion have been proposed to explain how this sad state of affairs came about. They can be divided into four main groups:

- (1) The original values, visions, and preferences are still to be commended (or at least not denounced), but there was a policy problem. The programs were simply not implemented in the way they should have been. Things go wrong. You feed good ideas into organizations, but the plan gets fouled up because of misunderstandings, the wrong allocation of resources, or political obstructionism.

- (2) A more sophisticated version of the first theory also leaves the original values unquestioned but places the blame for failure in the hands of the professional establishment. Acting as ever out of relentless self-interest and the imperative to expand at all costs, professionals will distort and blunt any radical impulse by exploiting it for their own ends. Thus, the police take over diversion programs; experts organize dispute settlements; professional therapists initiate self-help groups.

- (3) In yet another version of the first two theories, associated with David Rothman's well-known histories, there is a recurrent historical tension between "conscience" and "convenience." Again, there is the process of undermining and co-optation: organizations and professions absorb good ideas but transform them to meet managerial imperatives and wider functional needs. Moreover the ideas themselves — conscience, doing good, humanitarian reform — are open to some suspicion. There are limits to benevolence.

- (4) The final group of theories rests on a built-in omniscience about all liberal social reform. Armed with the right conceptual apparatus, we should have seen from the beginning that nothing good could have come from the original reform visions. It is obvious that these ideas have undeclared purposes, and it is equally obvious that they will "fail" because there are underlying historical processes (an extension of discipline, rationalization, or whatever) that unfold themselves despite and independent of the intentions and proclamations of reformers.

Each of these four theories makes good sense in its own way, but I am less interested here in the adequacy of the causal explanation than in the political preference that is derived from the analysis. What we find here is that the models that are analytically the weakest, those that insist on the naive distinction between theory (knowledge) and practice (power), are also those that allow for the most transparent reading of values. If you say that a good idea was badly implemented, the idea remains good. But if you say that all good intentions end up badly or (in the more sophisticated and radical of the theories) that good intentions do not matter too much anyway, then it is not too clear what you think about the values behind those intentions.

Why does all this matter? Simply becuase the proponents of the original destructuring and abolitionist ideas were not always "them", the people whom the theories are criticizing: the managers, bureaucrats, technicist criminologists, the powerful. They were us. *We* were the ones who wanted to abolish prisons, to weaken professional monopolies, to find forms of justice and conflict resolutions outside the official system, to undermine the power of the centralized state, to create possibilities for real community and social justice. Critical scholarship has well exposed the problems of this original agenda, but the very effectiveness of this demystification job is a little embarrassing. One has to distance oneself from those original ideas and reforms: dismiss one's enthusiastic support for them as matters of false consciousness or perhaps a product of overenthusiastic youthful exuberance. Life seems more complicated as you get older; about that early love you say "Well, yes, I wasn't really in love at the time; I only thought I was."

This distancing takes two forms. The first is to reassert the role of the intellectual as outsider and simply to resume the task of radical demystification. Critical theory continues exposing flaws, debunking, and showing that things are not what they seem, and, of course, are never *better* than they seem. At its extreme, this leads to the variety of radical impossibilism that asserts that all reforms are doomed and that despairs of the prospect of any real changes short of a total transformation of the social order. Thus *radical pessimism* joins the old conservative pessimism of the "realists of crime control" (people and society are beyond change; stay with the old remedies, however partial) and the newer neoliberal pessimism (benevolence invariably goes wrong; avoid harm rather than do good, settle for restricted goals).

This is an altogether familiar stance: pessimism combined with the dread of reformism. The second form of distancing, however, is rather strange: an actual reversal of earlier positions. Confronted on the one hand by the apparent failures of the radical visions of the 1960s and on the other by the hegemony of conservative ideology, an influential group of radical criminologists in Britain and North America has begun a massive stocktaking of its earlier theoretical and political perspective. The result has been the emergence of what has been called the *left realist, socialist realist,* or *radical realist* position.[7] By some irony the term *realist* — used less than a decade ago to denounce the bleak, unimaginative policies of conservatives and neoliberals — is now proudly asserted as a value.

This is not the place for even a summary, let alone a full evaluation, of this important new paradigm or its many implications for theoretical criminology. On the more limited question of what happened to the destructuring vision, two strands in the left realist position emerged. The first, at the metatheoretical level, draws directly on the changes in the wider left intellectual culture. The theories of the sixties — labeling, the early phase of the "new criminology" — are denounced as the product of "New Left excesses"; they are "romantic," "petty bourgeois," "Fanonist." Above all, the new theories were guilty of the thought-crime of "left idealism": they had been constructed merely by inverting the paradigms of positivism and correctionalism. But this idealist project simply did not reflect social reality. Crime is not a myth but a real threat to the powerless (the working class, women, minority groups); traditional positivist questions of causation still remain on the agenda; the point is not to abandon law and order but to construct a socialist version of law and order. The fight should be on the conservatives' own terrain, the reality of crime, and not on some promised land of the future.

This leads to the second strand in the left realist paradigm: a renewed appreciation of certain elements in the old system. The criminal law model, criminalization and punishment,[8] must be retained for street crime and expanded to cover the crimes of the powerful; the police must be democratized and socialized rather than attacked as oppressors; prisons have to remain; the weak must be given the full protection of the rule of law. The soft parts of the system — welfare, social work, treatment, rehabilitation — instead of being attacked as disguised forms of social control should be defended in the face of the conservative onslaught on the welfare state.

We are witnessing, then, a form of *radical regression* or what Cain calls "defensive formalism." Aware of the failures of the original vision (but too sophisticated to blame these on technical problems of implementation); contemplating a system that is still oppressive, unjust, and ineffective (but for which the inclusionary vision presents no immediate solution); confronted by vocal and organized victims (such as women who suffer from male violence) who want real protection (but by the full force of the state and not some mythical "community"); dissatisfied with mere debunking (and willing to suggest reforms that are part of a long-term political program); the left realists have arrived at a clear theoretical milestone. Clear and also convincing. Faced with the realities of social control in those societies that witnessed the destructuring impulse twenty years ago, demystification, pessimism, defensive formalism, and regression are all perfectly understandable responses. By any possible criterion — the safety and security of ordinary citizens, the welfare of the individual offender, the needs of the victim, a general sense of justice — things are bad.

My doubt is whether self-denunciation is the only way out of this slough of despond.

Enlightened by Memory

There are two alternative ways out of the slough of despond. One is political: a cautious reaffirmation of the original values behind the destructuring, abolitionist, and inclusionary visions. The other is analytical: a slightly different reading of the literature on social control. These solutions express what Cain nicely calls a "squeak of hope." As she notes, even the chorus of radical pessimism about informal justice (the despairing sense that the devil we know, formal justice, may have been better) "is occasionally punctuated by an attenuated left wing squeak of hope that by some dialectical feat a 'genuinely' human and popular form of justice may emerge."[9]

By "cautious reaffirmation" I mean simply the recognition that the values by which we judge the current system to be defective are much the same as those that informed the original vision. That is: the inclusionary ideals that looked appealing then are just as appealing now. It still makes sense to look for more humane, just, and workable alternatives to the criminal justice system's mechanisms of apprehension, judgment, and punishment. It still makes sense to say that mutual aid, good neighborliness, and real community are preferable to the solutions of bureaucracies, professionals, and the centralized state (and that this prospect touches genuine psychic and social needs, and is not just a trick to divert attention from real social conflict). Criticisms of the inhumanity and irrationality of the prison are as valid today as twenty years ago. It should not be impossible to imagine a way of stopping the relentless categorization of deviants, and so on.

In fact, even in some of the harshest of revisionist criticisms those original values are not completely negated. Abel, for example, after an effective demolition of what passes as "informal justice" recognizes that

> It is advocated by reformers and embraced by disputants precisely because it expresses values that deservedly elicit broad allegiance: the preference of harmony over conflict, for mechanisms that offer equal access to the many rather than unequal privilege to the few, that operate quickly and cheaply, that permit all citizens to participate in decision making rather than limiting authority to 'professionals', that are familiar rather than esoteric and that strive for and achieve substantive justice rather than frustrating it in the name of form.[10]

The memory of such values should now make it possible for us to approach the revisionist evaluations (and the rest of the literature on social control) in a somewhat different way. This requires a conscious suspension of the all-purpose assumptions that today's ideas are necessarily more radical (and more realistic!) than those of the past and that capitalist social democracies should be suspected precisely when they pretend to benevolence. Both these assumptions are often combined in what Foucault calls "a widespread facile tendency, which one should combat, to designate that which has just occurred as the primary enemy, as if this were always the principal form of oppression from which one had to liberate oneself."[11]

With such assumptions out of the way, we might cultivate instead (1) a sensitivity to success, however ambivalent, and (2) an experimental and inductive attitude.

What will happen if we look for success rather than expect failure, or at least formulate some pragmatic criteria for what counts as relative success? This is the strategy that Cain follows in her reevaluation of the informal justice literature. She acknowledges a particular set of values, looks at what the agencies are actually doing, and then extrapolates successes—however short-lived, unstable, and vulnerable—from the fleeting histories of "pre-figurative institutions" as they emerge and before they are co-opted. These are the type of defining characteristics of success that she finds in the history of informal justice: class identification is open and explicit; the client is constituted as a collective subject; so too is the opposition seen in collective, class terms; there is a long term "prophylactic" solution (e.g. education and politicization) and not just a resolution of the individual case; the agency operates beyond the courtroom (e.g. picketing, striking); agency workers are accountable to the collectivity for which they work (and not the individual client, employer, profession, or the state); the internal organization of the agency is democratic and nonspecialist. Cain then goes on to note the absence of these features in other forms of justice: professional, populist, and incorporated.

This is a commendable strategy for making the "squeak of hope" a little louder, although I altogether disagree with the particular value system that Cain uses, that is: What is good from a "class standpoint" or for "working-class interests." I would prefer a different set of criteria and one that is not dependent on the Marxist (or any other) intellectual's notion of what is another group's objective interests. And such criteria must allow for an ambivalent sense of what constitutes success for failure. For example: decentralization and inclusion can be said to have failed by leading to a greater (rather than, as intended, lesser) involvement in the business of deviancy control. But to the extent that this involvement comes from ordinary people and not licensed functionaries of the central state, this is just the type of success that should be encouraged.

The inductive attitude does not begin by listing abstract criteria or programmatic intentions that would have to be fulfilled in particular cases but, rather, starts with the cases themselves. We cannot speak in advance of fixed forms (autonomy, informality, self-help) that will always be "right" or political alliances that will always be "wrong." The policy arena becomes, rather, a site on which preferred values can be clarified.

We have to cultivate, that is, a pragmatic and experimental attitude. Experience and research should be used to find models that nearly work (in the sense of approximating desired values) and those that clearly fail (by undermining desired values). This means examining value preferences to see what policies they imply — what would decentralized community control actually look like? — but it does not mean judging results only in terms of their concordance with the original aims. The question is, "What is happening?" and not only "Is what is happening what was intended to happen?" This is a useful stance not just for the pragmatist of social policy but the analyst who is so trapped in the rhetoric of intended versus unintended consequences, that he or she misses those determinants of social policy that are external to the original value system.

The next question is *where* to look for success (however limited and ambivalent) and for opportunities to be inductive. And then, once these sites are located, what is their relationship to the wider social order? These questions have, of course, been posed in the social control literature, but the answers have been one-sided. The simple advocates of community and decentralization have been wrong to imagine that their projects can be kept apart from the wider power structure, while the demystifiers and critics are wrong to think that these projects will be totally contaminated by the outside world and can never offer glimpses of a different social order.

This debate makes sense only in terms of polarities that are as old as sociology itself: micro versus macro, reform versus revolution, autonomy versus dependence. In social control theory the most interesting versions of these debates come from (1) legal pluralism, with its theory of how to conceptualize the relationship between local normative orders and the wider social structure, and (2) Foucault, with his theory of microsystems of power whose logic is not reducible to the workings of capital.

I will return later to Foucault's theory of local power, but let me adapt from the legal pluralist literature the notion of "semi-autonomous fields."[12] These are social units that can generate rules, customs, and symbols internally and that have the means to induce compliance but that are vulnerable to rules and decisions from the outside world. Below are some fields in which the vision of decentralized community control can be examined (this is obviously not a survey of each subject).

1. The first and most obvious place to look is the actual record of experimentation with decentralized forms of community control and informal justice. This is the literature that I have already addressed, and I just want to discuss one altogether random example of how such fields may be used for value clarification. This is the experience of Community Boards and Citizens Panels in cities such as San Francisco.[13] On the one hand, the disputes that come before the Board are often trivial, the weaker participants might benefit more from formal legal settlements, and social conflicts might be prematurely neutralized. On the other hand, there is little sign of direct state control; the whole process is voluntary: the participants "donate" their conflict to the Board rather than to the state; disputes are resolved before they become actual "crimes"; the parties are encouraged to take full responsibility for their actions; there is no cost or professional lawyers; there is the possibility for a solution acceptable to both parties.

At the level of the wider social order the criticisms remain, but the field itself generates values and experiences that have their own autonomy.

2. The second field is to be found in the network of self-help, mutual-aid, and similar organizations that were set up by various victims' and deviants' movements over the past two decades. The model of self-help and mutual help, once confined to urban ethnic groups,[14] has taken many diverse forms: the "anonymous deviant" format (gamblers, addicts, alcoholics, overeaters) in which

organizations are sponsored, staffed, and controlled by deviants or former deviants; cooperative and nonprofessional forms of treatment and care, such as alternative health clinics, shelters for women who are victims of rape or domestic abuse, and communal homes for runaway teenagers.

This model has received surprisingly little attention in the literature as a form of social control. In one notable exception, Davis and Anderson usefully distinguish self-help and mutual help as a separate mode of control alongside custodial control and community care.[15] They divide this mode into forms with different degrees of pervasiveness in clients' (or "members'") lives, a continuum that ranges from various sectlike or cultlike organizations (religious, mystical, anti-drug) characterized by total and authoritarian control over members' lives to "transformative" groups (such as feminist health collectives) through to specific self-help groups (such as Weight Watchers).

The features of this model, as described by Davis and Anderson and other sympathetic observers, are quite similar to Cain's approved criteria of informal justice. These include: ideological commitment; politicization of the language of incompetence, dependence, and stigma; means chosen not in terms of pragmatic, bureaucratic, or professional criteria of efficiency but because they serve to express and dramatize the worldview of the members; an explicit antiprofessionalism (demystification of professional expertise, pooling of resources and knowledge); advocacy of wider social change (or, in some instances, secession from the dominant order); democratic internal organization (no formal hierarchy or division of labor, authority lies in the collective, minimum formal rules); a tendency for social control to be personalistic, moralistic, and based on holistic notions of change and commitment (self-criticism, thought reform, the use of dramatic myths such as "total abstinence from alcohol," "woman's absolute control over her body"); financial self-sufficiency; independence from the state; and decentralization.

This is not the place to consider the many intrinsic objections to these modes of control (such as the dangers of the authoritarian irrationality that leads to Jonestown) or their potential for co-optation into the state apparatus. Enough to note again that these are indeed models in practice of the vision of decentralized community control. If we take this vision seriously, these are just the places where its promise must be examined.

3. A third field consists of systems of private and workplace justice. These include the type of formal systems, such as workers' courts, workers' councils, and trade union assemblies, that are well documented in the standard literature on industrial self-management as well as the intricate informal systems of private justice studied in the more recent literatures on the hidden economy, workplace crime, and organizational deviance.

As with self-help and mutual help, this field offers extraordinarily rich possibilities to the student and/or advocate of decentralized control. There is now a wealth of factual material and also well-developed debates, for example, between those who argue for perpetuating the ingenious, spontaneous normative controls used by participants in the hidden economy and those who see dangers in formalizing self-control, thereby asking workers to police the very forms of resistance left open to them and to provide management with a convenient disciplinary tool removed from the protection of the rule of law.[16] This is a literature also sensitive to the question of the relationship between semiautonomous fields and the wider social order.

4. An allied body of research and theory, best covered by the legal pluralists themselves in their search for autonomous fields, deals with organizations that generate their own internal mechanisms of justice, regulation, and discipline. The best-documented examples include the army, professional associations, and educational institutions such as universities.

5. Another literature that is well developed in its own terms but hopelessly neglected by students of crime control deals with planned or actual communes, collectives, and other forms of utopian social orders. In the long historical record on these alternative forms of living and the intensive study of experiments such as the Israeli kibbutz, there is a wealth of material on the regulation and control of deviance. Questions of autonomy, dependence, and co-optation; the importance of the ideological commitment to the whole person rather than the isolated act; when internal controls take on the character of law; when exclusionary controls (such as expulsion) take over from the dominant inclusionary mode — these are all well-traversed subjects.

6. A related set of experiences is not at all defined and hardly exists as a separate "semi-autonomous field." It consists of the network of more or less spontaneous forms of communal living and working that developed out of the post-1960s movements: feminist, antinuclear, environmental. To the extent that these draw on the classic utopian and anarchist traditions, they are close to my previous category, but they are much less organized, encompassing, and coherent than, say, a commune or kibbutz. Steinert, who sees all this as a promising development for abolitionists, refers to the "re-emergence" in European countries over the past twenty or so years of "a sub-culture with its own infrastructure of meeting places, units of production and distribution, cultural activities, media and a distinct way of living."[17]

7. Finally, there lies the possibility of studying not any one particular type of semiautonomous field but contemplating whole societies that are characterized by nonstatist, noncentralized forms of social control (such as the traditional ancephalous society) or that allow such forms of control to flourish. There are encouraging if belated signs of criminological interest in the anthropological literature,[18] and the increasing interest in China allows for the study of historical swings from the decentralized, nonbureaucratic, nonstatist mode to an approximation of the Western model. In this context whole societies that

claim to socialist legality are also of interest. It must be said, though, that the lessons here have hardly been encouraging for the advocate of decentralized community control: guilt by association; the principle of equivalence; the privatization of the public domain (citizens using the official system to settle personal grudges) and the opening of private life to state scrutiny; the tendency toward pure instrumentality.

To anyone who is serious about the vision of decentralized community control, my suggestion is to contemplate these seven "fields" together in order to arrive at some general conclusions. In particular, what are the conditions for attaining success (as measured by our memory of those original values) and what are the limits that prevent it from being attained? The point of this exercise is not to be morally uplifting (the sociological role no more requires optimism then pessimism) but to do justice to the complexities of social reality.

My own provisional conclusion is rather simple and predictable: the further we move from the discourse of criminal justice, the more likely we are to find the conditions for realizing those values. Moreover, this type of success is achieved in those fields where social control is not viewed as a separate function.

The only way to extract this type of generalization (and its policy implications) is to avoid the terrible clutches of criminology. Foucault is right that this is not wholly possible—that we can never emerge from our own discources—but even within the confines of criminology, my sort of conclusion would be "acknowledged knowledge." On the first page of every textbook on deviance and crime is the truth that only the abolitionist movement has taken seriously: the criminal justice system is not the only form of social control. The left realists are correct in attacking the early phase of the critical paradigm for its idealist inversion of the assumptions of positivist/correctionalist criminology. But to return to the terrain of the traditional criminal justice model—however justified this might be on other theoretical and political grounds—is not just to abandon the vision of decentralized community control but to renounce a major weapon for creating an alternative criminology. You cannot, that is, have it both ways: statist criminal law and decentralization. To be realistic about law and order must mean to be unrealistic (that is, imaginative) about the possibilities of order without law. To take decentralization seriously means that you must be an abolitionist.

This is not simply because decentralization values are so difficult to realize within the interstices of the criminal jutice system but because the very nature of the system *must* undermine them. The realist-pessimist evaluations are, again, quite correct. Let us remind ourselves of those original values, which in the idealism of the sixties were seen even as basic human desires, frustrated by the culture. Thus:

(1) The desire for *community*: the wish to live in trust and fraternal co-operation with one's fellows in a total and visible collective entity. (2) The desire for *engagement*—the wish to come directly to grips with social and interpersonal problems. . . . (3) The desire for *dependence*—the wish to share responsibility for the control of one's impulses and the direction of one's life.[19]

These seem to me unlikely candidates for basic human desires, and there are even good reasons for rejecting them as absolute values. But there is no doubt that they cannot be fulfilled by the criminal justice system, even when it tries and especially when it tries. The criminal law is correctly characterized by the abolitionists as a state-run organization that maintains the monopoly on defining certain behavior as criminal and then organizing the punishment of such behavior by the deliberate infliction of pain. If we want to limit this monopoly, and decentralization is surely one way of doing so, then the last thing we should be doing is allowing the system to busy itself with community. We must take away, not give.

To express this another way: In "real" decentralized community control, we find not just those features revealed by a comparative survey of those "fields" (strong ties to parent social movement such as feminism, a strategy of political education, internal democracy, and so on) but the overriding criterion of an independent critical relationship to the state criminal law system. Left realists believe that this independent critical status can eventually be attained by fighting the system on its own terrain. But the essence of state power is not just the particular way it deploys its forces of criminalization and punishment but its initial normalizing power, that is, its radical monopoly to define what is right. As long as this exists, it is not enough to call for community control over the police or even citizen community patrols.

Thus "taking decentralization seriously" implies undertaking something like the two classic abolitionist projects. The first is to find alternatives to the criminal law in the civil law, tort and other forms of dispute and conflict resolution. The second is to specify and then achieve the type of structural conditions under which real community control can take place. These, for example, are Christie's conditions for a "low level of pain delivery", close personal knowledge; no group has any monopoly over power; those who pass judgments are vulnerable and accountable to their subjects; members of the group are interdependent; members share beliefs such as "each human body contains a sacred soul."[20]

Abolitionists are criticized precisely because they are romantic, naive, or disingenuous enough actually to take these projects seriously. And in truth much of this criticism is justified—though I doubt that abolitionists such as Christie or Hulsman mind being called romantics nor are they much impressed by the standard arguments in favor of the criminal law. My own position lies somewhere between the realist and abolitionist position. I would recommend a cautious reaffirmation of the values behind decentralized community control—"cautious" for these do not seem to me to be absolute values that cancel out all others. Instead of abolition, which *is* unrealistic, I would advocate *attrition*: a gradual wearing away of the criminal law, by a process of benign neglect, until it is used only when there is genuinely no alternative.

My caution derives from a number of ancient problems that are almost too obvious to itemize. They are all variations on the fallacy of extrapolating from the small homogenous social unit to the large, hierarchical total society. Thus:

- There are forms of harm, loss, and injustice inflicted by organizations, corporations, the state, and the powerful that are difficult to think of in terms other than "crime," and for which there are few effective substitutes for the criminal law model.
- Nonstatist, informal modes of control will not only leave the powerful untouched but, as the realists point out, leave the powerless and minority groups least protected. (The abolitionists would reply that they are not much protected now, but this hardly proves the case for informalism.)
- The ideology of the whole person that tends to govern successful forms of community control is not always desirable. We have only to look at the type of holistic judgments made, in their different ways, by religious cults, positivist criminology, and totalitarian political systems. Instead, we might prefer the more limited focus of the back-to-justice model. Neoclassicism, as Christie correctly points out, makes the act too important, but some acts are too trivial to have to bother about the person.
- Contrary to what abolitionists assert, not all acts designated as crime are actually forms of conflict, dispute, or trouble. Except by stretching these words beyond all recognition, we cannot translate crime control into these terms. The armed robber does not have a conflict with the security guard; the corporation dumping poisonous waste is not in dispute with the community; the violator of traffic regulations does not have any trouble.
- In a society in which the power to control is invested not just in the state but in the commercial market and in particular the hands of large corporate interests, nonstatist forms of decentralization cannot be valued in themselves. Nowhere is this better illustrated than in the growing critical literature on private security. At first sight, what could be better: autonomy from state control, decentralization, no positivist notion of disciplinary measures aimed at the individual soul, control embedded in a structure that appears consensual? But put this into practice, under the sole force of commercialism, and we have all the horrors that Shearing and Stenning describe in their nice analysis of Disney World: social control that is "embedded, preventative, subtle, co-operative and apparently non-coercive and consensual."[21]

Of course, the problem with Disney World (and the similar examples of shopping complexes, condominium estates, and the other "feudal-like domains" that students of private security have investigated) is that they represent only a part of the community package. They require no knowledge of the individual, they are authoritarian, they are not informed by any progressive ideology. These points are obvious — we all understand why Disney World is different from a kibbutz — but to be fair to the community vision, we have to take the whole package together and not judge the results of the component parts.

In any event, these are some of the standard objections to the abolitionist claims and aspirations. To the extent that such objections are correct, full realization of the vision of decentralized social control becomes impossible, undesirable, or both.

But this again is to leave the debate within the discourse of criminology. In the same way as the pragmatic search for value realization had to extend beyond what is called social control, so too does the theory of decentralization. My cautious reaffirmation of those sixties values and the sense in which they are unrealizable without full abilition (which in turn is an unlikely project) need grounding in a wider theory of power. This is something that neither conventional criminologists nor even radical social control theorists have undertaken.

Take the very notion of decentralization itself. This derives from a master metaphor that sees political power in terms of center and periphery. We are asked to imagine such things as deviants being drawn away from the center, or the periphery being awarded the power that belonged to the center. But this metaphor rests on a largely unexamined view of state power, which at times leans toward the most extreme form of elitist centralism, and at other times toward the most amorphous form of pluralism.

This produces some curious results in the social control literature. For example, most of the skeptical students of decarceration, community control, and informalism (including me) have relied heavily on Foucault to bolster our pessimism. The ritual quotations from Foucault were pulled out to prove that nothing could escape the awesome power of the state. Legal and disciplinary powers somehow "escape" from the center, filter out and disperse themselves, and then colonize the furthest extremities ("capillaries") of the social order. The dominant image is the Panopticon: a central vantage point that permits full surveillance of every peripheral point.

But this was surely a one-sided reading of a theory whose main thrust was to *deny* the privileged position given to the central state apparatus. Foucault is explicitly setting himself both against Hobbes's Leviathan and against Leninist theory in which the seizure of centralized state power is the whole point of politics.[22] For Foucault, the king's head has long been cut off: power is not wielded by a single subject, there is no central source of command, no practical center to political life. As Waltzer and Taylor both suggest, the images of microsystems of power not reducible to the workings of state or capital, of crosscutting alliances, strategies, and effects, all allow a reading of Foucault as being close to the old pluralism of U.S. political science but with this difference:

> Foucault is concerned not with the dispersion of power to the extremities of the political system but with its exercise in the extremities. For the Americans, power was dispersed to individuals and groups and then recentralized, that is brought to bear again at the focal point of sovereignty. For Foucault there is no focal point, but an endless network of power relations.[23]

No doubt the theory permits some contradictory readings here, but to wheel in Foucault to support a simple theory of a concentrated and centralized state power that infiltrates all other local forms of social control is hardly justified. Nor do Foucault's politics come near to traditional revolutionary centralism; there is no discernable sovereign state to take over or ruling class to replace. The same microphysics of power can and will reproduce itself in quite different political systems. In this sense Foucault is a reformist: each microsystem is not quite autonomous but it is "particular" and has to be challenged in its own terms.[24] And in his apparent preference for the ancephalous, androgynous, precategorical world that existed before the knowledge and power system of the modern state, he is certainly more of an abolitionist than a realist.[25] So instead of Foucault's being invoked to give theoretical dignity to demystification and realism, he could just as well be used to help celebrate the only successes that are possible: short-lived victories on limited terrains.

Be that as it may, my point here is that "taking decentralization seriously" implies not just a particular value preference but a more complicated theory than we admitted about the exercise of power in the modern state.

Summary

Let me retrace my steps through the "critical" literature on social control of the past two decades. My route was a somewhat tortuous one, full of diversions and deadends. This is the result of my own lack of commitment to any master plan (such as liberalism, left realism, or abolitionism), a failing, I would like to think, not of my own psyche but of the social world's refusal to correspond to any one theory.

In the 1960s most of the accepted systems and ideologies for the social control of deviants became the object of radical attacks under such organizing frameworks as destructuring, abolition, and inclusion. The desired alternatives came together in the vision of decentralized community control. Soon — with varying degrees of enthusiasm, commitment, and faithfulness to the original vision — experiments and reforms in this direction were carried out. When the results of these attempts were scrutinized a decade later, the situation was invariably found to be disappointing. The reforms had not been properly implemented, they failed in their own terms, they had even made matters worse.

In a general atmosphere of skepticism and retrenchment radical critics arrived at their own version of the "realism" that had come to dominate conservative and neoliberal rhetoric of crime control. This radical realism took two forms: the first was to continue debunking, exposing, and demystifying the pretensions of countercultural reformism; the second was to develop a new theory and political strategy more attuned to the current realities of crime. This took the shape of "regression" and "defensive formalism," less an enthusiasm to create alternatives to the prevailing systems of knowledge and power (such as the criminal law) than an attempt to exploit them for social justice and for working-class interests.

The price of realism is a certain loss of imagination. Before dismissing the prospect of decentralized community control as a hopeless detour and returning instead to the realist path, I suggested a serious examination of the various fields of social control in which the values behind the alternative vision may be realized. This led me to a cautious reaffirmation rather than denunciation of those values but, at the same time, to the reluctant conclusion that they cannot be achieved within the interstices of the statist criminal law mode. "Reluctant" because however appealing the prospect of abolition might be, it offers no realistic solution to all problems of crime control.

While theory might help, the old choice still remains: between visionary politics and realpolitik.

Notes

1. S. Cohen, *Visions of Social Control: Crime, Punishment and Classification* (New York: Basil Blackwell, 1985).
2. See, for example, Harold E. Pepinsky's proposal to replace "criminology" by the "sociology of justice": "The Sociology of Justice," *Annual Review of Sociology* 12 (1986): 93–108.
3. The phrase used by T. Platt and P. Takagi in their critique of the bleak pessimism of conservative crime control ideologists, "Intellectuals for Law and Order: A Critique of the New Realists," *Crime and Social Justice*, no. 8 (1977): 1–6.
4. I evaluate this literature in *Visions of Social Control*. On informal justice, see particulary R.L. Abel, "The Contradictions of Informal Justice," in *The Politics of Informal Justice*, vol. 1, ed. R.L. Abel (reviewed in chapter 11). On anti-psychiatry, see Peter Sedgewick, *Psychopolitics* (London: Pluto Press, 1982).
5. M. Cain, "Beyond Informal Justice," *Contemporary Crises: Law, Crime and Social Policy* 9, no. 4 (1985): 335–73.
6. Abel, "The Contradictions of Informal Justice," p. 305.
7. On the North American version of this position, see the journal *Crime and Social Justice* over the past four years; for example, Tony Platt, "Crime and Punishment

in the United States: Immediate and Long Term Reforms from a Marxist Perspective," *Crime and Social Justice*, no. 18 (1982): 34–45. The British version of radical realism may be found in Ian Taylor, *Law and Order: Arguments for Socialism* (London: Macmillan, 1982); John Lea and Jock Young, *What Is to Be Done about Law and Order?* (Harmondsworth: Penguin, 1984); and most explicitly, Jock Young, "The Failure of Criminology: The Need for a Radical Realism," in *Confronting Crime*, ed. J. Young and R. Mathews (London: Sage Publications, 1986).

8. I deal in chapter 13 with the way criminalization appears in the new realist literature.
9. Cain, "Beyond Informal Justice," p. 335.
10. Abel, "The Contradictions of Informal Justice," p. 310.
11. Michel Foucault, "Space, Knowledge and Power," interview in *Skyline*, March 1982; reprinted in *The Foucault Reader*, ed. P. Rabinow (New York: Pantheon Books, 1984), p. 248.
12. Sally Falk Moore, *Law as Process* (London: Routledge & Kegan Paul, 1978).
13. I draw here on information provided by Raymond Schonholz at the International Conference on Prison Abolition, Amsterdam, June 1985.
14. On the continuities between the organic systems of justice and self-help developed by urban ethnic minorities in the United States and later more self-conscious experiments in "justice without law," see Jerold S. Auerbach, *Justice without Law* (New York: Oxford University Press, 1983).
15. Nanette J. Davis and Bo Anderson, *Social Change: The Production of Deviance in the Modern State* (New York: Irvington, 1983).
16. For a review, from the point of view of the latter side of this debate, see Phil Scraton and Nigel South, "The Ideological Construction of the Hidden Economy: Private Justice and Work-Related Crime," *Contemporary Crises* 8, no. 1 (1984): 1–19.
17. Heinz Steinert, "Beyond Crime and Punishment," *Contemporary Crises* 10, no. 1 (1986): 28.
18. For one of the few criminology textbooks that makes a serious comparison between "order and trouble in simple societies" and the nature of state law, see Raymond Michalowski, *Order, Law and Crime: An Introduction to Criminology* (New York: Random House, 1985).
19. Philip Slater, *The Pursuit of Loneliness* (Boston: Beacon Press, 1970), p. 5.
20. Nils Christie, *Limits to Pain* (Oxford: Martin Robertson, 1981), pp. 81–91.
21. Clifford D. Shearing and Philip C. Stenning, "From the Panopticon to Disney World: The Development of Discipline," in *Perspectives in Criminal Law*, ed. A. N. Doob and E. L. Greenspan (Ontario: Canada Law Book, 1985), p. 347.
22. This is a reading of Foucault suggested recently by two liberal political philosophers: Michael Waltzer, "The Politics of Michel Foucault," *Dissent* 30 (1983): 381–490; Charles Taylor, "Foucault on Freedom and Truth," *Political Theory* 12, no. 2 (1984): 152–83.
23. Waltzer, "The Politics of Michel Foucault," p. 483.
24. For both Taylor and Waltzer, the problem of Foucault's political theory is not the absence of a central subject nor the presence of local power but that his explanation of the microphysics of power invokes some notion of an overall logic, fit, or "intelligibility." This then ends up as a form of functionalism.
25. On Foucault as an abolitionist, see Rolf DeFolter, "On the Methodological Foundations of the Abolitionist System: A Comparison of the Ideas of Hulsman, Mathiesen and Foucault," *Contemporary Crises: Law, Crime and Social Policy* 10, no. 1 (1986): 39–62.

13

The Object of Criminology:
Reflections on the New Criminalization*

My main title is deliberately vague: "The Object of Criminology." It could just as easily be "The Subject of Criminology." And in the contrasting meanings of the words *object* and *subject*, passive and active, lies my interest: the dual senses in which criminology has to accept a certain object (officially designated crime) as its subject matter, but at the same time the criminologist as an active subject is busy constituting what this object is or should be.

In more familiar terms this is the old problem of criminalization: How do certain elements of social life (acts, people, situations) come into the orbit of the criminal law? This is an old problem indeed: the stuff of chapter 1 of all criminology textbooks, the standard first three lectures in those "Introduction to Criminology" courses we have been giving for years. A reference to the Sellin-Tappan debate about whether the subject matter of criminology should be officially defined criminality or the wider category of violations of conduct norms; a few remarks about the difference between "crime," "deviance," and "social problems"; some amateur anthropology about cultural relativism versus universalism (with the obligatory references to murder and incest) and law versus custom; some jurisprudence (even more amateur) about law and morality, with the invariable footnotes to the Wolfenden-Hart-Devlin debate on the proper limits to the criminal sanction. And so on.

All this is familiar territory, the ritual bread-and-butter teaching to get out of the way (and then forget about) so that we can get on the with real business of theory, research, and policy. But "Practice What You Teach" is my motto here. If we tell our students that these are important matters, then we should treat them as important.

* "The Object of Criminology: Reflections on the New Criminalization." Extended version of paper given at the Annual Meeting of the American Society of Criminology, San Diego, 1985 on the occasion of being presented with the Sellin-Glueck award. (Not previously published).

I will do this not by entering into the substance of those old debates but by looking at the criminalization issue more as a matter in the sociology of knowledge. Or rather, following Foucault, the sociology of "knowledge/power": how the world of power constitutes certain objects as criminal and how criminological knowledge is implicated in this constitution. To arrive at the specific problem that interests me, I will take the liberty of rewriting the discourse of criminology in terms of two opposing impulses or tendencies. One will have to be called something like "criminalizing the normal" — how the category of crime becomes accepted. The other will be "normalizing the criminal" — how criminalization becomes questioned or even reversed. These are not, of course, equal "tendencies," nor do they always compete with each other. My exercise does some violence to the history of criminology, but it will serve to introduce the question that concerns me here: How do we make sense of today's attempt by the very same forces always most critical of the criminal law to themselves invoke the power to criminalize?

Before arriving at my question, let me attempt a breathless review of the three contexts in which criminalization/normalization appears in our literature: the analysis of primal criminalization; the notion of relativist moral enterprise; and the drift to normalization in the various new sociologies of deviance and criminologies of the sixties.

Primal Criminalization

I will use the term *primal criminalization* to cover the original construction of the categories of crime that we take to be synonymous with the emergence of the modern state. All histories of the state (and variously of capitalism, democracy, and modern society, if not of criminology) deal with this transformation: the move from custom to law; the restructuring of relationships in terms of contract; the creation of theft and the whole edifice of property law; the massive increase after the eighteenth century of the volume of criminalizable and punishable behavior.

This history is not my subject here, but it is worth noting how astonishingly few — up till the last decade — have been the cases used by criminologists to generalize about primal criminalization. Hall on theft, Chambliss on vagrancy, and not much else. These are quoted in all the textbooks and quite justifiably have attained classic status. But this leaves massive areas untouched: fraud, forgery, defamation, sexual offenses, and the whole catalogue of common law crimes. Standard progressivist histories of the criminal law (such as Radzinowicz's) are seldom cited, and these anyway are more informative on penalties than on the question of criminalization. There is little on *criminal* law of the scope of, say, Atiyah's work on the relationship between contract law and the rise of classical political economy.[1]

I say "up till the last decade" because a new legal historiography is now being written that calls for a major rethinking about the relationship between law and the state.[2] One version of the revisionist paradigm, the E.P. Thompson school, is already well known, though its implications are only just beginning to be registered by criminologists: a political reconsideration of the ideology of the rule of law and a theoretical reconsideration of how the "normal" activities of the working class became criminalized. Marx's famous two examples have been taken as paradigmatic: the 1842 essay on "The Law of the Thefts of Wood," describing the imposition of new penalties for the gathering by peasants of fallen wood, and the reference in *Capital* to the emergence of vagrancy laws to control itinerants displaced by the decline of the feudal system. Similarly, poaching, smuggling, piracy, and other such cases have now been added to the register of primal criminalization.

It is precisely this addition that has been the object of much lively debate about the eighteenth-century criminal law: revisionist historians such as Hay are now accused of generalizing from the atypical class-based forms of criminalization (such as the game laws) to the vast bulk of crimes (theft, rape, murder) where there already was a moral consensus about blameworthiness that had no class lines.[3] This is part of a wider historical debate—already a revision of revisionist history—that questions the whole notion of state monopoly of the punitive sanction.[4] Neither these theoretical debates nor the enormous current empirical interest in the history of crime and justice have really been integrated by criminology. Those breathless first chapters of our textbooks will look very different in a few years.

Another intellectual product of this decade, more difficult to absorb and from my point of view here even more challenging, is Foucault's theory of power and knowledge. Criminalization is not simply an exercise in power. It is one of the "dividing practices": the isolation of lepers in the Middle Ages; the confinement of the poor, insane, and itinerant; the classificatory schemes of clinical medicine; the birth of the prison; the rise of the "soft sciences," such as psychiatry and criminology, which combine a mode of manipulating people with a discourse of knowledge. This knowledge can never be pure. It subsumes, or in Foucault's term becomes an "alibi" for, the exercise of power.

Genuinely innovatory ideas take a long time to absorb and I do not believe that criminology is ready for the massive reordering of its intellectual history that Foucault's theory demands. Neither "pure" classicism nor "pure" positivism was (or could have been) self-reflective enough about the question of primal criminalization. The original classical school was concerned, of course, with the question of the proper powers of the state. But it could not have produced a sociology of how the change in power relationships from the seventeenth century to the nineteenth century created the primal criminal categories. Its questions were normative, not self-reflective: What should go into the criminal law, and how should it be administered in a clear, fair, and just manner? Positivism was obviously even less capable of being the object of its own attention: by separating crime from any contemplation of the state (as Matza correctly showed), positivism reified the category of crime. The program of nineteenth-century positivism could hardly have contemplated boundary disputes about what should be criminalized, nor have asked why and how primal criminalization had taken place. This is precisely why for Garafalo exactly one hundred years ago these were "natural crimes" and not mere "police crimes"; the legal categorization, that is, was obviously the same as the social consensus.

The sociological equivalent of "natural crime" became the notion of "consensus crime" as opposed to "conflict crime." Thus, Hall's typical definition: "The laws on homicide, theft, treason and incest e.g. have not been arbitrarily imposed . . . not only are they among the norms which appear to be practically universal, they also have rational, normal interrelations with economic and political institutions and changes."[5] In a current textbook (one of the few that gives detailed attention to the criminalization question) Hagen notes, though, that behavior placed in this consensus category is "neither immutably nor permanently criminal." He then goes on: "Nevertheless, the fact that some behaviors have been consensually defined as crimes for successive generations makes them of primary interest to some criminologists."[6] This runs together three quite separate issues: the status of any division between consensus (primal) and conflict (relativist) crime; the nature of moral sanctioning prior to and independent of criminalization; and the way in which certain behavior comes to interest "some" or all criminologists, and how this "interest" defines our subject.

It is the third issue that is my concern here: the role of the scientific discourse in creating its own object of study. Still less than the other two could this have been on the positivist program. The separation between the observer and the observed is one of the defining characteristics of positivism. It was only in the various antipositivist schools of the 1960s that the appropriateness of the criminal label became questioned and a more self-reflexive role assigned to the supposedly neutral "scientist." But this is running ahead of the story. We must first mention those forms of criminalization that were the product of a less "natural" exercise of state power and hence became more easily analyzed within a relativist paradigm.

Relativist Moral Enterprise

From the end of the nineteenth century onward the political base of criminalization was different from its primal form; it generated a different type of analytical literature, and it invoked a different role for the criminologist. The older categories of theft, violence, political crime, and public disorder were there and taken for granted; the newer ones were understood as the product of a different set of contingencies.

Consider this diverse list: protective factory legislation; juvenile delinquency laws (especially all "status offenses"); all laws regulating substance use and abuse (drugs, alcohol, tobacco); such legal prohibitions of sexuality as prostitution, pornography, and homosexuality; abortion and birth control; gambling. Each of these raises quite different issues for the student of criminalization, but unlike those primal crimes inseparable from the history of the modern state, they came to share certain common features when they were studied:

1. Things could have been different. In each case criminalization was an alternative either to tolerance or a form of control that already existed. Criminalization was neither natural nor inevitable. In the view of contemporary (but, more often, later) observers, it need not and should not have been chosen. This is clearly a relativist and not an absolute category; these are not "natural crimes." The observer further assumes (an assumption we will later have to question) that the phenomenon or behavior (say, the "nature" of heroin or the "fact" of domestic violence) is constant and fixed; only its categorization alters. Names such as evil, sickness, diversity, and crime can be (and are) interchanged for what is the "same" thing.

2. Such forms of criminalization could be more readily understood than primal or consensual crimes as being the end product of a particular social and political process. In the literature of the sixties this process came to be called "moral enterprise." Knowledge about these forms of criminalization (together with the overlapping theory of how the categories of deviance and social problems are created) began to share an emerging "social constructionist" paradigm. This was the story: a condition is exposed; the public becomes aware of it; the powerful find an interest in doing something about it; policies are formulated; the condition is finally criminalized.

3. The meta theory, then, was firmly relativist and pluralist. There was no moral consensus from which criminalization could be rationally deduced. These forms of crime (and allied categories of deviance and social problems) were merely *labels* that emerged as part of an ongoing process called "the social construction of reality." Labeling theory, of course, was the best-known version of this epistemological pluralism.

Now, there were and are obvious differences within the literature. These were not so much, as Hagen suggests, between the "moral functionalists," who saw law as the product of consensus and a *good* solution to a set of social and economic problems, and "moral Marxists," who saw law as an instrument of domination and a *bad* solution to social and economic problems. This division applies more to the debate about the origins and the status of natural, consensual, primal crimes. For relativist crime, the theoretical division was between those who talked about free-floating pressure groups, moral entrepreneurs, or interest groups and those who wanted to ground these forces more firmly in the political economy.

But whether the politics was pluralist (free-floating moral enterprise) or coercive (ruling-class interests), the value agenda seemed the same. Both sides saw these forms of criminalization as "bad": the category had been fixed in an irrational or arbitrary way, out of prejudice or just plain ignorance. In almost no case was the enterprise judged in positive or even neutral terms. All these campaigns and crusades were the product of either the misplaced paternalism, dogooding, and middle-class morality of the Progressives (and their descendants) or of the cruder forces of reactionary politics, class, status, power, and discrimination. "Kookiness and racism" was one well-known explanation of the origins of the Harrison Act. In the same way that C. Wright Mills twenty years earlier had dissected the "professional ideology of social pathologists" (the view that all the world should be a large Christian village), so the sociologists of the 1960s brought their liberal, cosmopolitan, universal values to explaining and judging relativist crime. All these behaviors — smoking dope, homosexuality, abortion, gambling, prostitution, pornography — not only should not have been criminalized in the first place but should now be regarded as perfectly normal.

Varieties of Normalization

The very same criminology that had taken for granted the primal criminal categories or (in the case of the Progressives) joined campaigns to criminalize new areas of life or produced knowledge that made criminals into special beings contained (and still does) diametrically opposite tendencies. These I will call "normalization."

To confuse matters, note that Foucault uses the term *normalization* in precisely the opposite way to this commonsense meaning. Positivist social science produces knowledge that replaces and incorporates the judicial penalty (classicism) by creating a system of finely graded intervals that distribute individuals around a norm. This normative rationality (in psychiatry, sexology, criminology) undermines legal rationality (the binary opposition between permitted and forbidden) by creating new categories and gradations of normality, anomaly, and perversion that the techniques of discipline are designed to eliminate (but, of course, never do).

Although it eventually also produced its own forms of normalization (in Foucault's sense), the naturalist movement within criminology can be understood as "normalizing" in my commonsense sense. Matza's *Becoming Deviant* remains the most eloquent guide to this variety of normalization. This was the meaning of naturalism: not (as in natural law theory) that crime was naturally crime but that crime was natural. The Durkheimian argument about the normality of deviance and crime; the Chicago School's stress on crime as part of a natural process (of growing up, of urban growth); the Mertonian theory of anomie as a natural by-product of industrial society; Sutherland's insistence that learning criminal behavior followed the same rules as learning normal behavior; motivational-accounts theory,which actually is constructed on the deviants' own attempts to normalize ("neutralize") their action – these are all well known. But these are not the forms of normalization that interest me here. They move from "pathology" to "diversity" (in Matza's terms) but they do not question the criminal category itself. This had to wait for the three post-1960s paradigms of labeling theory, critical criminology, and abolitionism.

(i) In labeling theory, with its central focus on definition and reaction and its unabashed relativism, the initial commitment to criminalize is merely one possible form of social imputation ("signification"). The subsequent fitting of acts or actors to the already-constructed category is seen as a *failure* of "normalization" (the term explicitly used by Lemert). In the normal run of things primary deviance (or rule breaking) is unreacted to, unsignified, unclassified, explained away, or tolerated.

This is not the place to examine the baroque twists of labeling theory. What is important for us here is the implication that for many (if not all) forms of relativist criminalization (primal forms were ignored), what had happened was a gigantic set of category errors. These phenomena should simply not have been called crime at all; they should have been normalized.

This was one of the rationalizations of what I have called the great "destructuring impulse" of the 1960s.[7] In its weak (physical) form, the adverse effects of the category error were to be mitigated by dismantling or bypassing the apparatus of crime control: decarceration, diversion, divestment, decentralization, deformalization. In the stronger (idealistic) form that interests me here, the error itself was to be reversed. Drawing on a mixture of pragmatic, civil libertarian, and theoretical reasons, a rhetoric of decriminalization became firmly established. The criminal law had overreached itself into areas in which it did not belong, most notably, "crimes without victims," a concept very much a product of this period. The extension of the criminal law into these areas was inefficient, distracting, corrupting, expensive, criminogenic, and abusive of civil liberties. These areas were "not the law's business."

These boundary disputes or category errors were to be rectified by a form of epistemological politics. Names had to be changed. The paradigmatic case became the decision (by a *vote!*) of the American Psychiatric Association to no longer designate homosexuality as a diagnostic category. This was demedicalization, but criminalization could also – so we persuaded ourselves – be canceled by a similar process. The agenda of the day was *reverse moral enterprise*: not adding to but subtracting from that part of the moral fabric of society patrolled by the criminal law. The alternative was another label or, most radically, doing nothing at all: varieties of legalization, radical non-intervention, tolerance, or normalization.

(ii) In the tougher successors of labeling theory—the various new, conflict, radical, critical, and Marxist criminologies—the challenge to criminalization takes some different forms. In the first place the base for criminalization lies no longer in some vaguely pluralist notion of pressure group politics and moral enterprise but in the deepest recesses of the political economy. Those morally relativist areas (victimless crimes and so on) are of only marginal interest, and the enterprise of normalizing them was dismissed as liberalism, bourgeois idealism, amoral hipsterism, libertarianism, and zookeeping. The point is to excavate down to the base of primal criminalization, there to find not "nature" but the very basis of the capitalist social order.

Two further strands of argument appeared that will soon be of importance to us. The first, later to be denounced as a symptom of "left idealism," was that public concern about the primal categories of street crime was the product of mystification and false consciousness (the processes analyzed by liberal deviancy theory as stereotyping and moral panics). "Real" crime was elsewhere: the crimes of the powerful. So: victimless crime is unimportant, street crime is exaggerated, state and business crime are wrongly underplayed.

The second argument moved from a radical critique of the state's power to criminalize toward visualizing a society without such criminalization. Thus, for the authors of *The New Criminology*, "Deviance is normal. . . . The task is to create a society in which the facts of human diversity . . . are not subject to the power to criminalize."[8] In more orthodox Marxism this radical vision of normalization may be found in the recently revived writings of the Bolshevik jurist Pashukanis. The legal form is a homology of the commodity form; the future socialist society would see not so much a victory of proletarian, socialist law but of socialism *over* law. There would be a literal withering away of law, "the disappearance of the judicial factor from social relations."[9]

The later movements within radical theory and the nature of criminal law in socialist states are other matters. What we must note here is that in its early phases, at least, the radical paradigm shared with labeling theory a critical stance toward the taken-for-granted nature of the criminal category. Radical theorists were interested in different crimes, used different theories, and had very different criteria for what should be criminalized, but radicals and liberals seemed united in their skepticism about the orthodox (positivist) acceptance of criminalization as a fact of life.

(iii) I would have liked to be able to devote more time to my third variety of normalization, abolitionism, because it is not only far more radical and internally consistent than the others but also much less familiar to a North American audience.[10]

Different versions of the abolitionist paradigm appear in the work of each of a group of European criminologists—Nils Christie, Thomas Mathiesen, Herman Bianchi, and Louk Hulsman—and (in a more allusive way because he was never interested in "policy") in Foucault. Not just prisons have to be abolished but the *whole* apparatus and the *very concept* of criminal justice. Detailed arguments are presented in support of this abolitionist stance, but often (disingenuously sometimes) a total indictment of penal law and the penal system is seen as commonsensical and obvious: everyone has heard this news. The penal system does not answer people's "real needs"; it removes conflict from those actually involved; it causes suffering and pain, unjustly and unequally; far from being a solution to anything, it is the problem. The task of criminology is to find ways of settling conflict or dealing with undesirable behavior right outside the criminal law. Decriminalization thus becomes *the* central strategy for criminologists, "the process by which the competence of the penal system to impose sanctions in reaction to a certain form of behavior is withdrawn."[11]

The abolitionist position is most consistently associated with Hulsman's work. Words such as *crime, criminal, criminality*, and *criminal justice* are part of what he calls the "penal dialect" (close to Foucault's "discourse"). Only inertia and habit prevent us from abolishing this dialect entirely and replacing it with the language of *regrettable acts, undesirable behavior, problem situations, conflicts, trouble, harmful events*. On the one hand, this might sound an abstract, even metaphysical view, as in the anti-psychiatry discourse where *mental illness* always appears in quotation marks because it is not really illness, or in Foucault's attempt to visualize a pre-categorical world in which the classificatory schemes of the human sciences have not yet been created. On the other hand, this is a highly concrete vision. We are invited to describe these events and situations as they actually occur in our homes, streets, and neighborhoods. For abolitionists, the criminologist is not a metatheorist but takes part in real policy-making: writing blueprints on decriminalization for governments and for bodies such as the Council of Europe, or devising practical experiments in alternative forms of communal living, dispute settlement, and conflict resolution.

This type of practical utopianism rejects any criminology that bases its worldview on the definitional activities of the very system that is its subject of study. This "makes it necessary to abandon as a tool in the conceptual frame of criminology the notion of crime. Crime has no ontological reality. Crime is not the object but the product of criminal policy."[12] Criminalization—which deems a certain "occurrence" undesirable, attributes it to an individual, uses punishment to control this individual, assigns acts to scales of gravity and justice—is merely one of many ways of constructing social reality. It must be rejected in favor of quite different alternatives. We must start from zero. The discourse of jurisprudence, criminal law, courts, prison, and police can have no privileged status whatsoever.

Abolitionism is clearly the most consistent and extreme of the three varieties of normalization and anticriminalization I have listed here. It is also the only one that is politically alive, for some strange things were to happen with the liberal and radical versions.

The New Criminalization

If all those diverse varieties of normalization — naturalist sociology, labeling theory, libertarian non-interventionism, the early phase of critical criminology, abolitionism — were movements of reformation, then the end of the seventies witnessed the start of the counterreformation. Mainstream criminology does not interest me here. Certainly, it went through a massive change during this period — the abandonment of the traditional positivist interest in causation in favor of matters of technology, administration, and management — but this move left the criminalization question attended. It is the moves within liberal and radical circles that concern me, and here we began to witness two rather remarkable developments: the virtual disappearance of decriminalization from the agenda, and along with it any attempt to take a critical stance toward the concept of crime; and the support given by criminologists to campaigns (moral enterprise) directed at reinforcing and extending criminalization, particularly in the areas of corporate behavior, environmental issues, and then pornography, violence against women, and other issues raised by the feminist movement.

The rest of my paper consists of reflections about these "new" forms of criminalization.

Let me begin with the trajectory within academic criminology. The starting point is Sutherland. If differential association theory "normalized" crime by locating it in causally familiar language, then the debate about white-collar crime was "knowledge/power" in the enterprise of criminalization. The call was to criminalize those unpatrolled areas of corporate behavior previously regarded as merely antisocial or for the criminal law to replace the civil law as the regulator of corporate morality. All contemporary literature about white-collar and corporate crime retains the original element of moral enterprise: behavior regarded as ordinary business practice should no longer be so normalized. In the same way as gathering firewood became theft two centuries ago, so must the predatory activities of the business class now become criminalized.

Epistemological politics again, this is the meaning of the title of Sutherland's famous 1945 paper "Is 'White Collar Crime' Crime?" But the category error this time was not that the criminal label had been applied too often (over-criminalization) or in the "wrong" places (such as victimless crime) but that it had not been applied in enough of the right places. To expose these places became the object of the crusading, muckraking strand in American criminology that Sutherland's polemic inspired. To label these exposed places as "really" criminal was to be both conceptually correct and politically progressive.

For a long time this polemic was submerged in criminology. "Pure" 1960s deviancy theory was too deconstructionist — decriminalization, noninterventionism, civil rights — to mount crusades to strengthen the criminal law. White-collar crime, if mentioned at all, appeared alongside street crime in a much more pragmatic context. It was a question of priorities, allocation of scarce resources. The "honest politician" should play down victimless crimes to free resources for the fight against violent and predatory crime and — usually an afterthought — white-collar crime.

When the Berkeley version of radical criminology appeared on the scene, though, the conflict moved well beyond minor boundary disputes in the interest of "priorities." The question of what should be called crime was not pragmatic nor merely theoretical; it was a central human rights issue. The criminal law must be seen not in its usual restricted, liberal terms but as a guarantee of certain basic human rights. A denial of these rights should properly be called criminal. Exploitation, imperialism, racism, and sexism were the *true* crimes.[13]

Taken literally, the human rights model is a program for the criminalization of all forms of power in the modern state. But taken rhetorically and combined with the muckraking and reformist element in the white-collar crime debate, a new discourse of criminalization began to take shape. It was to be consolidated by the most powerful ideological force of the past decade, feminism — or more particularly, the strand in feminism that sought to use the criminalizing power of the state for instrumental and symbolic ends.

I do not want to give the impression that a homogeneous new paradigm, "new criminalization," has emerged. The attempt over the past twenty years to construct an alternative criminology has taken aboard so many diverse intellectual and political strands, normalizing and criminalizing, that we must expect to find all sorts of internal disagreements and inconsistencies. Sometimes these are merely differences of emphasis, but in the internal polemics of alternative criminology two distinct positions emerged: left idealism and left realism.

The first position we have already encountered. The traditional categories of primal crime (coded as "street crime" or "working-class crime") must be demystified. These are not the real crimes: the damage and fear they cause are exaggerated (by the media, by moral panics, by law and order campaigns that the state uses to maintain its political hegemony). The criminal law in its origin, content, and enforcement is selective, class biased, and unjust, a tool to protect private property, to strengthen ruling-class power, to control and maintain a permanent social underclass. The real crimes are the crimes of the powerful:

corporate crime, state crime, environmental crimes. The normalized depredations of the powerful must be properly criminalized. The criminological task is political, to join the power struggle against the powerful, and intellectual, to create a new liberatory knowledge of the "real" crime problem.

Left realism is a counterposition that has emerged only in the past four or five years.[14] It consists largely of retraction and self-criticism by former left idealists. The polemic line runs like this: the "New Left-inspired" approach to crime and justice that gave rise to the first wave of critical criminology was "dangerous," "irresponsible," "politically immature," "romantic," "utopian," "voluntarist," "anarchist," "libertarian," and "Fanonist," the product of a "primitive analysis," a "confused approach to strategy and tactics," and a "petty bourgeois worldview." In particular, it was wrong to gloss over the significance of street crime (and even more wrong to interpret it as primitive rebellion), wrong to see the criminal law a mere expression of ruling-class interest, wrong to see the police as oppressors.

Instead, the left realists argue, we must begin with the real facts of working-class crime and victimization. Because of their powerlessness and social disorganization, the working class and racial minorities are doubly vulnerable not just to crimes of the powerful but also to predatory street crimes. Primal crime is not only real enough but one of *the* politically crucial issues for the Left: socialism is about the protection of the vulnerable and the establishment of social justice. And to the patterns of vulnerability clearly shown by orthodox victimization studies (the suffering, divisiveness, and demoralization caused by street crime) must be added the patterns of vulnerability shown up by feminist victimology: domestic violence, rape, pornography, and other forms of exploitation, harassment, and denial of human rights.

This focus on the victim restores one side of the triangle of criminal, victim, and state instead of dealing exclusively with the dialectical relationship between crime and state social control. Further, "The central tenet of left realism is to reflect the reality of crime . . . its origins, nature and impact."[15] In its left realist phase the object of radical criminology had become criminalization rather than crime. This only created a separate paradigm that could not possibly compete with liberalism or conservatism. It is *crime* that now must be taken seriously. Unremarkable as this conclusion might sound to those who have not taken these particular theoretical journeys, the conceptual drama of the change should not be missed. "The tide is turning for radical criminology," proclaim the left realists.[16]

This is not the place to analyze the whole significance of this turn nor to deal with its particular strengths: its political potential and its revival of interest in the traditional causal questions abandoned by both left idealism and the now-dominant managerial criminology. Nor can I consider the theoretical generology being appealed to in support of the renewed radical faith in criminalization (which Heinz Steinert has rather cruelly called the "amazing new left law and order campaign").[17] Important here has been E.P. Thompson's argument that the rule of law was an unqualified human good, a liberating weapon to be used for political action in defense of the interests of the powerless. This "defensive formalism," in turn, is one tendency within radical sociology of law, the other being varieties of informalism and idealist destructuring ("justice without law"). The left realists are the vanguard in alternative criminology of a more orthodox socialism: their realism, formalism, and belief in a strong centralized state being set against the visionary, libertarian, and decentralist tendencies of the small abolitionist faction.

In any event, whether it self-consciously proclaims itself left realist or not, alternative criminology today defines its object in the shadow of these debates. These, very crudely, are the available positions in decreasing order, I suppose, of "realism": accepting a rational core in the public definition of the crime problem; extending this core conception to include a range of neglected victims; without denying the existence of the core, emphasizing instead the seriousness of crimes of the powerful and seeking to extend the net of criminalization; demythologizing the core and using old idealist or new abolitionist ideas to decriminalize certain forms of existing crime. I will take two recent counter-texts from what might be loosely called alternative criminology to find traces of all these positions.

In the first, from the United States, Pepinsky and Jesilow build their entire text by exposing the myths that surround working-class crime.[18] The point of the law is, surely, to protect us from harm and deprivation, but the poor bear the brunt of criminalization while others more deserving of punishment remain untouched. Pepinsky and Jesilow's project is to show that crimes of the powerful—white-collar crime, environmental offenses, safety offenses, and (their particular animus) unnecessary medical treatment—cause more harm, deprivation, and loss than street crime.

Box, from England, gives a more thorough account of the same evidence.[19] Yes, "conventional" crimes do have victims whose suffering is real; these crimes should be understood and controlled so that fewer people are victimized: "A radical criminology which appears to deny this will be seen as callous and rightly rejected" (p. 3). But these conventional crimes of the young working-class male constitute *a* crime problem, not *the* crime problem: "Maybe what is stuffed into our consciousness as *the* crime problem is in fact an illusion, a trick to deflect our attention away from other even more serious crimes and victimizing behaviors which objectively cause the vast bulk of avoidable death, injury and deprivation" (p. 3). Box then builds up the appropriate evidence about corporate crime, police crime, rape, and sexual assault on females.

There are interesting and important differences between these two texts. Pepinsky and Jesilow seem more "idealist" than Box in that they are prepared to extend their redefinitional enterprise to harms, deprivations, wrongs, and violations well outside the conventional criminal law, to "the business executive in a Brooks Brothers suit who denies another pay rise" and all sorts of other normalized business and professional activities. They advocate a type of epistemological populism to determine priorities: "Just as it is open to legislators to rewrite the law, it is open to citizens to reconsider what kinds of taking and killing they want to define as wrong and right" (p. 4).

Box is more concerned to use the criminal law's own strict internal criteria to establish harm (and hence what should properly be criminalized). The problem as he sees it is that standard definitions of murder, rape, robbery, assault, theft, and other serious crimes are so constructed as to exclude many similar and, in important ways, identical acts that are committed more frequently by the powerful and that "objectively and avoidably" cause more harm, injury, and suffering. For example, only some kinds of avoidable killing are defined as murder; others—resulting, for example, from inadequate safety standards, environmental pollution, inadequately tested drugs—are not. And only one kind of nonconsensual sexual act is defined as rape.

Pepinsky and Jesilow are again more "idealist" (or rather, closer to abolitionism) in that they are skeptical about simply extending criminalization to more people and actions. Criminalization, they note at one point, is "a relatively bad choice for responding to most of the wrongs people do" (p. 5). Consequently, they want to decrease the scope of the criminal justice system, to teach citizens how to live without law enforcement, to develop new mediation mechanisms, and overall, to "lessen the force of criminal justice by benign neglect" (p. 90).

Box, on the other hand, has no such minimalist program. He agrees with the left realists that radicals must recapture the law and order, street-crime terrain from the conservatives. The attack on crimes of the powerful is a strategy of opening up a "second front" (p. 34). And in opening up this front, he is prepared to use all the conventional weapons of the criminal justice system and, indeed, even to consider, in order to prosecute and convict corporations, "abandoning judicial practices which protect the accused from arbitrary or unjust conviction or which ensure they receive the benefit of the doubt" (p. 69). Incapacitating executives by imprisonment is also a good idea; "The fear of imprisonment may instill the fear of rape into young, smooth, neat corporate executives . . . and lead to a dramatic and welcome improvement in their behavior" (p. 71).

My "new criminalization" heading covers, then, all sorts of varying positions: a pure left realist position on street crime (that is, the socialist version of law and order), a massive extension of the power to criminalize in order to open a second front against the crimes of the powerful, a qualified use of the criminal sanction for the most damaging wrongs, reserving a minimalist or abolitionist position for other crimes, and many other variations on these themes.

Excluding Pepinsky and Jesilow's "benign neglect" theme and other equivalent antistate and decentralist ideas that may be heard (outside the European abolitionists, that is), the realist program has now come to dominate the literature on alternative criminology. Unlike in the texts of the mid-sixties to the mid-seventies, the fateful decision to criminalize either is not the object of much critical attention or, in selected cases, is supported with crusading zeal.

And Some New Problems

So far, so good. Or rather, so far, so bad. For if I did not think there were any problems in these recent developments, I would not have had a subject for this paper. By "problems" I mean, first, a series of unresolved questions about what is happening in the real world of criminalization and moral enterprise. Is it true that there is a growing tendency to campaign for the criminalization of "new" areas of social life and for the "heavier" criminalization of existing ones? If so, what accounts for this tendency? Under what conditions are the campaigns successful? Can variations be observed between societies? Can some optimal level of criminalization be determined (does it ever make sense to talk about "overcriminalization")? And so on.

We lack the most elementary answers to these questions. We can make all sorts of macrosociological generalizations about the striking trend in the history of the criminal law for the modern state to require legal institutions to assume responsibilities (ideological and coercive) that were once the domain of "society." Or, we can refine this observation, as Habermas and others have done, by noting the extension of regulatory and administrative (as opposed to penal law) into the political economy, leading to a greater integration of state and society. We can also talk about the greater use of symbolic law, to reaffirm basic social values rather than achieve instrumental ends. But such generalizations are at a very high level of abstraction. They can be plausibly countered by equally abstract suggestions, for example, that the orthodox criminal law is becoming *less* important as a form of social control.

If abstract theory is not very helpful, neither is hard empiricism. It is surprising how few researchers have simply classified and counted changes in the net volume of criminalization in any society. The research by Berk and his colleagues on the Californian penal code between 1955 and 1971 is one of the few of this kind.[20] They counted a massive net increase in criminalization. Some areas were removed from the criminal code, but never in this period was there any overall decriminalization. Would this pattern be repeated in other states? What would comparisons between countries show? And how would the net rates vary between types of offenses?

I want to concentrate, though, on a second series of "problems", not on what is actually happening but on my sociology of knowledge question about how criminologists are framing and participating in the business of criminalization. How, for example, do we account for the apparent death of liberal non-interventionist criminology? What has happened to all those impressive arguments in favor of decriminalizing consensual crimes, arguments that figured so prominently in criminology for a decade and then somehow faded away from the discourse?[21] Are the accepted wisdoms of that earlier period — that criminal laws unsupported by widely shared moral beliefs are ineffective and counterproductive, that law enforcement is biased, that justice does not happen — now to be reversed? Why was it once radical to demystify and now radical to be realistic?

There are all sorts of lines of response to such questions. On the issue of victimless crime, for example, one argument might be that the victories have been won, that there is nothing left to fight. This is patently not the case. A simple roundup of the original victimless crime categories will show that with the single possible exception of homosexuality, most areas show no dramatic moves to decriminalization (drugs, vagrancy, gambling, prostitution); in others such as abortion, earlier victories are under threat; and in others (pornography) there have been moves to more criminalization. What has to be explained about the sixties is not permissiveness but the ideology of permissiveness, a myth that flourished despite increased state control and a myth that justified later tightening up.[22]

A more serious line of argument is the radical critique that the whole theory and strategy of decriminalization was misconceived, and that concepts such as victimless crime have no justification. This was part of the broader onslaught against labeling theory for supposedly advocating "repressive tolerance,"[23] and for its "benign neglect" of the objective conditions that give rise to such real social problems as heroin use. Moreover, these crimes were not at all victimless (the many victims were merely not immediately visible) or consensual (this romanticizes human choice; these are not people freely engaged in willing transactions) or harmless (real social harm and damage could be found).

There is some force to these objections, as there is to two more general criticisms of liberal noninterventionism: first, that giving more freedom and privacy in limited areas of consumption, reproduction, and sexuality benefit only selected members of the privileged classes; and second, that the historical role of liberalism, far from being protective, has been to remove the defenses of the weak in the name of some abstract notion of freedom. And these objections no doubt apply to such libertarian slogans as "total freedom from state interference to use your body." As Schur, however, points out in a recent reevaluation of the victimless crime concept, neither the abstract moral claims (about rights, harms, victims, or whatever) nor the sociological objections about repressive tolerance nor any dislike of "ghettos of deviance" address themselves to the original debate.[24] The original issue was an empirical matter in the sociology of law: What were the actual consequences of trying to enforce the criminal law against behaviors that (whatever their "real" moral or social meanings) lacked the property of most other crimes, the presence of a complaining victim to initiate the enforcement? The empirical point was to show the actual and likely costs of this particular legal policy: secondary deviance, black markets, corrupt law enforcement, victimization by the law, and so on. This sociological model, Schur reminds us, emphasizes that certain predictable and observable consequences are likely to follow from the attempted criminalization of consensual exchanges, regardless of what conclusion we might reach about harm or rights.

Even if the essence of the behavior or its moral status could be made absolutely clear (and the current debates about the "harm" of pornography or the "victim" of abortion show how unlikely is this prospect), and even if the utilitarian costs were finally reckoned up, the actual choice of policy (criminalization or decriminalization) will not logically follow. The decision remains political. As does the decision whether to deal with the original structural causes, to devise new forms of control, or to work at both these levels.

In any event the various problems intrinsic to the victimless crime concept do not in themselves explain today's apparent lack of interest in decriminalization. It is not that either radical or liberal criminologists are actually *supporting* the New Right and the renewed moral crusades against "victimless crimes" but rather that their preoccupations are elsewhere: street crime or "new" crimes. In radical theory the justification for this move is "realism." It is hard to see what has happened in liberal theory. One might have expected that the ideology of neoliberal skepticism (about benevolence, paternalism, good intentions, state intervention) would have encouraged an even greater concern with areas of such apparently misguided state intervention.

In both radicalism and liberalism, though, these internal theoretical leaps are responses to external political changes: the dominance of law and order rhetoric and the continued prominence of the crime problem; the visibility and militancy of the "new" victims; the preoccupations of the old "soft" deviants with defensive battles (to retain liberal abortion laws, gays trying to prevent legal repression in the wake of the AIDS epidemic); the dramatic elevation of the drug problem (with the disappearance of any evangelism on behalf of recreational drug use). All this can be summed up by the change of slogans and demands at the local community level; the same neighborhoods and minority groups that in the sixties were shouting, "Police brutality" and "Off the pigs" are now demanding more police protection as a basic right. Such is the political context that has shaped the new criminalization. That is: simple and persuasive as it sounds, this model cannot be explained in its own terms, wholly within its academic trajectory. Similarly, the new criminalization cannot be accepted as the final answer to the puzzle of determining criminology's proper object. Such a solution is persuasive more in the normative than the analytic sense. Our values, that is, might lead us to support wholeheartedly all forms of the new criminalization without our ever being able to explain their social base or political ramifications.

This becomes quite obvious as soon as we try to draw up a shopping list of the areas of social life that are putative candidates for new (or heavier) criminalization or, alternatively, decriminalization. Consider the following list:

- Marijuana use; vagrancy; juvenile status offenses; gambling; euthanasia
  Some liberals: in favor of full decriminalization
  Most radicals: indifferent
- Prostitution
  Some liberals: full decriminalization
  Most radicals and feminists: decriminalization but not legalization
- Abortion
  Most liberals and radicals: full decriminalization
- Rape; all forms of sexual violence against women
  All liberals: support for existing criminalization
  All radicals and feminists: further and heavier criminalization
- Pornography
  Some liberals: decriminalization except for hard-core pornography (sado-masochism, etc.)
  Most radicals and feminists: further and heavier criminalization (all forms of exploitation of women)
- Incest
  Nearly all liberals and radicals: support or extend existing criminalization
  A few radicals: decriminalize under certain conditions
- Corporate crime; environmental crimes; state crime (torture and other abuses of power)
  Liberals: cautious criminalization
  Radicals: massive criminalization
- Tobacco; teenage drinking; dangerous foods
  Some liberals in favor of new criminalization
- Heroin
  No one knows

I need hardly point out that this list is totally useless. It does not specify place or time; it gives no idea of the strength of these various forces; there could be strong objections to an item appearing in any particular category; the same item can plausibly appear in several categories, and so on. This is just my point. And the picture becomes really complex when we add to my caricature of current "liberal" and "radical" positions any historical sense of the actual moves for and against criminalization of any items on the list. Three particular complexities are worth singling out:

1. the *Changing forces* problem: the way in which similar forces might at one time support criminalization and another time decriminalization for the behavior in question.
2. the *Strange alliances* problem: the way in which criminalization or decriminalization may be supported for opposite political reasons, and on the basis of quite different conceptions of the essence of the behavior in question.
3. the *Unintended consequences* problem: the way in which campaigns supported for one set of reasons might result in policies that might have an opposite set of results.

Commercial sex — prostitution and pornography — provides an obvious arena for illustrating such complexities.

1. *Changing forces.* The current liberal, radical, and feminist attacks on commercial sex have their precedents in the late-nineteenth-century campaigns against male vice and the double standard. The moral entrepreneurs of the Progressive period — ladies rescue committees, antivice and social purity leagues — campaigned against prostitution, pornography, white slavery, and homosexuality as manifestations of undifferentiated male lust. The prostitute was the fallen woman, the weak, exploited victim of male sexuality. Using the model of slavery, these campaigns were abolitionist: they opposed legalization, supported severe state repression, lobbied for more criminal sanctions, encouraged stricter law enforcement.

By the 1960s commercial sex became seen in quite different terms: the campaign was against not for repression. In liberal and progressive thought pornography became a right, a matter of choice and privacy, part of an emancipatory campaign toward free, liberated sexuality. Prostitution also was caught up in the rhetoric of rights and civil liberties. The prostitute remained a victim, not of an unrestrained male libido but of the unjust criminal justice system. The attack was on the discriminatory laws that hurt the weakest most. Decriminalization of both pornography and prostitution was supported.

Within a decade these positions changed. The "second wave" of feminist thought turned bitterly against the whole liberal conception of pornography as harmless, victimless, or consensual. The liberal fallacy was to isolate sex from society and history. Pornography became analyzed in terms of male power and violence, sexism and patriarchy, the degradation and subordination of women.[25] There was indeed a victim: the woman used in the production of pornography. And there was indeed danger: pornography was "the theory that underlies the practice of rape." It becomes imperative, then, to strengthen and extend the protective and symbolic power of the criminal law.

In the case of prostitution the switch in forces was not so dramatic.[26] The decriminalization stand remained, in the sense that some feminist groups continue to support prostitutes against legal harassment and discrimination. But feminist theory about prostitution has developed in such a way that the negative rather than positive features of the phenomenon are emphasized; not autonomy and choice but the commodification of sexuality, the ownership of female sexuality as the core of the gender system, the element of sexual exploitation and slavery. Thus, full legalization and state regulation are opposed and the long-term position is abolitionist, not in the nineteenth-century sense (through total legal prohibition) but through eventual attrition following the realization of the general feminist program. Meantime, the institution of prostitution is not supported, though individual prostitutes are defended as "righteous deviants" and their male clients criminalized.

2. *Strange alliances.* In each of these three periods — the end of the nineteenth century, the 1960s, and the present — the control of commercial sex has attracted a complex set of social forces. Historians of the early campaigns note the convergence of feminists, personal rights activists, organized religion, socialists, antisuffragists, repressive moralists, male-dominated corporate philanthropy, bohemians, and puritans.[27] The 1960s "crimes-without-victims" banner attracted mainstream liberals and civil rights advocates (attracted by the Millsian conception of the proper limits of the law), all-purpose libertarians, feminists stressing equality and freedom of choice, and socialists of the left idealist type, attacking discrimination and repression. Now, radical feminist campaigners against pornography sometimes find themselves in alliances with right-wing groups from the Moral Majority; antifeminist conservatives; profamily, antisex lobbyists; and traditional procensorship groups.[28]

3. *Unintended consequences.* Again, this has been a constant historical threat. Current feminist critics looking back at the nineteenth-century social purity campaigns see them as classic examples of reform gone wrong. Instead of protection, the most vulnerable women (poor, members of ethnic minorities) became subject to more harassment, repression, and exploitation. Instead of advancing the causes of feminism, patriarchy was even further morally legitimated. As Walkowitz comments about one reform episode: "Begun as the libertarian struggle against the state sanction of male vice, the repeal campaign helped to spawn a hydra headed campaign against sexual deviation of all kinds."[29] Similarly, the current feminist campaign against pornography might have to face the unintended consequence of helping build a new power base for extreme moral conservatives and antifeminist forces.

I list these three examples from the arena of sexual politics as "problems" not in the sense that they are seen only by the smart, outside observer or that they do not have solutions. Feminist literature is already fully aware of these paradoxes, and there is a well-developed body of theory to explain them —

whether in terms of ideological contradictions, organizational pressures, or political strategy. Current studies, for example, of campaigns to change rape laws by criminalizing all degrees of nonconsensual sexual contacts have noted just these problems: the undesirable price to be paid for using the criminal law to achieve symbolic aims; "success" being less a feminist victory over patriarchy than a coincidence of very different feminist and state interests; how a mere extension of the traditional criminal justice system reproduces male patronage and reinforces the neo-classical tendency to concentrate all social policy into punishing individual acts; the way in which laws created to achieve equal justice are enforced in such a way as to extend state control over the traditional underclass.[30]

Reviewing such problems in the wake of the success of the Canadian feminist movement in changing the rape laws, Snider reflects: "Since this system [criminal justice] does not increase public safety, does not change authoritarian, sexist and competitive values into sensitive, humanitarian and co-operative ones, the purpose of progressive reformers such as feminist groups ought to be to weaken rather than strengthen it."[31] This is not, of course, to argue that all forms of criminalization must be rejected, still less that victims of sexual domination should not be protected or offenders not punished. The point is that campaigns for legal reform should not forget the standard problems: co-optation; the difficulty of finding universal definitions; questions of rights. There is real danger that in the emerging discourse of the new criminalization, these subtleties will disappear, as if decades of critical theory about the criminal law did not exist.

Sexual politics is only one of the more visible areas for observing these confusions. There are many other latent areas that can still catch us by surprise. Take, for example, the endless possibilities of using the criminal law to enforce religious belief. For most of the Western world, it seems a very long time ago when the gravest crimes included sacrilege, defilement of sacred things, idol worshipping, defamation of God, sorcery, and summoning spirits. But attempts to criminalize the teaching of evolutionism are not so far away; in my supposedly "Western" country, Israel, doctors can be punished for performing autopsies, and the selling of pig meat might soon be a criminal offense; in many countries "deprogrammers" (erstwhile liberals) are rescuing their children from semireligious cults like EST, Scientology, and the Moonies, and trying to have these organizations banned. Marx perhaps only slightly exaggerated the drama of criminalization: "At the same time, when the English stopped burning witches at the stake, they began to hang forgers of bank notes."

No theory can fully anticipate the future twists and turns of the social world. Here, though, are four theoretical projects that might help us in understanding the present.

The Theory of Criminalization

One source of confusion might lie in our very conception of criminalization. We have many good theories about *why* acts are criminalized and some good descriptions of some traditional criminalization campaigns (though whether these apply to newer criminalizing enterprises, I will have to consider). But our discourse overall is organized in the terms of the menu or shopping list metaphor of classical jurisprudence. There is a list of crimes, each with its tariff; some behaviors get added to the list, thus becoming criminal; others get taken off, thus becoming noncriminal.

For most purposes, such as the standard consensus versus conflict debates about the origins of the law,[32] this model will do, but often it takes for granted the very category that is the problem. Some things like pornography or obscenity are already legal definitions in themselves, the product of previous campaigns. The problem is not simply whether one adds them to the list but how they were constructed in the first place. These are not words that refer to fixed acts or persons but to situations and conflicts that are now being judged in a different way. When we are asked to include as a crime a previously normalized form of sexual encounter, say, the male use of "persuasion," we are adding a new item to the list *and* seeing it in terms of the already-existing item of rape.

Another problem is the way criminalization relates to the overall exercise of power in modern society. Foucault has taught us to question three common assumptions about power: that it is centrally focused, based on and always relating back to the privileged position of the state; that it is a property, something that X has and Y does not; that it always operates in negative, repressive terms — a force that says no. Criminalization rather must be seen in terms of a complex set of strategies, maneuvers, and relationships in which the power to ban, to say no, is not its only effect. Foucault suggested that the so-called repression of sexuality in the eighteenth and nineteenth centuries actually created new spaces to talk about sex. Similarly, the current criminalizing campaigns in the realm of sexual politics cannot be judged in purely negative terms. A new knowledge is being created, new objects can now be openly spoken about; not the old "perversions" of normal sexuality that preoccupied Krafft-Ebing and Freud but new deviations from the desired norm: how the male boss talks to the female secretary, the posture of the model in the beer advertisement, the wording of the lyrics of a popular song, and so on.

Criminalization plays a paradoxical role in this overall discourse. In the rhetoric of moral enterprise — old and new, liberal, conservative, and radical — we find time and time again the statement that crime is not the "real" problem. In the same way that the positivists assured us that the real problem was not delinquency (action or infraction) but neglect, deprivation, poverty, or whatever, so the new criminalizers deconstruct the categories of crime and criminal and talk about racism, sexism, patriarchy, capitalism, abuses of power, and the like.

Both the old and the new rhetoric are correct. The classical and neo-classical models make the abstract act too important. Criminalization is the process of identifying an act deemed dangerous to the dominant social order and designating it in law as criminally punishable. This fateful decision produces a peculiar illusion (peculiar because we know very well that it is an illusion): that acts of conduct were divided originally into positive/negative, criminal/virtuous. The criminal law draws a simple line of demarcation. Unlike social norms that we know as subtle, continuous, and negotiable, we start to talk about a dichotomous variable, crime/noncrime. In principle (as the Soviet criminologist Yakovlev points out) an act cannot demonstrate a little of both properties. Strictly speaking, there cannot be degrees of criminality. "Such is the principled peculiarity of the rule of law which places the latter apart from other social norms and values. Moral judgements do have their gradations and transitions; legal prescriptions are single and accurate ones."[33]

Why am I making such heavy weather here of what is so sociologically obvious? Simply because a nonreflective stance toward criminalization (as exhibited by many new realists and criminalizers) will always face a particular theoretical (and political) paradox. The more clearly one exposes the subtle, continuous, and pervasive nature of the social danger to be attacked, the more difficult becomes the use of the "single and accurate" system of criminal law as one's weapon. It is because crime/non-crime is a dichotomous variable that the ambition of the criminal law model (especially in its current neo-classical phase) is to apply the same yardstick in unique and different situations. And this, as abolitionists argue, is precisely the weakness of crime as a form of social control.

These are not just nice theoretical debates but matters of immediate policy interest. Criminalization is a particular reaction to a defined social problem. The empirical question is, Under what conditions do certain people consider that a given conflict requires state intervention, and if it does, should this intervention take the form of criminal justice (rather than another system, for example, civil law)? The political question is why and how this preference becomes reality. The pragmatic question is, What do we gain by defining the problem in terms of crime?

The way we define a problem gives us certain goals for knowing what its solution is.[34] If we define the road safety problem in terms of the quality of life for accident victims and their families, the solution is better health care, insurance, or victim compensation. But these will not count as solutions or make no sense at all if the problem is defined only in terms of accident-prone drivers or the number of detected traffic offenses.[35] Thus, defining a problem in terms of crime, provides a particular notion of what counts as a solution:

no crime, or less crime (though it is never clear *how* much less). But this is only one possible cognitive frame. Crime is not a property inherent in any social problem and its peculiar defect — as decades of criminology have shown — is that its criterion of solution is particularly elusive. It becomes more elusive the more we try to stretch the category. If we define more acts of sexual exploitation as crime, the result cannot be less crime but more crime. And if we succeed in raising consciousness about those acts, then more of them will be reported. These points are perfectly banal, but why are they so seldom considered by the new criminalizers?

This leads me on to a final problem in this section: the supposed realism of the new realists. How does one explain, except entirely in its own terms, the apparent abandonment by critical criminology of interest in the question of how rules are constructed in favor of either a renewed appreciation in the liberal ideology of the rule of law or the attempted construction of a socialist law and order policy, a new version of the old penal dialect? In one sense this is simply a regression to the tendency in the social sciences to give almost exclusive attention to crime as a response to troublesome behavior.[36] But the turnabout here has to be explained more specifically.

The explanation probably lies in the ambiguity of the original talk about the possibility of a crime-free society. The argument that crime is a product of capitalism and will disappear under socialism could mean one of two things: the disappearance of crime is seen either as the disappearance of the causes, problems, and conditions that trigger, or call for, the criminalization process *or* is seen as the disappearance of the criminalization process as an answer to those problems. It seems clear now that the first interpretation has won out. To capture the law and order terrain from the conservatives, the left realists have to reemphasize traditional causal questions, to insist, that is, on the first of those senses in which capitalism is criminogenic. This has meant less reflection about the criminalization process itself, an abandonment, that is, of the second possibility. This might be politically expedient and sociologically sensible — but it does close off one way of imagining a very different social order.

The Politics of Liberalism

The internal movements within radical theory are of minor significance in the overall terrain of criminal justice politics. This cannot be said for liberal theory. In fact, the history of our subject has been inextricably tied up with the history of liberalism, and one of the great unwritten projects in criminology is to understand the evolving ambiguities in liberal thought and their influence on crime control policy and thinking.

In classical liberal thinking about crime not only was a privileged position given to state power but a particular notion of the state was used. This was the limited state: acting as a combination of traffic officer (preventing collisions) and night guard (looking after life and property). The debate about the proper limits of the state's power to criminalize still derives from this original conception: hence the philosophical appeal to Bentham and Mill in the original debate about victimless crime; hence the permanent appeal of utilitarianism in criminological thinking.

The past twenty years of criminal justice politics should have done enough to dispel the notion that this restricted interpretation of liberalism will help very much. For one thing, post-Keynesian liberalism has always been more interventionist than those traditional metaphors apply. And there has also been the tension between different conceptions of liberty. Classic ("minimalist") liberalism was closer to what Berlin called "negative liberty": the state intervenes only to protect the individual's liberty from being infringed upon by others. This, crudely speaking, is the base of primal criminalization. Progressive, post-progressive, *and* radical ideologies, on the other hand, appeal also to a concept of "positive liberty." The benevolent, paternalistic state not only is protective but wants to liberate human potential (for happiness, self-fulfillment, true self, or whatever). And this difference between positive and negative liberty is only one aspect of the great debate that has opened up within liberal thinking over the past decade between defenders of the more traditional mode (Rawls, Nozick, Dworkin) and of the newer "communitarian" version (Taylor, Walzer, Macintyre, Sandel).[37]

Criminologists would be well advised to study this literature, if only to see how far the debate in liberalism has moved from the old questions about tolerance, privacy, and the limits of state intervention that shaped the decriminalization debates. Take again the troublesome area of sexual politics: pornography, prostitution, and sexual violence. Within feminist literature a debate already exists between those who would extend the use of the law for symbolic and instrumental reasons and those who doubt whether the conventional criminal justice system can be turned around and used in the fight against sexism (as if assuming that the state is a neutral force with no ideological character of its own). But within criminology this debate has hardly been registered. We still talk of decriminalization within the old liberal discourse of atomistic individual against the state, while the real political forces "outside" have long used a quite different model of the relationship between individual and society.

Consider, for example, the historical shifts along the continuum of determinism/voluntarism. The original Progressives wanted to save the weak and the vulnerable: women, along with children, were victims of circumstances, determined beings. Protection and repression were in their best interests. The rhetoric of decriminalization, on the other hand, needed rational, voluntaristic beings: the woman free to choose a "career" of prostitution, to participate in or consume pornography — all without benevolent state interference. The current wisdom simultaneously reinvokes the woman as determined (the victim of the legal process or of patriarchy) and calls for state intervention to protect negative liberty (against exploitation) and allow positive liberty (for self-liberation). In current feminist literature on pornography there is none of the free choice espoused by neo-classical criminologists nor any traditional liberal idea of the minimum state. Pornography totally *determines* sexuality (by conditioning males into violent, misogynous, and exploitative attitudes). The future society has to be systematically rescripted; this cannot take place under market liberalism; therefore the state has to adopt an active, interventionist role.

The apparently puzzling alliances and battles in the field of sexual politics can be understood in terms of these increasingly open contradictions of liberalism. This, of course, is true in other areas where criminalization is being contested, for example, the use of the criminal law to protect minorities from discrimination and to criminalize racial incitement. A student in France produces a Ph.D "proving" that the Holocaust never happened. Should he be defended (as he was by some *radicals*) in terms of the liberal doctrine of academic freedom or should "denial of the Holocaust" be made into a new crime?

The liberal position on freedom of speech has always been even more exposed in the realm of class politics. Here, Left and Right retain their traditional objects of social censure. Thus, the Right supported and the Left (including, by the way, left realist criminologists) opposed the use of the criminal law against the striking miners in Great Britain in 1984-85. Even though the strike was technically a civil dispute (between the National Union of Miners and the Coal Board) the police used criminal law in an instrumental way to undermine the pickets (reviving medieval laws to allow the setting up of roadblocks to prevent strikers' crossing of counties, obscenity laws to allow the arrest of pickets verbally abusing blacklegs, municipal laws to allow the imposition of curfews on whole communities). If the Left was politically consistent in opposing this, liberals—those that remain—had no clear position on criminalization.

Beyond the terrain of class politics it has become clear that the issues raised by the New Left, ecological, antinuclear, and women's movements—with their common faith that the personal is political—defy conventional categorization in left, center, and right terms. It is not at all clear where criminalization fits in the "new map of the geography of cultural politics."[38]

The Sociology of Moral Enterprise

The study of moral enterprise was the product of the liberal sociology of deviance paradigm of the 1960s. The concept made sociological sense but it also owed its immediate appeal to the notion that moral entrepreneurs were not people "like us." As I noted earlier, moral enterprise was a concept used not only in the neutral sense—Becker's definition of creating a new part in the moral fabric or society—but also to denote a process clearly devalued from the standpoint of the liberal, permissive worldview.

The question that now suggests itself is whether the theory of moral enterprise can be used to analyze the new criminalizing of the 1980s. For example, have the areas of corporate crime, environmental crime, crimes against women, and so on provided (as one observer suggests about campaigns against teenage drinking) "new careers for moral entrepreneurs"?[39] There is some resistance to even putting such questions because the sociology of moral enterprise evokes such negative connotations for contemporary liberals and radicals. Who wants to be associated with moral panics, social purity, moral prophylaxis, puritanism, or middle-class morality? There is also, as I suggest in the next section, a reluctance among criminologists to acknowledge their own role in the politics of redefinition. Let me, however, suggest a few senses in which the question is at least worth putting and is not, at first glance at least, altogether outrageous or irrelevant. I will then move to the obvious differences between the old and new forms of moral enterprise.

First, there is little doubt that the new enterprise contains a high degree of indignation, zeal, and emotional commitment. Students of the white-collar crime polemic note Sutherland's original "religious commitment that, at its best, demands that the ethic of Christianity be maintained in human and business relations."[40] The reference to Christianity aside, the contemporary literature on corporate crime, for all its conceptual sophistication (explaining how organizations are responsible for deviance and illegality) shows the same fundamentalist zeal.[41] In the radical feminist literature on pornography this sort of commitment defines the nature of the whole enterprise.

Second, it is clear that the end point and the criterion for success of both the old and the new forms of enterprise are successful criminalization. The point of the exercise is not simply consciousness raising or social-problem definition but a specific commitment to change a previously normalized condition or behavior into a punishable criminal offense.

Third, there are striking similarities in the rhetoric and strategy of the campaigns:

- The attempt to increase public awareness through the use of the mass media and other publicity techniques (slide shows of sadistic pornography, tours of Time Square, pickets of *Playboy*).
- The attempt to expose the behavior in question as being underreported, unnoticed, and normalized, but now increasing at an alarming rate.
- The emphasis on victimization, fear, damage, threat, and potential danger.
- The cognitive pyramid technique in which the behavior in question is presented as inextricably linked with other conditions: pornography with rape; rape with other sexual abuses, such as harassment at work and child abuse. And all with some overarching condition such as sexism or exploitation.[42]

- The use of atrocity stories and a rhetoric of exaggeration. For example, one criminologist refers to corporate crime as "minor acts of genocide,"[43] and the vocabulary of the Holocaust, Nazism, fascism, and totalitarianism is routinely used in the campaigning literature against pornography.[44]

To examine these parallels — particularly the last group, those at the level of rhetoric — might be a useful way of understanding some common problems in criminalization campaigns. Note, for example, the cognitive pyramid theory. When this appears in traditional forms of moral enterprise, it is usually so crude — take the "dope-causes-crime" equation — that it can easily be exposed by the smart social scientist. The new campaigns, however, use a version of the theory so knowledgeable, theoretically sophisticated, and politically wise that it cannot be exposed by the outside observer. Indeed, the criminological theory and the campaign theory are identical, often produced by the same people. And the theory *is* beyond refutation: rape and pornography, of course, are connected with the prevailing structure and ideology of sexism; corporate crime, of course, cannot be separated from the nature of capitalism and free enterprise; and so on.

But such analysis, however correct, presents the entrepreneur with the dilemma I identified earlier: If the problem can be defined only in such complex terms, how to use the simple definitions of the criminal law? This is parallel to Becker's dilemma of the rule enforcers who simultaneously have to inflate the problem to obtain resources (give us more money, or else things will get worse) *and* claim that the problem is under control (we are doing a good job under the circumstances). The dilemma for the entrepreneur, old and new, is this: the more he or she succeeds in cognitively inflating the problem into a much wider, deeper phenomenon, the more difficult it becomes to use criminalization with its limited, specific, and dichotomous definitions as a solution. The more "radical" the cognitive claims are, the more obvious this problem becomes. For example, that predatory criminal rape is different only in degree from normal sexual behavior in patriarchal society; that there is an element of rape in all sexual behavior; that the rapist is the man next door. Or that corporate crime can be defined in terms of the normal exploitative practices of the business firm; because all profit-making organizations extract surplus value in excess of the cost of labor, they are all ultimately criminal, that is, the profit-making goal makes the corporation inherently criminogenic. I will return to this problem when dealing with the special role of criminological knowledge in the new enterprise. In theory, though, this is a problem shared by old and new forms.

We must now consider the many obvious ways in which the traditional moral enterprise literature is of little use in understanding the new criminalization. There are few actual studies of contemporary radical criminalizers,[45] but it is obvious at first sight that criminological campaigns against corporate crime, international organizations trying to criminalize human rights offenses, feminist campaigns against pornography and to extend the definition of sexual violence do not fit the standard descriptions of moral enterprise.[46]

The traditional profile — of the muckraker, purity reformer, symbolic crusader, urban progressive, do-gooder, social hygienist, and others — is of a group of status discontents trying to defend symbolically the dominance and prestige of a life-style to which they are committed and that they see as threatened. As their own claims to respect and honor diminish, they seek public acts and symbols (alcohol use, pornography) to reaffirm a lost value system. This they do either by assimilative reform (convert the sinner) or coercive reform (new laws to prohibit deviant behavior). Their social background is variously described as rural, religious, less formally educated, female, lower middle class. Their political base and worldview is seen as conservative, dogmatic, populist, hostile to minority groups. They might even share a particular personality constellation, the Authoritarian Personality Type — dogmatic, rigid, harsh, and punitive, based perhaps on a particular type of childhood. In short, these groups are not liberals (though they might appeal to one particular version of liberalism by talking about freedom and the common good).

Now, clearly, in the same way that the theories of traditional criminology cannot explain the crimes of the powerful — so the theories of traditional moral enterprise cannot deal with the newer forms. The campaigners come now from a different social base and would (quite rightly) be outraged to have their politics analyzed as stemming either from status discontent or a personality syndrome derived from a childhood socialization characterized by violence. Moreover, the campaigners are not defending a lost moral order but building a utopian vision of an order that should be. Note also that analysts of traditional moral enterprise see the liberal elite (themselves) as permissive and universalistic, while the masses are reactionary and punitive, easily misled by irrational, populist campaigners. But now the new criminalizers are the liberal elite and are engaged in raising the consciousness of a (falsely conscious) mass to be more rather than less punitive about certain areas of life. And this is seen as rational, instrumental politics rather than the irrational, symbolic politics of the old moral crusaders.

These negative comparisons suggest, incidentally, that moral enterprise theory perhaps did not even apply to the old campaigns. In the worldview of the 1960s liberal values were seen as forming or about to form a new consensus from which right-wing morality was a minority deviation. Liberal hegemony had been established over such aberrations as Prohibition and soon "reverse moral enterprise" would triumph over current prohibitions: marijuana, homosexuality, abortion. Movements such as Born Again Christians, the Moral Majority, and the post-1970s "backlash" against gay rights and free abortion were seen as revivals of the old discredited morality. The problem with this analysis is that liberal hegemony might never have been established, not after Prohibition, and not even in the "permissive" sixties. The Moral Majority might be a moral majority, and from their hegemonic point of view it has always been the liberals and the radicals who have been moral entrepreneurs, struggling against the tide to defend a minority view.

Be that as it may, undoubtedly some serious work needs to be done to understand the social and political base of the new criminalization and the nature of its appeal. In comparison with the old-style enterprise and then the reverse moral enterprise of the sixties, one of the most interesting themes is the changing status of the victim. In the literature of the 1960s (liberal and left realist) the tendency was to play down the significance of the victim (exaggerated for street crime; absent, by definition, for victimless crime). The focus was not on the victim's problems but on the deviant's problems. He or she became a heroic figure struggling against labeling, resisting stigmatization, challenging the categories of devaluation. In the politics of deviance, gays, prisoners, and prostitutes were all engaged in active stigma contests with the powerful.[47]

By the 1980s the focus shifts entirely to the victim. There are victims everywhere and victimology becomes the growth area for criminologists. Mainstream victimology shows the extent to which the working class suffers from crime: this strengthens the paradigm of administrative criminology and also forms the basis for the left realist position. Radical victimology shows up the hidden victimization by the powerful: corporations, governments, males. Instead of denying the victim or celebrating the active deviant, a massive new enterprise is devoted to exposing the hidden victims everywhere: children, the elderly, women, workers, consumers, drivers. Criminology and moral enterprise devote themselves not to raising the consciousness of deviants struggling against an oppressive social order but to raising consciousness among victims, potential victims, and hidden victims. The point is not to make people realize their strength but to realize their weakness. Like all forms of consciousness raising, this is not easy. "What makes the detection of the crimes of the wealthy harder is that their victims are usually unaware that they have been victimized."[48] Instead of relying on surveys to support the criminalization of those who victimize most, this "demands a program of sensitizing people to the numerous ways in which they are victimized but remain relatively ignorant of their victimization."[49]

Again, we can understand this movement in its own terms, or set it in a wider cultural and political context, for example, Lasch's "survival mentality," the cultural tendency to normalize crisis and to see the self as victim or potential victim. "The victim has come to enjoy a certain moral superiority in our society."[50] Each group vies for privileged status: Who has suffered most? In this moral evolution of the victim — facilitated by victimology and by the indiscriminate use of the term *victim* till it loses all meaning — the appeal is not to universal rights of citizenship (the traditional basis for social equality in liberalism) but to the special experience of being a victim.

One of the most fascinating (and neglected) areas for studying current forms of moral enterprise is the emergence of "abuses of power" or "human rights offenses" as special categories of crime. Criminologists have justifiably given much attention to traditional political crimes *against* the state (issues such as the widening of definitions of terrorism, new techniques of surveillance and control, erosions of civil liberties, and so on). The last few years, however, have seen a sustained attempt to translate the human rights agenda into the creation of new criminal offenses by the state against its citizens.

More visible in Western Europe than in the United States and in international rather than purely national arenas, the enterprise here takes a weak and strong form. The weak form calls for stricter law enforcement and stronger punishment of state agents responsible for torture, slavery, "disappearances," illegal arrests, and other such legally defined human rights violations or abuses of political power. This merges into a stronger and more radical rhetoric in which governments, multinationals, police and military officials, lawyers, doctors, and (sometimes) parents and husbands are all classified together in terms of their powers over other weaker human beings. Power is abused against "collective victims"—the poor, political dissidents, women, children, migrant workers—in ways that would be considered criminal if committed by those not in control.[51]

The two most notable features of this enterprise are its scope and political tone. Its scope goes not only beyond the primal crimes that have always interested international agencies (illicit drug traffic, terrorism, kidnapping, hijacking, and the like) but beyond crimes of the powerful that elicit universal condemnation (the kidnapping and selling of women into prostitution; slavery; the selling of Third World children to supply factories and brothels; the dumping of dangerous drugs by multinationals; torture; mass killings; genocide) into the generalized categories of racism, sexism, and exploitation. And what is notable about the political tone is that the rhetoric of criminalization does not use the old justifications of deterrence, social defense, or retribution but is phrased explicitly within the vocabulary of human rights. The criteria for determining the object of criminalization, that is, correspond to those of the most radical form of leftist criminology: "guardians of human rights" and not "defenders of order." And this, remember, coming not just from organizations such as Amnesty International but conservative criminology (the International Association for Penal Law, International Society for Social Defense, International Society of Criminology, World Society of Victimology, and others) and various UN organizations such as UNSDRI.

There is, to be sure, something incongruous in the spectacle of government officials meeting solemnly all over the world to seek the criminalization of practices that they themselves employ or support. And the agencies and mecha-nisms of law enforcement being proposed (such as "universal penal jurisdic-tion"[52]) might have no power at all. Nonetheless, these are potentially powerful sources of criminalization, and to my knowledge, no criminologist has begun to study their history, social base, and possible effects.

The Question of Knowledge

What part does the social scientist play in the process of criminalization, old or new? The most restricted role would be the traditional positivist one: the supplier of knowledge for making informed decisions. Unlike the moral philosopher who has to consider what would reasonable men or women deem the appropriate sanction were they to make this decision behind Rawls's "veil of ignorance," the social scientist lifts this veil. What would those men and women say if only they knew what we could tell them?

This will do up to a point, the point being reached when the "same" knowl-edge does not have the same meaning to everyone, when its claim to be knowl-edge is contested, or when it can be used in quite different ways. In the history of the use of empirical knowledge in determining what should be criminalized, these points have long been reached. Although there are still many social scien-tists who believe otherwise, it must surely be clear by now that the debate, for example, about victimless crime cannot be resolved in purely empirical terms. As Wilson pointed out in comparing the results of the Violence Commission (in favor of regulation) and the Obscenity Commission (against regulation), it is *inherently* unlikely that social science can either show harmful effects or prove that there are no harmful effects. And anyway, utilitarian proof would not determine the decision. "These are moral issues and ultimately all judge-ments about the acceptability of restrictions on various media will have to rest on political and philosophical considerations."[53]

The problem, however, is much more complicated than this simple division between facts (technically difficult to establish) versus values (which produce decisions). The question is how power determines what counts as knowledge and how such knowledge will be used. It is in these terms that we understand the "facts" of abortion: at what point is a fetal protoplasm disposed of and at what point is a human being killed?

A large part of the enterprise of the new criminalization is devoted to estab-lishing an alternative knowledge: Who are the real victims? What is harm? Some of this work involves digging out new facts, some involves reinterpreting old facts. Feminist scholarship on pornography, for example, has thrown up little that is new (in comparison, for example, to the mass of new evidence on corporate crime) but much in the way of demystification of old knowledge. The conventional wisdom about pornography's being harmless must now be seen as the product of the "machismo" of traditional media research, a bias that makes all the old data "dirty."[54]

The extreme relativist would doubt whether data could ever be wholly clean. This is not my position. We have to understand, though, that the new criminalizers base their campaigns on different kinds of truth claims. The facts, for example, that corporations kill more people each year than the number of deaths listed as criminal homicide, that more people are injured through avoidable occupational hazards than by street crime, that more money is lost on a single massive corporate crime than the total losses over a year from ordinary theft — these are relatively clean data. Whatever conclusions we draw from them, their truth claims can be established one way or the other. But to claim as new knowledge that normal sexual encounters merge imperceptibly into sexual assaults and that rape is merely the most serious of these is much more difficult to establish either way. This is not to say that it is wrong or should not be done, merely that it belongs to a different order of truth.

In both cases — that is, where alternative knowledge is relatively "clean" in the positivist sense or else more dependent on a different idea of what constitutes knowledge — the special appeal to criminalization remains problematic. As I have suggested already, the more complex and plausible is the new knowledge, the more difficult it is to know just *what* to criminalize. Do we simply expand the definition of corporate crime to include those forms of death, injury, and financial loss that are not as yet criminal (or even administrative or civil offenses) but are still violations of human rights? One criminologist answers honestly enough: "This clearly raises enormous philosophical and political issues and may, if pushed to an extreme position, risk losing any sympathetic reception for the study and control of corporate crime from those of liberal sensibilities."[55] Similarly, the campaign to substitute feminist for legalistic definitions of rape — to include, for example, sexual access gained by "verbal violence," financial pressures, or fradulent declarations — might be tempered by a sense of what is politically realistic in male-dominated society.

But what is "extreme" and what is "realistic"? Criminologists might reply that this is hardly their problem. This is correct — but it is also to ignore the hidden political agenda at the very source of much criminological knowledge. Consider again the tensions between, on the one hand, normalizing a phenomenon and thus subjecting it to complex cognitive and moral evaluation and, on the other, criminalizing it and thus subjecting it to simple evaluations. In most of the cases we have considered here this tension is left unexplored because the observer does not see any necessary contradiction between an explanation (in terms of pervasiveness, complexity, or whatever) and a moral judgment. And there *is* no such contradiction: "appreciation" does not mean that there cannot be "correction." But there is a set of political preferences that cannot easily be reduced to truth claims: in favor of using the criminal law to solve certain social problems and in deciding what is realistic or extreme to include in the definition of crime.

My point is simply that such preferences are often undeclared. Compare, for example, the occupational crimes of the powerful and the powerless. In the first case criminalization is unreservedly supported despite or because of the demonstration of the actual normality of the activities in question. To take a specific case: the criminological campaign against and study of arson. Brady's research has provided convincing evidence of the extent of the problem, the need for greater public awareness, and the need to use the criminal justice system (tougher law enforcement, putting deterrence to work, using computer technology in detection, counteracting the proarson lobby, and so on). But all this extensive evidence points not to the untypical, deviant nature of the offense but precisely the opposite: "Arson is primarily an outcome of routine business practices in the banking, insurance and real estate industries."[56]

Compare this to the growing literature on "occupational crime" by ordinary, powerless workers: cheating, fiddling, pilfering, and the like. The *scale* of loss and damage is less than corporate crime, but all the ethnographies of workplace crime point to much cumulative harm and loss, invisible damage, and unaware victims. And the deviance is the outcome of "routine" normalized workplace practices. Yet, for most criminologists producing this knowledge, all this constitutes an argument *against* criminalization and in favor of using informal workplace controls—through trade union workers' courts, factory councils, and so forth—right outside the criminal law.[57]

In this example it is relatively easy to see how the observer's political predilections lead to favoring criminalization in one case (against big business) and informal controls in the other (for the ordinary worker). What is less clear is how these predilections affect the type of knowledge that is produced about the phenomenon. I know of only one good account in the new criminalization literature of the relationship between political enterprise and the production of knowledge. This is Pitch's analysis of how rape emerged as an issue in the Italian feminist movement and what general problems it poses for critical criminology.[58]

Pitch starts by asking whether a genealogy of rape can be constructed independent of how it is observed, defined, or legislated about. Rape became a social problem and a political issue through the activities of the women's movement. However real its effects and consequences, rape is also a socially constructed event: the aim of consciousness raising was to widen traditional legal definitions to encompass different and more subtle forms of male violence. The inside story (from the women's movement) about how and why all this happened is different from that produced by the outsider social scientist. This raises the epistemological problem: What is the reality of the phenomenon itself? Critical criminologists working in the social control paradigm have produced different answers to such questions: relativism (if something is defined as real, then it is real); demystification (there is a reality, but it is not the same as that constructed by the powerful); left realism (social construction must have an objective base).

Why are these metaissues so important? Simply because to deal with the central problems of *etiology* and *policy*, one must have some idea of the reality of the phenomenon (in this case, rape) independent of the definitions of the offender, victim, social control agent, campaigning movement, or mass media. No plausible causal explanation or policy preference can be based solely and literally on the perceptions of any one or all of these "others." This, however, is just what critical criminologists did by accepting (uncritically) the particular explanations and policy preferences of the women's movement. This also meant awarding a legitimacy to state institutions as the regulator of behavior, accepting the denunciatory and symbolic functions of the criminal law, supporting retribution and deterrence. The whole discourse of criminalization was unquestioned, and the alternative notions of justice that emerged from the radical critique of the previous decade disappeared. Penal law was granted a legitimacy by the same intellectual forces that had spent so much time trying to undermine it. To admit this, "critical criminologists would have to face a particular embarrassment: whose side should they choose, women's or progressive penal reformers?"[59]

For Pitch, then, rape is an example to expose the "epistemological inconsistencies and ambiguities" within the paradigm of critical criminology: acknowledging the socially constructed nature of social problems but forgetting this when convenient. Until these ambiguities are resolved, the only choice for the critical criminologist is "that of explicitly recognizing the crucial intervention in his/her analyses of his/her political choices."[60]

A charge similar to Pitch's "epistemological inconsistency," but without the political argument and with some tedious ethnomethodological rhetoric, has recently been leveled against the whole social constructionist literature on social problems. What Woolgar and Pawluch call "ontological gerrymandering" takes the form of the following common strategy: identifying a particular condition or behavior (their example is child abuse), noting various definitions or claims about the condition, then stressing their variability and explaining this in terms of changing social circumstances, implying that the condition does not vary. The trick, "ontological gerrymandering," is to assume that only the variable definitions have a problematic truth (sin, crime, illness) but that claims about the condition itself (its unchanging nature over time or its changing amounts) can be taken on faith, as common sense.[61]

"Epistemological inconsistency" and "ontological gerrymandering" aside, all this is surely just another round in the old sociological debate about facts and values. This is even clearer in the social problems literature than in criminology.

The social constructionist paradigm sees social problems as the result of collective definitions, "claims making," rather than objective conditions.[62] In the pure version of this paradigm, whether the sociologist is viewed as a detached, disinterested, and unbiased expert is an empirical and political question: Has he or she succeeded in establishing this credential? Sociologists, in this view, should not concern themselves with the validity of the participants' truth claims but only their viability. The only question is how such claims are created, demonstrated, and established. Nor should sociologists be asked to choose "whose side are we on?"; they should rather, in Gusfield's words, remain "on the side." It is presumptuous to claim any technical expertise and moral vision that supersedes those of the people. The "public," through the due political process, creates the knowledge of what constitutes a social problem.

The question "What is a social problem?" then, mirrors the continuing debate about the real object of criminology, with its history of competing "claims-making activities" about what should be crime. But if there is one thing that unites all radical factions — old left idealists, left realists, and abolitionists — it is a rejection of this social constructionist solution. From the beginning critical criminologists wanted to be participants in the business of claims making, determiners of truth and upholders of values, and not just analysts "on the side." The original attacks on absolutism and positivism were made not in the name of relativism or detached value neutrality but in terms of a different set of values. This political commitment was the essence of alternative criminology. It continues (in the name of socialism, feminism, or whatever), as does the belief in the truth of the new alternative knowledge about victimization, harm, or rights.

What this means is that criminologists who have chosen the critical over the administrative paradigm will always be playing the dual role of knowledge producers and moral entrepreneurs. In this they are not very different from natural scientists working in such fields as risk analysis: creating the knowledge to decide what is "acceptable mechanical risk" or "acceptable level of radiation." In both cases political choice will become more rather than less relevant in arriving at this knowledge.[63]

Conclusion

My aim in this paper has been to observe the criminalization issue as it weaves its way through the discourse of criminology, particularly the various new criminologies of the last two decades. Current controversies — between mainstream and periphery, abolitionists and realists — are only new rounds in the same battle that started with the birth of the subject: constructing and deconstructing "crime," that elusive object of criminology.

I am not necessarily arguing against criminalization as a solution to social problems. Abolitionists — as well as criminalizers — present simplified responses to reality: they reduce complex demands for social change in many realms of social life into all-purpose solutions that are meant to apply everywhere. The abolitionist critique of the penal law is (to me) convincing and its model of the good society appealing. It bypasses, however, some major political realities and struggles of our time. And to the victim of rape, environmental pollution, or terrorism, it can hardly look relevant.

The strength of left realism, on the other hand, is its apparent relevance. It responds to the realities of street crime by elevating the victims' demands for protection and justice into a socialist program for reconstructing social democracy. And it seeks to extend the demand for protection and justice by criminalizing the depredations of the powerful. But, however politically expedient and morally sensitive this solution might seem, it is prone to theoretical amnesia. What is gained by giving up the romantic and visionary excesses of the 1960s is lost by forgetting the truisms of the new criminology of that decade: that rules are created in ongoing collective struggles; that "crime" is only one of many possible responses to conflict, rule breaking, and trouble; that the criminal law model (police, courts, prisons) has hopelessly failed as a guarantee of protection and social justice for the weak; that crime control bureaucracies and professionals become self-serving and self-fulfilling. These are truths that have not been refuted. Abolitionists might take these truths too literally by trying to translate them into a concrete program of social policy. Realists, however, convert too literally victims' conceptions of their problems into the language of crime. This is to reify the very label that (still) has to be questioned and to legitimate the very system that needs to be weakened. We gain political realism but we lose visionary edge and theoretical integrity.

The mere existence of these emerging paradigms in critical criminology, however, is more important than trying to score debating points on behalf of either side. Faced by the hopeless bankruptcy of mainstream managerial criminology with its endless rounds of "new" solutions to the crime problem and its final abandonment of any social and political program, the various critical factions have more in common than what divides them. As long as all three sides of the crime triangle — offense/offender, victim, and social reaction/state — are kept in focus, both abolitionists and realists are viable alternatives to mainstream criminology. Each fights a different battle against the old enemy: realists concede the existence of the traditional terrain of crime (and fight there for such goals as social justice and democratic control of the police) while simultaneously opening up a front against "new" crimes; abolitionists are trying to find a different terrain and form of battle altogether.

In both cases these three areas will have to be contested: first, the area containing objects now called crime that are candidates for possible decriminalization; second, the area of crimes that are not seriously proposed as candidates for decriminalization; third, those forms of rule breaking, conflict, problems (and other noncriminal categories) that are possible candidates for criminalization. Our theoretical questions still concern the relative size of these areas, what belongs in each one, and the permeability of the boundaries between them.

I have offered four theoretical projects that might help us with such questions: the theory of criminalization itself, the nature of liberalism, the basis of moral enterprise and the uses of criminological knowledge. Each of these projects needs to be grounded in a concrete political reality. Thus, looking back at the past decade, we must understand the variable ways in which criminalization appears in the demands of social and political movements. Crime is a response to social conflict that simplifies and reduces complexities. This is why it exerts such a powerful attraction for movements that strive for political recognition and legitimacy. The sixties and seventies saw the emergence of all sorts of collective movements that abandoned the traditional terrain of class politics to operate instead in the welfare system, the personal and sexual areas, the environment and ecology.

These groups had the dual problem of acheiving symbolic and instrumental goals as well as establishing and imposing their own autonomous identity. Criminalization was and is a powerful way of doing this. "There should be a law against it" and "It should be a crime" are rallying calls no less for the new than for traditional forms of moral enterprise. We should also note the particular success of these post-1960s movements in reconstituting the term *violence* by uncovering and emphasizing victimization, by creating such concepts as institutional violence, by using the rhetoric of liberation, and by changing legal categories (for example, redefining rape in terms of violence rather than sex).

Another context for studying criminalization is not the rarefied world of critical criminology in the West but actual crime control policy in socialist societies. In the Soviet Union, for example, we have to understand the historical reasons for the total eclipse of Pashukanis's vision of a society without law by the radical instrumentality of Soviet law under Stalin. This period was marked by a massive criminalization to achieve political ends: new areas of social life were criminalized (not meeting grain quotas; absenteeism, lateness, tardiness, or negligence at work; acts that might weaken family life); law enforcement officials mobilized into a proactive stance to seek out certain forms of misbehavior; criminal justice seen as a tool to create a new kind of person.[64] This period of radical instrumentality ended after 1945, but these and subsequent developments are worth studying to understand what an "overcriminalized" society might look like.

Another project, even more remote sounding to most criminologists, is the study of social control outside the formal state punitive system. I have already noted how revisionist historians are reconsidering the original base of primal criminalization. Similarly, current students of social control have been increasingly drawn to informal decentralized systems (see chapter 12): the market (consumerism, commodification, advertising), welfare and regulatory law, private security, civil law, and other such areas outside the scope of the criminal law.

Whatever these projects might show, if the study of the criminalization teaches us anything, it is the need for a middle way between the general and the specific. For those attracted to general theories and causes — whether abolitionism, left realism, liberalism, or whatever — the lesson is to look for the specifics of each phenomenon: its history and its current form. For those immersed in any specific campaign, the point is to remember the general nature of criminalization, and the particular combination of knowledge and power that is likely to produce it.

Fifty years ago, Sellin argued that as social scientists, criminologists cannot afford to allow nonscientists to fix the terms and boundaries for the study of crime. But this is nothing like the problems that arise when we "scientists" try to fix these terms and boundaries ourselves.

Notes

1. P. S. Atiyah, *The Rise and Fall of Freedom of Contract* (Oxford: Clarendon Press, 1979).
2. For a useful bibliography and guide to current issues, see David Sugerman, "Law, Economy and the State in England, 1750–1914, Some Major Issues," in *Legality, Ideology and the State*, ed. D. Sugerman (London: Academic Press 1983), pp. 213–66.
3. John Langbein, "Albion's Fatal Flaws," *Past and Present* 98 (1983):96–120.
4. See Michael Ignatieff, "State, Civil Society and Total Institutions," in *Social Control and the State: Comparative and Historical Essays*, ed. S. Cohen and A. Scull (Oxford: Martin Robertson, 1983).
5. Jerome Hall, *Comparative Law and Social Theory* (Baton Rouge: Louisiana State University Press, 1963), p. 613.
6. John Hagen, *Modern Criminology* (New York: McGraw-Hill, 1985), p. 54.
7. Stanley Cohen, *Visions of Social Control: Crime, Punishment and Classification* (Cambridge: Polity Press, 1985).
8. Ian Taylor et al., *The New Criminology* (London: Routledge & Kegan Paul, 1973), p. 282.
9. E. B. Pashukanis, *Law and Marxism: A General Theory* (London: Ink Links, 1978), p. 61. For a recent guide to Pashukanis, see R. Warrington, "Pashukanis and the Commodity Form Theory," in *Legality, Ideology and the State*, ed. D. Sugerman (London: Academic Press, 1983), pp. 43–67.
10. For an accessible introduction to the most straightforward of the European abolitionist school, Louk Hulsman, see Jacqueline de Celis and Andre Normandeau, "Alternatives to the Criminal Justice System: An Abolitionist Perspective" (International Centre for Comparative Criminology, Universite de Montreal, 1984).
11. This definition comes from one of the most important policy documents influenced by the abolitionist movement: European Committee on Crime Problems *Report on Decriminalization* (Strasbourg: Council of Europe, 1980).

12. Louk Hulsman, "Critical Criminology and the Concept of Crime" (Paper given at the International Conference on Prison Abolition, Amsterdam, June 1985). Hulsman's paper and other evaluations of abolitionism appear in a special issue of *Contemporary Crises: Crime, Law and Social Policy* 10, no.1 (1986).

13. Herman and Julia Schwendinger "Defenders of Order or Guardians of Human Rights?" in *Critical Criminology*, ed I. Taylor et al. (London: Routledge & Kegan Paul 1975).

14. The key sources are various papers (by Platt, Taylor, Hunt, and others) in *Crime and Social Justice* 18 (Winter 1982) and 19 (Summer 1983); Ian Taylor, *Law and Order: Arguments for Socialism* (London: Macmillan, 1981); John Lea and Jock Young, *What Is to Be Done about Law and Order?* (Harmondsworth: Penguin, 1984). The most explicit statement of the left realist position is Jock Young, "The Failure of Criminology: The Need for a Radical Realism," in *Confronting Crime*, ed. R. Mathews and J. Young (London: Sage Publications, 1986), pp. 4–30.

15. Ibid., p. 21.

16. R. Mathews and J. Young, eds. "Introduction" to *Confronting Crime* (London: Sage Publications, 1986), p. 1.

17. Heinz Steinert, "The Amazing New Left Law and Order Campaign," *Contemporary Crisis* 9, no. 4 (October 1985).

18. Harold E. Pepinsky and Paul Jesilow, *Myths That Cause Crime* (Cabin John, Md.: Seven Locks Press, 1984).

19. Steven Box, *Power, Crime and Mystification* (London: Tavistock, 1983).

20. Richard A. Berk et al., *A Measure of Justice: An Empirical Study of Changes in the California Penal Code, 1955–71* (New York: Academic Press, 1977).

21. The golden years for the victimless crime/overcriminalization concepts were from the mid-1960s to the mid-1970s. The Wolfenden Report appeared in 1957, followed by the key works in the debate: Hart's *Law, Liberty and Morality* (1963); Schur's *Crimes without Victims* (1965); Packer's *The Limits of the Criminal Sanction* (1968); Kadish's "The Crisis of Over Criminalization" (1968); Morris and Hawkins, *The Honest Politician's Guide to Crime Control* (1970); and Geiss's *Not the Law's Business* (1972). These are the works still quoted, and no major defense of their argument has appeared since then.

22. See various papers in National Deviancy Conference, ed., *Permissiveness and Control: The Fate of the Sixties Legislation* (London: Macmillan, 1980).

23. Ronald Bayer, "Heroin Decriminalization and the Ideology of Tolerance: A Critical View," *Law and Society* 12 (Winter 1978): 301–18.

24. Edwin M. Schur, "'Crimes without Victims': A 20 Year Reassessment" (Paper presented at Annual Meeting of the Society for the Study of Social Problems, Washington D.C., August 1985) and "The Criminology and Politics of Victimless Crime" (Paper presented at symposium, Simon Frazer University, May 1986).

25. For an accessible summary of feminist antipornography thought, see Laura Lederer, ed., *Take Back the Night: Women on Pornography* (New York: Bantam Books, 1982). In my discussion here I have not even begun to consider the differences *within* current feminist ideology. The existence of these differences only strengthens my argument about the complexity of the criminalization question. On pornography, see Varda Burstyn, ed., *Women against Censorship* (Vancouver: Douglass & McIntyre, 1985); Ann Snitow et al., *The Politics of Desire* (New York: Monthly Review Press 1983).

26. For a review of the literature, see Michael Musheno and Kathryn Seeley "Prostitution Policy and the Woman's Movement: Historical Analysis of Feminist Thought and Organization," *Contemporary Crises* 10, no. 3 (October 1986).

27. For a review of such work, see Judith Walkowitz, "The Politics of Prostitution," *Signs* 6 (1980): 123–35.
28. A popular recent account of the strange-alliances problem in the United States is Mary Kay Blakely, "Is One Woman's Sexuality Another Woman's Pornography?" *MS* (April 1985): 37–47.
29. Walkowitz,"The Politics of Prostitution," p. 130.
30. Such are the problems noted by Laureen Snider, "Legal Reform and Social Control: The Dangers of Abolishing Rape," *International Journal of the Sociology of Law* 13 (1985).
31. Ibid.
32. For a recent review, see William J. Chambliss, "The Criminalization of Conduct," in *Law and Deviance*, ed. H. Laurence Ross (Beverly Hills, Calif.: Sage Publications, 1981), pp. 45–64.
33. Alexander Yakovlev, "The Social Functions of the Criminalization Process," in *Selected Issues in Criminal Justice*, no. 4 (Helsinki: Institute for Crime Prevention and Control 1985), p. 30.
34. See David Dery, *Problem Definition in Policy Analysis* (Lawrence: University Press of Kansas, 1984).
35. For a model account of how such social problems are cognitively framed, see Joseph R. Gusfield, *The Culture of Public Problems: Drinking, Driving and the Symbolic Order* (Chicago: University of Chicago Press, 1981).
36. Malcolm Spector, "Seven Ways to Control Toublesome Rascals," in *Law and Deviance*, ed. H. Laurence Ross (Beverly Hills, Calif.: Sage Publications, 1981).
37. Some of the landmarks in this debate are to be found in Michael J. Sandel, ed., *Liberalism and Its Critics* (Oxford: Basil Blackwell, 1984).
38. Christopher Lasch, *The Minimal Self: Psychic Survival in Troubled Times* (New York: Norton, 1984), p. 198. Lasch's own new map of cultural politics distinguishes between the party of the super ego (the restoration of traditional authority); the party of the rational ego (the enlightenment, liberal view); and the New Left (personal politics, new consciousness, feminist awareness). Compare this to Davis's typology of sexual ideologies: Jehovanist (the traditional view, stressing repression, prohibition, and pollution); Gnostic (the liberatory view, aimed at shattering all taboos and boundaries); and Naturalist (the social scientific, secular view of sex, which plays down its effects, positive or negative, and sees it in strict behavioral terms): Murray S. Davis: *Smut: Erotic Reality/Obscene Ideology* (Chicago: University of Chicago Press, 1983).
39. Robert L. Chauncey, "New Careers for Moral Entrepreneurs: Teenage Drinking," *Journal of Drug Issues* 10 (1980): 48–70.
40. Gilbert Geiss and Colin Golf, Introduction to Edwin H. Sutherland's *White Collar Crime: The Uncut Version* (New Haven: Yale University Press 1983), p. xviii.
41. Thus, Susan Shapiro reviews four recent criminological texts on white-collar crime under the heading "The New Moral Entrepreneurs: Corporate Crime Crusaders," *Contemporary Sociology* 10, no. 3 (May 1983): 304–7. She quotes one of these authors to the effect that criminologists should become "dedicated persons who embark on an impassioned crusade in behalf of" white-collar crime.
42. Diana Russell, *Sexual Exploitation: Linking Rape, Child Abuse and Workplace Harassment* (Beverly Hills, Calif.: Sage Publications, 1984).
43. Box, *Power, Crime and Mystification*, p. 79.
44. See, for example, Lederer, *Take Back the Night*.
45. Though there is some literature on legal activism in the 1960s and 1970s in areas such as environmental and consumer protection. See Joel F. Handler, *Social Move-*

ments and the Legal System: A Theory of Law Reform and Social Change (New York: Academic Press, 1978).

46. The classic studies are Joseph R. Gusfield, *Symbolic Crusade: Status Politics and the American Temperance Movement* (Urbana: University of Illinois Press, 1966), and Louis A. Zurcher et al., "The Anti Pornography Campaign: A Symbolic Crusade," *Social Problems* 19 (Fall 1971): 217–38.

47. Edwin Schur, *The Politics of Deviance: Stigma Contests and the Uses of Power* (Englewood Cliffs, N.J.: Prentice-Hall, 1980).

48. Pepinsky and Jesilow, *Myths That Cause Crime*, pp. 81–82.

49. Box, *Power, Crime and Mystification*, p. 223.

50. Lasch, *The Minimal Self*, p. 67.

51. For current examples of rights rhetoric in the institutions of international crime control, see papers and resolutions from the Seventh United Nations Congress on the Prevention of Crime and the Treatment of Offenders (1985).

52. See *Outlawing an Ancient Evil: Torture* (New York: UN Department of Public Information, 1985).

53. James Q. Wilson, "Violence, Pornography and Social Science," *Public Interest* (Winter 1971): 61.

54. Thelma McCormack, "Machismo in Media Research: A Critical Review of Research on Violence and Pornography," *Social Problems* 25, no. 5 (June 1978): 542–54; Pauline B. Bart and Margaret Jozsa, "Dirty Books, Dirty Films and Dirty Data," in *Take Back the Night: Women on Pornography*, ed. Laura Lederer (New York: Bantam Books, 1982), pp. 201–15.

55. Box, *Power, Crime and Mystification*, p. 22.

56. James Brady, "The Social Economy of Arson: Vandals, Gangsters, Bankers and Officials in the Making of an Urban Problem," in *Research in Law, Deviance and Social Control*, vol. 6, ed. S. Spitzer and A. T. Scull (Greenwich, Conn.: JAI Press, 1984), p. 200.

57. Needless to say, the "same" evidence produced by criminologists doing research on workplace crime can be used by traditional (right-wing) moral entrepreneurs to campaign for the heavier criminalization of these activities. In Britain this is just what happened in the case of "welfare scrounging."

58. Tamar Pitch, "Critical Criminology, the Construction of Social Problems and the Question of Rape," *International Journal of the Sociology of Law* 13 (1985): 35–46.

59. Ibid., p. 45.

60. Ibid., p. 41.

61. Steve Woolgar and Dorothy Pawluch, "Ontological Gerrymandering: The Anatomy of Social Problems Explanations," *Social Problems* 32, no. 3 (1985): 214–27.

62. Joseph W. Schneider, "Social Problems Theory: The Constructionist View," *Annual Review of Sociology* 11 (1985): 209–29. The original theory of social problems as claims making is set out in Malcolm Spector and John Kitsuse *Constructing Social Problems* (Menlo Park, Calif.: Cummings, 1977).

63. Two observers of the field of risk analysis note that although radicals of an earlier decade fought against the politicization of research, now — under such slogans as "responsibility in science" — radicals in the scientific community are taking on a more activist, adversarial role, intervening in public debate about acceptable risk: Mary Douglas and Anton Wildavsky, *Risk and Culture: An Essay on the Selection of Technical and Environmental Dangers* (Berkeley: University of California Press, 1982), especially chs. 3, 4.

64. Peter Solomon, "Stalinist Justice in the Era of Radical Instrumentality" (forthcoming).

14

Bandits, Rebels, or Criminals:
African History and Western Criminology*

It has long been a cliche in the social sciences to talk about the insulation of disciplines and subdisciplines from one another. We all know what it is like to study a phenomenon — poverty, crime, the family — from within one academic paradigm and then come across a quite different view of the "same" phenomenon. The result is usually self-pity: "If only I had known what they were up to," or alternatively, "If only they had known what I was up to."

For Africanists — or specialists in any other field where subject matter rather than disciplinary boundaries provides some collective identity (conferences, journals, teaching) — this, I assume, is less of a problem. A subject such as crime in colonial Africa would naturally attract sociologists, anthropologists, and historians who would have little excuse for not knowing what each other meant by, say, "colonialism." For those of us in the strange business of criminology, however, the problem of insulation has been endemic, chronic, and the subject of much rumination. Ever since its emergence as a separate body of knowledge and power at the end of the nineteenth century, criminology has claimed a monopoly over its self-constituted subject matter and also an "interdisciplinary" character that embraces unto itself sociology, psychology, criminal law, psychiatry, and much else.

The faith of positivist criminology was that there was a "thing" out there — crime — whose existence and pathological nature were self-evident. The causes

* "Bandits, Rebels and Criminals: African History and Western Criminology," from *Africa: Journal of the International African Institute*, Vol. 56 No. 4 (1986), pp. 468–483.

This was a review essay of two books: Donald Crummey (Ed.), *Banditry, Rebellion and Social Protest in Africa* (Portsmouth, N.H.: Heinemann, 1985) and Yves Brillon, *Crime, Justice and Culture in Black Africa* (Cahiers No. 3, Centre International de Criminologie Comparee, Universite de Montreal, 1985).

of this phenomenon were then to be uncovered through the paradigm of the natural sciences, and its pathology ameliorated through a combination of technology and benevolence. The mid-1960s onslaught on conventional criminology — from interactionist sociology of deviance, labeling theory, and then various new, radical, critical, or Marxist criminologies — was to challenge this positivist faith and also to open up the subject to the mainlands of the social sciences. The results have been exciting, confusing, and like most such intellectual movements, extremely uneven. At its centers of power the old criminology remains unchanged. And although the new criminology imported all sorts of ideas from the mainland, its own productions remain unknown to other social scientists.

Which leads me to the purpose of this review: to see how these two books about crime in Africa might look from the perspective of recent criminology. The books could hardly be more different. Donald Crummey's quite excellent collection, (*Banditry, Rebellion and Social Protest in Africa*) consists of seventeen papers by historians all sympathetic to popular history, radical history, and history-from-below; all interested in criminality only in its relationship to resistance, rebellion, and protest; and all inspired one way or the other by Hobsbawm's classic characterization of the social bandit. Yves Brillon's study, (*Crime, Justice and Culture in Black Africa*) comes from a Western (French-Canadian) criminologist not particularly influenced by the new criminology nor much interested in the political significance of crime but using the insights of anthropology to free himself from ethnocentricism.

Let me first give a highly condensed account of those hidden developments in criminology that should be of interest to Crummey and his fellow historians.

Politics in the New Criminology

The dominant thrust of the new criminologies was to reverse the positivist separation of crime from the state, that is, to introduce politics into criminology. The dual victory of the bourgeois state and of criminology itself had been to constitute the criminal question as belonging to a realm of knowledge and power not part of the normal political process of democracy. By the end of the nineteenth century this victory was complete: welfare, justice, punishment, treatment, and criminology were not "politics."[1]

The crime-state separation was challenged from two directions relevant to this review. The first was theoretically "cleaner" and relatively unproblematic: to insist (in conventional Durkheimian terms) on the relative nature of crime and deviance; to reject, therefore, any reification of crime as the product of a universal etiological sequence; to direct attention away from behavior and toward definition, reaction, and social control. At the micro level this meant accounting for the construction, application, and effects of deviant and stigmatic labels. At the macro level this meant explaining the origins of laws and punishments, converting criminology, in effect, into the sociology of law. For Marxists, the project was to create a political economy of law and punishment. For Foucault—an overwhelming influence in recent years—the problem was to locate the whole discourse of crime in terms of the birth of the state and of the "human sciences" themselves.

Those interests find little equivalent attention among Crummey's historians; their object is behavior, not definition. More obviously relevant is the second of the new criminology's political directions: not only explaining the (obvious) politics of law but trying to decode the political meanings of criminal action itself.

The point here was to repudiate the dominant positivist image of criminals as determined, pathological beings driven to action by forces beyond their control. An alternative image was proposed: criminality as more meaningful, rational, and intentional. At the extreme—and here is where the theoretical troubles start—the criminal emerges as a crypto-political actor, crime becomes an embryonic form of social protest. This replacement of images was part of a wider "deviant imagination": the 1960s cultural revolutions against conventional cognitive boundaries and moral authorities. Vandals, soccer hooligans, sex offenders, drug takers, even schizophrenics—all became candidates (unwittingly in most cases) for attribution of meaning and political significance. Romantic, sentimental, and misguided as this enterprise might now sound ("Homage to Catatonia," as it was dismissed by a later critic), it allowed important comparisons and insights. And it opened up the field to outside influences.

One such influence was the new social history. It was at this point that E.P. Thompson, Hobsbawm, and Rude were "discovered" and adopted (no doubt without their blessing) by the new criminology. For surely the enterprise of rescuing today's deviants from the wastebin of social pathology was exactly parallel to these historians' attempts to rescue machine breakers, food rioters, poachers, and smugglers from—in E.P. Thompson's ringing phrase—"the enormous condescension of posterity." For criminologists, the lesson from this revitalized social history was that crime was central to understanding the historical transformation to capitalism. The message from Thompson on the Black Act, from Captain Swing, from *Albion's Fatal Tree*, and, of course, from Hobsbawm's primitive rebels and social bandits seemed clear enough: to listen to experience in its own terms, from below, is to find its hidden significance. The criminologist's question becomes, "How would 'our' hooligans appear if they were afforded the same possibilities of rationality and intelligibility, say, as those of Edward Thompson?"[2]

This is not the place to look at the criticisms within and against radical social history nor the fate of their equivalents in the new criminology.[3] Enough to note the two historical borrowings that criminologists fitted into their own emerging concerns. The first was to understand the problem of definition (criminalization) in terms of the emerging requirements of capitalist political economy — for example, the transformation of customary rights into crime. The second was to restore (or attribute) political meaning to crime. A number of related ideas become common here:[4] *boundary-blurring* (the erosion of the boundaries between crime and politics and the disciplines used to comprehend them); *convergence* (the similarity in behavior and social labeling of certain forms of crime and marginal politics); the *politicization* of deviance (the "stigma contests" through which certain deviant groups seek to define themselves in political terms);[5] and, most explicitly from social historians like Hobsbawm, *equivalence*, however different from political activity it seems — and however crude, primitive, inarticulate, or even hopeless — crime under certain conditions serves equivalent functions to such recognized political forms as protest and resistance.

This takes us to Crummey's volume.

African History

For the criminologists sensitized to the political importance of crime, *Banditry, Rebellion and Social Protest in Africa* will be an invaluable source. A certain amount of decoding, though, is required. With the exception of the editor's comprehensive review of the literature and Ralph Austen's skeptical account of the relevance of Western models of resistance and heroic criminality to Africa, few of these historians are explicitly concerned with the theoretical connections between crime, law, and the state that have so preoccupied the new criminology. They devote a few paragraphs to Hobsbawm and perhaps some other literature on social banditry and then, correctly, get down to the business of their history.

These excellent pieces of work, then, each demand attention in their own terms, and I am sure that I am doing some damage to their authors' intentions by extracting only those themes of criminological interest. This also means ignoring altogether those chapters where the starting point is not "crime" precisely because these are histories of clearly identified and uncontested forms of protest, resistance, and rebellion (for example, the black women's struggle against the Orange Free State Pass Laws in 1913, the 1912 rebellion in Rwanda, the 1894 revolt against Italian overrule in Eritrea, or the famous Bambatha rebellion).

Of course, it is just the continuity (similarity? equivalence? convergence?) between crime and politics in precolonial, colonial, and postcolonial Africa that the editor and his contributors assume. "The Great Beast — the title of Crummey's introduction — is the uncontrolled, outraged reaction of the people, popular violence that can be understood only "in the light of other kinds of popular protest and politics" (p. 1). The task is to make this light clear, to rescue the beast from the "class prejudice" that would dismiss it as disorder, anarchy, mere crime.

As the editor sets them out, every element in this rescue operation by African historians is paralleled in not only the revisionist history of early modern Europe but also the first phase of revisionist criminology: a sympathy with the underclass that suffers and resists domination; an identification of that other beast, the Leviathan of the modern state, which claims a monopoly on the legitimate use of violence and then turns it against the people; the claimed relationship between primary accumulation and property law, theft as "the most primitive form of protest" (Engels).

I will view these themes in the case studies of crime and social banditry and then raise some more general and methodological issues.

The Social Criminal

Banditry, resistance, protest, and *rebellion* are all terms that can be defined by social science and in terms of behavior alone (or its attendant consciousness or subsequent consequences). Crime, on the other hand, is one of many possible definitions (others include conflict, dispute, trouble, deviance) that can be attached to certain behaviors or events, but only by a legitimate authority (usually the state). Crime is infraction and not just action.

Contrary to his own analysis and those of his contributors, Crummey oversimplifies the problem, then, by stating that "crime is inherently a form of protest, since it violates the law" (p. 3). As it stands, this assertion makes no sense—in Africa or anywhere else. There are many forms of crime, that is, actions classified as such by the state, which are not "inherently forms of protest." Violation of law cannot *in itself* be taken as an indicator of protest. Crummey is aware of this when he notes that crime may be accompanied by many forms of consciousness, and that "class based laws" engender a particular form of defiance.

These two qualities—the political base of the law and the type of consciousness that might accompany its infraction—are among the many we look for in claiming to connect crime with politics. These claims may be strong and ambitious or weak and modest. Thus, consider the difference between these possibilities: all crime is inherently political; some crimes are political in the sense that they are informed by a particular consciousness (such as resistance or protest) or that the law has a particular character (such as class domination or sexual repression); crime is a primitive precursor of more sophisticated political forms (progression); crime sometimes serves the same social function as politics (equivalence); crime can take on a political shape (politicization); or, the weakest claim, crime is better understood if we place it in a political context.

Each of these claims has quite different implications and imposes different standards of proof. Without being made explicit, examples and permutations of all of them may be found throughout Crummey's collection. Thus, Larry Yarak's careful account of some twenty cases of murder and theft in the Gold Coast town of Elmira in the early nineteenth century makes only quite modest claims about the political significance of crime. His use of the criminal records (which are remarkable detailed, by the way, compared to their modern equivalents) results in a nuanced picture of the social divisions and class structure under the Dutch regime. As the editor comments, however, "Theft allows valuable inferences about inequality in Elmira, but tells little about resistance" (p. 4). And the murder cases, which show so well the tensions and resentments between the various strata (master and slave, trader and Dutch official), only allow Yarak to find "an unmistakable social dimension" (p. 33). Given the structure of the hearings before the Dutch Council, we have to be very careful about attributing motivation; the historian cannot easily distinguish "social crime" from "crime without qualification."

Now unless *social* is to be given the particular meaning associated with Hobsbawm's distinction — the social bandit versus the ordinary bandit, a distinction in which *social* really means *political* — it is not remarkable to find evidence for "social crime." All crime is social. This is not to detract from the value of this sort of analysis but to note that concepts such as protest and resistance imply more than "social."

A series of far more radical claims about the political nature of crime is found in William Freund's history of theft among the Birom tin miners of Northern Nigeria. For the new criminology, this is a most suggestive chapter, containing as it does variations of all the main claims about the relationship between property crime and political resistance. These claims fall into two main groups. First, there is the notion that much theft arose from the Birom rejection of the capitalist notion of property. Even if the "persistent community appropriation of tin ore" failed to achieve the ideological coherence of so much European resistance to the capitalist infringement of property rights, still it "contained the germ of a populist 'moral economy' that conflicted with the political economy of the mining companies and the state" (p. 50). The second set of claims deals with the actual historical relationships between periods of tin theft and heightened political consciousness and organization. The possibilities here seem endless: theft is the *equivalent* of militancy and appears before it (a *progression* from a primitive to a more sophisticated form); theft occurs at some periods *instead* of militancy; theft "grew alongside" militancy (that is, of the Birom Political Union and the unions in the late 1940s and 1950s). Strikes in one period apparently encouraged theft to expand, then at another period a decline in militancy was coupled with an extension of illicit activity.

Freund is aware that the range of these relationships (and the different ways they can be interpreted) must cast doubt on Engels's famous claim that crime was "the earliest, crudest and least fruitful" form of rebellion. As he notes: "The relationship of theft to social protest, when placed in the general context of the resistance of labour to the prerogatives of capital, is thus rather more complex than the pure progression which Engels once proposed" (p. 59). Yes, though Freund sometimes misses these complexities by implying that in the long historical period he covers tin theft continued to have the same meaning, continued to evidence the same clash between populist and statist moral economies. He quotes in a footnote Peter Linebaugh's suggestion that *direct appropriation* is a more accurate and less pejorative term than *theft* but dismisses this usage as too cumbersome. It is not, however, a matter of terminology nor is the historical continuity implied by this contemporary report self-evident: "Villagers do not and never have seen tin theft as a violation of any moral code which makes sense to them. Obtaining tin by theft is merely a modest recompensation for the expropriation of land and difficulties faced by Birom farmers; it expresses the belief that wealth has been appropriated unjustly by outsiders" (p. 57).

The fact that villagers disliked even applying the word *stealing* to what they were doing says little about the quality of this act as a form of "social protest." White-collar criminals, corporate executives, and government officials—like the Nigerian entrepreneurs who stole in the Nationalist Era as a way to share in mine profits—also do not like being called thieves. We cannot take the offender's denial of criminality *in itself* as an indicator of other social meanings (such as expropriation, redistribution, recompensation, liberation, or protest).

Similar issues are raised by "Fire on the Mountain," David Prochaska's fascinating account of Algerian reactions to French colonialism at the end of the nineteenth century. This chapter will be of particular interest to criminologists because it is the only one that explicitly deals with definition and control as well as behavior itself. By the same token, it is the best illustration of the Thompson-Hay model: the criminalization of customary activity and the resistance implied by subsequent violation of the law. As if in evidence of the blurred boundary between crime and politics, the editor includes this chapter in the "Protest and Resistance" rather than the "Criminality" section, although its "crime"—setting forests alight—could (and was) just as easily be called "arson" as the "expropriations" of Freund's Nigerian miners could be called "theft."

The historical base of criminalization was the massive expropriation of Algerian lands (especially forests for cork oaks), their transfer to French legal ownership, and the application of a legal code with its own agencies of enforcement. One object of the sanction, and the new political economy it protested, was *kcar*: the controlled burning of forests, which had been a fact of

life for centuries of forest dwellers. *Kcar* was rational, part of a four-year ecological cycle in which the lower limbs of trees and underbrush were burned
to open up clearings in the forest, and traditional: part of complex cosmology
that defined the nature of communal land.

How did the Algerians respond to the combined assault on their traditional
political economy by land expropriation and the application of the forest code?
Besides writing petitions and other forms of conventional protest, they burned
the forests down; dramatic, "monster" forest fires followed each set of expropriations. But no single explanation works for all these forest fires, and Prochaska
has to move cautiously through the varying accounts preferred by the three
parties to the conflict. First, the Algerians themselves, who yielded when they
had to, put up with things, used subterfuge, or started fires either as conscious
forms of protest and revenge or as a continuation of the normal practices of
kcar (which sometimes led to uncontrolled fires). Second, the settlers and business interests, who expressed no doubt about the political meaning of the action: the arsonists were bandits, their torch the equivalent of the "assassin's
ambush" or the "rebel's gun." The threat of resistance powered by religious
fanaticism created a powerful myth of Algerian banditry. Third, the government, which shared the same concerns but also understood that the majority
of fires originated from *kcar* rather intentional sabotage.

It is not a question of weighing one explanation against the other; they form
a single matrix. The French attempt to suppress *kcar* and its political economy
(by legal codes and severe collective punishments, such as fines and confisca-
tion) led the Algerians (or some of them) to respond in ways that could be
called arson, revenge, banditry, protest — or continuation of traditional practice. As Prochaska explains it: the French said, "You can live in the forest as
long as you don't set fire to it"; the Algerians said, "How can we live in the
forest without setting fire to it?"

We can begin our model at the point at which traditional practice becomes
defined as rule breaking and is criminalized, and then becomes (and/or is perceived to be) protest. Or we can begin with the criminal category (arson) that
is "really" protest but that is criminalized. Either way we have what sociologists of deviance would call "deviancy amplification" or a "control circuit,"
that is, a spiral of control → deviance → further control → further deviance,
and so on, each stage with its characteristic myths and hostility. Or in Prochaska's
more familiar language, a war of attrition.

I will come back later to the complex interaction between the attribution
of politicality by self and other. What is always at issue in the politics of deviance is the eventual definition of reality that the powerful succeed in imposing.
A nice illustration of the massive gap that can exist between the original meaning
of action and the definition that the powerful prefer emerges from Allan
Roberts's chapter on "terrorists" of the late nineteenth century, the Tabwa lion-

men. His analysis does not raise the same issue as Freund's or Prochaska's because this was not a developed colonial political economy. (The editor rather obscurely refers to "a clear case of incipient criminality in the context of an incipient state.") The clear gap was between what Roberts calls the missionaries' "sublimely obtuse interpretation" (their total refusal, that is, to accept that the killers were theriomorphic men) and the range of possible explanations of the killings. Even if this was not social banditry, the crimes had some heroic status and certainly should be understood in their social contexts (local power struggles, the effects of famine, the advent of the Europeans): "The theriomorphic strategy was available for use by a variety of actors in many different circumstances among which might be resistance to European colonizers" (p. 80).

In Search of the Social Bandit

If "crime is inherently a form of protest" and banditry is "simply a form of criminality common to agrarian societies," then banditry is a form of protest. Once again, though, the editor's syllogism is contradicted, both by his own comments and by the six chapters that deal with social banditry.

There can be no doubt about the stimulus produced by Hobsbawm's original distinction: between ordinary criminal bandits and social bandits who rise above predatory crime and direct their activities to redress the wrongs of peasants, upon whom they depend for protection and support, and who in turn idolize them as avengers, redistributors, and protectors. Despite the rich literature elsewhere, however, "Africanists have done little with bandits," notes Crummey. His volume fills this gap, though what is striking at first sight is an immediate skepticism about whether the category of social bandit is of any use at all to Africanists. In his own chapter about nineteenth-century Ethiopian banditry, Crummey makes a comment about the myth of the bandit Kassa that might be more general: "We hear overtones of social banditry, but only by standing far back. As we approach they vanish" (p. 140).

I sense, however, that the editor and at least most of his contributors would still like to retain these overtones, despite their own negative evidence that points only to unredeemed, ordinary bandits, as much as criminologists would like "their" criminals to show some social consciousness. Only Austen is explicitly pessimistic about the whole enterprise of "importing" Hobsbawm into Africa, and he states flatly that the concept of social bandit just does not apply. He offers, though, a typology of heroic criminality in Africa that gives crime a very explicit set of political meanings and that vindicates, he asserts, Hobsbawm's project of seeing criminal deviance as the expression—in however archaic a sense—of a positive alternative to dominant social values.

The typology is based on the relationship between "social crime" and the evolution of the state, "beginning with a rural situation in which segmentary self-help provides an alternative to official authority and concluding with the self-conscious use of criminal action to overthrow modern governments" (p. 90). The five resultant types are the self-helping frontiersman; the populist redistributor; the professional underworld; the picaro-trickster; and the urban guerrilla. Populist redistribution is, of course, closest to social banditry but, according to Austen, is not found in African reality or folklore, and anyway is more a means of influencing the modern state than opposing it with archaic peasant values. This distinction seems to me less important than its undoubted political character.

In a curious way — because he goes beyond the vague notion of "social crime" and insists that crime expresses values that are *alternatives* to the dominant social order — Austen actually comes closer to expanding rather than restricting Hobsbawm's original project. Thus, even professional criminals "in both their actions and legends . . . represent a form of opposition to established order with its own social meaning" (p. 94). This might be true in the sense that such criminals challenge the capacity of the state to maintain its official version of the social order. It is surely not true, however, in terms of values or intentions. This type is much closer to the "innovative capitalists" who are criminology's main subjects: more "meanly parasitical" than "heroically radical" in Austen's terms.

Austen makes two further general points that are surely applicable to all these histories. The first is that the social milieu of criminal events cannot be assumed to be the same as the heroic legends that grow around them. The second is that more explicit attention must be given to the nature of the state. Hobsbawm, after all, identified the modern state as a minimum condition for social banditry: a stratification system that transcends segmented tribal or kinship groups. The vocabulary of deviance in Africa, Austen argues, is (was?) seldom state versus criminal or legitimate versus illegitimate acquisition or property.

The substantive chapters on banditry, then, turn out to be less significant for any signs of social banditry — even its "overtones" are absent — than for illustrating the opaque relationship between forms of crime and phases in the development of the state. Thus, Ray Key on pre-nineteenth-century Gold Coast shows how mercantilism created the conditions for widespread banditry and brigandage as far back as the seventeenth century, before the arrival of colonial rule and capitalist relations of production. (A reading of current Western historical criminology sometimes gives the impression that theft is purely an artifact of capitalist political economy.)

Two chapters on Ethiopia, Crummey on the nineteenth century and Tim Fernyhough on the twentieth, find a somewhat different (and ironic) political significance in banditry. In a feudal-type society not colonized and with limited capitalist penetration, banditry became an institution dominated by the ruling class. It was a form of political competition used to gain status, office, and power (Ethiopia's first two modern monarchs both came to the throne through *sheftenat*). These lives of plunder, outlawry, and armed defiance show few links of a progressive or socially redeeming nature with the peasants, who, next to the merchants, were the main victims of bandits. By providing an alternative avenue to mobility, banditry diffused class conflict. And eventually the *sheftenat*, a term that conveys both a criminal and a political meaning (venal highwayman and prominent nobleman), eventually lost its connection with the nobility and became wholly criminalized.

If the Ethiopian bandits became nobles rather than rebels, then the Bushmen had a stranger fate. In Robert Gordon's terrible history, the Bushmen — whose very name, he argues, originally meant "bandit" — pass from exploitation by the Cape settlers, then by the German administration, and then on to their eventual taming and "praetorianization": employment by the occupying South African army as trackers in pursuit of SWAPO guerrillas. Not social bandits, not noblemen but mercenaries studied by the army ethnologists from the Afrikaans universities.

Consciousness and Legitimation

Any theory of the political significance of crime, whether in criminology or history, has to solve the vexatious problem of the correspondence between consciousness and legitimation. That is, the relationship between, on the one hand, the language, subjective meaning, and motivation through which people comprehend (or describe) their own action and, on the other, the credibility and acceptability awarded to these accounts by significant others, in particular the state and its accredited agents of control. Very crudely, there are four logical possibilities: (1) the "pure-political" deviant whose own account (e.g. in terms of "rebellion") is accorded legitimacy; (2) the "pure-ordinary" deviant who neither offers nor is assigned any type of political motive; (3) the "unknowing-political" deviant who does not show any apparent political consciousness but who is awarded this by others (e.g. the juvenile delinquent recruited by radical criminologists into the class war); and (4) the "contested-political" deviant whose own political account is not honored by others (e.g. the dissenter in the Soviet Union labeled as schizophrenic).

This typology is obviously very crude because of the different meanings of *legitimacy* here (agreement? credibility? comprehension?) and because the range of possible "others" is so great. Those last two contested categories have to be subdivided according to reactions from different audiences: peer group, movement or party, legal system, mass media, state, or outside social scientists. Such a typology, nonetheless, allows us to visualize the reality negotiation that results from every episode of deviance and control.

This, in turn, allows us to ask two questions. The first is more clearly methodological: What is the status of actors' subjective meanings as revealed by our standard sources (interviews, public statements, oral histories)? How can these claims be checked in the light of other evidence, notably the action itself? The second question is more political: Under what conditions are claims actually legitimated and offered concrete political support?

In the relevant historical and criminological literature, these questions have not always been separated out, leaving it unclear where any case would fit into my self/other typology. In his original account, for example, Hobsbawm was more clearly concerned with the second criterion (legitimation by others) than any questions of subjective meaning. Banditry is social protest when "it is regarded as such by the poor who consequently protect the bandit, regard him as their champion, idealize him and turn him into a myth." He was not much interested in what sociologists of deviance call "initial motivation." Thus, "It does not greatly matter whether a man began his career for quasi political reasons like Giuliano . . . or whether he simply robs because it is a natural thing for an outlaw to do."[6]

In this case, popular recognition precedes (and might then *cause* changes in) self-recognition. The powerful, we can assume, will always be more grudging in their recognition. Their normal interest, that is, must be to depoliticize. It was, for example, obviously more convenient for successive settlers to pathologize Bushmen crime rather than see it as a reaction to colonial domination. But what are we to make of this extraordinary statement that Gordon found in a police report about a woman who killed her three boys: "She says that she will not bring up boys in order that they have to work for white men"?

The methodological problem here is to do justice to social meaning without romantically elevating it into something we would *prefer* it to be. Paradoxically, it is a chapter located firmly (and properly) in the section "Protest and Resistance" that offers the most sensitive guide to the problem of attributing political consciousness. Leroy Vail and Landeg White take a clearly subjective source: creations of the people themselves in the form of 200 popular songs recorded in colonial Mozambique. The songs show with great clarity and power the people's bitter hostility to the colonial order, their awareness of abuses of power, official violence, Portuguese prodigality. Vail and White's aim is not to show the limits of this type of popular consciousness nor even to demonstrate Eric Wolf's point that "transcendental ideological issues appear only in a very prosaic guise." The point rather is to show the falseness of the contrast in African history between *resistance* and *collaboration*, terms that do little justice to what people thought, how they made sense of their previous experience and the realities of colonial power.

In "elevating the peasantry to its new legitimacy," the old political vocabulary was shifted onto the economic terrain. This allows for the elevation to "resistance" of any activity that frustrates the operations of capitalism: theft, desertion, work evasion, low productivity, or whatever. This, they say, is to do violence to language and to beg the question of what happens when the "same" activity is practiced by the peasantry in the new revolutionary states. Further:

> Even more worrying is the naivete of so much resistance psychology, with its accompanying political moralizing. Human reactions to exploitation are enormously diverse. The moment we go beyond the kinds of organized resistance that are politically or militarily visible and try to deduce from people's behaviour their attitudes, perceptions and cultural values, we find ourselves in areas where terms like "resistance," "collaboration," "subjective consciousness," "false consciousness," and the like lack the necessary nuances [p. 195].

This is a severe restriction. Vail and White are surely correct in noting, however, that resistance and collaboration are not always the right or the most interesting ways of classifying behavior: "Any competent novelist would have no difficulty in devising twenty different narratives describing twenty different ways of coping with exploitation and each of the twenty heroes and heroines — their days mixed up with a mixture of semi-resistance and semi-collusion would have an equal claim on our attention" (p. 195).

Legitimacy, not consciousness, occupies Terence Ranger's excellent account of the relationships between peasants and guerrillas in the liberation struggle in Zimbabwe during the seventies. His criterion for banditry is not "lack of coherent political motivation" but illegitimacy and criminality. He describes a long and complex struggle for legitimation in which the possibilities of bandit/criminal, social bandit and guerrilla/freedom fighter were continually at stake. In the early years, thus, the choice between politics and crime ("legitimacy and animality") was this: "which of these men with guns represented the people and were seen to behave like heroic men; which resorted to force against the people and were seen to behave like beasts?" (p. 379). To gain legitimacy, the guerrillas had to adopt codes of right conduct, discipline, rules against stealing from or harassing the people.

We may extract four possibilities from Ranger's historical account: (1) the unequivocal guerrilla — recognized by the party leadership and accepted as such by the peasants; (2) the unequivocal bandit — individuals and gangs operating under cover of the war, repudiated by the party and feared by the peasants; (3) the fighters regarded by the party as guerrillas but who are not (yet) accorded this legitimacy by the peasants, who see them rather as bandits (because they break disciplinary rules, get drunk, are guilty of harassment); (4) an equivocal category close to social banditry — renegade terrorists accepted and helped by the peasants but not recognized by the party.

When the liberation movement come to power after 1980, there was theoretically no need for guerrillas or social bandits. Armed groups outside the service of the state, like those operating in parts of Matabeleland, could only be unredeemed bandits and were not claimed by any party or liberation movement. Yet, suggests Ranger, they were in some areas at least, accepted by peasants. A strange return of the social bandit.

African Criminology

To move from radical historiography of Africa to conventional Western criminology of Africa is less like seeing the same territory with a different guide than using a different map altogether. Until very recently this map has come from "comparative criminology" (usually little more than the euphemism used when Anglo-Saxon academics look at societies other than their own).

In terms of this paradigm, crime in the Third World in general and Africa in particular is conceived wholly within modernization theory.[7] In this theory the Third World is simply passing through the stage completed by the West in the early phases of industrialization; crime is a result of rapid social change, the by product of overrapid modernization, and can be explained in terms of "universal processes that cross cultural lines" (such as anomie, urban drift, or social disorganization).

In the past few years this perspective has been challenged by the countertheory of radical criminology.[8] This inverts all the assumptions of modernization theory: Third World development is not simply a retarded replay of Western European history; the dominant processes are colonialism, imperialism, and dependency; crime is "an integral ally of capitalist penetration into the Third World";[9] colonial law creates new categories of crime and provides labor for capital.

Like many revisionist endeavors in their early stages, these countertheories have sometimes been rather facile, as if simply using terms like *dependency* and *modes of production* will magically lead to understanding. The theories are also more convincing when dealing with definition (the criminalization of customary activity, the use of law to control wage labor) than behavior.

Mahiber's recent argument, for example, that "much of the history of crime in Third World societies is a history of political conflict precipitated by colonial law," turns out to be less of a challenge to conventional criminology than she claims.[10] She analyzes the Black Power Movement in Trinidad as a form of "nation building" and shows how, during the 1970 State of Emergency, these activities threatened the interests of the neocolonial elite, leading to legal repression and criminalization. This case might indeed show that "Black Power crises were not really crimes."[11] The example is familiar enough: the powerful try to delegitimate popular demands for social change by labeling them as criminal. But this tells us very little about those forms of crime not at all associated with the boycotts, protests, and other unambiguously political activities of the Movement.

At least, however, there is here a theory and a depicted social reality that historians would recognize. In the conventional criminology of Africa not the slightest trace of those key questions about crime and politics will be found. They cannot easily be posed within the modernization paradigm nor by the international bodies that control the cultural capital of comparative criminology through the United Nations and similar social defense organizations.

Brillon's book emerges from one of the most visible organizations in this field: the Montreal-based International Centre for Comparative Criminology, which since 1970 has carried out research in West Africa based in the Ivory Coast. I have criticized elsewhere (chapter 10) the overall direction of this type of work: the evangelical peddling of made-for-export Western criminology and the paternalistic vision of social control guided by professionals and experts who have to tell backward African societies about the crime problem they do not realize they have. I noted also, though, that the Center's actual research was not insensitive to local conditions and, at best, showed a cultural relativism and a disenchantment with the replication of discredited Western solutions.

It is this best side that is shown in Brillon's book. The product of collaboration with the Criminological Institute at the University of Abidjan, it starts with a candid admission: "The criminologist is ill equipped to analyse deviance and criminal behaviour in the African countries" (p. 11). Brillon recommends instead a new interdisciplinary solution, "ethno-criminology." Two separate social orders must be understood. First, the traditional African systems of law and justice, based on "indigenous ancestral practises" and studied by "juridic anthropologists," and then the new penal codes, judicial procedures, and social defense policies studies by Western criminology.

Little of this will be news to Africanists, and compared with the sophisticated theoretical genealogy of Crummey's volume, this is elementary stuff. There is the ubiquitous assumption that the same "evolutionary process" that took centuries in Europe and North America is now "condensed" in Africa, thus allowing the clash between two social orders to be observed. There is no overall theory of colonialism or dependency, and little mention of the significance of capitalist penetration or changes in political economy. There is no sense at all of any political struggle or conflict, let alone protest, resistance, or rebellion. Ethnographies are cited, but aside from Bohannan's early work there is no awareness of recent anthropological theory about law, order, and conflict resolution. And despite his own evidence to the contrary, Brillon continues to see crime and other "social pathologies" as indicators of anomie.

Despite these theoretical shortcomings, though, this is a study from which Africanists have much to learn. They might find little new in the substance of Brillon's chapters on criminal infractions in traditional African societies or on traditional juridic systems, but the grid of Western criminology that he places over this familiar material yields a surprisingly interesting picture. He classifies infractions into five types — sorcery, then crimes against public authority, life and bodily integrity, morals, and patrimony — concentrating on examples such as homicide where motivation (sorcery, theft, adultery) gives the actor immunity because customary laws do not define them as a crime. He then deals with traditional judicial procedures — conflict resolution, vendettas, conciliation, restitution, trial by ordeal, and so on — in terms of their emphasis on compensation of the victim. This again is familiar material, and Brillon does not speculate on its recent appeal to Western criminologists who seek to abolish the punitive criminal law model in favor of "traditional" forms of conflict resolution.

The best parts of the book, however, deal not with traditional patterns of deviance and control but with criminology "proper." Using original research material from Abidjan and the rest of the Ivory Coast supplemented by data from elsewhere in Francophone Africa, Brillon's real subject becomes the socially constructed nature of criminal statistics. Unlike Crummey's historians, whose subject is behavior and not definition and who are consistently (and surprisingly) uncritical about using official criminal records as actual records of behavior, Brillon correctly refuses to see statistics as reflecting "criminality."

The model is familiar. The state system of social control (criminal law) is overlaid and imposed on the traditional order, but the people continue using the traditional jurisdiction to settle disputes and conflict because it is more accessible and more comprehensible, and can be used in an opportunistic way. The result: criminal statistics that mask the "true" volume and nature of crime. The model leads Brillon into some fruitful directions. He sees crime statistics as an index of "juridic acculturation." The formal system acts as a filter (political in character because it aims to incriminate behavior that does not fit the ideology of the nation-state or its economic interests). The flow of acts into the system means the increasing absorption of deviance and its "conversion" into crime. This happens through "regulation" and "indication" (the definitions of modern justice achieve hegemony) and what Brillon nicely calls "magnetism": "the new institution, its attraction strengthened by the coercive measures conferred by political and legislative power, will direct, steal and lure clients who were formally subject to other systems or institutions" (p. 127).

Magnetism in turn depends on such banal matters as proximity of villages to courts, police deployment patterns, local power structures, and so on. The solemn figures of comparative criminology — the standard comparison of crime rates per 100,000 of the population — then, tell us little about criminality. To know that in 1972 the crime rate in Zaire was 107 per 100,000 and in the Ivory Coast 410, and in Ghana 1072 without knowing anything about each flow system, gives us only what Nils Christie calls "dead data."

The same dead data form the base of standard African criminological research whose "banality" Brillon tellingly criticizes. These studies deplore the absence of adequate statistics, but instead of using them as indicators of the functioning of the criminal justice system, go on to use this "castrated," "deAfricanized" data to replicate and elaborate all sorts of (usually out-of-date) Western theories. Thus, papers are still produced such as "The Role of Family Structure in the Development of Delinquent Behaviour Among Juvenile Delinquents in Lagos" (a real title!). These "prove" that broken homes "cause" delinquency – rather than talk about social context (of families, rural exodus, age structures) or selection process (failure of self-regulating control agencies, degree of isolation, exposure to official sanctions) or nature of the delinquency (the most common arrest being the illegal sale of goods on the street).

Such criticism should, but of course will not, stop the nonsense of this type of criminological research. And historians have much to learn about criminal statistics as indicators of the deployment of social control resources.[12] But Brillon does not travel far enough down his own theoretical track. He claims that his "ethno-criminology" allows us to "get at" all the hidden crime that is absorbed by a parallel system that "leaves no trace that would enable us to collate, assess and quantify these crimes" (p. 148). But this begs the policy question of *why* we should want to do this, and the theoretical question of how an act can be a crime before it has reached the system that has a monopoly on this definition.

Conclusion

Although apparently dealing with the same subject, crime and violence in colonial Africa, these books are worlds apart from each other in theory, method, audience, intentions, and hidden politics. Yet, comparing them is more than an exercise in the sociology of knowledge, more than a study of how intellectual discourses are constructed.

The problems of an "ethno-criminology" that has no history or politics might be obvious. But what can sophisticated social historians of Africa learn from this criminology? In one sense the real value of Crummey's volume is that it is so free from the intellectual baggage of positivist criminology. We directly approach crime and banditry through the discourses of popular history and political economy without having to pass through the terrain of pathology, determinism, and punishment. Seldom would theories of differential opportunity, subculture of violence, or status frustration have added very much.

But something *is* missing. Crime in colonial Africa consists not just of the high drama of bandits, highwaymen, brigands, rebels, and outlaws but the low drama of children being arrested for begging on the streets or stealing food from the market stalls. These are the people – the poorest, the weakest, the most isolated – who find themselves defined as criminals. Then there are those other dramas of magic, sorcery, ritual crime, infanticide, personal insult, self-defense and vigilantism. And yet another type of high drama: the crimes of the multinationals and the CIA, genocide, state crime and death squads, corruption and bribery.

Now, of course, it is no real "criticism" against social historians of Africa that they do not talk about banal everyday delinquency or traditional offenses or crimes of the powerful. These were not their subjects. But some awareness of the bread and butter of criminology and the advances in alternative criminology might nonetheless help. It might prevent the cavalier assumption that because the law is political (in the sense of originating in the demands of the political economy), than all law violation is a sign of resistance, rebellion, or protest. It might help understand how notions of individual rights, private property, and personal safety are understood not only in terms of legal domination. It will offer some useful models to comprehend the dialectic between individual acts of rule breaking and organized ideologies and systems of social control. And above all, it will show the intractable problems in the concept of crime.

Notes

1. A model historical account of this transition is David Garland, *Punishment and Welfare: A History of Penal Strategies* (London: Gawer, 1985).
2. Geoffrey Pearson, "Goths and Vandals: Crime in History," *Contemporary Crises* 2, no. 2 (1978): 34.
3. Such an account would have to deal with a rather strange current twist in radical criminology. The early search for incipient signs of resistance, heroism, and rebellion in working-class criminality is now being repudiated in favor of a realization of the divisive, demoralizing, and antirevolutionary character of crime, the fact that the powerless are its main victims. Those earlier attempts are dismissed as romantic, idealist, and Fanonist. This emerging "radical realist" position — which also appeals to E.P. Thompson, but this time for his appreciation of the historical victories of the rule of law — has some fascinating implications for popular social history.
4. See chapter 5.
5. Edwin M. Schur, *The Politics of Deviance: Stigma Contests and the Uses of Power* (Englewood Cliffs, N.J.: Prentice-Hall, 1980).
6. E.J. Hobsbawm, *Primitive Rebels* (New York: Norton, 1959), p. 19.
7. See references in chapter 10 (Clifford; Clinard and Abbott) and Louise Shelly, *Crime and Modernization: The Impact of Industrialization and Modernization in Crime* (Carbondale: Southern Illinois University Press, 1981).
8. See especially Colin Summer, "Crime, Justice and Underdevelopment: Beyond Modernization Theory," in *Crime, Justice and Underdevelopment*, ed. Summer (London: Heinemann, 1982), pp. 1–39.
9. Ibid., p. 33.
10. Cynthia Mahiber, *Crime and Nation-Building in the Caribbean: The Legacy of Legal Barriers* (Cambridge, Mass.: Schenkman, 1985), p. 3.
11. Ibid., p. 183.
12. Erikson's study of seventeenth century Massachusetts remains the best such historical account of deviance and social control: Kai T. Erikson, *Wayward Puritans: A Study in the Sociology of Deviance* (New York: John Wiley & Sons, 1966).

Part Four

Conclusion

15

The Last Seminar*

Introductory Note: Readers will no doubt take the following narrative to be a work of fiction, a "short story." As such, its appearance in a serious sociological publication will be regarded as controversial, to say the least. In fact, though, the text represents a true account, as told to me by Professor ____, a well-known sociologist. He recorded this story when I interviewed him at the beginning of 1978 in the ____ Psychiatric Hospital, where he had then spent two years. The interview was conducted as part of the ongoing Social Science Research Council-funded project on "Personal Identity and the Life-Cycle in the Seventies." The transcript was only slightly edited by me, mainly to remove some embarrassing personal references, and the text was then revised by Professor ____ himself, in accordance with the reverse feedback life history method. The final style—including the rather erratic grammar—was his own choice.

More literary-minded readers might be interested to know that the following lines (by John Berryman) were stuck on the wall of our ex-colleague's hospital room:

It seems to be dark all the time.
I have difficulty walking.
I can remember what to say to my seminar
but I don't know that I want to.

Professor ____ (who is now making a steady recovery from a condition diagnosed apparently as "crypto meta-psychosis") generously suggested that my name appear as author of the narrative as he himself "wouldn't be needing any more items for his c.v. anymore."

* "The Last Seminar" from *Sociological Review*, Vol. 27 (February 1979), pp. 5–20.

The Last Seminar

There were two beginnings, I suppose. The one when they started moving in and the other when we started noticing them. I'm not sure what the gap between these two moments was, probably not very long. Perhaps they started moving in right from the beginning of the year, the academic year I mean, in the first week of October. That would have been the obvious time if they had all planned it together. Though even at this stage, even after all that has happened, I have no real evidence of any collaboration, any collusion between them. At the end they certainly saw each other, but that was all.

Anyway, it was toward the end of January, a few weeks after the start of the second term when I first noticed anything. (This was in the Spring Term — universities do not have winter, only Autumn, Spring, and Summer terms.) I was just coming to the end of a lecture on prison history when my eyes moved to somewhere near the middle of the lecture room, where a man in his early forties was looking at me very intensely. He was not making any attempt to take notes but seemed to be concentrating, or at least playing very well at concentrating. His eyes never left my face.

I could not remember seeing him at my lectures in the previous term, but this was not in itself surprising. Students often walked in and out of lecture courses. It was also not unusual to find those who claimed that it had taken them a whole term to get it together to find the right times and rooms. But somehow this man did not look that sort of student. "Mature students" (all those over twenty-one) were usually better organized. In a strange way, he seemed familiar. What must have struck me — even then, I suppose — was that he looked very much like a prisoner. There was a certain grayness of the complexion, something about the hairstyle, but more obviously the clothes; that tight gray jacket didn't look quite like the standard army surplus stuff.

I wanted to talk to the man after the lecture, but he disappeared through the back exit. I was hardly conscious of thinking about him again till a week later, when I saw him standing at the far end of a queue in the refectory. Again his grayness seemed obvious — his complexion as well as his clothes — and also, seeing him standing up for the first time, a curious slouch. That slouch in the nineteenth-century etchings of prisoners walking around exercise yards rather than the familiar student posture. I lost him in the crowd, but that afternoon asked S. (who was teaching the course with me) whether he knew the man. I also enquired around among the students. No one could place him.

For some intangible reason, I started feeling uneasy about the man's presence. His official existence on the campus had to be recorded somewhere and eventually I found a trace in the registry. Yes, a man named Jeff Bridges had registered late for the course. The office remembered him vaguely as a mature student. This must be him.

The morning after the canteen sighting—later, I thought in terms of sightings—I was in my office opening the mail when D. came in. I assumed that she'd come to discuss her paper (on the labeling of mental illness), which she'd given me to comment on a few weeks earlier. I was just rehearsing a plausible account for not having looked at the paper yet, when she started to tell me about something else. She was worried that one of her students was having some sort of breakdown. This student had sat in the front row of her lecture the day before, rocking back and forth in his seat. Every now and then he moaned softly. D. had stopped her lecture and asked him if he was all right, but he appeared to be in some sort of trance and did not respond. The rest of the students with their normal affected tolerance were embarrassed but pretended not to be. D. assumed that the student was in the middle or just coming out of some weird drug experience. She resumed her lecture and after a while the moaning subsided, though he continued rocking.

Unlike in my encounter with Bridges, D. had recognized the student. He'd come to classes most of the first term, not saying a word or doing any work. D. had given him an extension for his essay on the usual grounds of "personal problems." Now, after the lecture she tried to talk to him, but he just stared right through her and walked out of the room moaning. The student's personal counselor was on sabbatical leave, so D. phoned the Health Center directly to make inquiries. They had no record of the student's having consulted them. D. and I discussed various courses of action and agreed to refer the matter to the chairman. I thought that she was making a fuss about nothing, and that the student had just got hold of some bad dope too early in the morning.

I still didn't think of connecting any of this with Bridges and for the rest of the week nothing unusual happened. Then Bridges, who I thought had been deliberately avoiding me, walked up to the desk at the end of a class in which he had participated with his usual intense stare.

"You don't know anything about it, do you? It's all a game to you."

I asked him what he meant.

"Prison," he said, "You think because you've spoken to a few cons you understand it all. Well, you don't, you just don't." He was slowly shaking his head. The tone was polite but condescending. I'd heard that tone before.

"How do you know?" I asked.

"Because I've been inside, that's why. I don't want to talk about it now." He was already moving out of the room. He turned round at the door. "Didn't you know there were two of us in your class?"

What could be going on? A knot of anxiety started tightening in my stomach. Something of that intangible unease was beginning to take on a shape. The shape moved with me as I walked very quickly, almost running, down the stairs to the Admissions Office. There had to be more information on Bridges somewhere. And yes, there was his application form, with a clear gap in his biography of five years in which he'd written "Army." Nothing on the file about how he'd been admitted or who had interviewed him. I then searched through all the other forms of students registered for the course. There was someone called Derek Meehan with a similar form: three years covered by "Army," no record of an interview. I could place him — a thin kid in his early twenties who had sat next to Bridges that morning.

But why was I getting so agitated? It was not that unusual for ex-prisoners to be accepted for a sociology degree. But surely it was strange that I hadn't been told about these two before. And how did they suddenly appear this term? My mind also went back to the obscurely threatening way Bridges and Meehan had been watching me during the morning seminar. I could now remember Meehan's supercilious grin.

Something very strange was happening. I went along the corridor to D.'s room. Perhaps — I couldn't think how — her moaning student was connected with this. She hadn't seen him again, but one of his roommates had reported that he was just lying around in bed all day still moaning softly. And another student, a girl named Jenny Carson, who'd appeared perfectly normal in the first term, had started acting the same way in a seminar the previous day. She'd sat through the hour with her head sunk on the table and wouldn't speak at all. D. had heard that morning that Jenny had made a suicide attempt during the night. She'd taken an overdose and was now just coming 'round in the Health Center.

D. was obviously worried by all this, but I did not tell her my suspicions that our visits could be connected. Two criminals appearing in a course about crime, two mental breakdowns in a course on mental illness. This had to be more than coincidence. My first thoughts went toward some sort of hoax, a stunt engineered by the Students Union or one of the political groupings to ridicule or discredit D. and myself in some way. Or even the whole Department. Had the others seen anything strange? But this was ridiculous. Even they wouldn't go to such lengths for a joke. And the suicide attempt was real enough.

I started making inquiries. At first people didn't want to tell me anything. Then it came out that some strange things had been happening to most of my colleagues. L.'s class on "Social Change in Latin America" had been disrupted several times by a Chilean student. He would stop her in midsentence, not with the usual theoretical questions about the revolutionary potential of the lumpen proletariat but with detailed factual statements. He contradicted or brought up to date the information in the texts of lectures: about the size of certain guerrilla forces, exact military tactics that had been followed, the composition of various political groups. He'd sat in one class holding what L. thought was a plastic model of a hand grenade. Plastic model like hell.

And M., who'd written several books and articles about the trade union movement and spent time studying car assembly workers, had noticed two men wearing "Ford" overalls hanging around the corridor outside his office. There were some other sightings. I can't remember them all now. J., who was teaching a course on underdevelopment with someone from Economics, had taken leave for a week because he'd been hallucinating images of malnourished children standing in lines outside the refectory. I phoned his wife. J. was in bed and didn't want to talk about things. She thought he'd been overworking and needed a rest; the visions were obvious symptoms of stress.

It was time to go home myself and put these pieces together. We couldn't all be just hallucinating from overwork. That couldn't be. But on the other hand, the visits, the sightings did seem to be private in some way. People had seen their own visions but couldn't see one another's. Was it just a collection of private guilt trips, psychic visits from those whom we had written about, researched, studied? They were entering our heads to remind us of their corporeal existence, of the fact that our careers had been constructed out of their presence. But this was no sort of explanation. I had actually seen Bridges and Meehan, and their lives had been recorded on a file. And that girl, Jenny, had really tried to kill herself. Why shouldn't the guerrilla, the starving kids, the car workers, all the others be real as well? And Christ knows how many more of them were around the place. "Them"—what can I mean by that?

I couldn't bring myself to talk to anyone. Not till I could get some more information, put things together. They might think I was going crazy otherwise.

And now things started happening faster. It was the next day, I think. I'd parked my car and started walking to the buildings when I noticed Bridges and Meehan sitting in an old van in the middle of the car park. There were two other men with them, both of them wearing the dark-navy boiler suits of the campus maintenance staff. Another of the eternal attempts by students to "politicize" the campus workers? Even in the old days that would have been a tenuous explanation. Now the sight of two ex-criminals sitting in a van talking to these two workers, whom I'd never seen before, just didn't make sense. Was there some extraordinary criminal escapade planned? But that wouldn't account for the Latin American guerrilla, the catatonics, the pot-bellied children.

That morning there were more sightings. Many more. M. was convinced that two engineers who'd come to his office to repair the central heating system were really car assembly workers. D.'s husband phoned to say that she was taking the week off because more of her students seemed to be having mental breakdowns. J. was still at home with his "hallucinations" of starving children. F., who had been doing some evaluative research on a homeless families project, had come to his office to find a woman and two children sitting on the floor on a pile of old suitcases and boxes. They claimed they'd been sent there by the project, but F. said that nobody there knew about them. There must have been more sightings like this but I can't remember them now. I was rushing around, checking out all these stories. The pattern was always the same. I could see all the visitors or at least some evidence, traces of their existence, but the others could see only their own visions.

And sometimes they were not aware even of their own visits. Early that day, when I was desperately trying to understand something, the mind flicking from one theory to another, I became convinced about one constant pattern. Those of us who had done any empirical research were being infiltrated by our subjects. ("Infiltrated," is that the right word? I'm still not sure how to describe what was being done to us. Penetrated? Visited? Invaded?) I could not explain how this had happened, but they were certainly here, taking revenge against us for writing about them. And I was privileged to see it all. But shit, some of us had been left untouched: the theorists, meta-physicians, philosophers. Why hadn't they been visited? If anyone deserved to be punished for living off other people's misery (this must be what was happening), surely it must be they. I had watched them for years, with their abstractions and theories, their texts and commentaries, their condescending smirks as they sat silently through seminar after seminar. How could they be left alone while we were being tormented like this?

Later – I don't know exactly when, things became too confusing to carry any sense of sequence – I realized the truth. They had been visited long before us. Probably from the beginning of the year. But they hadn't realized it. They never became really aware of any visitors. There had been nothing physically different about the theorists' new "students." No strange clothes, props, biographies. They looked just like ordinary students. But for months they had been handing in essays and making contributions to seminars which were nonsense. Literal nonsense, I mean. Garbage. Word salad. This is one of the more lucid parts of an essay which was handed in to E. for his graduate course on "Epistemology and Sociology." I found the charred remains of the essay toward the end, when the fires had started.

> The resolution proposed by Lacan differs substantially from the way it is perceived in Althusser's early writing, although the problematic – in its less obvious dialectical manifestation – remains the same in all other respects. Taking the split (the primordial structural 'break') between object and reality as being fundamentally irreconcilable with the way the ego dissociates itself from its own "being in the world," the thesis (or more accurately, *anti-thesis*) takes on a dimension which bourgeois sociology cannot completely situate given the limitations imposed by its positivistically inspired method.

There was more like this, much more. There must have been some other pages of the essay destroyed by the fire because I couldn't find any ending. On another kind of paper, there was a note clipped to the essay in E.'s handwriting.

O.K. for a first draft. But I don't think you pay enough attention to the purely *linguistic* implications of the Lacanian argument. Expand that section. Note also how Habermas (using, I think, a hitherto untranslated paper by Lorenzer) explicates on the way translation rules and decoding practices conform to a particular "rhetoric of decipherment." I've also marked parts on your draft where you rely a bit too heavily on purely secondary sources.

I began — much later, of course, when there was more time to think — to make sense of what I'd felt for a long time. These people had already entered the circle of the damned. Words had taken over. "Hollow eyed and high" (Whose words are those?), they had long ago driven each other mad with those theories, models, paradigmatic shifts. Commentaries on commentaries on commentaries. All sense of the world gone, washed away with the excreta of the Left Bank. No words could have any impact on them anymore. They had been visited long ago.

But no use at the time to try explaining this to E. or any of them. E. had no sense of humor and was anyway always going on about his sort of work not being appreciated in the Department. And how could I have explained it to him anyway? That some alien beings had taken possession of the minds of otherwise perfectly ordinary students? The limitations of positivism, indeed. How *could* bourgeois empiricism grasp any of this? K. might listen. He read a lot of science fiction and could have made the necessary epistemological leaps. But the time never came to talk with him. It never came.

At some point during all this I decided that I should talk to the Rector. I had no idea of what he could do. Just a compelling sense that someone At The Top should know. I gave him an edited account of everything I'd seen, trying to stay calm, very calm. His reaction was astonishing. Just a series of coincidences, he thought. No point in bothering about it. These things would die down as they always did on the campus. He didn't understand. And the next morning I realized just how little he did understand. Could bear to understand. That was the morning Dr. C. phoned me from the Health Center. Would I come to see him about something too complicated and confidential to discuss on the phone. I knew it had to be something about the visits. He would certainly have heard about the breakdowns, the suicide attempt.

It was about the sightings, but not in the way I thought. I can't remember how the conversation went, too much has happened since then. The main point was that the Rector and two of my colleagues had phoned Dr. C. to say that they were worried about me. All my investigations and reports of the visits seemed irrational, quite paranoid. I was having delusions, ideas of reference produced by the strain of the term. Why didn't I take a few weeks' holiday; the Chairman had offered to cover for my teaching. This was incredible. I just wanted to laugh. They couldn't deliberately be trying to discredit and isolate me. No, it really would be paranoid to assume that. They themselves weren't part of any plot, they just didn't understand. Christ knows, I was only just beginning to put things together myself.

I tried for a while to convince Dr. C. that there was a pattern out there and that I wasn't imagining it at all. No use pushing this line too hard, though. The more details I gave about the sightings and the more I tried to make the obvious connections, the crazier I sounded. Better keep quiet and play their game a while until the evidence piled up. It was obviously all going to build up to some Gotterdamerung crisis and they would have to see things then. So I told Dr. C. that I would take it easy. He gave me the standard campus dosage of Librium. I might need it for the days ahead.

How long could it go on? Others could still see only their own private visions. I could see them all. And when would the visitors start seeing each other? The criminal, the ill, the poor, the mad, the desperate. They were stalking the corridors, the lecture rooms, the offices. I knew about them. They were there. You must believe me. Yes, because later that same day I knew for the first time that the visitors were starting to do things that others had to notice. They were leaving their traces. I was phoned at home by the Rector's secretary, summoned to come back immediately to the campus.

There had been some sort of power failure in most of the buildings and the Rector's office was lit by a few candles. The Registrar and a few old-guard professors were crouched around the desk in the half-light. There had been some worrying *incidents* they thought I might be able to shed some light on. One of the cleaners had found a student hanging in his room. Parts of his body had been removed. Empty meths bottles and cans of baked beans had been found in the library stacks and there were other signs of people's having slept there. A fire had been started in the computer center. An Iranian engineering student had apparently been kidnapped. The Dean had received a ransom note written on the back of a reading list for T.'s course on "Twentieth Century Politics." It was obvious that there had been other "incidents" (they kept using that word). All this, of course, was strictly confidential. Things must be hushed up or else the media would start nosing around.

I told them about some of my sightings. But I wasn't going to put things together for them. They'd either blame me or just refuse to understand. They had already decided anyway to go along with the Rector's proposal to shut the campus down a week before the term was due to end. Find some excuse to declare an early vacation, get the students off campus, and things would just blow over. I couldn't tell them that these "students" wouldn't go. That nothing would blow over.

I left them in the darkness where they sat arranging the early closure. The place would be kept open till the end of the week. A typical piece of academic planning. But I knew that the visits would continue. Or perhaps some point had already been made, some horrible existential lesson already been learned and the visitors would fade away into the emptiness. This was possible. We would then just continue as before, but with our consciousness expanded. That was all that mattered: new ideas, new thoughts, new guilt. Then we could continue as before with only a change in the drumbeats of the mind. I use that figure of speech because I saw the drummers then. In the corridor as I left the office two black drummers stood, wearing only loincloths and some blue stones round their neck. A steady, African rhythm and I knew that I was the only one hearing it and seeing them. Heart of darkness returns home.

One more day now before the early end to the term. I had no plan beyond survival and the continued attempt to make sense of things. There was nothing more an intellectual could do. There never has been. But emotions kept flooding in to block the thought processes. Anxiety, fear about what the visitors might do next. Already breakdowns, kidnappings, a death. And who knows what had been successfully covered up? That morning I saw the ex-prisoners walking about in the chemistry laboratories. The number of black and Latin American students seemed to be increasing each hour. I wandered around the campus all morning seeing these things. In the bar during the lunch hour, two women in their forties, with exaggerated makeup and short skirts, were moving from table to table. I believe they were prostitutes looking for customers. Somewhere in a corner an old man collapsed on the floor where he lay screaming and trembling.

No matter. Things might be just speeding up a bit before they finally calmed down. Like objects gathering in the eye of the tornado. Then there would be quiet and peace and we could go on with our jobs. Ignore the sightings for a while, that was the thing. I walked back to my office with a deliberately normal stride. The corridors were empty and there were loud explosions and shouts from the square. I thought I smelled smoke. The drumbeats had returned.

But I had to keep walking, walking purposefully back to my office. There was no point in allowing myself to be totally demoralized by all this. It was up to us, to me, to maintain some semblance of normality. Even if the place was going to shut down soon — temporarily, of course, temporarily — we had to keep on with the educational process. The university had survived worse troubles than these. If I cracked up, let go, then everyone else would. The normal students must still be around somewhere. Of course they were.

I checked my timetable; there was an urban sociology seminar in five minutes and I had to be there. I picked up my notes and the student list from my desk and went toward the seminar room. The corridor was deserted. I had to go to the toilet on the way. One of the cubicle doors was open and a young man was lying on the floor, his head propped on the toilet seat. His trousers were around his ankles, dirty underpants, one sleeve rolled up, a hypodermic syringe in the other hand. Mouth open, glazed eyes staring vacantly ahead. The Lenny Bruce death scene. Piled on the floor, next to some empty glass capsules are some paperbacks. I can see two titles: *Beyond Alienation* and *One Dimensional Man*.

I hurry past the cubicle. This is now becoming pure fantasy stuff. That guy just wasn't there. Standing in front of the urinal, I unzip my fly and start pissing. A student (a student?) appears from somewhere and stands next to me. He reaches for my cock and holds it. "No, no," I'm shouting, squirming away, running out the door.

The corridor was still quiet. It must be the only place where nothing was happening. No matter, a job had to be done. All this business would be cleared up in time. The main thing was not to panic. If things were skidding a bit, go with the skid and don't slam the brakes on.

Would anyone turn up for the seminar? The room looked strange because all the chairs and tables had been removed. There were some holes in the wall where the blackboard had been ripped out. In one corner a girl sat huddled against the wall, her head sunk between her thighs. I think it was D.'s catatonic student. Underneath the venetian blinds sat a peasant woman—Mexican? Spanish?—breast-feeding a baby. A little boy of three or four was watching. This now must be a grotesque dream. For the first time since it all started, I felt that I really couldn't go on. The mind could just not function any more. Jesus God, there was nothing in my contract that said that I had to teach under these conditions.

The door opened and Jerry Robson walked in. He was one of those amiably vague students who seemed to turn up at random to most courses. A gentle sort of refugee from the sixties, living out some cultural composite of what hippie students might have been like. He'd probably just got out of bed and hadn't realized that anything unusual was happening on the campus. He didn't appear to find anything strange about the seminar room either and just sat down on the floor and began looking through his copy of *The Sun*, waiting for the proceedings to start. I couldn't think of what to say to him but muttered the standard formula about waiting a few minutes to see if any other students would turn up. He seemed satisfied with this information and didn't even look around the room.

Where now the peasant woman had finished feeding. She and the little boy were loudly spitting out some sort of pips on the floor. The girl in the corner was tearing out chunks of her hair. No one else was going to come, that was clear. For what it was worth, I should work out some readings and essay titles to give Robson.

Just then there was a series of staccato thuds from the square outside the window. Machine-gun fire? That can't be possible. I looked out of the window. There was a cloud of dense smoke all over the square. Drumbeats and screams from somewhere else. Coming out of the library entrance, into the smoke, were three figures in long white gowns and hoods. They were carrying piles of books to a point in the square where the smoke was thickest. Suddenly there came a loudly amplified announcement in Spanish. As the echoes died away, I could hear an anthem or marching song. There was a burst of machine-gun fire from near the Law Building. A bullet went through one of the window panes just above the peasant woman's head. She seemed not to notice anything. Neither did Robson or the children.

It was time to cut my losses. There was no doubt in my mind now that all this was real, that I wasn't going insane. But what was to be gained from seeing it through to the end? Wherever that may be. Besides, it was now becoming physically dangerous to stay on the campus much longer. Who knows when some assassin might burst into the seminar room? And if things became a bit more structured, what side would I be on? I could not even work out what the sides were. Yes, perhaps the authorities were right to shut the place down for a while. Though God knows what this would even look like. And there was no way this would all just fade away.

Staying in the seminar room was not possible anymore. The infant was now sleeping on the floor. The little boy had got hold of a box of chalk and was drawing everywhere—walls, blackboard, floors. Crosses, crosses all over the place, with the occasional matchstick figure hanging from them. The woman was looking intensely at me and I understood the look. She started unbuttoning her dress and slid down flat onto the floor with her legs wide apart. The catatonic girl was still huddled in the corner and suddenly started to vomit. Trickles of yellow slime moving down the edge of the floor. It was about time to end the seminar.

Robson decided on this precise moment to start rolling a joint. He had been something of a caricature of himself in the old days, but even more grotesquely than I remembered from then, he began acting out a stage hippie role. "Too much, man, too much" he muttered as he lit up. I wasn't too clear whether he was just stoned or else had come to the conclusion that the sociology department had somehow arranged this whole freak show for his benefit. Some sort of laboratory demonstration which he just had to sit back and observe. I was getting angry at his lack of response.

"Can't you see that something a little *odd* is happening? You'd better get out of here—the whole place is going to shut down or blow up. Or something." But it was no use talking to him.

"Take it easy, man. You academics are so messed up with all your head trips you just can't go along with things. I'm going to stick around to see what's going to happen. Roll with the punch."

Let him stay, then. I took one more look around the seminar room. There was thick smoke gathering outside and I could just see across the square that the library windows had been blacked out. Sandbags were appearing round the bookshop. In the room the girl had stopped vomiting and the little boy was dragging his bare toes through puddles of the stuff. The peasant woman was pointing to her naked crotch with one hand and holding up the fingers of the other calling out some amount in pesetas. The smell was unbearable: smoke from outside, the vomit, fumes of grass. I said goodbye to Robson. There was no way of getting through to him now.

Running quickly down the corridor that was now totally deserted – my room was at the far end – I passed R.'s room, which had been totally vandalized. The door was ripped off its hinges, filing cabinets open on the floor, torn books thrown round all over. A quotation, in R.'s writing, was chalked on the blackboard. Some of the words had been rubbed out. "The dialectic is the a priori reconstruction of the world process and thus the motive of conception ____ consciousness. It is creative, god like ____ utterly free from assumptions, ultimately even a kind of ecstasy" (Husserl).

Ecstasy, indeed. The dialectic was opening. But could we have imagined it happening like this? I moved quickly to my office with the vague idea that I had to save something from there. The door was daubed with three large swastikas and the names of some football teams, but the room itself was just as I left it earlier on. What could I save? First, these notes about the sightings (always the good sociologist). And some books? I ran my eyes along the familiar shelves.

How about all that stuff on "extreme situations"? *Social Reactions to Stress* and the complete publications of the National Institute of Disaster Research, *Society in Crisis* – ha, ha, I wouldn't be needing any of those. And nothing, nothing at all from "theory." Nor sociology of religion. And certainly not philosophy of the social sciences. Nor, God help us, the social structure of modern Britain. Then *The Homeless Mind, The Raw and the Cooked, The Structure of Social Action*, what could all these titles *mean*? And not much Marxism that I would want to read again. And then those long shelves on deviance, crime, mental illness, suicide, prostitution, prisons, delinquency, drugs, social pathology, social problems, alcoholism, rape, violence, abortion, death. God help me, no. Just a few, just a few books worth saving from all this: Paul Goodman, Laing, Jules Henry, Bateson, certainly Albert Memmi. Yes, I might read some of these again. And there was a book of Diane Arbus photos that a student had given me . . . this would be suitable. She had been visited too.

Then my squash racket and a pair of shorts – why not? Though Christ knows what could be happening in the squash courts by now. I threw about a dozen books into a plastic bag. Let them have the rest.

It was not going to be easy to leave the campus. The foyer of the Social Science Building was the first problem. There was a stink of ether and Dettol everywhere, and the whole area seemed to have been turned into a geriatric ward. Old men and women were lying on rubber sheets all over the floor. Under the notice board of the Revolutionary Students Federation an old woman stood with plastic tubes coming out her nose. Other tubes strapped on her arms led to a bottle of some yellow liquid which she was carrying in her hand. Some of the old people were coughing and spitting blood on the floor. Others were screaming and crying. In the background there was the rhythmic sound of African work songs — miners? roadworkers? convicts? — which seemed to be coming from the typing pool office leading off the foyer.

I picked my way through the bodies. Half of me was concentrating just on moving, moving through patches of white gowns, striped pajamas, plastic tubes, dried blood. At the same time some other part of me was thinking about where everyone else had got to, my colleagues, the administration, the real students. Surely, they were seeing all this as well. That terrible acid head rush when you're sure you're coming out of the trip, only to know in some part of you that this very sureness might be itself part of the trip.

No, I couldn't afford such thoughts. This had to be real . . . I was not cracking up, I was not tripping. Concentrate, concentrate on getting through the bodies. Hit them away when they get too thick, when they come at you. But the door seemed to get further and further away, the smell stronger, the screams louder.

At last the door. Across the square now, and move along the Chemistry Building to the parking lot. Crouching and swerving like in the war movies. There must be snipers in one of the buildings. Every now and then a dull thud as one of the sand bags around the library gets hit. Past the windows of the Film Centre now, and pressed up against the glass are the faces and pot bellies of those children from the Oxfam Biafra posters. This cannot be real.

And now the parking lot. Wandering through it are groups of M.'s car assembly workers with wrenches, screwdrivers, and hammers in their hands. They are slowly smashing up all the cars. Glass from shattered windows, hubcaps, wheels, whole engines are strewn all over the ground. In the gathering darkness, I just manage to pick my way through the debris to my Renault at the far end. None of the workers appears to notice me. Into the car and throw all the stuff onto the back seat.

A glow of dim light is now visible around the sports field. As I slowly drive past I see groups of African tribesmen (Hausa? Yoruba? Azande? Nuer? Xhosa? I get the books mixed up). They are lighting fires all around the field. The soccer goalposts are being hacked away, presumably for firewood, and a goat is chewing at the netting. Some of the car workers are watching the fires, and one group — I think I see Bridges and Meehan with them — is walking toward the fires. They are brandishing spanners, car jacks, and pieces of metal. Words, "Kill the black bastards," come through the darkness. I think this is the first time that the different groups recognize one another's presence. But what can I do? Who is to be rescued?

Harder down on the accelerator now and getting onto the road alongside the campus. Some sort of shantytown must have been built overnight. Tin shacks with bits of clothing hanging from them are spread out on the lawn all the way up to the library. A stench of manure in the air. A little girl, Latin American looking, like the woman in the seminar room, is crouched shitting or pissing on the footpath leading up to the buildings. I've made the road just in time. In the rearview mirror I can see a group of men in khaki uniforms emerging from behind the oak trees. They are building a road block with pieces of wood and metal.

I drove faster. No idea where my colleagues or anyone else might be. Was I the first or the last to leave? No matter. There was no turning back now.

H C S. P94